Approaches to Teaching
the Works of
Inca Garcilaso de la Vega

Approaches to Teaching the Works of Inca Garcilaso de la Vega

Edited by

Christian Fernández

and

José Antonio Mazzotti

The Modern Language Association of America
New York   2022

© 2022 by The Modern Language Association of America
85 Broad Street, Suite 500, New York, New York 10004-2434
www.mla.org

To order MLA publications, visit mla.org/books. For wholesale and international orders, see mla.org/Bookstore-Orders.

The MLA office is located on the island known as Mannahatta (Manhattan) in Lenapehoking, the homeland of the Lenape people. The MLA pays respect to the original stewards of this land and to the diverse and vibrant Native communities that continue to thrive in New York City.

Approaches to Teaching World Literature 169
ISSN 1059-1133

Library of Congress Cataloging-in-Publication Data
Names: Fernández, Christian, 1960– editor. | Mazzotti, José Antonio, 1961– editor.
Title: Approaches to teaching the works of Inca Garcilaso de la Vega / edited by
    Christian Fernández and José Antonio Mazzotti.
Description: New York : The Modern Language Association of America, 2022. |
    Series: Approaches to teaching world literature, 1059-1133 ; 169 |
    Includes bibliographical references.
Identifiers: LCCN 2021033769 (print) | LCCN 2021033770 (ebook) |
    ISBN 9781603295574 (hardcover) | ISBN 9781603295581 (paperback) |
    ISBN 9781603295598 (EPUB)
Subjects: LCSH: Vega, Garcilaso de la, 1539–1616. —Study and teaching (Higher) |
    Incas—Peru—Historiography. | Peru—History—1548–1820—Historiography.
Classification: LCC F3444.G3 A67 2022 (print) | LCC F3444.G3 (ebook) |
    DDC 985/.019—dc23
LC record available at https://lccn.loc.gov/2021033769
LC ebook record available at https://lccn.loc.gov/2021033770

CONTENTS

PART ONE: MATERIALS

Classroom Texts   3
The Instructor's Library   5
Monographs and Critical Studies   6
Collections of Essays in Spanish   8
Background and Related Topics   9
Online Resources   11

PART TWO: APPROACHES

Introduction   19
   Christian Fernández and José Antonio Mazzotti

**The *Royal Commentaries* and Inca Garcilaso's Earlier
and Later Works**

León Hebreo's *Diálogos de amor* as a Gateway to Inca Garcilaso's Opus   25
   Damian Bacich

At the Crossroads of the Early Modern World: *La Florida del Inca*
   in the Hemispheric American Studies Classroom   34
   Ralph Bauer

Inca Garcilaso Reads Cabeza de Vaca   53
   Rolena Adorno

Teaching the Picaresque with the *Historia general del Perú*   65
   Sara L. Lehman

Natural History and the *Comentarios reales*   76
   Yarí Pérez Marín

Identity and Gender in the *Royal Commentaries*

Inca Garcilaso and Transnational Identity in Colonial, Postcolonial,
   and Neocolonial Contexts   94
   Michael J. Horswell

Writing as an Indian: Teaching the Other Inca Garcilaso and
   His Native Sources   105
   Rocío Quispe-Agnoli

Teaching Inca Garcilaso in the Context of Indigenous Writing, Thought,
   and Culture   115
   Isabel Dulfano

Weaving Gender into the *Royal Commentaries*   130
  Raquel Chang-Rodríguez

Inca Garcilaso on Women   140
  Sara V. Guengerich

The *Royal Commentaries*, Language, and Visual Representation

Inca Garcilaso and the Power of Language   150
  Margarita Zamora

Incan Resonances in Inca Garcilaso's Prose   160
  José Antonio Mazzotti

Incomparable Cosmologies: Character and Motive in the March
  to Cajamarca   175
  Sara Castro-Klarén

Teaching the *Royal Commentaries* with Visual Representations
  of the Exploration, Conquest, and Colonization of Peru   193
  Giovanna Montenegro

Learning from Mistakes: Interpretation in the *Comentarios reales*   201
  Sarah H. Beckjord

Inca Garcilaso across the Disciplines

The Andes in Appalachia: Inca Garcilaso in a Hemispheric Curriculum   211
  Kimberly Borchard

Inca Mummies and Mountaintop Sacrifice: Ethnohistory and the
  Comentarios reales   224
  George Antony Thomas

Religion in the *Royal Commentaries*   233
  James W. Fuerst

"Between the Tree of Memory and the Bark of History":
  Revisiting Inca Garcilaso's Sites of Memory   247
  Dinorah Cortés-Vélez

Casting Inca Garcilaso, Comparatively Speaking   257
  Nhora Lucía Serrano

Notes on Contributors   267

Survey Respondents   273

Part One

MATERIALS

Classroom Texts

Inca Garcilaso de la Vega's *Comentarios reales de los Incas* (*Royal Commentaries of the Incas*) was translated into French and English in the seventeenth, eighteenth, and nineteenth centuries, but those translations are outdated and difficult to access. The complete modern English translation is the one done by Harold V. Livermore in 1966, which includes both the first part, or the *Royal Commentaries*, and the second part, known as *Historia general del Perú* (*General History of Peru*). The first volume includes a foreword by the historian Arnold J. Toynbee and an introduction by Livermore, who also wrote an introduction for the second volume. The publisher of the edition, the University of Texas Press, also published a translation of *La Florida del Inca* (*The Florida of the Inca*) by John Grier Varner and Jeannette Johnson Varner, with a short preface, in 1951.

The first literary work of Garcilaso's was published in Madrid in 1590. *Diálogos de amor*, the translation into Spanish of León Hebreo's *Dialoghi d'amore* (*Dialogues of Love*), has not been translated into English, but since it is an important piece of work that is necessary for the understanding of the process of writing for Garcilaso, we should mention here the more recent translation from the original Italian *Dialoghi* by one of the contributors to this volume, Damian Bacich, and Rossella Pescatori. There is a previous English translation from the Italian, published in 1937, but, given the discrepancies in the sixteenth-century Italian editions, the last translation by Bacich and Pescatori is the most appropriate because it includes an introduction with up-to-date research and bibliography on the subject.

Anthologies or selections from the works of Garcilaso for undergraduate courses are more common and comprehensive in the original Spanish, but for English-speaking students there is an abridged version of the *Royal Commentaries* extracted from the Livermore translation mentioned above. This one-volume version has been edited by the historian Karen Spalding, who also wrote an informative introduction to the volume.

There are several anthologies or selections from the works of Garcilaso, but in some cases they are difficult to acquire or are out of print. There are two recommended selections in Spanish. The first, titled *Comentarios reales*, is prepared by one of the most important scholars on Garcilaso studies, Enrique Pupo-Walker, and contains selections of *Diálogos de amor*, *La Florida del Inca*, and both the *Comentarios reales* and the *Historia general del Perú*. It also contains material for a more comprehensive view of the entire oeuvre of Garcilaso, together with a long and important introduction by one of the experts on his works. The second is an extensive selection by Mercedes Serna, from the University of Barcelona, of those chapters from the first part of the *Comentarios reales* that are most appropriate for the study of the work as literature.

For students with knowledge and interest in reading Garcilaso's works in the original Spanish there are several editions. The most studied and edited work of Garcilaso's is the first part of the *Comentarios reales*, of which three modern editions are still in circulation. The first was published in two volumes by the Biblioteca Ayacucho in 1976. This press was created by the Venezuelan government to publish the cultural and literary patrimony of Latin America. The volumes were edited, with a prologue and a chronology, by the late Aurelio Miró Quesada, who at the time was the leading scholar on Garcilaso. The second edition was published in Mexico in 1991 by Fondo de Cultura Económica and edited by the Peruvian scholar Carlos Araníbar, who prepared an analytical index and an extensive glossary for this edition. Araníbar modernized the Spanish, changed some words, and divided the paragraphs to make them more accessible to the modern reader, but the true importance of this edition is the excellent glossary, in which Araníbar explains many topics and the historical context of Garcilaso's work. The third in this list, published by Espasa in 2013, was edited by Mercedes López-Baralt, also a leading scholar in colonial and Andean studies, and combines the *Comentarios reales* in one volume with *La Florida del Inca*, an extensive introduction by López-Baralt, textual notes, and a glossary. *La Florida del Inca* has also been published in Spain, edited by Sylvia Lynn Hilton with an introduction and a short bibliography.

The best modern edition in Spanish of both the *Comentarios reales* and the *Historia general del Perú* is the one edited by Ángel Rosenblat. The *Comentarios reales*, in two volumes, is preceded by a prologue by Ricardo Rojas, and the *Historia general*, in three volumes, is preceded by a study of this work by José de la Riva Agüero, one of the first Peruvian scholars dedicated to the study of Garcilaso's life and works. The introductions in this edition are outdated, but the edition of the texts is recommended.

There is not an English translation of the complete works of Garcilaso. The first edition of his complete works in Spanish was *Obras completas del Inca Garcilaso de la Vega* (1960–65), which included the two parts of the *Comentarios reales*, *La Florida del Inca*, Garcilaso's translation of Hebreo's *Dialoghi d'amore*, and his genealogy on his family ancestry, *Relación de la descendencia de Garci Pérez de Vargas* (*Account of the Lineage of Garci Pérez de Vargas*). This last work is the only manuscript by Garcilaso that has survived and was posthumously published in 1929 in Spain in the *Revista de historia de la genealogía española* (*Journal of History of Spanish Genealogy*) and reproduced in Peru the same year in the *Boletín bibliográfico* (*Bibliographical Bulletin*) of San Marcos University. In 1951 a facsimile edition with its corresponding transcription was published in book form by Raúl Porras Barrenechea.

On the four hundredth anniversary of the publication of *La Florida del Inca*, *Comentarios reales*, and *Historia general del Perú*, the Fondo Editorial de la Universidad Inca Garcilaso de la Vega dedicated ten years to publishing all the works of Garcilaso. It published the first part of *Comentarios reales* in 2007, *La Florida del Inca* in 2009, *Segunda parte de los* Comentarios reales (*Second Part of the* Royal Commentaries) in two volumes in 2013, and *Traducción de los*

Diálogos de amor *de León de Hebreo, y otros escritos* (*Translation of the* Dialogues of Love *by León Hebreo, and Other Works*) in 2015. This last volume includes *La descendencia de Garci Pérez de Vargas*, the only two letters known of Garcilaso's addressed to the antiquarian Juan Fernández Franco, and a short prologue to a sermon by Alonso Bernardino, a work that Garcilaso published. All the volumes are preceded by prologues by the Peruvian scholar Ricardo González Vigil, also an expert on Garcilaso's works.

However, the last edition of Garcilaso's *Obras completas* is the one published in 2015 by the Ministerio de Relaciones Exteriores (Ministry of Foreign Relations) of Peru. This has been a decade's work by Carlos Araníbar under the direction of the Centro Cultural Inca Garcilaso. Araníbar has modernized the Spanish, punctuation, accentuation, and paragraphing to make the text more accessible to modern readers and has included textual notes, indexes, and an extensive, up-to-date bibliography. The first volume includes *Diálogos de amor, La descendencia de Garci Pérez de Vargas*, and *La Florida del Inca*; the second volume contains the first part of *Comentarios reales*; and the third volume includes the second part of *Comentarios reales* and two letters by Garcilaso to his friend Fernández Franco. This last volume also includes the entire book on Garcilaso by Aurelio Miró Quesada. Along with *Obras completas del Inca Garcilaso de la Vega*, these two editions are the only ones published in Peru that include all the works of Garcilaso in the original Spanish and give the twenty-first-century reader an up-to-date introduction to Garcilaso's works and bibliographies.

The Instructor's Library

The bibliography of the works and life of Garcilaso is extensive since scholars started to research and write about Garcilaso, analyzing and interpreting his works, at the beginning of the twentieth century, mostly in Spanish. However, the bibliography in English has been increasing in the last decades. Here we provide a selection of the most important and the latest bibliography in English of mainly monographs, followed by a bibliography in Spanish selected with the same criteria.

The most recent, important, and useful selection of articles in English on Garcilaso is *Inca Garcilaso and Contemporary World-Making*, edited by Sara Castro-Klarén and Christian Fernández. This volume has been designed for classroom use in different disciplines or in disciplines with interdisciplinary approaches. It contains eleven articles, an introduction, an afterword, and a short biography of Garcilaso written by leading scholars on colonial, postcolonial, Andean, and Garcilasian studies. The instructor can use the entire book or select specific articles from the book, which is available in print and digital format from libraries in the United States and around the world.

Another collection of essays on Garcilaso is *Garcilaso Inca de la Vega: An American Humanist*, edited by José Anadón. These fifteen essays are short because they are a selection of papers read at a conference in homage of José Durand, one of the leading scholars on Garcilaso studies.

The best and the only biography of Garcilaso in English is *El Inca: The Life and Times of Garcilaso de la Vega*, authored by John Grier Varner. There is not a modern or proper biography in Spanish; the closest to a biography in that language is *El Inca Garcilaso y otros estudios garcilasistas*, by Aurelio Miró Quesada. The Peruvian scholars Miró Quesada, Raúl Porras Barrenechea, and José Durand dedicated their lives to the study of the life and works of Garcilaso and made major contributions on this subject in countless articles and books, and they were the most prepared to write a biography of Garcilaso in Spanish, but none of them wrote one or even a monograph on Garcilaso. However, the abovementioned book by Miró Quesada is still the best Spanish-language resource on the life of Garcilaso.

Monographs and Critical Studies

In English

The most recent book in English on Garcilaso is James W. Fuerst's *New World Postcolonial: The Political Thought of Inca Garcilaso de la Vega*. This is an important contribution to the studies on Garcilaso and the first monograph dedicated to studying the *Royal Commentaries* from a political theory perspective. José Antonio Mazzotti's *Incan Insights: The Inca Garcilaso's Hints to Andean Readers* is the English translation of his book *Coros mestizos del Inca Garcilaso* and is a seminal book in Garcilasian studies. Margarita Zamora's *Language, Authority, and Indigenous History in the* Comentarios reales de los Incas is another important book that examines the *Royal Commentaries* in the context of the Renaissance European world. In *Garcilaso de la Vega and His Sources in* Comentarios reales de los Incas, Frances G. Crowley studies the main sources Garcilaso used in the writing of the *Royal Commentaries*, such as Pedro de Cieza de León, Agustín de Zárate, Francisco López de Gómara, Blas Valera, and José de Acosta. Donald G. Castanien's *El Inca Garcilaso de la Vega* can be considered a short biography and used instead of the longer and more detailed book by Varner. *La Florida del Inca and the Struggle for Social Equality in Colonial Spanish America*, by Jonathan D. Steigman, is a short monograph dedicated to the study of *The Florida of the Inca*.

In Spanish

The newest monograph in the last four decades, *El Inca Garcilaso en su siglo de oro* (*Inca Garcilaso in His Golden Age*), by Fernando Rodríguez Mansilla, is a return to traditional approaches on Garcilaso from the perspective of Spanish peninsular literature. Enrique Cortéz's *Biografía y polémica: El Inca Garcilaso y el archivo colonial andino en el siglo XIX* (*Biography and Polemics: Inca Garcilaso and the Colonial Andean Archive in the Nineteenth Century*) studies the relation between Garcilaso's texts and their reception in the nineteenth century. *El Inca en la ficción literaria* (*The Inca in Literary Fiction*), by Miguel Hugo Maguiño Veneros, is the only monograph dedicated to the study of Garcilaso as the main fictional character in novels and short stories such as *Diario del Inca Garcilaso, 1562–1616* (*Inca Garcilaso's Diary, 1562–1616*), by Francisco Carrillo Espejo, and *Poderes secretos* (*Secret Powers*), by Miguel Gutiérrez. Raquel Chang-Rodríguez's *Cartografía garcilasista* (*Garcilaso's Cartography*) examines the geocultural landscapes of Garcilaso, emphasizing his *Relación de la descendencia de Garci Pérez de Vargas*. In *El Inca Garcilaso, traductor de culturas* (*Inca Garcilaso: Translator of Cultures*), Mercedes López-Baralt examines Garcilaso's works from the perspective of anthropology. *Incas ilustrados: Reconstrucciones imperiales en la segunda mitad del siglo XVIII* (*Enlightened Incas: Imperial Reconstructions in the Second Half of the Eighteenth Century*), by Fernanda Macchi, studies Garcilaso's work's impact in the eighteenth and nineteenth centuries and also the process of its translation into French and its impact in French thought. In *Inca Garcilaso: Imaginación, memoria e identidad* (*Inca Garcilaso: Imagination, Memory and Identity*), Christian Fernández studies how the process of memory works in the construction of the historiographical discourse of the *Comentarios reales*. As mentioned above, Mazzotti's *Coros mestizos del Inca Garcilaso: Resonancias andinas* (*Inca Garcilaso's Mestizo Choirs: Andean Resonances*) is the original version of the book that, with a few revisions, he published in English as *Incan Insights: El Inca Garcilaso's Hints to Andean Readers*. *Memoria del bien perdido: Conflicto, identidad y nostalgia en el Inca Garcilaso de la Vega* (*Memory of Things Past: Conflict, Identity and Nostalgia in Inca Garcilaso de la Vega*), by Max Hernández, is a psychoanalytic study of Garcilaso through his works. *Traducción, escritura y violencia colonizadora: Un estudio de la obra del Inca Garcilaso* (*Translation, Writing and Colonizing Violence: A Study of Inca Garcilaso's Works*), by Susana Jákfalvi-Leiva, is a linguistic analysis of the process of translation. Enrique Pupo-Walker's *Historia, creación y profecía en los textos del Inca Garcilaso de la Vega* (*History, Creation and Prophecy in Inca Garcilaso de la Vega's Texts*) is a study of the fictionalization of the historical discourse. *Inca Garcilaso: Clásico de América* (*Inca Garcilaso: Classic of America*) is a collection of nine articles by José Durand, and even though it is not a monograph, we include it here for its importance in Garcilaso studies. Finally, an important recent book in French is *Un Inca platonicien:*

Garcilaso de la Vega, 1539–1616 (*A Platonic Inca: Garcilaso de la Vega, 1539–1616*), by Carmen Bernard. Bernard is one of the leading historians specializing in Latin America working in France.

Collections of Essays in Spanish

This section includes the collections of essays published in the last ten years as the result of conferences, symposia, and celebrations for the life and works of Garcilaso. We include only the most available.

The issue of *Revista de crítica literaria latinoamericana* (*Journal of Latin American Literary Criticism*) titled *El Inca Garcilaso en dos orillas* (*Inca Garcilaso in Two Worlds*) is a volume with twenty-two articles on Garcilaso covering many aspects of his works, including Garcilaso in literature, in movies, and on the Internet, among other topics of interest for cultural studies. A long-awaited collection is *Los mundos diversos del Inca Garcilaso y la academia actual* (*The Diverse Worlds of Inca Garcilaso and the Current Academy*), coedited by Fermín del Pino-Díaz and Amalia Iniesta Cámara, which brings together thirty articles covering many aspects of Garcilaso's works and includes a six-essay section with recent information about new editions, international readership and dissemination, and other related issues. In 2016 Eduardo González Viaña and José Antonio Mazzotti edited a collection of the best articles and creative work on Garcilaso published in recent years, titled *Garcilasismo creativo y crítico: Nueva antología* (*Fiction and Criticism on Garcilaso: New Anthology*). Also in 2016, Mazzotti published a collection of thirteen of his articles on Garcilaso, written between 1996 and 2016, under the title *Encontrando un Inca: Ensayos escogidos sobre el Inca Garcilaso de la Vega* (*Encountering an Inca: Selected Essays on Inca Garcilaso de la Vega*); an expanded edition came out in Cuba in 2018 with an updated bibliography. These essays cover all the books by Garcilaso, from *Diálogos de amor* to the second part of the *Comentarios reales*, underlining the transatlantic epistemologies and background of Garcilaso in his depiction of New World cultures. Carmen de Mora, Guillermo Serés, and Mercedes Serna edited eighteen articles in the volume *Humanismo, mestizaje y escritura en los* Comentarios reales (*Humanism, Mestizaje and Writing in the* Royal Commentaries). In 2010 Mazzotti edited twenty articles in a volume titled *Renacimiento mestizo: Los 400 años de los* Comentarios reales (*Mestizo Renaissance: 400 Years of the* Royal Commentaries). Also in 2010, Raquel Chang-Rodríguez published *Entre la espada y la pluma: El Inca Garcilaso de la Vega y sus* Comentarios reales (*Between the Sword and the Quill: Inca Garcilaso de la Vega and His* Royal Commentaries) with ten articles, an introduction, and a "coloquio" about Garcilaso with the renowned Peruvian novelist Mario Vargas Llosa. Two important collections of articles were published in celebration of the four hundredth anniversary of the publication of *La Florida del Inca*, *Nuevas lecturas de* La Florida del Inca (*New Readings of* The Florida of the Inca), edited by Carmen de Mora and Antonio Garrido Aranda, and *Franqueando fronteras: Garcilaso de la Vega y* La Florida del Inca (*Opening Borders: Garcilaso de la Vega and* The Florida of the Inca), edited with an introduction and a chronology by Chang-Rodríguez.

Background and Related Topics

In the last thirty years, bibliography on colonial Latin America has grown exponentially, and Garcilaso is still one of the main authors whom scholars are interested in studying. The works of Garcilaso are always studied in conjunction with other colonial chroniclers and writers treating similar or related topics, such as Felipe Guaman Poma de Ayala, Bartolomé de Las Casas, Blas Valera, Pedro Sarmiento de Gamboa, Titu Cusi Yupanqui, and Juan de Betanzos, among many others. Some of the issues that Garcilaso's texts illuminate are the conquest of the Amerindians, colonialism, memory and the writing of history, racism, injustice, historical writing, Andean religions, transatlantic issues, and many others. The plethora of sources on these topics makes it impossible to list most of the books published; however, they are most useful for teachers who are trying to develop a variety of syllabi in different disciplines and levels of undergraduate and graduate courses.

Anthologies are always helpful for teachers and students, and we recommend three of them with a selection of articles dedicated to different chronicles and different topics. *Amerindian Images and the Legacy of Columbus*, edited by René Jara and Nicholas Spadaccini, contains a long introduction and twenty-three articles with a wide range of topics on different authors. *New World Encounters*, edited by Stephen Greenblatt, includes fourteen articles that cover not only Spanish American authors but also French and Portuguese colonial issues. *Coded Encounters: Writing, Gender, and Ethnicity in Colonial America*, edited by Francisco Javier Cevallos-Candau and others, contains fourteen articles with topics related to issues of gender and ethnicity, among others.

Monographs about the conquest and clash of cultures in Peru are plentiful, but John Hemming's *The Conquest of the Incas*, a detailed account of the wars of conquest, is still the best choice in English. A more recent approach to the same area of study is *Andean Worlds: Indigenous History, Culture, and Consciousness under Spanish Rule, 1532–1825*, by Kenneth Andrien. This book covers not only the conquest but also its consequences until the independence of these countries from Spanish rule. Two important monographs by Sabine Mac-Cormack are *Religion in the Andes: Vision and Imagination in Early Colonial*

Peru and her intervention on the same topics with a transatlantic twist, *On the Wings of Time: Rome, the Incas, Spain, and Peru*. Taking a similar transatlantic approach are a short but fundamental volume, J. H. Elliott's *The Old World and the New 1492–1650*, and the author's latest extensive study on the subject, *Empires of the Atlantic World: Britain and Spain in America, 1492–1830*. The first book can be used in undergraduate courses, but the second not only expands the time frame that the study covers but also includes Great Britain and introduces imperial studies, a more recent field, which makes this volume most useful for graduate courses.

Indigenous identity, mestizaje, ethnicity, and racial difference are important topics in Garcilaso studies, and we recommend some of the more recent monographs on these issues: *The Mestizo Mind: The Intellectual Dynamics of Colonization and Globalization*, by Serge Gruzinski; *Global Indios: The Indigenous Struggle for Justice in Sixteenth-Century Spain*, by Nancy E. van Deusen; and *The Disappearing Mestizo: Configuring Difference in the Colonial New Kingdom of Granada*, by Joanne Rappaport.

For comparative studies with other texts and authors, Rolena Adorno's *Polemics of Possession in Spanish American Narrative* studies not only colonial authors such as Guaman Poma de Ayala and Álvar Núñez Cabeza de Vaca but also contemporary authors such as Gabriel García Márquez, among others. Related to Andean sexuality in colonial times, Michael J. Horswell's *Decolonizing the Sodomite: Queer Tropes of Sexuality in Colonial Andean Culture* is a good choice for graduate courses. The last of the books we recommend in this section of volumes on Andean culture is Sara Castro-Klarén's *The Narrow Pass of Our Nerves: Writing, Coloniality and Postcolonial Theory*. This book studies a vast range of topics and authors from the perspective of postcolonial theory and can be used for graduate courses in which the purpose is to study Andean colonial cultures, Garcilaso, and Guaman Poma de Ayala.

More general monographs that deal with several issues resulting from the conquest of the Americas, but can be applied to the case of Peru and Garcilaso's texts, include David A. Brading's *The First America: The Spanish Monarchy, Creole Patriots, and the Liberal State, 1492–1867*, which covers a vast range of topics on the conquest of Mexico and Peru and dedicates chapters to specific authors, among them Garcilaso and Guaman Poma de Ayala. Walter Mignolo's *The Darker Side of the Renaissance: Literacy, Territoriality, and Colonization* is one of the most important books on colonial studies and can be used for graduate courses. The same goes for Tzvetan Todorov's *The Conquest of America: The Question of the Other*, one of the first studies that approaches Spanish American colonial texts from a new perspective. And lastly, *The Fall of Natural Man: The American Indian and the Origins of Ethnology*, by Anthony Pagden, deals with issues of barbarism, Aristotle's theory of natural slavery that Spaniards used to classify indigenous peoples of the Americas as slaves, and comparative ethnology in Las Casas, Juan Ginés de Sepúlveda, José de Acosta, and Joseph-François Lafitau.

Online Resources

The best online resource in Spanish on the life and works of Garcilaso is the site *Biblioteca Virtual Miguel de Cervantes*, which has a section on Garcilaso, free to access ("Inca Garcilaso de la Vega"). Garcilaso traveled to Spain from Peru in 1560 and lived in the town of Montilla and the city of Córdoba until his death in 1616; since all his works were published in Portugal and Spain, most of the documents related to him are in Spain. The page dedicated to Garcilaso is maintained by the University of Alicante and includes all the author's first editions in digital files. It also has other chroniclers' works and bibliographies, as well as an extensive list of digitized articles on Garcilaso and a section of images that includes his portraits; pictures of his houses in Montilla, Córdoba, and Cuzco, Peru; videos of conferences and homages; and many other images that can be used in class. It also has links to external Web pages on Garcilaso. The instructor can use this resource either for undergraduate classes or for graduate courses. For lower-level classes, the instructor can use images and some short videos or conferences. For upper-level classes and graduate seminars, the digitalized first editions are an excellent resource.

If the instructor wants only the digitized version of the first edition of the first part of the *Comentarios reales*, the John Carter Brown Library provides one (brown.edu/Facilities/John_Carter_Brown_Library/exhibitions/peru/peru/ind_inca.php). A digitized version of Livermore's English translation of both parts of the *Royal Commentaries* is available online at the University of Michigan by subscription (fulcrum.org/concern/monographs/xw42n814p).

The 2017 film *Inca Garcilaso, el mestizo*, directed by Fátima Entrenas and Miguel Ángel Entrenas, uses a screenplay by Mazzotti and Carlos Clementson. It is an eighty-minute fictional movie in Spanish, and versions with English ("Inca Garcilaso with English Subtitles") and French subtitles are available ("Inca Garcilaso Movie"). It narrates the most important moments of Garcilaso's life, especially those that influenced him to write his masterwork, the *Royal Commentaries*, and can be used in courses of all levels.

WORKS CITED

Adorno, Rolena. *The Polemics of Possession in Spanish American Narrative*. Yale UP, 2007.

Anadón, José, editor. *Garcilaso Inca de la Vega: An American Humanist: A Tribute to José Durand*. U of Notre Dame P, 1998.

Andrien, Kenneth. *Andean Worlds: Indigenous History, Culture, and Consciousness under Spanish Rule, 1532–1825*. U of New Mexico P, 2001.

Bernard, Carmen. *Un Inca platonicien: Garcilaso de la Vega, 1539–1616*. Fayard, 2006.

Brading, David A. *The First America: The Spanish Monarchy, Creole Patriots, and the Liberal State, 1492–1867*. Cambridge UP, 1991.

Carrillo Espejo, Francisco. *Diario del Inca Garcilaso, 1562–1616*. Editorial Horizonte, 1996.

Castanien, Donald G. *El Inca Garcilaso de la Vega*. Twayne, 1969.

Castro-Klarén, Sara. *The Narrow Pass of Our Nerves: Writing, Coloniality and Postcolonial Theory*. Iberoamericana/Vervuert, 2011.

Castro-Klarén, Sara, and Christian Fernández, editors. *Inca Garcilaso and Contemporary World-Making*. U of Pittsburgh P, 2016.

Cevallos-Candau, Francisco Javier, et al., editors. *Coded Encounters: Writing, Gender, and Ethnicity in Colonial America*. U of Massachusetts P, 1994.

Chang-Rodríguez, Raquel. *Cartografía garcilasista*. Universidad de Alicante, 2013.

———. *Entre la espada y la pluma: El Inca Garcilaso de la Vega y sus* Comentarios reales. Pontificia Universidad Católica del Perú, 2010.

———. *Franqueando fronteras: Garcilaso de la Vega y* La Florida del Inca. Pontificia Universidad Católica del Perú, 2006.

Cortez, Enrique E. *Biografía y polémica: El Inca Garcilaso y el archivo colonial andino en el siglo XIX*. Iberoamericana/Vervuert, 2019.

Crowley, Frances G. *Garcilaso de la Vega and His Sources in* Comentarios reales de los Incas. Mouton, 1971.

Durand, José. *El Inca Garcilaso de la Vega: Clásico de América*. Septentas, 1976.

Elliott, J. H. *Empires of the Atlantic World: Britain and Spain in America, 1492–1830*. Yale UP, 2006.

———. *The Old World and the New, 1492–1650*. Cambridge UP, 1970.

Fernández, Christian. *Inca Garcilaso: Imaginación, memoria e identidad*. Universidad Nacional Mayor de San Marcos, 2004.

Fuerst, James W. *New World Postcolonial: The Political Thought of Inca Garcilaso de la Vega*. U of Pittsburgh P, 2018.

Garcilaso de la Vega. *Comentarios reales*. Edited by Mercedes Serna, Castalia, 2000.

———. *Comentarios reales de los Incas*. Edited by Daniel Dillon Alvarez, Universidad Inca Garcilaso de la Vega, 2007.

———. *Comentarios reales de los Incas*. Edited by Carlos Araníbar, Fondo de Cultura Económica, 1991.

———. *Comentarios reales de los Incas*. Edited by Aurelio Miró Quesada, Biblioteca Ayacucho, 1976. 2 vols.

———. *Comentarios reales de los Incas*. Edited by Ángel Rosenblat, Emecé Editores, 1943. 2 vols.

———. *Comentarios reales: La Florida del Inca*. Edited by Mercedes López-Baralt, Espasa Calpe, 2003. Biblioteca de Literatura Universal.

———. *Comentarios reales: Selección*. Edited by Enrique Pupo-Walker, Cátedra, 1996. Letras hispánicas 410.

———. *La Florida del Inca*. Edited by Sylvia Lynn Hilton, Historia 16, 1986. Crónicas de América 22.

————. *La Florida del Inca*. Edited by Carmen Zevallos Choy, Universidad Inca Garcilaso de la Vega, 2009.

————. *The Florida of the Inca: A History of the Adelantado, Hernando de Soto, Governor and Captain General of the Kingdom of Florida, and of Other Heroic Spanish and Indian Cavaliers*. Translated by John Grier Varner and Jeannette Johnson Varner, U of Texas P, 1951.

————. *Historia general del Perú (Segunda parte de los* Comentarios reales de los Incas*)*. Edited by Ángel Rosenblat, Emecé Editores, 1944. 3 vols.

————. *Obras completas*. Edited by Carlos Araníbar, Ministerio de Relaciones Exteriores, 2015. 3 vols.

————. *Obras completas del Inca Garcilaso de la Vega*. Edited by P. Carmelo Sáenz de Santa María, Atlas, 1960–65. 3 vols.

————. *Relación de la descendencia de Garci Pérez de Vargas (1596)*. Ediciones del Instituto de Historia, 1951.

————. *Royal Commentaries of the Incas and General History of Peru*. Translated by Harold V. Livermore, U of Texas P, 1966. 2 vols.

————. *Royal Commentaries of the Incas and General History of Peru: Abridged*. Edited by Karen Spalding, translated by Harold V. Livermore, Hackett, 1966.

————. *Segunda parte de los* Comentarios reales. Edited by Carla Gonzáles Márquez, Universidad Inca Garcilaso de la Vega, 2013. 2 vols.

————. *Traducción de los* Diálogos de amor *de León de Hebreo, y otros escritos*. Universidad Inca Garcilaso de la Vega, 2015.

González Viaña, Eduardo, and José Antonio Mazzotti, editors. *Garcilasismo creativo y crítico: Nueva antología*. Axiara / Academia Norteamericana de la Lengua Española, 2016.

Greenblatt, Stephen, editor. *New World Encounters*. U of California P, 1993.

Gruzinski, Serge. *The Mestizo Mind: The Intellectual Dynamics of Colonization and Globalization*. Translated by Deke Dusinberre, Routledge, 2002.

Gutiérrez, Miguel. *Poderes secretos*. J. Campodónico, 1995.

Hebreo, León. *Dialogues of Love*. Translated by Cosmos Damian Bacich and Rossella Pescatori, U of Toronto P, 2009.

Hemming, John. *The Conquest of the Incas*. Harcourt, Brace, Jovanovich, 1970.

Hernández, Max. *Memoria del bien perdido: Conflicto, identidad y nostalgia en el Inca Garcilaso de la Vega*. Sociedad Estatal Quinto Centenario, 1991.

Horswell, Michael J. *Decolonizing the Sodomite: Queer Tropes of Sexuality in Colonial Andean Culture*. U of Texas P, 2006.

"Inca Garcilaso de la Vega." *Biblioteca Virtual Miguel de Cervantes*, cervantesvirtual .com/portales/inca_garcilaso_de_la_vega.

Inca Garcilaso, el mestizo. Directed by Fátima Entrenas y Miguel Ángel Entrenas, Cátedra Intercultural, U of Cordoba, 2017. DVD.

"Inca Garcilaso Movie—French Subtitles." *YouTube*, translated by Claude Rigault and uploaded by Jessica Liodos, 29 Jan. 2020, youtube.com/watch?v =dohE1vuZEEY.

"Inca Garcilaso with English Subtitles." *YouTube*, translated and uploaded by Jessica Liodos, youtube.com/watch?v=Dfqxb-S8IRM&feature=youtu.be.

Jákfalvi-Leiva, Susana. *Traducción, escritura y violencia colonizadora: Un estudio de la obra del Inca Garcilaso*. Maxwell School of Citizenship and Public Affairs, 1984.

Jara, René, and Nicholas Spadaccini, editors. *Amerindian Images and the Legacy of Columbus*. U of Minnesota P, 1992.

López-Baralt, Mercedes. *El Inca Garcilaso, traductor de culturas*. Iberoamericana/ Vervuert, 2011.

Macchi, Fernanda. *Incas ilustrados: Reconstrucciones imperiales en la segunda mitad del siglo XVIII*. Iberoamericana/Vervuert, 2009.

MacCormack, Sabine. *On the Wings of Time: Rome, the Incas, Spain, and Peru*. Princeton UP, 2007.

———. *Religion in the Andes: Vision and Imagination in Early Colonial Peru*. Princeton UP, 1991.

Maguiño Veneros, Miguel Hugo. *El Inca en la ficción literaria*. Universidad San Ignacio de Loyola, 2014.

Mazzotti, José Antonio. *Coros mestizos del Inca Garcilaso*. Fondo de Cultura Económica, 1996.

———. *Encontrando un Inca: Ensayos escogidos sobre el Inca Garcilaso de la Vega*. Axiara / Academia Norteamericana de la Lengua Española, 2016.

———. *Encontrando un Inca: Ensayos escogidos sobre el Inca Garcilaso de la Vega*. Expanded ed., La Habana, Editorial Universidad de la Habana, 2018.

———. *Incan Insights: El Inca Garcilaso's Hints to Andean Readers*. Iberoamericana/ Vervuert, 2008.

———, editor. *Renacimiento mestizo: Los 400 años de los* Comentarios reales. Iberoamericana/Vervuert, 2010.

Mignolo, Walter. *The Darker Side of the Renaissance: Literacy, Territoriality, and Colonization*. U of Michigan P, 1995.

Miró Quesada, Aurelio. *El Inca Garcilaso y otros estudios garcilasistas*. Ediciones Cultura Hispánica, 1971.

Mora, Carmen de, and Antonio Garrido Aranda, editors. *Nuevas lecturas de* La Florida del Inca. Iberoamericana/Vervuert, 2008.

Mora, Carmen de, et al., editors. *Humanismo, mestizaje y escritura en los* Comentarios reales. Iberoamericana/Vervuert, 2010.

Pagden, Anthony. *The Fall of Natural Man: The American Indian and the Origins of Ethnology*. Cambridge UP, 1982.

Pino-Díaz, Fermín del, and Amalia Iniesta Cámara, editors. *Los mundos diversos del Inca Garcilaso y la academia actual*. Universidad Nacional Agraria La Molina, 2017.

Pupo-Walker, Enrique. *Historia, creación y profecía en los textos del Inca Garcilaso de la Vega*. José Porrúa Turanzas, 1982.

Rappaport, Joanne. *The Disappearing Mestizo: Configuring Difference in the Colonial New Kingdom of Granada*. Duke UP, 2014.

Rodríguez Mansilla, Fernando. *El Inca Garcilaso en su Siglo de Oro*. Iberoamericana/ Vervuert, 2019.

Steigman, Jonathan D. *La Florida del Inca and the Struggle for Social Equality in Colonial Spanish America*. U of Alabama P, 2005.

Todorov, Tzvetan. *The Conquest of America: The Question of the Other*. Translated by Richard Howard, Harper and Row, 1984.

van Deusen, Nancy E. *Global Indios: The Indigenous Struggle for Justice in Sixteenth-Century Spain*. Duke UP, 2015.

Varner, John Grier. *El Inca: The Life and Times of Garcilaso de la Vega*. U of Texas P, 1968.

Zamora, Margarita. *Language, Authority, and Indigenous History in the* Comentarios reales de los Incas. Cambridge UP, 1988.

Part Two

APPROACHES

Introduction

Christian Fernández and José Antonio Mazzotti

Approaches to Teaching the Works of Inca Garcilaso de la Vega brings together
key essays to showcase methods of teaching the works of Inca Garcilaso from
different perspectives and disciplines. We have selected twenty essays by the
most distinguished and established students of Garcilaso's oeuvre and by young
scholars who bring new approaches to teaching his works. Thus far, most of the
abundant scholarship on this author is in Spanish. This volume shows an English-
speaking academia the importance of Garcilaso's work in Latin American culture and in postcolonial studies at large. It also explains the masterful discursive methods (which incorporate both Andean and Renaissance influences) that
Garcilaso used to find appropriate frames of representation for Andean culture
in his time. The volume highlights and disseminates the recent cutting-edge
scholarship and teaching approaches that have appeared in Latin American colonial studies in the Americas and in Europe. At the center of this reexamina-
tion one finds that Garcilaso's wrestling with writing culture is an attempt to produce a corpus that could encompass and translate the intelligibility of his view
of the Andean world to present and future readers all over the world. In this
sense, Garcilaso constitutes one of the first American-born cultural translators
and undoubtedly an early modern representative of a distinctive New World
identity.

As interest in the work of Garcilaso grows in university departments in the
fields of Spanish, Romance languages, English, comparative literature, American studies, ethnic studies, anthropology, art history, Latin American studies,
and cultural studies, we hope teachers will welcome this volume in English on
Garcilaso's oeuvre, mainly on the *Comentarios reales*, or *Royal Commentaries*,
now considered a foundational masterpiece of Latin American literary and historiographical traditions.

Garcilaso's *Royal Commentaries* and *La Florida del Inca* (*The Florida of the
Inca*) have an established place in the Spanish American literary canon. At least
since 1766, when these works were included in the Royal Academy of the Spanish Language's *Diccionario de autoridades* (*Dictionary of Authorities*) as an example of Spanish language and style, Garcilaso has been considered a master of
Spanish prose. In recent years, some of the most influential textbooks and literary anthologies in English have included the works of Garcilaso: *The Heath Anthology of American Literature* (Lauter), Susan Castillo and Ivy Schweitzer's *The
Literatures of Colonial America: An Anthology*, Carla Mulford's *Early American
Writings*, and *The Norton Anthology of American Literature* (Baym), to mention
just a few. Garcilaso's works as literary artifacts provide to teachers a plethora of
topics for the study, analysis, and interpretation not only of Garcilaso's language
and discursive style but also of a wide range of issues, such as the "discovery" of

the other, the conquest and colonization of the Americas, imperialism, race and racism, the conflict of languages and translation, and the formation of the self in Renaissance Europe and the Americas.

The essays are divided into four sections that deal with the broad themes in Garcilaso's main book as well as his other works (*Dialogues of Love*; *The Florida of the Inca*, an original history of the conquest of what is now the southern United States; and *General History of Peru*, the second part of the *Royal Commentaries*) and their importance in several disciplines. Since the public and readers of this volume are mainly teachers in American universities in different disciplines, most of the essays focus on teaching the materials in English translation. In general, Spanish American colonial writers are taught in Spanish to students only in their third or fourth year of college studies, but given the fact that this volume's focus is English-language settings, it can also be used in first- and second-year classes, or any class where students do not need to have a working command of Spanish. We recommend and will use the standard translation by Harold V. Livermore.

Garcilaso published the first part of his classic text *Royal Commentaries* in 1609. Since its publication, the *Royal Commentaries* has come to represent a Latin American tradition of art and thought and a model for historiographical narratives that has remained provocative and suggestive both in the Americas and in Europe.

In order to communicate the importance and the hybrid nature of his writing, a few lines on Garcilaso's life are in order. Born in Cuzco in 1539, he was the son of Capitán Garcilaso de la Vega y Vargas, a Spanish conquistador, and Chimpu Ocllo, an Incan princess. He was raised primarily by his mother and her Incan relatives, who belonged to the *panaka*, or royal family, of the emperor Tupac Yupanqui. Garcilaso learned the Quechua language in infancy and developed fluency in Spanish probably after the age of six. Those early years were pivotal for Garcilaso's historical work a few decades later, in which he declares that the main sources for his account were the oral versions he had heard from his maternal relatives (in Quechua, of course), his own observations of Incan monuments and rituals, and the letters from old classmates who were also first-generation mestizos and Indians from noble families growing up in Cuzco.

His father died in May 1559 and left him a moderate fortune of four thousand golden pesos to travel to Spain. A few months later, in January 1560, Garcilaso left Cuzco for Spain to pursue grants and exemptions for the services both his father and his mother had rendered to the crown. Once his attempts to receive any rewards from the crown failed, he met his paternal uncle Alonso de Vargas, who protected and supported him and treated him like a son. He lived in Montilla with his uncle and aunt, and between 1569 and 1570 he enlisted in the army of Don Juan de Austria and pursued a military career. After his uncle died in 1570, he remained in Montilla and started his self-education, reading the classics and several Renaissance authors in Spanish and Italian. He completed his translation into Spanish of the Italian canonical treatise about love and desire *Dialoghi di amore*, the *Dialogues of Love*, by the Jewish Spanish exile León Hebreo, and published it in Madrid in 1590, with great success. It is still considered today the best Spanish translation of Hebreo's masterpiece.

We can presume that it was during those formative years in Montilla that he also read what Spanish historians had written about the Incas. A possible motivation for reading these accounts was that historians such as Francisco López de Gómara, Agustín de Zárate, and Diego Fernández (el Palentino) had written that Garcilaso's father had helped Gonzalo Pizarro (brother of Francisco Pizarro) in his rebellion against the crown between 1544 and 1548, having facilitated Pizarro's victory at the battle of Huarina in 1547. In 1563 the Consejo de Indias (the crown's administrative entity that handled all matters related to the Spanish possessions in the New World) had denied Garcilaso's requests to receive compensation for his father's services during the conquest of Peru.

Garcilaso resolved to take up his quill and construct his version of Incan history and the conquest after concluding that the Spanish accounts were all either incomplete or false in some way. He did so by displaying a masterful command of Renaissance historiographical rhetoric, by recalling the stories and myths he had heard from his Quechua-speaking relatives during his early years, and by gathering information from mestizo friends who had remained in Peru. Writing in a peculiar, nuanced, and polyphonic style, he not only permanently modified later readers' understanding of Incan history and administration but also created and articulated a new American identity. He called this new subjectivity "mestizo" to differentiate himself from both the Spaniards and the indigenous people. However, many times he also called himself an "Indian" and an "Inca": his literary name, Inca Garcilaso, adopted in the 1580s, is a testimony to his efforts to juxtapose his double identity (his birth name was Gómez Suárez de Figueroa). In 1591 Garcilaso moved to Córdoba, where he wrote his major works, *The Florida of the Inca* (published in 1605) and the *Royal Commentaries* (1609 and 1617).

It is important to appreciate the thread that runs throughout his works. In *Dialogues of Love*, Garcilaso shows an affinity for a Neoplatonic philosophy that accepted the possibility of more than one valid universal truth. To Garcilaso, this philosophical framework would be most useful in advancing the idea that the Incas held some beliefs that could stand as truth despite their lack of Christian knowledge. Garcilaso also implicitly linked radical kabbalah ideas, as presented by Hebreo, with four paradigms of Andean mythology and a circular conception of time related to an Andean cosmogonic understanding of time and space. In *The Florida of the Inca*, Garcilaso eloquently describes the humanist dimension of some conquistadores as well as several indigenous leaders (mainly the Seminole from Florida and other groups of today's Georgia, South and North Carolina, Alabama, and Texas). He also presents the conquistador Hernando de Soto as a paradigm of a just ruler and as a leader who honored the common good. This paradigm of a Spanish *dux populi* (leader of the people) would prove very useful in depicting some of the conquistadores in the *Royal Commentaries*.

In the first part of the *Royal Commentaries*, Garcilaso elaborates a positive pre-Christian portrait of the Incas and their administration as a model for a harmonious society that was not only a reflection of the past but also a subtle political proposal for his own colonial time. In the second part of the work, *General History of Peru*, Garcilaso praises the first conquistadores for the same qualities he sees in de Soto in *The Florida of the Inca*. The work concludes with the execution of Túpac Amaru I in 1572, which marked the end of the main line of the Inca dynasty. The first part had begun with the foundation of Cuzco and the empire by the first two Incas, Manco Capac and his wife-sister, Mama Ocllo. In this sense, the work in its two parts is a dynastic history of a royal family, employing many elements of Renaissance rhetoric as well as some layers of meaning that can be better understood with an Andean approach determined from different disciplines.

It is indisputable that since its publication more than four hundred years ago and the translations that followed—the French and English translations were especially influential—Garcilaso's history of the Incas and the Spanish conquest of the Andes has remained the indispensable source on the matter. The *Royal Commentaries* has not only retained its place as a masterpiece in the Spanish language and a foundational text in the construction of Latin America as a distinct culture, but it has also managed to stay relevant in debates on imperial policies, intercultural analysis, and intersemiotic communication. The work has also shed light on the use of the archives related to the Incan royal family, as well as European chronicles, for the purpose of presenting the past as difference.

At the turn of the twentieth century, the Spanish polymath Marcelino Menéndez y Pelayo accused Garcilaso of displaying an exaggerated imagination (Cortez). In 1973 the Peruvian ethnohistorian María Rostworowski pointed out the factual historical inconsistencies of Garcilaso's description and understanding of Andean culture in general and of Inca government, religion, costumes, ritual, art, and architecture in particular. However, Garcilaso's account retains its place as the indispensable source for many modern disciplines, from archaeology to history and linguistics. Let us not forget that throughout colonial times and into the period of independence, Garcilaso was widely read among elites in Spanish America. In fact, the *Royal Commentaries* is directly credited with having been one of the inspirations for the indigenous uprising of Túpac Amaru II in 1780, as well as a constant companion to the two most important liberators of Spanish America, José de San Martín and Simón Bolívar (see Durand). Besides remaining the most trustworthy source on Inca culture, and despite his partiality toward the side of the Incan aristocracy to which his mother belonged, Garcilaso's historiographical project—how to make intelligible the radical differences in Inca culture to a European mind entrenched in seeing otherness from the exclusive perspective of self—has attracted the continued interest of cultural historians in Spain, England, France, and the United States. This inquiry into mutual intelligibility across differences and epochs continues to engage Garcilaso's modern readers.

At the same time, an analysis of the rhetorical mechanisms that characterize Garcilaso's works, and a recognition of the hybrid nature of his writing style, all suggest the importance of taking an innovative approach to the *Royal Commentaries*, one appreciative of the hidden and transatlantic complexities of this notable Latin American author. In fact, one can only fully understand the role of the *Royal Commentaries* in Latin American culture by acknowledging Garcilaso's different cultural experiences and migrations (from Peru to Spain; from his mother tongue, Quechua, to his father's Spanish) and the migration of subsequent generations of Latin Americans. The complexity of his writing attests to the unique nature of his style and his configuration of the Andean world before and after the conquest. Today, Garcilaso remains an inspiration for indigenous movements in Latin America for his defense of nature and of the human dignity of the indigenous people, despite his Cuzco-centric and pro-Incaist agenda.

This volume brings together twenty essays by scholars and teachers from various fields who are working from the groundbreaking perspectives created by the postcolonial and decolonial turns. These authors include very well-established and respected specialists in Garcilaso studies, midcareer scholars, and more recent graduates entering the discipline. This wide range of authors brings different methodological and theoretical approaches to the study and teaching of the works of Garcilaso. We also have chosen essays that can be read in conjunction with other related essays in the volume, making it more useful for both the teacher and the student.

Some of the pedagogical issues that emerge from the essays are related to the historical and cultural context in which Garcilaso wrote. Garcilaso lived before the Enlightenment, and the importance of Catholicism for his worldview and that of his readers is not to be underestimated. He wrote keeping in mind that his readers would have a strong religious consciousness, and he constantly declares himself a sincere believer of the "true" faith. There was also a firm ecclesiastical control that would not allow any suspicious references that could disseminate heretical or idolatrous ideas. For this reason, it is key to understand that in order to present Incan religion or ancient Andean myths without distortion, Garcilaso had to show them in a coded format. Today, readers can access those mentions by familiarizing themselves with information from history, archaeology, Quechua linguistics, and ethnography. However, the fact that Garcilaso's *Royal Commentaries* presents some of those references in its subtext does not eliminate the overwhelming evidence of his Catholic beliefs. For a just assessment of Garcilaso, we need to frame his works within a syncretic understanding of his narrative style. Some of the essays will emphasize the European aspects of Garcilaso's works; others will stress their Andean roots and meanings; but both cultural backgrounds complement each other.

Another pedagogical issue that emerges from the essays is the relation between an early-seventeenth-century author such as Garcilaso and contemporary issues like migration, multiculturalism, and indigenous rights. As we know, Garcilaso has traditionally been depicted as a mestizo with predominant European values and culture. However, some of the essays will demonstrate that he preserves many traces from his Andean origins and has a great deal to say regarding identity formation under a dominant culture and language. Garcilaso's own migration can help to illuminate aspects of the experience of millions of Latin American immigrants in the United States and Europe today. Issues of language loyalty; conceptions of nature, space, and time; and emotional and cultural links to the country of origin are all important in considering the social process and cultural transformation of minority groups in Western societies today.

WORKS CITED

Baym, Nina, editor. *The Norton Anthology of American Literature: Beginnings to 1820.* 6th ed., vol. 1, W. W. Norton, 2002.

Castillo, Susan, and Ivy Schweitzer, editors. *The Literatures of Colonial America: An Anthology.* Blackwell, 2001.

Cortez, Enrique E. "Canon, hispanismo y literatura colonial: El Inca Garcilaso en el proyecto de historia literaria de Marcelino Menéndez Pelayo." *MLN,* vol. 123, no. 2, Mar. 2013, pp. 277–97.

Durand, José. "Presencia de Garcilaso Inca en Túpac Amaru." *Cuadernos Americanos,* vol. 6, no. 18, 1989, pp. 172–77.

Garcilaso de la Vega. *Royal Commentaries of the Incas and General History of Peru.* Translated by Harold V. Livermore, U of Texas P, 1966. 2 vols.

Lauter, Paul, editor. *Heath Anthology of American Literature.* 7th ed., vol. 1, Wadsworth Cengage Learning, 2014.

Mulford, Carla, editor. *Early American Writings.* Oxford UP, 2002.

Rostworowski, María. *Historia del Tahuantinsuyo.* Instituto de Estudios Peruanos, 1988.

———. *History of the Inca Realm.* Translated by Harry B. Iceland, Cambridge UP, 1998.

León Hebreo's *Diálogos de amor* as a Gateway to Inca Garcilaso's Opus

Damian Bacich

También por aprovechar los años de mi edad y servir a los estudiosos, traduxe de italiano en romance castellano los diálogos de filosofía entre Filón y Sofía, libro intitulado León Hebreo, que anda traduzido en todas lenguas.

In order to make the most of my [middle] age and be of use to scholars, I translated from Italian into the Castilian vernacular the book of philosophical dialogues between Philo and Sophia, entitled León Hebreo, which has been translated into every language.
—Inca Garcilaso de la Vega, *Historia general del Perú*[1]

Those familiar with the work of Inca Garcilaso de la Vega know that his first foray into publishing was the 1590 translation of the *Dialoghi d'amore* (*Dialogues of Love*), by León Hebreo. And while it may seem easy to dismiss his Spanish translation, *Diálogos de amor*, as nothing more than Garcilaso's youthful dabbling in the trendy Neoplatonism of his times, which also captivated the youthful Miguel de Cervantes and other writers, it would certainly be unwise. There is much more to the story than this, since the *Diálogos* represents a key moment in Garcilaso's personal and professional itinerary, as has been demonstrated by numerous scholars. As such, it is my contention that including this work in curricula that deal with Garcilaso can greatly enrich students' understanding and experience of his later, more prominent works, most notably the *Comentarios reales de los Incas* (*Royal Commentaries of the Incas*).

I teach at a large urban public university that confers bachelor's as well as master's degrees and serves students from a broad variety of social and educational backgrounds. I have used selections from the *Diálogos* in undergraduate courses and graduate seminars on translation, transatlantic cultural exchange, and colonial Hispanic American literature, all of which feature Garcilaso and his works. I have found that introducing students to the *Diálogos* is an excellent aid for framing the conversation around Garcilaso, his motivations, and his milieu.

Diálogos de amor

Though now not well known, the *Dialoghi d'amore* was an important and influential text in its time. Written in Tuscan dialect and first published in Rome in 1535, the work was widely read in Renaissance Italy, and its popularity spread throughout Europe and the Mediterranean in the second half of the cinquecento. By the mid-seventeenth century it had been translated into French, Hebrew, Latin, and Spanish. Among those directly influenced by the *Dialoghi* were writers such as Cervantes, Michel de Montaigne, Alessandro Piccolomini, Philip Sidney, and Baruch Spinoza. The book's appeal in part stemmed from a combination of its eclectic subject matter (a fascinating mixture of Neoplatonic philosophy and Hebrew kabbalah) and its accessible vernacular style, at a time when many such treatises were written in Latin.

Framed as a conversation between two lovers—Philo, a tutor and suitor, and Sophia, his beloved yet evasive interlocutor—the work falls into the dialogue genre that achieved great popularity during the early modern period. The three conversations, or dialogues, around which the book is structured are titled "On Love and Desire," "On the Universality of Love," and "On the Origin of Love" (Hebreo, *Dialogues*). The first and shortest of the dialogues centers around the interplay and distinction between love and desire, touching on the practical and concrete spheres of life such as family, power, and wealth. The conversation begins with Philo's provocative statement, "El conocerte, o Sofía, causa en mí amor y deseo" ("Knowing you, Sophia, provokes in me love and desire"; Garcilaso, *La traducción* 1; Hebreo, *Dialogues* 1), thereby setting a tone that mixes sensuality with spirituality and that characterizes the entire work. As the object of Philo's advances, Sophia keeps her suitor at a distance and engaged in conversation by alternating between expressions of interest and skepticism, encouraging him to consider notions such as moderation versus extremes, the contemplative versus the active life, and reason versus passion. For Hebreo, through the voice of Philo, sensual love is intimately tied to spiritual or intellectual love and is essential for understanding the love of the divine, which is what all philosophical systems aim toward.

The second dialogue, which deals with love as a universal force, has a markedly encyclopedic character, touching on subjects such as astrology, meteorology, and zoology, and the two interlocutors delve into the theories of thinkers from Plato and Aristotle to Maimonides and Ibn Gabirol. For Philo, love in the physical order is organized around a male-female principle of attraction, whereas the universe itself is recapitulated in the human body, giving rise to the image of the microcosmos-macrocosmos, so dear to Giovanni Pico della Mirandola. Philo attempts to show Sophia how throughout the centuries there have been numerous attempts to express such abstract ideas, and a centerpiece of this dialogue is Philo's discourse on the uses of myth and allegory, or what Plato referred to as the lies of the poets (377d). Drawing heavily from Boccaccio's *Genealogia deorum gentilium*, Hebreo outlines the ways that allegorical readings of Greek and Roman myths have been used to encapsulate scientific, philosophical, and theological truths. The ancient fables, in particular those that take the form of poetry, are a privileged vehicle for the conservation and transmission of knowledge, especially about the harmonious relations of love in the cosmos. Hebreo's discussion of the uses of allegory provides a framework for Garcilaso to use in presenting Inca mythology to a European audience and gives him the authority to adopt a comparative approach that effectively puts Andean mythology on par with the gods of Greek and Roman antiquity. By analyzing Hebreo's explanation of the allegorical senses of myth and fable, students come to understand the purposes that early modern readers expected fable and fiction to serve, acting as intersection between philosophy, ethics, history, and religion. They can also develop a sense of the intellectual underpinnings to Garcilaso's discussion in chapter 27 of book 2 of the *Comentarios reales* of the role of the *amautas*, the wise men of Inca society, charged with preserving the ancient knowledge: "supieron componer en prosa, también como en verso, fábulas breves y compendiosas por vía de poesía, para encerrar en ellas doctrina moral o para guardar alguna tradición de su idolatría" ("One of these abilities was the composition in prose and in verse of short and concise fables of a poetic kind to summarize moral doctrine or preserve some tradition of their idolatry"; *Obras* 2: 125; *Royal Commentaries* 1: 130).

Hebreo's third dialogue is the lengthiest (twice as long as the second dialogue and four times as long as the first) and also the densest, in which the discourse reaches speculative heights. In it, the two lovers discuss topics such as divine and human intellect, the world soul and the human soul, the essence and nature of love, and whether love is eternal or coeval with the world itself. This dialogue is marked by a clear attempt to synthesize major philosophical currents of the Middle Ages and early Renaissance—Platonism, Aristotelianism, humanism, and kabbalah. An important discussion in this dialogue centers around a retelling of Plato's androgyne story from *Symposium* and the analysis of the allegorical elements it contains (Garcilaso, *La traducción* 286–88). Not only can it serve as a case study in the application of multiple meanings to a fable, as described in the second dialogue, but it provides an interesting parallel to Garcilaso's tale of the giants in chapter 9 of book 9 of the *Comentarios reales*: the androgynes, like Garcilaso's giants, sought to do battle against the gods, only to be punished for their rebellion.

The third dialogue ends with the two lovers promising to meet again for a fourth and final colloquy. Like many lovers' promises, this one seems to have not been kept: the fourth dialogue never materialized, and since the work was published posthumously, a great deal of speculation developed over the years as to its existence. Whether Hebreo intended to write a fourth dialogue or simply wanted to leave readers in suspense, the frustratingly ambiguous ending only served to heighten the work's air of mystery and hermeticism.

León Hebreo

Part of the mystery surrounding *Dialoghi* for early modern readers was the identity of its author, thought to be deceased by the time of its publishing in 1535. Most knew him thanks to his attribution as "Leone Ebreo" (León Hebreo in Spanish) and therefore had a vague idea that he was of Jewish descent. Some Italian versions, such as the elegant editions of the Aldus Manutius press, described him as a *medico*, in reference to his profession, and a Christian convert. What many did not know was that the author was one of the most illustrious exiles of Spain's 1492 expulsion of the Jews, and the details of his life and career in some ways provide interesting parallels to those of his Andean translator. For students unaware of Spain's history of intolerance against Moors, Jews, and American Indians, into which both Garcilaso and Hebreo were born, familiarity with Hebreo's biography can provide a useful introduction to the dynamics that marginalized constituencies faced during Spain's imperial expansion.

Born Yehuda Abravanel in Lisbon in the early 1460s, the man we know as León Hebreo was a scion of one of Spain's most influential Sephardic families, one that proudly traced its lineage to the biblical King David. His father, Isaac Abravanel, was arguably the most important Jewish writer of the fifteenth century, having penned numerous works of biblical exegesis, apologetics, and philosophy; Dom Isaac (as he was known to his contemporaries) was afforded princely status in the Portuguese Jewish community and was a key member of the king of Portugal's inner circle. Accused of complicity in a plot against the royal family, Isaac Abravanel was forced to flee Portugal with his family in the early 1480s and took up residence in Castile, where Yehuda eventually became physician to the Catholic monarchs Ferdinand and Isabella. At court the Abravanel family's prestige and Yehuda's skill as a doctor afforded him an elevated position and entry into the highest spheres of power. With the Alhambra Decree, which expelled all Jews from Spain, however, Yehuda Abravanel found himself forced to either accept baptism or once again leave behind the life he had built. Unwilling to abandon his ancestral beliefs, and despite the urgings of King Ferdinand, who held him in high esteem, Abravanel chose to join the rest of his family and leave Spain for the Italian peninsula. The price he paid was high. Ferdinand offered to exempt Abravanel from the decree of expulsion if he were to allow his son Isaac (named for Abravanel's father) to be baptized. Abravanel refused and arranged to send his son to Portugal for safekeeping, only to have him eventually taken and baptized after Portugal expelled its Jewish population in 1495. It is unlikely that father and son ever saw each other again, and Abravanel would eventually compose the poetic *Lament on Destiny* (*Lamentación o queja del destino*) about his suffering over the loss of young Isaac (Miró Quesada 113).

The Abravanel family would find a home in Naples, yet soon volatile political circumstances and a wave of anti-Jewish policies would converge to deny Yehuda Abravanel stability. Between 1495 and 1510 he would reside in Genoa and Venice before returning to Naples. He likely spent time in Florence and in Rome, but after 1521 there are no further records of Abravanel's whereabouts. When *Dialoghi d'amore* was eventually published in 1535, it was generally believed that Abravanel had passed away some years earlier, though the location of his final resting place remains a mystery. And though he yearned to return to the Iberian Peninsula of his birth, if only to reconnect with his estranged son, it was in Italy that Abravanel was introduced to the intellectual circles of the Renaissance and was able to interact with prominent humanists, likely absorbing the ideas that led to his drafting of that unique combination of humanism and kabbalah known as *Dialoghi d'amore*.

Dialoghi d'amore *in Spanish*

If *Dialoghi d'amore* took root in Italy, it is in the Spanish-speaking world that the work had a lasting impact. The Italian editions were known and read both in Spain and in the Spanish colonies soon after publication. The work's influence was also felt in the numerous tracts and treatises on the theme of love that filled the bookshelves of the literate. Works written in a similar vein as Hebreo's, such as Maximiliano Calvi's *Del tractado de la hermosura y del amor* and the anonymous *Diálogo de amor intitulado Dórida* typified an interest in Neoplatonism as a literary framing device. Hebreo's influence was also felt in so-called mythological manuals, such as Juan Pérez de Moya's *Philosofía secreta* and Pedro Sánchez de Viana's Spanish translation of Ovid's *Metamorphoses*, which took their cues from the mythological exegesis found in the second dialogue.

In addition to the Italian editions circulating, two published Spanish versions already existed when Garcilaso chose to write his. As with Garcilaso's, each of these versions used translation as a means to offer a distinct vision of Hispanic identity and the notion of empire. The first, published in Venice in 1568, was translated by Guedella Yahia, a descendant of Portuguese Jews in Italy, who sought to rescue the Abravanel name from oblivion and reaffirm the author's dual identity as both Jewish and Spanish. The work, although dedicated to Philip II, was aimed at readers in the Sephardic diaspora around the Mediterranean seeking to maintain their Spanish identity in exile and seems to have circulated among them, even making its way to the library of Baruch Spinoza. The second, prepared by Carlos Montesa, a law professor from Zaragoza, and published in 1584, manipulated Hebreo's text so as to remove some of the more overtly sexual aspects of the work and the more ambiguous passages, as well as any reference to Judaism. Curiously enough, this second edition carried a dedication to Francisco Gasca Salazar, the apostolic inquisitor of Aragon and cousin of Pedro de la Gasca, the man responsible for restoring the kingdom of Peru to the Spanish crown after the rebellion led by Gonzalo Pizarro. The translation prominently displayed a Latin inscription on the frontispiece: "Cesari Restitutis Peru Regnis Spolia Tiranorum" ("The kingdoms of Peru, spoils of the tyrants, restored to the emperor"), the motto of the coat of arms awarded to Gasca by Charles V. Chroniclers of the uprising such as Francisco López de Gómara had accused Garcilaso's father of loaning a horse to Pizarro during the rebellion, an allegation that dogged Garcilaso throughout his life. If Garcilaso knew of this translation, with its prominent association of Peru with sedition and rebellion, it is not surprising that he chose to produce his own "Peruvian" version, with the elaborate title *La traducción del Indio de los tres diálogos de amor de León Hebreo, hecha de italiano en español por Garcilaso Inga de la Vega, natural de la gran ciudad del Cuzco, cabeza de los reynos y provincias del Piru* (*The Indian's Translation of the Three Dialogues of Love by León Hebreo, Made from Italian into Spanish by Garcilaso Inca de la Vega, Native of the Great City of Cuzco, Capital of the Kingdoms and Provinces of Peru*).

In the dedication of this work to Philip II of Spain, Garcilaso provided four justifications for producing a translation of his own: the first, out of admiration for Hebreo, his wisdom and brilliance; the second, as a tribute in demonstration of the fealty of the king's vassals in the New World, especially those of Peru and the city of Cuzco in particular, as capital of the Inca empire; the third, as a way of faithfully serving the king with the pen after having spent years serving him under arms (emphasizing the familiar theme of *armas y letras*); and the fourth, as an offering on behalf of both sides of his family: his mother's noble Inca lineage and his paternal ancestors, who served the Spanish crown for generations, including Garcilaso's father, who, according to Garcilaso, served the crown in Peru both in peace "administrando justicia" ("administering justice") and "en la guerra contra los tiranos que en diversos tiempos se levantaron" ("in the wars against the tyrants, who at various times rose up"), thus countering the aforementioned charges of insurrection (*La traducción*). This final justification serves to establish Garcilaso as a spokesman for the mestizos of Peru, a role he would consolidate in his later works. The dedication also contains a preview of his planned literary projects, most notably *La Florida del Inca* and the *Comentarios reales*. For students, these reasons offer insight into the multiplicity of ends that translation can serve. Far from a merely utilitarian act—the transfer of a message from one code to another so as to communicate effectively—Garcilaso's translation involved a primordial attempt at fashioning and affirming an identity, an identity that would be further developed in the *Comentarios reales*.

Inca Garcilaso and Translation

As a translation, Garcilaso's *Diálogos* was a tour de force, surpassing both previous Spanish versions in elegance of style and fidelity to the original Italian. Garcilaso even added a series of marginal notes, some borrowed from the 1564 Latin translation by Juan Carlos Sarraceno, and others that expressed his particular glosses of the text and guided the readers toward textual interpretations he favored. Garcilaso's version eventually eclipsed the others, thanks to the renown of its author and the quality of its production. Its popularity, however, was not enough to save *Diálogos* from the inquisitorial censure.

In his prologue to the *Historia general del Perú (General History of Peru)*, published in 1617, Garcilaso informs his readers that "La Santa y general Inquisición destos reinos, en este último expurgatorio de libros prohibidos, no vedándolo en otras lenguas, lo mandó recoger en la nuestra bulgar, porque no era para vulgo" ("The Holy and general Inquisition of these kingdoms, in this latest index of prohibited books, while not banning it in other languages, ordered it removed from circulation in our vernacular"; *Obras*; *Royal Commentaries*). The idea that *Diálogos* was deemed unsuitable for a general readership can awaken students to the reality of the Inquisition and help ignite a conversation on the uses and abuses of censorship, specifically in early modern Spain and Spanish America. It can also serve to highlight the ways that Spaniards and colonial subjects both lived under and subverted the regulation of literary texts. Garcilaso, when his book was officially suppressed, did not resign himself to consigning it to oblivion. Instead he chose to reprint his dedication to Philip II from *Diálogos* within the prologue of the *Historia general*, thereby ensuring that the work would claim its own space within his more expansive Peruvian epic.

Though the *Comentarios reales* would cement Garcilaso's place in the pantheon of Spanish-language authors, *Diálogos de amor* remains a singular work, worthy of study by anyone interested in Garcilaso's overall opus. In uniting the voices of two constituencies that profoundly shaped the Hispanic world, the Jews of Sepharad and the mestizos of the Americas, two groups viewed with suspicion and hostility, Garcilaso provided a space to dialogue with the dominant culture that had marginalized them. Like Garcilaso, Hebreo came from a prominent family yet found himself on the margins of empire. Like Garcilaso, his greatest work was produced far from his native land. And like Garcilaso, he made recourse to literature as a way to influence his time and context. By highlighting the ways *Diálogos de amor* connects to *Comentarios reales* and how Garcilaso and Hebreo parallel and complement each other, instructors have the opportunity to offer students a holistic and more complete approach to Garcilaso's overall body of work.

What to Use in Class

The *Diálogos de amor* is a long and densely written work that would be extremely challenging as a stand-alone text for students in an undergraduate course. Based on the above, I find the following passages from Garcilaso's translation to be useful as an introduction or companion to his *Comentarios reales*: the dedication to King Philip II, "Sacra Católica Real Majestad, defensor de la fe" ("Holy Catholic Royal Majesty, defender of the faith"), the allegorical senses of fable in the second dialogue (67–68), and the myth of the androgyne in the third dialogue (169–78). Finally, an account of the life of Hebreo can be found in various sources, in both Spanish and English, such as chapter 5 of Aurelio Miró Quesada's *El Inca Garcilaso y otros estudios garcilasistas*, "La traducción de los *Diálogos de amor*" (109–27), and the section on Hebreo in John Charles Nelson's *Renaissance Theory of Love* (84–102).

NOTE

[1] Translations in this essay not otherwise attributed are my own.

WORKS CITED

Calvi, Maximiliano. *Del tractado de la hermosura y del amor.* Por Paulo Gotardo Poncio, 1576.

Diálogo de amor intitulado Dórida. Burgos, 1593.

Garcilaso de la Vega. *Obras completas del Inca Garcilaso de la Vega.* Edited by P. Carmelo Sáenz de Santa María, Atlas, 1960. 4 vols.

———. *Royal Commentaries of the Incas and General History of Peru.* Translated by Harold V. Livermore, U of Texas P, 1966. 2 vols.

———. *La traducción del Indio de los tres diálogos de amor de León Hebreo.* Garcilaso, *Obras completas*, vol. 1.

Hebreo, León. *Los diálogos de amor del maestre León Abarbanel.* Translated by Guedella Yahia, Venice, 1568.

———. *Dialogues of Love.* Translated by Cosmos Damian Bacich and Rossella Pescatori, U of Toronto P, 2009.

———. *Philographia universal de todo el mundo, de los diálogos de León Hebreo.* Translated by Carlos Montesa, En casa de Lorenzo y diego de Robles, hermanos, 1584.

Miró Quesada, Aurelio. *El Inca Garcilaso y otros estudios garcilasistas.* Ediciones de Cultura Hispánica, 1971.

Nelson, John Charles. *Renaissance Theory of Love: The Context of Giordano Bruno's Eroici Furori*. Columbia UP, 1958.

Pérez de Moya, Juan. *Philosofía secreta*. Casa de Francisco Sánchez, 1585.

Plato. *The Republic*. Translated by Benjamin Jowett. *LibreTexts*, 12 Mar. 2020, human .libretexts.org/Courses/Los_Medanos_College/Classical_Greek%3A_ Philosophy_Reader_(E_F_Haven)/Ch._07_The_Republic_By_Plato_ (Translated_by_Benjamin_Jowett).

Sánchez de Viana, Pedro. *Las transformaciones de Ovidio, traducidos del verso latino*. Por Diego Fernández de Córdova, 1589.

At the Crossroads of
the Early Modern World:
La Florida del Inca in the Hemispheric
American Studies Classroom

Ralph Bauer

Inca Garcilaso de la Vega is an important figure in the literary history not only of Spain and Latin America but also of the early Americas and the early modern world more broadly. Although his works best known beyond the Iberian Peninsula were his *Comentarios reales de los Incas* and *Historia general del Perú*,[1] his earlier work *La Florida del Inca* is of similarly great significance for the literary history of the New World, especially the literary history of early American borderlands and what literary and cultural critics have called *zonas de contacto* (contact zones). An embellished history of Hernando de Soto's failed expedition to extend the Spanish empire into southeastern North America, *La Florida* tells the story of the fierce struggle for control over a territory that would remain coveted and contested by native as well as various Euro-American imperial and national powers for some three hundred years to come. First published in Lisbon in 1605, *La Florida* was well known not only in Portugal and Spain but also in England and France, both of which had imperial ambitions in North America. It was translated into French in 1670 by P. Richelet as *Histoire de la Floride; ou, Relation de ce qui s'est passé au voyage de Ferdinand de Soto, pour la conqueste de ce pays*. This translation was republished numerous times in the eighteenth century, and it was used as the source of the German translation by Heinrich Ludewig Meier under the title *Geschichte der Eroberung von Florida*, also republished several times, at a time of considerable German interest in and immigration to North America.

A text that indelibly shaped early modern ideas about North America, including its lands and its native populations, Garcilaso's *La Florida* occupies a prominent place on the crossroads of various national and regional literary histories. Written in Spanish and published in Portugal by a Peruvian mestizo about a territory that would eventually be claimed by the United States, it equally belongs to the literary histories of Peru, Latin America, Spain, and the United States. Synthesizing many of the ethical, religious, legal, political, and epistemological questions that had emerged over the course of the first hundred years of European contact with the Americas—questions about the rights of conquest generally and the nature of the Spanish conquest particularly, as well as questions about the relation between barbarism and civilization, paganism and Christianity, nature and grace, language and truth—it represents the culmination of the great sixteenth-century Spanish tradition of the *crónica de Indias*, the chroni-

cles of the European discovery and conquest. On the one hand, it thus presents
a retrospective dialogue with an ideologically diverse body of canonical texts in
the history of the European discovery and conquest that can be productively incorporated in the colonial (Latin) American curriculum—from the writings of
Christopher Columbus and Hernando Cortés to those of Bartolomé de Las Casas and Bernal Díaz del Castillo. As a history of La Florida, in particular, it stands
in dialogue with a diverse body of texts written in various languages about a territory that was still hotly contested at the end of the sixteenth century, during
the time when Garcilaso wrote—from the accounts of Álvar Núñez Cabeza de
Vaca to those of René Goulaine de Laudonnière. More generally, as a crucial
text about early American borderlands, it illustrates issues of intercultural contact, conflict, translation, and transculturation that put it in dialogue with a great
number of sixteenth- and seventeenth-century narratives of "anti-conquest"
chronicling the emergence of an incipiently "modern" experience—narratives
of shipwreck, captivity, orphanage, and disaster written in virtually all Western
European languages about the New World—from Hans Staden's captivity narrative about his time as a prisoner of the Tupinamba tribe in Brazil to John Smith's
history of Virginia and Mary Rowlandson's narrative about her captivity among
Native Americans in New England.[2]

On the other hand, *La Florida* also points forward in literary history to the
emergence of a distinctly American form of local patriotism as it would develop
throughout the Western Hemisphere—first within various imperial contexts
and later in national contexts—by giving voice to the concerns of the first generation of American-born criollos and mestizos.[3] *La Florida* is therefore transi-
tional and transformational by standing not only between ideological and geopolitical perspectives but also between competing and successive intellectual and
aesthetic traditions—humanist thought and the philosophies of the Reformation, Counter-Reformation, Renaissance, and baroque periods. It thus connects
the sixteenth-century tradition of the *crónica de Indias* with seventeenth-,
eighteenth-, and nineteenth-century representational practices—from Carlos
de Sigüenza y Góngora's baroque celebrations of the piety of Cortés to the neo-
classical celebrations of the noble savage in the revolutionary poetry of José
Joaquín de Olmedo and Joel Barlow, as well as the Romantic fictions and histories of Félix Varela, James Fenimore Cooper, and William Hickling Prescott.
Finally, as the history of a *failed* European conquest of a Native American
territory—a Native American territory that had already withstood three previous European attempts at conquest—*La Florida* is a crucial text in the history of
Amerindian anticolonial resistance, an important chapter not only in the literary
history of modern Creole nation-states but also in the story that Anna Brickhouse
has called "the unsettlement of America" (93–144). Thus, Garcilaso's *La Florida*
occupies a crucial place in the making of early modern culture from multiple perspectives that can productively be integrated in various hemispheric American
studies curricula.

La Florida del Inca *and the Textual Struggle for North America in the Sixteenth Century*

The full title of the first Spanish edition published in Lisbon was *La Florida del Ynca: Historia del adelantado Hernando de Soto, gouernador y capitan general del reyno de la Florida, y de otros heroicos caualleros españoles è indios; escrita por el Ynca Garcilasso de la Vega, capitan de su magestad, natural de la gran ciudad del Cozco, cabeça de los reynos y prouincias del Peru.* "La Florida" in Garcilaso's account is not synonymous with the modern state of Florida; rather, at the time when Garcilaso wrote this history, in the 1580s and 1590s, the name was used to designate a vast and unexplored territory of the North American mainland north of the Gulf of Mexico between the Atlantic shoreline and what the Spaniards called the province of the "Seven Cities of Cíbola" (roughly, what today is the southwest of the United States). As Garcilaso himself put it,

> La descripcion dela gran tierra Florida, sera cosa difficultosa, poderla pintar tan cumplida, como la quisieramos dar pintada, porque como ella por todas partes sea tan ancha y larga, y no esté ganada, ni aun descubierta del todo, no se sabe que confines tenga. Los mas cierto, y lo que no se ignora es, que al medio dia tiene el mar Oceano, y la gran isla de Cuba. Al Septentrion (aunque quieren dezir que Hernando de Soto entró mil leguas la tierra . . . no se sabe donde vaya a parar, si confine con la mar o con otras tierras. Al levante viene a descabezar con la tierra que llaman de los Bacallaos, aunque cierto Cosmographo Frances pone otra grandissima provincia en medio, que llama la nueva Francia, por tener en ella si quiera el nombre. Al poniente confina con las provincias de las siete ciudades, que llamaron assi sus descubridores de aquellas tierras.
>
> (*La Florida* 2–3)

> It will be difficult for us to paint as complete a picture of the vast land of Florida as we should like because, this region being as yet unexplored and unconquered, its confines are still a mystery. A most certain fact, which we cannot ignore, is that to the south of it lie the ocean sea and the great island of Cuba; but even though it is said that Hernando de Soto penetrated a thousand leagues into its interior . . . we are still ignorant as to whether or not it is limited on the north by more lands or by the sea itself. To the east, it is cut off at a place called the Land of the Codfish, but a certain French cosmographer states that between Florida and this land there lies another which he calls New France. On the west, it is bound by the Provinces of the Seven Cities, so called by their discoverers [i.e., Francisco Vázquez de Coronado and his men] who found them in the year of 1539.   (*The Florida* 6–7)[4]

Before de Soto's *entrada* (an expedition of conquest and exploration), there had been three previous attempts to explore and conquer this territory. In 1513 there had been the expedition of Ponce de León, who had given the land the name "La Florida" because of the abundance of flowers there and because he had landed there on Easter, which is known in Spanish as Pascua Florida. Moreover, there had been the expeditions of Lucas Vásquez de Ayllón in 1524 and Pánfilo de Narváez in 1528. All these previous expeditions had started on the western shore of the Floridian peninsula but ended in failure as they progressed into the interior of the North American continent. Similarly, the de Soto expedition ended in utter disaster after de Soto himself succumbed to a fever in 1542 following many ordeals and battles on a long trek that had taken the expedition through what are today the states of Florida, Georgia, the Carolinas, Tennessee, Alabama, Mississippi, Louisiana, Arkansas, Oklahoma, and Texas. Only about half of the seven hundred members of the expedition survived to return to New Spain.

Garcilaso had never himself set foot on the shores of North America, so he could not speak with the authority of an eyewitness. Instead he relied on the eyewitness accounts provided by others for the basic historical facts of the expedition, including that of Alonso de Carmona, one of the participants in the expedition, and a written account by Juan Coles found by Garcilaso in the establishment of a printer in Córdoba. The majority of the information came from an unnamed noble Spaniard, probably Gonzalo Silvestre, another survivor of the de Soto expedition who had made his way back to New Spain and from there to Peru, where he had befriended Garcilaso's father, the Spanish captain Garcilaso de la Vega y Vargas. Garcilaso did not begin writing his history of the de Soto expedition until the late 1580s, almost thirty years after having permanently left his Peruvian homeland for Spain and some fifty years after the expedition had taken place. Most likely his interest in the subject matter was piqued by de Soto's connection to his Andean homeland: before embarking on his North American expedition, de Soto had been one of the original conquistadores of Peru who had landed with Francisco Pizarro on the Pacific coast at Tumbes in 1532 and had taken hostage the Inca ruler Atahuallpa during the massacre that the Spaniards perpetrated in the city of Cajamarca. He had been a close associate of Garcilaso's father, who had also been a conquistador. De Soto had returned to Spain after the conquest of Peru and had petitioned for and received permission from the crown to conquer La Florida; if successful, he would be rewarded with the governorship of that territory, an office for which there was illustrious competition, namely Cabeza de Vaca, the chronicler of the previously unsuccessful attempt to conquer La Florida by Pánfilo de Narváez. But whereas Cabeza de Vaca had offered a very unflattering image of the conduct of the Spanish conquistadores in America in his account, *Naufragios*—and although Garcilaso himself drew heavily on Cabeza de Vaca's *Naufragios*—Garcilaso's account of de Soto (who was notorious for his brutal treatment of Amerindians) emphasized the heroic, pious, and magnanimous character of the expedition and its leader.[5]

Explaining why de Soto petitioned Charles V for the governorship of a kingdom that he first had to conquer, Garcilaso writes:

> Esto hiço Hernando de Soto movido de generosa embidia, y zelo magnanimo delas hazañas nuevamente hechas en Mexico por el Marques del Valle don Hernando Cortes, y en el Peru por el Marques don Francisco Pizarro, y el Adelantado don Diego de Almagro, las quales el vio y ayudo a hazer. Empero como en su animo libre y generoso no cupiesse ser subdito, ni fuesse inferior a los ya nombrados en valor y esfuerço para la Guerra, ni en prudencia y discrecion para la paz, dexò aquellas hazañas aunque tan grandes, y emprendio estotras para el mayores, pues en ellas perdia la vida y la hazienda que en las otras auia ganado.   (*La Florida* 2)

> Hernando de Soto was moved to make this request by an openhearted envy of and a magnanimous enthusiasm for the recent accomplishments of the Marquis del Valle Don Hernando Cortés in Mexico and those of the Marquis Don Francisco Pizarro and the Adelantado don Diego de Almagro in Peru. The latter accomplishments he had seen and helped to make possible, but being a liberal and free-spirited man, it was not in his nature to serve as an inferior, and indeed he was not inferior to the individuals mentioned, either in valor and strength in time of war or in wisdom and discretion in time of peace; so he forsook those noble exploits, important as they were, and set out upon others which for him proved to be of even more serious consequences, for in them he lost his life, not to speak of his previously earned fortune.   (*The Florida* 6)

In part, Garcilaso's lionization of de Soto must be seen in light of the exemplary role that he is meant to play as a character in Garcilaso's Christian humanist historiographic rhetoric. Modern historians have often quarreled about the factual accuracy of Garcilaso's account of the de Soto expedition, but it is important to consider that, in the sixteenth century, history was a branch of rhetoric, and standards of historical truth depended not only (or even primarily) on factual accuracy but also on verisimilitude in conveying an author's general idea of a person, a place, or an event, beyond the particular facts. Its primary purpose was that of edification, of teaching a lesson about the past, the present, and the future (in accordance with the three branches of classical rhetoric, known as judicial, demonstrative, and deliberative). For example, literary historians have amply noted Garcilaso's attempts to create Cuzco and the Inca state in the image of Rome in his *Comentarios reales*.[6] Similarly, Garcilaso's representation of de Soto and his expedition must be seen in the light of the general idea that Garcilaso wished to convey of what the Spanish conquest of America was all about—the heroic (albeit, in this case, tragically unsuccessful) attempt to Christianize pagans—in order to inspire future attempts to win innumerable souls for the Catholic faith, thereby stopping the incursions that had been made into the

Americas by rival missions, especially by French and English Protestants. De Soto hereby serves in *La Florida* as an exemplum of an entire generation of original conquistadores whose conduct in America had been the subject of a highly polemical debate in the second part of the sixteenth century. Indeed, Garcilaso's characterization of de Soto (quoted above) immediately blends into a defense of an entire generation of first conquistadores.

> De donde por auer sido assi hechas casi todas las conquistas principales del nuevo mundo, algunos no sin falta de malicia, y con sobra de embidia se han mouido a dezir que a costa de locos, necios, y porfiados sin auer puesto otro caudal mayor, ha comprado España el señorio de todo el nuevo mundo, y no miran que son hijos della, y que el mayor ser y caudal que siempre ella huuo y tiene, fue produzirlos y criarlos tales que ayan sido para ganar el Mundo Nuevo y hacerse temer del Viejo.   (*La Florida* 2)

> Since almost all of the principal conquests of the New World have been accomplished under similar conditions, some people, moved by malice and excessive envy, have accused Spain of having bought dominion over the whole of the New World at no greater outlay of fortunate than the expenditure of stupid and persistent madmen. But such malicious and envious persons fail to consider that these same stupid and persistent individuals have been the sons of Spain, a nation whose best fortune lies in the men she has produced, men reared to conquer the New World and at the same time make themselves feared by the Old.   (*The Florida* 6)

The designation of the original conquistadores as "madmen" had gained currency especially in the wake of the fierce attacks launched by Dominican theologians and jurists such as (most prominently) Bartolomé de Las Casas in the 1540s and 1550s, who made the cruelty of the Spanish conquest proverbial not only on the Iberian Peninsula but throughout the entire early modern world. After Las Casas's *Brevísima relación de la destrucción de las Indias* (*Short Account of the Destruction of the Indies*) had been translated into English, French, Dutch, and German in the 1570s and 1580s, it was conveniently appropriated by northern European Protestant imperialists, such as Richard Hakluyt, Sir Walter Raleigh, and Samuel Purchas, to call into question the justness and legitimacy of the entire Spanish conquest of America and to justify their own incursions into the Western Hemisphere, from which they had been excluded by the papal bulls collectively known as *Inter Caetera* issued by Pope Alexander VI in 1493. Even if the pope had the divine authority to donate the New World to Spain and Portugal (also a point of contention among Protestants, of course[7]), English imperialists argued that the divine mission of evangelizing the American Indians had been betrayed by the Spanish conquistadores' greed and cruelty—even Las Casas had prophesied that God would punish Spain for its betrayal—and they pointed to the repeated Spanish failures to subdue La Florida in order to prove that God had providentially saved La Florida from the Spaniards to preserve it for English settlers. And so, whereas the rest of the Americas had been raped by the proverbially cruel Spanish conqueror, La Florida remained "a riche and beautifull Virgin," as Purchas put it, waiting for "an English bridegroome, who as making the first love, may lay the justest challenge unto her" (643).

In part, Garcilaso's heroic portrayal of de Soto can thus be understood as his attempt to "correct" and counteract the Protestant historiographic tradition that has come to be known as the "Black Legend" (see Gibson; Chang-Rodríguez). This anti-Spanish propaganda and the imperial contest in the New World were fueled in part by the rising religious sectarianism that had erupted in Europe in the wake of the Protestant Reformation. Garcilaso's reference in his geographical description (quoted above) to "a certain French cosmographer" who had stated that to the north of La Florida was another territory called "New France" highlights his awareness that northern European powers were at the gates of Spain's empire in America, notwithstanding the Alexandrine bulls that had granted to Spain a monopoly of access to all lands west of Brazil. Most likely, this unnamed geographer was André Thevet, whose *Cosmographie universelle* had been published in Paris in 1575 and whose map of North America had prominently displayed "Nouvelle-France" to the north of La Florida (fig. 1).[8] Thevet

Figure 1. André Thevet, *Cosmographie universelle*. Paris, 1575. Detail. Courtesy of the John Carter Brown Library at Brown University.

was himself a Catholic and a Franciscan monk who was highly critical of some of his Protestant countrymen who had begun to establish colonies in the New World, especially in Brazil. But Garcilaso's reference to Thevet subtly draws attention to what he discreetly omits from his geographic description of La Florida. Clearly he was aware of the French colony that had been established at Fort Caroline, near what today is Jacksonville, Florida, by the Huguenots under Jean Ribault and that had been destroyed by Pedro Menéndez de Avilés in 1565. René Goulaine de Laudonnière's account of these events, published in 1586 under the title *L'histoire notable de la Floride située ès Indes Occidentales, contenant les trois voyages faits en icelle par certains capitaines et pilotes français*, compared the extremely bloody and ruthless manner in which Menéndez de Avilés had proceeded against the French colony with the slaughter of Amerindians by Spanish conquerors familiar from the writings of Las Casas. In French Huguenot accounts, Amerindians and Protestants were similarly victimized by Catholic cruelties. Another French Huguenot, Jean de Léry, in his account of his experiences in Brazil entitled *Histoire d'un voyage fait en la terre du Brésil, autrement dite Amerique*, even compared the atrocities that (French) Catholics had perpetrated against Protestants in France with the cannibalism practiced by the Tupinamba in Brazil.

The 1590s, while Garcilaso was at work on *La Florida*, saw a steady flood of anti-Catholic and anti-Spanish propaganda pouring from the presses of the Flemish Calvinist publisher and engraver Theodor de Bry, operating in Frankfurt. In 1590 de Bry published—in Latin, German, English, and French—the first part of his multivolume series of New World travel accounts, *Americae*. It was a republication of Thomas Harriot's account of the first English colony on Roanoke Island, on the outer banks of North Carolina—a territory that was technically part of La Florida, as described by Garcilaso. As if this had not tweaked enough noses in Spain, the year after, in 1591, de Bry republished Laudonnière's account, in Latin and German, complete with lavish copperplate engraving of watercolor paintings by Jacques le Moyne prominently depicting "Charlesfort" on the Florida peninsula (fig. 2) and Laudonnière in friendly dealings with the native Timucuans (fig. 3). In 1593 de Bry published volume three of *Americae*, which included de Léry's comparisons of Tupinamba cannibalism and Catholic atrocities in Europe, as well as the Protestant captivity narrative of Hans Staden. Subsequent volumes featured Walter Raleigh's "discovery" of Guiana and the indictments of Spanish cruelties by the Italian chronicler Girolamo Benzoni. Finally, in 1598, de Bry published a stand-alone volume titled *Narratio regionum Indicarum per Hispanos quosdam devastatarum verissima*, a Latin translation of Las Casas's *Brevísima relación*, complete with de Bry's famous engravings illustrating the butchering of innocent Native Americans by Spanish conquistadores (fig. 4). In this context, it becomes clear why Garcilaso chose to write, rather anachronistically, not a general history of La Florida but the history of a single Spanish expedition that had taken place half a century before. In Garcilaso's *La Florida*, de Soto functions as a metonymy not only of the character of the Spanish

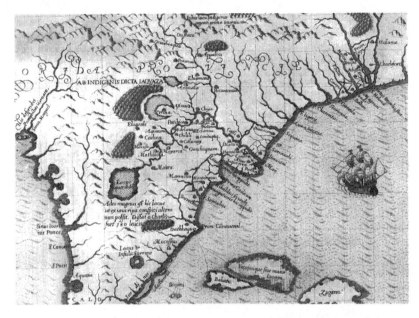

Figure 2. Fold-out engraved map from Theodor de Bry, *Der ander Theil, der newlich erfundenen Landschafft Americae, von dreyen Schiffahrten, so die Frantzosen in Floridam . . . gethan: Eine vnter dem Hauptman[n] H. Laudonniere, anno 1564.* Frankfurt, 1603. Courtesy of the John Carter Brown Library at Brown University.

Figure 3. Theodor de Bry, *Der ander Theil, der newlich erfundenen Landschafft Americae, von dreyen Schiffahrten, so die Frantzosen in Floridam . . . gethan: Eine vnter dem Hauptman[n] H. Laudonniere, anno 1564.* Frankfurt, 1603, p. ii. Courtesy of the John Carter Brown Library at Brown University.

Figure 4. Theodor de Bry, *Narratio regionum Indicarum per Hispanos quosdam devastatarum verissima*. Frankfurt, 1598, p. 50. Courtesy of the John Carter Brown Library at Brown University.

conquest but of Catholicism at large in the face of the attacks by Protestant propagandists and in the context of overwhelming crisis for Spain's empire in America.

Inca Garcilaso, Creole Patriotism, and Mestizaje in the Early Americas

More immediately, Garcilaso's representation of de Soto must also be seen in the light of his very personal connection to the issue of the original Spanish conquest through his father, who was, like de Soto, one of the original conquerors of Peru. Garcilaso had left his homeland at age twenty and arrived in Spain in 1560 in order to seek recognition and compensation from the Council of the Indies for the role that his father had played in the Peruvian civil wars of the 1540s, in particular in the rebellion of Gonzalo Pizarro against the Spanish viceroy who had been sent to Peru in order to enforce the New Laws of 1542. While these laws were primarily intended to roll back some of the rights, titles, and privileges that the crown had initially conferred upon the original conquistadores—such as the right to pass down their titles to an encomienda to their descendants—they were ostensibly implemented for the protection of the American Indians, and Las Casas's indictments of the cruelty and greed of the original conquistadores provided a convenient pretext for this change in policy. Unfortunately for Garcilaso, however, the record of his father's unequivocal loyalty to the crown in this conflict was less than spotless, and his petition was denied by the council and repeatedly fell on deaf ears at the court of Philip II. While Captain Garcilaso had not overtly supported Pizarro's insurgency, he appears to have been personally acquainted and even friendly with the insurgent. Although the captain had joined the loyalist forces, he found himself in the wrong place at the wrong time when he was captured by Pizarro and placed under house arrest. Several historians of the conflict averred that Garcilaso's father had ample opportunity to escape but refrained because he harbored sympathies for Pizarro and his cause. Worse, some of these historians reported that a victorious Pizarro was later seen riding into Cuzco on Captain Garcilaso's horse, which had allegedly been loaned to him in a demonstration of the captain's sympathies.[9]

Although these circumstances put Inca Garcilaso in a situation that was particularly unfavorable to the outcome of his personal petition for compensation, his attempt to redeem the generation of his father by creating the character of de Soto as an exemplum of piety, honor, and loyalty spoke for an entire first generation of American-born Creoles, mestizos, and their descendants who felt that certain rights and privileges were owed to them on merit of their fathers' service to the crown, God, and empire. In both Spanish and British America alike, filiopietism was thus intimately bound up with a position of privilege in a social hierarchy that had emerged from a culture of conquest. Garcilaso's history of La Florida is therefore comparable to many celebrations of colonial patriarchs authored by colonial Creoles not only in Spanish America, such as Carlos de Sigüenza y Góngora's *Piedad heróica de don Hernando Cortés, marqués del Valle*, but also in British America, such as Cotton Mather's *Magnalia Christi Americana*, the famous Puritan divine's collection of hagiographies of New England's "founding fathers."

As Garcilaso's literary and rhetorical attempt to correct the historiographic *idea* of his father's generation of first conquerors, *La Florida* engaged not only with previous accounts of the same expedition[10] but also with accounts of previous *entradas* into La Florida—accounts by chroniclers such as Gonzalo Fernández de Oviedo, Francisco López de Gómara, and, most important, Álvar Núñez Cabeza de Vaca. But again, this story of the Spanish attempt to conquer La Florida served merely as a metonymy for the Spanish conquest of America more generally. In its positive portrayal of de Soto as an exemplar of the Spanish conqueror, *La Florida* is comparable to the histories written by many other apologists of the Spanish conquest, including many of the histories written by the conquerors themselves, such as Bernal Díaz del Castillo's *Historia verdadera de la conquista de la Nueva España* (not published until 1632 but written roughly at the same time as *La Florida*). These texts emphasized the treachery and tyranny of Native American lords; the unnatural cruelty and perversion of Amerindians' cultural practices, such as cannibalism and human sacrifice; and the Amerindians' resistance to Spanish attempts at Christianization in order to shore up the conquerors' pretensions that they had served in a just war and therefore merited certain titles and privileges, such as the encomienda. This expectation harked back to the medieval Christian Reconquista and effectively elevated to a neofeudal aristocratic status many Spaniards who had descended from families that were less than illustrious back in Spain. If those rights and privileges had been under assault in the aftermath of the New Laws, it was partially due, Garcilaso knew, to the political fallout of the historiographic debate surrounding the legitimacy of the Spanish conquest and the character of the original conquistadores.

But what sets Garcilaso's *La Florida* apart from the written accounts by many of the conquerors and their Creole offspring is that his lionization of the first generation of patriarchs extended not only to the European conquistadores but also to the Native Americans, to whom he, a mestizo, felt an affinity through the lineage of his mother. Thus, he concludes his preface with the hope that his book will bring honor to "los Indios mestizos, y criollos del Peru, para que viendo ellos el favor y merced que los discretos y sabios hazian a su principiante, se animassen a passar adelante en cosas semejantes, sacadas de sus no cultivados ingenious" ("the mestizo Indians and the creoles of Peru, so that seeing a novice of their own race receive the favor and grace of the wise and learned, they would be encouraged to make advancements with similar ideas drawn from their own uncultivated mental resources"; *The Florida* xlv). His history synthesizes the ideologically highly bifurcated sixteenth-century tradition of the *crónica de Indias* by drawing not only on the apologists of the conquest but also on its harshest critics, such as Las Casas, who had portrayed Native American elites as the natural and legitimate lords of the New World presiding over well-ordered societies perfect in everything except for their want of the Christian gospel. *La Florida* lends support to this position by arguing that the alleged Native American treachery and violent resistance was in fact a consequence of Spanish injustices and cruelties perpetrated by some individuals who had tragically poisoned the Amerindians' natural proclivity to accept Christianity. In elaborating this argument, Garcilaso pays particular homage to Cabeza de Vaca and his *Naufragios*, the literary ancestor in the historiography of *La Florida*, which had approached the polemic about the nature of the Spanish conquest by distinguishing between two types of conquistadores: on the one hand, the defenders of violent conquest, who are false Christians, such as the governor Pánfilo de Narváez, and, on the other, the advocates of Las Casasian "peaceful conquest," who are true Christians, such as Cabeza de Vaca himself (Adorno 254–69; see also Bauer, *Cultural Geography* 30–76). A case in point is Garcilaso's treatment of Narváez's interactions with native Floridians ten years before de Soto's arrival. In *La Florida*, he relates the story of a Spanish captive named Juan Ortiz, who was but a boy when he arrived in La Florida with an expedition that had been sent in search of survivors of the earlier expedition of Narváez (pt. 1, bk. 2). Ortiz was captured by the people of Hirrihigua, a native lord who harbored a profound hatred for all Spaniards and inflicted terrible punishments on Ortiz, partially roasting him and sparing his life only upon the pleas of Hirrihigua's sympathetic daughter. This story of a European captive redeemed by a Native American daughter invites a comparison with John Smith's account of his own captivity among the Powhatans of Virginia and his delivery by Pocahontas (Voigt 303–05, 321–23). Of course, the crucial differences between Garcilaso's and Smith's accounts are that the former attributes Hirrihigua's cruelty to the outrages previously committed by Narváez. Thus, the reader learns that Narváez had cut off Hirrihigua's nose and fed his mother to the dogs. Garcilaso writes:

> Empero (como la injuria no sepa perdonar) todas las vezes que se acordaua, que a su madre auian echado a los perros y dexadola comer dellos: y quando se iua a sonar y no hallaua sus narizes, le tomaua el diablo por vengarse de Juan Ortiz, como si el se las huviera cortado.   (*La Florida* 33)

> Outrage knows no forgiveness, and each time that Hirrihigua recalled that the Spaniards had cast his mother to the dogs and permitted them to feed upon her body, and each time that he attempted to blow his nose and failed to find it, the Devil seized him with the thought of avenging himself on Juan Ortiz, as if that young man personally had deprived him of his nostrils.   (*The Florida* 68)

The other difference is that Ortiz is ultimately delivered from his captivity not by the young Indian maiden (as was Smith) but by a neighboring cacique named Mucozo, who grants Ortiz refuge after he escapes from Hirrihigua (with the daughter's help) and who refuses to return the captive despite paying a considerable price for his fortitude, as he is in love with Hirrihigua's daughter and plans to marry her. Garcilaso writes:

> Destos dos Caçiques, que con mucha instancia y porfia pedian a Iuan Ortiz, lo defendio Mocoço con tanta generosidad, que tuuo por mejor perder (como lo perdio) el casamiento que aficionadamente desseaua hazer con la hija de Hirrihigua. . . . El buen Mocoço, el qual, aunque barbaro lo hizo con este Christiano mui de otra manera, que los famosissimos varones del triumuirato que en Layno lugar cerca de Bolonia, hizieron aquella nunca jamas bastamente abóminada, proscripcion y concierto de dar, y trocar los parientes, amigos, y valedores, por los enemigos y aduersarios; y lo hizo mucho mejor, que otros Principes Christianos, que despues acà han hecho otras tan abominables, y mas que aquella, considerada la innocencia de los entregados, y la calidad de algunos de ellos, y la fe, que deuian tener, y guardar los entregadores: que aquellos eran Gentiles, y estos se preciauan

del nombre y religion christiana. . . . Basta representar la magnanimadad
de un infiel, para que los Principes fieles se esfuerçen a le imitar y sobrepu-
jar, si pudieren. . . . Dios, y la naturaleza humana muchas vezes en desier-
tos tan incultos, y esteriles produzen semejantes animos, para mayor confusion y verguença de los que nascen, y se crian en tierras fertiles y
abundantes de toda Buena doctrina, sciencias, y religion Christiana.

(*La Florida* 35–36)

Indeed this Cacique defended Juan Ortiz with such generosity, he chose
to abandon all possibility of a marriage with Hirrihigua's daughter, whom
he ardently desired and subsequently lost. . . . The good Mucozo, who although a barbarian, behaved toward this Christian in a manner far different from that of the famous Triumvirate of Laino (a place near Bologna),
which made a never-sufficiently abominated proscription and agreement
to exchange relatives, friends and protectors for enemies and adversaries.
And too, his behavior was much more admirable than that of other Christian princes who since then have made bargains equally odious, if not more
so, when one considers the innocence of those delivered up, the rank of
some of them, and the fidelity which their deliverers should have had and
respected. For the betrayed were infidels, whereas their betrayers took
pride in the name and doctrines of Christianity. . . . It suffices to represent the magnanimity of an infidel so that princes of the Faith may make
efforts to imitate and if possible surpass him—not in infidelity. . . . But in
virtue and similar excellences. . . . God and human nature many times produce such souls in sterile and uncultivated deserts to the greater confusion and shame of people who are born and reared in lands that are fertile
and abundant in all good doctrines and sciences, as well as the Christian
religions.

(*The Florida* 73–74)

In accounting for Garcilaso's defense of pagan civility, scholarship has generally emphasized the importance of Italian humanist and Neoplatonic influences
upon his historical works, pointing to the formative role that his early translation of León Hebreo's Neoplatonic *Diálogos de amor* played on his subsequent
works. While Italian Neoplatonism is doubtlessly an important influence on Garcilaso's portrayal of friendship in *La Florida*, it is important to see his reception
of Italian humanism and Neoplatonism in the Counter-Reformation context in
which he wrote in Spain. With regard to his attitude toward paganism in general and Native American paganism in particular, Garcilaso's humanist Neoplatonism and neoclassicism were thoroughly mediated by the Jesuit education he
had received both in Peru and after his arrival in Spain, first in Montilla and
later in Córdoba. Jesuit theology had provided a great synthesis of various religious and philosophical currents of the sixteenth century designed to counter
the intellectual challenges posed by humanism and the Protestant Reformation.
On the one hand, Jesuit theology had resurrected the Dominicans' long Thomist

tradition of neoscholastic natural law philosophy as it had thrived in the so-called School of Salamanca—the writings of Francisco de Vitoria, Domingo de Soto, Luis de Molina, and Francisco Suárez (the former two being Dominicans and the latter two being Jesuits). Based on the writings of Thomas Aquinas, these theologians argued (against Franciscan nominalists and later against Calvinists) that civility and the Rights of Dominion did not depend on grace but ultimately derived from natural law and human reason in which "all mankind is one." One of the central concepts of their philosophy was that of synderesis, signifying the innate principle in the moral consciousness of every person that directs the agent to good and restrains them from evil as a consequence of human reason. The act of conversion and the process of salvation represented in this theological tradition are merely the perfection of natural tendencies already innate in universal human reason (see Hanke; Brading; Fernández-Santamaria; Hamilton).

On the other hand, the Jesuit influence on Garcilaso's thought is also evident in his attitude toward Native American paganism. Christian Fernández has drawn our attention to the importance that the language of Hermeticism ("la lengua mercurial" [111]) plays in the visual and verbal rhetoric of Garcilaso's work. Indeed, Christian Hermeticism had played an important role in the Jesuits' conceptualization of Native American paganism throughout the New World. Ultimately derived from Marsilio Ficino's claim (in the introduction to his translation of the *Corpus Hermeticum* in Florence in 1471) that the Egyptian sage Hermes Trismegistus was the same person as Moses remembered under a different name, the Jesuit missionaries argued that all pagan religions were faint memories of the one true God. Garcilaso's *La Florida* therefore presents an interesting point of comparison to the vast archive of Jesuit writing about the New World in various languages, from José de Acosta's *Historia natural y moral de las Indias* in the sixteenth century to the reports from Canada known as the Jesuit Relations during the seventeenth century and the works of such "enlightened" Jesuit writers of the eighteenth century as Joseph-François Lafitau, the "father of modern ethnography," who, in his *Moeurs des sauvages américains*, argued that "nothing more greatly resembles the Caduceus of Mercury" than the Huron peace pipe (2: 325). Christian Hermeticism thus provided the foundation for a syncretist understanding of Native American paganism that in turn provided the theological foundation of the cultural mestizaje throughout the Americas in the seventeenth and eighteenth centuries (fig. 5).

Tempering the humanist optimism regarding human agency in the world and its role in divine providence with a profound Counter-Reformation sense of the sovereignty of an inscrutable divine will and an emphasis on the individual's experience of dislocation, captivity, exile, and disaster as an allegory of the uncertainties of human worldly existence at large, *La Florida* chronicles the emergence of a modern consciousness that makes it eminently comparable to narratives dealing with captivity, shipwreck, and disaster, such as Cabeza de Vaca's *Nau-*

Figure 5. *Allerhand so lehr-als geist-reiche Brief, Schrifften und Reis-Beschreibungen*. Augsburg und Grätz: Verlag Philips, Martins, und Joh. Veith seel. Erben, Buchhändlern, 1726–1761. Courtesy of the John Carter Brown Library at Brown University.

fragios, Staden's narrative of his captivity among the Tupinamba of Brazil, and Francisco Núñez de Pineda y Bascuñán's *Cautiverio feliz*, about his captivity among the Mapuche Indians of southern Chile. The theme of aborted conquest ending in captivity and disaster is not only prominently displayed in *La Florida* with the demise of de Soto himself, but it also bookends the narrative, with the account of the captivity of Juan Ortiz toward the beginning and the martyrdom of the twenty-four missionaries who lost their lives trying to convert the Florida natives toward the end. In the case of *La Florida*, however, written by the mestizo son of a European father and an Indian mother, this theme of aborted conquest also frequently, as Lisa Voigt has shown (99–153), conveys additional ideas about intercultural communication, translation, and hybridization. Like his character Ortiz, Garcilaso is himself a cultural go-between who crosses territories, oceans, and languages to mediate between cultures at the crossroads of various cultural geographies and literary histories, thereby participating in the creation of a modern world.

NOTES

[1] Both works were disseminated throughout Europe, being translated into English, French, and Dutch during the seventeenth century and cited by such influential early modern English writers as Francis Bacon, Samuel Purchas, and John Dryden. On the translation of the works of Garcilaso, see Chang-Rodríguez; see also Garcés. On the disseminations of Garcilaso's works in the eighteenth century, see Macchi. Greene has characterized the early modern literary world as a "transatlantic family" (226), pointing out that Garcilaso was a relative not only of the Spanish Renaissance poet and diplomat Diego Hurtado de Mendoza but also of the English Renaissance poet Philip Sidney.

[2] For a good comparative discussion of these issues in narratives of captivity across linguistic boundaries, see Voigt.

[3] For a discussion of *La Florida* in this light, see Brading 257–58. For discussions of other important Spanish American texts in the history of a Creole identity, see Mazzotti, *Agencias*; for a hemispheric perspective, see Bauer and Mazzotti.

[4] I cite here and throughout from the digital facsimile edition of *La Florida* at the *Internet Archive*. *La Florida del Inca* is available in multiple languages and formats, including open-access digital editions.

[5] On the relationship between Garcilaso's *La Florida* and Cabeza de Vaca's *Naufragios*, see Adorno 279–307. On the mediation of violence in *La Florida*, see Rabasa 199–225.

[6] On verisimilitude in the *Comentarios reales* in the Renaissance tradition of Italian humanist historiography, see MacCormack 58–59; Pupo-Walker; Zamora.

[7] See Bauer, *Alchemy* 184–201, esp. 194; Gibson; García Carcel.

[8] The invention of the name "New France" is usually attributed to the Verrazano brothers, but given the date and popularity of Thevet's *Cosmographie universelle*, and given the fact that Garcilaso refers to the cosmographer as being "French," I suspect that Thevet is the cosmographer to whom he referred.

[9] For a more detailed treatment of these events, see Varner and Varner xxxi.

[10] These include, most notably, the eyewitness account written in Portuguese by an anonymous "Fidalgo" ("Gentleman") of Elvas, entitled *Relação verdadeira dos trabalhos que o governador D. Fernando de Souto* and published in 1557; the other account was written by de Soto's personal secretary, Rodrigo Ranjel, and included in Gonzalo Fernández de Oviedo y Valdés's *Historia general y natural de las Indias*. However, since the volume that contained Ranjel's account was not published until the nineteenth century, it is unlikely that Garcilaso was familiar with it. The third account, written by the tax collector of the expedition, Luis Fernández de Biedma, was an official testimony given to the Council of the Indies in 1544 but also was not published until the nineteenth century and therefore was not likely known by Garcilaso. All these accounts, including Garcilaso's *La Florida*, can be found in English translation and digital format in the *Early Americas Digital Archive* (eada.lib.umd.edu/text-entries/florida-of-the-inca/).

WORKS CITED

Adorno, Rolena. *The Polemics of Possession in Spanish American Narrative*. Yale UP, 2007.

Bauer, Ralph. *The Alchemy of Conquest: Science, Religion, and the Secrets of the New World*. U of Virginia P, 2019.

―――. *The Cultural Geography of Colonial American Literatures: Empire, Travel, Modernity.* Cambridge UP, 2003.

Bauer, Ralph, and José Antonio Mazzotti, editors. *Creole Subjects in the Colonial Americas: Empires, Texts, Identities.* U of North Carolina P, 2009.

Brading, David A. *The First America: The Spanish Monarchy, Creole Patriots, and the Liberal State, 1492–1867.* Cambridge UP, 1991

Brickhouse, Anna. *The Unsettlement of America: Translation, Interpretation, and the Story of Don Luis de Velasco, 1560–1945.* Oxford UP, 2014.

Chang-Rodríguez, Raquel. Introduction. *Franqueando fronteras: Garcilaso de la Vega y La Florida del Inca,* edited by Chang-Rodríguez, Pontificia Universidad Católica del Perú, 2006, pp. 15–38.

Fernández, Christian. *Inca Garcilaso: Imaginación, memoria e identidad.* Universidad Nacional Mayor de San Marcos, 2004.

Fernández-Santamaria, J. A. *The State, War, and Peace: Spanish Political Thought in the Renaissance, 1516–1559.* Cambridge UP, 1977.

Garcés, María Antonia. "The Translator Translated: Inca Garcilaso and English Imperial Expansion." *Travel and Translation in the Early Modern Period,* edited by Carmine G. Di Biase, Rodopi, 2006, pp. 203–25.

García Carcel, Ricardo. *La leyenda negra: Historia y opinion.* Alianza Editorial, 1992.

Garcilaso de la Vega. *La Florida del Ynca: Historia del adelantado Hernando de Soto, gouernador y capitan general del reyno de la Florida, y de otros heroicos caualleros españoles è indios; escrita por el ynca Garcilasso de la Vega, capitan de su magestad, natural de la gran ciudad del Cozco, cabeça de los reynos y prouincias del Peru.* Pedro Crasbeeck, 1605. *Internet Archive,* archive.org/details/lafloridadelynca00vega.

―――. *The Florida of the Inca: A History of the Adelantado, Hernando de Soto, Governor and Captain General of the Kingdom of Florida, and of Other Heroic Spanish and Indian Cavaliers.* Translated by John Grier Varner and Jeannette Johnson Varner, U of Texas P, 1951.

―――. *Histoire de la Floride; ou, Relation de ce qui s'est passé au voyage de Ferdinand de Soto, pour la conqueste de ce pays.* Translated by P. Richelet, Geruais Clouzier, 1670. 2 vols.

Gibson, Charles. *The Black Legend: Anti-Spanish Attitudes in the Old World and the New.* Knopf, 1971.

Greene, Roland. *Unrequited Conquests: Love and Empire in the Colonial Americas.* U of Chicago P, 1999.

Hamilton, Bernice. *Political Thought in Sixteenth-Century Spain: A Study of the Political Ideas of Vitoria, De Soto, Suárez, and Molina.* Clarendon Press, 1963.

Hanke, Lewis. *All Mankind Is One: A Study of the Dispute between Bartolomé de Las Casas and Juan Ginés de Sepúlveda in 1550 on the Intellectual and Religious Capacity of the American Indians.* Northern Illinois UP, 1974.

Lafitau, Joseph-François. *Moeurs des sauvages amériquains, comparées aux moeurs des premiers temps.* Saugrain / Charles Estienne Hochereau, 1724. 2 vols.

Macchi, Fernanda. *Incas ilustrados: Reconstrucciones imperiales en la segunda mitad del siglo XVIII.* Iberoamericana/Vervuert, 2009.

MacCormack, Sabine. *On the Wings of Time: Rome, the Incas, Spain, and Peru.* Princeton UP, 2007.

Mazzotti, José Antonio, editor. *Agencias criollas: La ambigüedad "colonial" en las letras hispanoamericanas.* Instituto Internacional de Literatura Iberoamericana, 2000.

Pupo-Walker, Enrique. *Historia, creación y profecía en los textos del Inca Garcilaso de la Vega.* José Porrúa Turanzas, 1982.

Purchas, Samuel. *Purchas His Pilgrimage; or, Relations of the World and the Religions Observed in All Ages and Places Discovered, from the Creation unto This Present: Contayning a Theological and Geographical Historie of Asia, Africa, and America.* William Stansby, 1613.

Rabasa, José. *Writing Violence on the Northern Frontier: The Historiography of Sixteenth-Century New Mexico and Florida and the Legacy of Conquest.* Duke UP, 2000.

Varner, John Grier. *El Inca: The Life and Times of Garcilaso de la Vega.* U of Texas P, 1968.

Varner, John Grier, and Jeanette Johnson Varner. Introduction. Garcilaso, *The Florida of the Inca*, pp. xxi–xxxiv.

Voigt, Lisa. *Writing Captivity in the Early Modern Atlantic: Circulations of Knowledge and Authority in the Iberian and English Imperial Worlds.* U of North Carolina P, 2009.

Zamora, Margarita. *Language, Authority, and Indigenous History in the* Comentarios reales de los Incas. Cambridge UP, 1988.

Inca Garcilaso Reads Cabeza de Vaca

Rolena Adorno

In *La Florida del Inca* (*The Florida of the Inca*), Inca Garcilaso de la Vega tells the story of the Hernando de Soto expedition to conquer territories in what is today the United States. One of his most important literary interlocutors was the account of the Pánfilo de Narváez expedition told by Álvar Núñez Cabeza de Vaca in his *Naufragios*. In succession, each expedition had been contracted to settle the vast lands to the north of New Spain called "La Florida." Historically, both expeditions were colossal failures; they ended in disaster for the Spanish expeditionary forces and the indigenous communities they attacked. Cabeza de Vaca created his account of the Narváez expedition to solicit a royal contract to lead his own expedition to La Florida, and Garcilaso recounted the de Soto expedition to dignify the historical reputation of its leader while enhancing that of his own father; de Soto and the captain Garcilaso de la Vega y Vargas had served together in the conquest of Peru.

Literarily, Garcilaso's narration of 1605 followed the lead of Cabeza de Vaca's of 1542. Having no military triumphs to recount, they created episodes of native spiritual epiphany—that is, scenes in which acts and gestures of native submission were taken as proof of autochthonous American peoples' readiness to convert to Christianity. Citing Cabeza de Vaca, Garcilaso created episodes of native-Spanish cooperation to highlight his claims about the native peoples' predisposition to accept the Christian gospel. Garcilaso later would emphasize this spiritual readiness in reference to the Andean peoples in his *Comentarios reales de los Incas* (*Royal Commentaries of the Incas*), thus casting in a positive light the Inca portion of his dual Spanish-Andean lineage. Garcilaso's most intriguing account, however, is one in which he begins by following Cabeza de Vaca regarding the spiritual readiness of the natives but then departs from Cabeza de Vaca's tales of native cooperation to tell instead how they held their ground and created a menacing standoff with the Spanish conquistadores. Here Garcilaso adds a new narrative element that Cabeza de Vaca could not represent: the Indians' natural love of homeland, which Garcilaso shared and which would find its most vibrant expression in his *Comentarios reales*.

Garcilaso's reliance on Cabeza de Vaca's account is not an isolated case in the early writings on the Indies. It represents a central phenomenon in that tradition by which authors sought to lend credibility to their own accounts by relying on the authority of accounts that preceded them. When authors deliberately echoed previously published, well-known works, they sought the confirmation of the deeds they memorialized less in the supposed veracity of historical testimony than in the plausibility consecrated by the narrative tradition of earlier chronicles and accounts of conquest. Garcilaso's *La Florida* offers such an instance of textual density.[1]

The early-sixteenth-century Spanish concept of "La Florida" is central to this discussion. It encompassed the vast northern territory that rimmed the Gulf of Mexico from today's Soto la Marina River in Tamaulipas in northern Mexico to the Florida cape. At the time of the Narváez expedition in the 1520s, La Florida spread as far north and west as the Spanish imagined the North American continent to extend. With Francisco Vázquez de Coronado's expedition in the early 1540s, the portion of La Florida consisting of today's southwestern United States was designated by the Spanish as "Cíbola."

For Garcilaso, writing in the 1580s and 1590s, La Florida was almost as vast as it had been in Cabeza de Vaca's day. He acknowledged that its dimensions were unknown:

> [N]o se sabe qué confines tenga. Lo más cierto, y lo que no se ignora, es que al mediodía tienen el mar océano y la gran isla de Cuba. Al septentrión, aunque quieren decir que Hernando de Soto entró mil leguas la tierra adentro, como adelante tocaremos, no se sabe dónde vaya a parar, si confine con la mar o con otras tierras. Al levante, viene a descabezar con la tierra que llaman de los Bacallaos, aunque cierto cosmógrafo francés pone otra grandísima provincia en medio, que llama la Nueva Francia, por tener en ella siquiera el nombre. Al ponente confina con las provincias de las Siete Ciudades.   (*La Florida* 13)

> [I]ts confines are still a mystery. A most certain fact, which we cannot ignore, is that to the south of it lie the ocean sea and the great island of Cuba; but even though it is said that Hernando de Soto penetrated a thousand leagues into its interior (as we shall see later), we are still ignorant as to whether or not it is limited on the north by more lands or by the sea itself. To the east it is cut off by a place called the Land of the Codfish, but a certain French cosmographer states that between Florida and this land there lies another which he even calls New France. On the west, it is bound by the Provinces of the Seven Cities.   (*The Florida* 6–7)

The immensity of the Floridian territories as well as European readers' ignorance of them served Garcilaso in the claims he made about the geographical areas traversed by the Narváez and de Soto expeditions and the indigenous groups found in them.

With his dual patrimony in mind, Garcilaso emphasizes the need to praise the great deeds of the Indians as well as those of the Spaniards: "y que no hagamos agravio a los unos por los otros, dejando de decir las valentías de la una nación por contar solamente las de la otra, sino que se digan todas como acaecieron en su tiempo y lugar" ("and that we not do injury to either race by recounting the valiant achievements of one while omitting those of the other, but instead tell all things as they occurred and in their proper time and place"; *La Florida* 322; *The Florida* 460). In this light, his identification of Cabeza de

Vaca as an eyewitness authority on La Florida and its peoples was central. There was no written authority more unequivocally sympathetic to the Indians of La Florida and their potential for Christian civilization than Cabeza de Vaca.[2]

The heart of Garcilaso's reading of *Naufragios* is Cabeza de Vaca's assertion about the coastal native peoples of northwestern Mexico, between the Río Yaqui and the Río Petatlán (today's Río Sinaloa):

> Y mostravan grandíssimo plazer con nosotros, aunque temimos que llegados a los que tenían la frontera con los cristianos y guerra con ellos nos avían de maltratar y hazer que pagássemos lo que los christianos contra ellos hazían. Mas como Dios Nuestro Señor fue servido de traernos hasta ellos, començáronnos a temer y a catar como los passados y aun algo más, de que no quedamos poco maravillados, por donde claramente se vee que estas gentes todas, para ser atraídos a ser christianos y a obediençia de la Imperial Magestad, an de ser llevados con buen tratamiento, y que éste es camino muy çierto y otro no. (Cabeza de Vaca 157)

> And they showed very great pleasure with us, although we feared that when we arrived at the ones who held the frontier against the Christians and were at war with them, they would treat us cruelly and make us pay for what the Christians were doing to them. But since God our Lord was served to bring us to them, they began to fear and respect us as the previous ones had done, and even somewhat more, about which we were not a little amazed, by which it is clearly seen that all these peoples, to be drawn to become Christians and to obedience to the Imperial Majesty, must be given good treatment, and that this is the path most certain and no other. (Adorno and Pautz 1: 240)[3]

As part of his discussion of Floridian customs, Garcilaso readjusted and then repeated Cabeza de Vaca's sweeping affirmation about there being neither idolatry nor human sacrifice in La Florida: "Estos indios son gentiles de nación e idólatras. Adoran al Sol y a la Luna por principales dioses, mas sin ningunas ceremonias de tener ídolos ni hacer sacrificios ni oraciones ni otras supersticiones" ("The Indians are a race of pagans and idolaters; they worship the sun and the moon as their principal deities, but, unlike the rest of heathendom, without any ceremony of images, sacrifices, prayers, or other superstitions"; *La Florida* 18; *The Florida* 13). Idolaters, yes; but practitioners of human sacrifice, no. Cabeza de Vaca had been unequivocal: "[P]orque dos mil leguas que anduvimos por tierra y por la mar en las barcas, y otros diez meses que después de salidos de cativos sin parar anduvimos por la tierra, no hallamos sacrificios ni idolatría" ("[I]n the two thousand leagues that we traveled by land and through the sea on the rafts and another ten months that we went through the land without stopping once we were no longer captives, we found neither sacrifices nor idolatry"; Cabeza de Vaca 168; Adorno and Pautz 1: 262). Like Cabeza de Vaca, Garcilaso postulated the absence of sinful customs and crimes against nature among the indigenous peoples: "Los que dicen que comen carne humana se lo levantan, a lo menos a los que son de las provincias que nuestro gobernador descubrió; antes lo abominan, como lo nota Álvar Núñez Cabeza de Vaca en sus *Naufragios*, capítulo catorce, y diez y siete" ("People who say that the Indians eat human flesh attribute this practice to them falsely, at least to those of the provinces our Governor [Hernando de Soto] discovered. They on the contrary abominate this practice, as Álvar Núñez Cabeza de Vaca notes in his *Naufragios*, chapters fourteen and seventeen"; *La Florida* 19; *The Florida* 15). Nevertheless, the aristocratic Garcilaso does not rule out altogether the possibility of the existence of cannibalism in La Florida; he suggests, "Pueden ser que la coman donde los nuestros no llegaron, que la Florida es tan ancha y larga que hay para todos" ("It may be, however, that the Indians do eat human flesh in places where our men did not penetrate, for Florida is so broad and long that there is space enough within it for anything to happen"; *La Florida* 19; *The Florida* 16). Cabeza de Vaca had written about five Narváez expeditioners who

> llegaron a tal estremo que se comieron los unos a los otros hasta que quedó uno, que por ser solo, no huvo quien lo comiesse. . . . Deste caso se alteraron tanto los indios y huvo entre ellos tan gran escándalo que sin duda que si al principio ellos lo vieran los mataran, y todos nos viéramos en grande trabajo. (Cabeza de Vaca 89–90)

> came to such dire need that they ate one another until only one remained, who, because he was alone, had no one to eat him. . . . the Indians became very upset because of this and it produced such a great scandal among them that without a doubt, if at the start they had seen it, they would have killed them, and all of us would have been in grave danger.
> (Adorno and Pautz 1: 104, 106)

Garcilaso cited Cabeza de Vaca as an authority not only on the benign and well-disposed character of the Florida Indians but also, from time to time, on their resistance to the Spaniards. When Garcilaso insisted on the Indians' willingness to mislead de Soto's armed soldiers to discourage them from advancing farther, he derived valuable support from Cabeza de Vaca. In the Indians' effort to thwart the invaders' penetration of their homeland, Garcilaso concludes that, even though the Narváez expedition had not penetrated as far inland as de Soto's, his account does not contradict that of Cabeza de Vaca.[4] Here the adversarial relationship denotes the Indians' fierce and uncompromising loyalty to their homeland, which was a value that Garcilaso dramatized to great effect in the *Comentarios reales* with regard to the Incas. There as here, the only value to override that of patriotism—that is, a natural love of homeland and the will to defend it—was the desire to receive the "greater truth" of the revelation of the Christian gospel. Garcilaso stopped short, however, of making any claim about the identity of Amerindian and Christian deities, such as Cabeza de Vaca had done regarding the Indians of Sinaloa, when he boldly proclaimed, "[A]quel que ellos dezían nosotros lo llamávamos Dios" ("[T]he one to whom they referred we called God"; Cabeza de Vaca 166; Adorno and Pautz 1: 258). Garcilaso pursues this line more emphatically and directly when he claims that the natives of La Florida were now engaged in carrying out exemplary customs, thanks to the visible spiritual legacy that the Narváez survivors had inspired in lands they had not even reached. Garcilaso asserts that there were wooden crosses adorning the dwellings in the province he calls Guancane and that these could be explained by the

> noticia de los beneficios y maravillas que Álvar Núñez Cabeza de Vaca y Andrés Dorantes y sus compañeros, en virtud de Jesu Cristo Nuestro Señor, había hecho por las provincias que anduvieron de la Florida los años que los indios los tuvieron por esclavos, como el mismo Álvar Núñez lo dejó escrito en sus comentarios. (*La Florida* 336)

> news of the benefits and marvels Álvar Núñez Cabeza de Vaca and Andrés Dorantes and their companions had performed in virtue of Jesus Christ Our Lord within the provinces of Florida through which they had traveled during the years they were held in bondage by the Indians, as Álvar Núñez himself has recorded in his *Comentarios*." (*The Florida* 482)[5]

Garcilaso insists:

> Y aunque es verdad, que Alvar Núñez y sus compañeros no llegaron a esta provincia de Guancane, ni a otras muchas que hay entre ellas y las tierras donde ellos anduvieron, todavía pasando de mano en mano y de tierra en tierra, llegó a ella [la provincia de Guancane] la fama de las hazañas obradas por Dios por medio de aquellos hombres. (*La Florida* 336–37)

> And even though it is true that Álvar Núñez and his companions did not come to this particular province or to a number of others which lie between it and the lands where they traveled, still the fame of the deeds performed by God through these men eventually, by passing from hand to hand and from land to land, reached the province of Guancane.
> (*The Florida* 482)

Garcilaso's account echoes an episode in which Cabeza de Vaca had told how the Indians of northwestern coastal Mexico were instructed to receive the Christians by offering them food and provisions and by carrying crosses but no weapons (Adorno and Pautz 1: 260; Cabeza de Vaca 167). Garcilaso's episode thus recreates Cabeza de Vaca's account about a province that not only was not reached by Narváez, as Garcilaso indicates, but does not appear in any of Garcilaso's citations of the firsthand de Soto expedition accounts that he knew.[6] In narrating the passage of the Spanish force through the province of Guancane, Garcilaso claims that de Soto departed westward from Guancane in search of "el Río Grande" ("the great river"), evidently the Mississippi River, down which the expedition would hope to sail to "el mar del norte," the Gulf of Mexico (*La Florida* 337–38; *The Florida* 484–85). Garcilaso asserts that even though he had identified the route that the army traveled from one province to another, he had not shown the latitude of those provinces or traced the men's exact course because his unnamed informant was neither a cosmographer nor a sailor and knew nothing of such matters. He adds that the army carried no instruments to take land elevations and none of its members knew how to go about looking into it. Furthermore, their anger and disappointment at finding neither gold nor silver left them ill-disposed to query such matters. With this apology Garcilaso begs the readers' indulgence for such important omissions, adding that he wished he had no need to seek such pardon.

Did Garcilaso make up the term and place he called "Guancane"? The toponym did not come from the language, Caddo, of the people of the area in question, which lay along the Mississippi River and to the west of it (Swanton 53). Was it a variant of a toponym in Quechua in Garcilaso's native Peru? Upon narrating in his *Comentarios reales* the conquests carried out by the second Inca ruler Sinchi Roca, Garcilaso makes reference to a "people and nation" called Huancani, and, it turns out, the settlement Huancané, located in the province of Huancané in the Department of Puno, exists in Peru to the present (*Obras* 2: 65; *Royal Commentaries* 1: 105; see also Espinoza Galarza 189, 244, 318).

For the reader of Garcilaso's era, however, *Guancane* might have seemed to be a word in the Taíno language of the Antilles. Although the juxtaposition of two consonants (such as the *nc* in *Guancane*) is not found in that language, its words would have seemed more familiar to the seventeenth-century reader than those of the Quechua language because of the wider publication and circulation of materials about the Caribbean than about the Andes at that time. The island of Guanahaní, the site of Christopher Columbus's landing on 12 October 1492, is a first example, and in the Taíno lexicon, similar names were cited by Columbus and his chroniclers: the inlet of Guanaba, the islands of the Guanajas (or Guanajos), the settlement of Guanica on the island of San Juan (Puerto Rico), the island of Guanín, and so forth.[7]

In Guancane, in spite of the crosses that greeted the passing Spanish army, de Soto and his soldiers dared not pause in their advance because of the unmistakable hostility of the inhabitants of this province who silently watched them pass:

> Al fin de ellas llegaron a otra llamada Gua[n]cane, cuyos naturales eran diferentes que los pasados, porque aquéllos eran afables y amigos de españoles, mas éstos se les mostraron enemigos, que nunca quisieron su amis-

tad, antes, en todo lo que pudieron, mostraron el odio que les tenían y desearon pelear con ellos, presentándoles la batalla muchas veces.

(*La Florida* 336)

[T]hey came to another province called Guancane. Here the natives differed from those in the past, for whereas the others had been affable, these proved to be hostile and showed no desire for friendship. Instead, they demonstrated their hatred in every way possible, many times presenting themselves for battle."   (*The Florida* 482)

Garcilaso concludes, "Tardaron los españoles ocho días en atravesar esta provincia de Guancane y no reposaron en ella día alguno por excusar el pelear con los indios, que tanto ellos deseaban" ("The Spaniards took eight days to cross this province, not resting a single day within its confines because of their desire to avoid a conflict with these people who were so eager to fight").

The province of Guancane presents a unique case in *La Florida*: Garcilaso claims that its natives showed evidence of being influenced by the hearsay reports received about Cabeza de Vaca and his three companions, whom they had never seen, while at the same time manifesting a hostile attitude toward the armed Christians who now passed through their territory. De Soto's men, fearing this hostility and finding themselves vulnerable because of the lack of mounted horsemen, did not dare stop to rest a single day but continued their march, trying to pass through undetected or at least without provoking the Guancanians, who knew well how to defend their land and people from soldiers on foot. Although Garcilaso does not announce it as such (nor would he have dared to do so), he had created a conquest-free Amerindian utopia. This becomes apparent when we compare this episode with the one that concludes *La Florida*.

Upon drawing his work to a close, Garcilaso makes reference to an Indian lord of vassals who returned to his native Florida after having been taken to Castile and back. The lord organizes an attack against the Christians while at the same time promising to assist them in the task of converting his vassals to Christianity (*La Florida* 447–48; *The Florida* 641–42). Once again, Garcilaso echoes Cabeza de Vaca in the gesture of the native lord calling forth his people, as Cabeza de Vaca had so dramatically done in his re-creation of similar events in the province of Culiacán in northwestern Mexico. But in *La Florida* this happens *a la inversa*: the natives entrap and ambush the Christians, murdering the priests and friars who await their arrival. After the massacre, they seize a chest filled with breviaries, missals, books of scripture, and sacred vestments. Leaping gleefully about, wearing the vestments and ridiculing them, three Indians seize a crucifix from the chest. Then something miraculous occurs. As they look upon the cross they suddenly fall dead. In this tableau created by Garcilaso to draw to a close his narration of the de Soto expedition, "Spaniards and Indians lie dead, one next to the other, in a land soaked with the blood of both races" (Vaccarella 114; see also *La Florida* 447–48; *The Florida* 641–42).

Seen in relation to this ruinous yet paradoxically miraculous ending, the Guancane episode seems to be a minor event: there is no violent encounter between the Spaniards and the Indians, there is no submission to the Spanish, either forced or voluntary, and there is no spiritual apotheosis. I suggest that the non-encounter at Guancane serves as Garcilaso's secret signature to *La Florida*: the Guancanians' natural love of homeland emboldens them to hold off the Spaniards at the same time as they ostentatiously display the cross, the fundamental symbol of Christianity; in Guancane Indians appear with crosses in their hands, not weapons, but they do not submit themselves to the Spanish.

In the nonexistent province of Guancane, the scene of the silent march of Spanish soldiers crossing a landscape populated by potential enemies whose homes display the Christian cross is utopian in two senses. In its literal sense, it is "no place." In its symbolic sense, it is utopian because the natives of the province, the lords of vassals as well as the vassals themselves, reside tranquilly in their homes and work peacefully in their fields but are poised to defend their lands and themselves from invaders. In Garcilaso's Guancane the narrative equilibrium is one of internal native harmony and external tension against the potential invaders. The tension is grave and ominous, and the stability that reigns can be broken at any moment. At any moment the weakened, horseless Spanish army can become the victims of the Guancanians' aggression; at any moment the scene can erupt into a bloodbath like the kind that concludes *La Florida*, in which Spaniards and Indians lie dead "in a land soaked with the blood of both races."

In teaching these paired episodes of Garcilaso and Cabeza de Vaca, I often conclude by presenting fragments of well-known twentieth-century Latin American narratives for the students' further consideration. My aim is to help them grasp the principles of continuity and consistency in the transformative life of a literary culture, to learn that Spanish colonial-era narratives constitute an integral dimension of the origins of Latin American literature and its heritage. For Cabeza de Vaca, I focus on the figure of the protagonist-narrator and its resonances in Jorge Luis Borges's short story "El etnógrafo" and Abel Posse's novel *El largo atardecer del caminante*.[8]

For Garcilaso, I choose the role of place and—as the reader may have guessed—Guancane. Garcilaso's Guancane captures a moment of unstable and threatening equilibrium in the life of a community. Although it apparently did not exist empirically, its symbolic value is coherent and powerful. As such, it anticipates the fictional creation of the preeminent towns and communities we know in the modern Latin American novel, notably Comala, in Juan Rulfo's *Pedro Páramo*, and Macondo, in Gabriel García Márquez's *Cien años de soledad* (*One Hundred Years of Solitude*).[9]

Within the world ruled by Pedro Páramo with the collusion—out of fear or indifference—of the residents of Comala, the ruined pueblo functions as the setting from the beginning of the novel. Its reign of silence is achieved by Páramo's destruction of the town and its infernal, suffocating "airless heat." In fact, two days after his arrival in Comala, Juan Preciado dies of asphyxiation. The novel ends with the scene of the much earlier death of Páramo, who saw in that moment of sightless epiphany that "la tierra en ruinas estaba frente a él, vacía" ("the ruined, sterile earth lay before him"; Rulfo, *Pedro Páramo* [2008] 178; *Pedro Páramo* [1994] 128). The land lies in ruins, its paradise lost, thanks not to the violence of nature but to that of humanity.

If the world of Comala is presented to the reader after its destruction, the Macondo of García Márquez's *Cien años* appears from prior to its foundation until the moment it disappears, enveloped in a great wind, for all time. If the heat and silence and consequences of Páramo's rape of the town Comala produce a static, asphyxiating environment, without movement and without air, Macondo brings with it a vibrant and organic dynamism. If Comala is a corpse, Macondo is a tender infant, then an adolescent, and, later, an adult who breathes air that is life-giving until that air is transformed into a biblical, destructive force that carries itself and Macondo away, off the face of the earth.

If Comala is a cadaver abandoned by the violence that destroyed it, Macondo is a creature whose conception and birth were produced in the same crucible. That is, its foundation was provoked by the consequences of an act of remembered violence: the return of the ghost of Prudencio Aguilar, murdered by José Arcadio Buendía, inspires in Buendía a vision of founding a new town where it will be possible to live in peace (García Márquez, *Cien años* 108–12; *One Hundred Years* 21–25). The trajectory of Macondo's history is characterized by a double violence. Political violence is created by a municipal government that is alternately arbitrary and benign, by twenty years of civil war at the national level, and by a government external to the town that is ever more powerful and arbitrary, ever more intrusive yet ever more distant. Economic violence is constituted by foreigners' discovery of the sweetness of the Macondo region's natural bounty (the banana groves) and its conversion into an exploitative industry that in the last instance is the source of the destruction of all the resources—natural and human—of Macondo. These narrative events reiterate the conquistadores' and entrepreneurs' exploitation of the Americas, starting with, but not limited to, the Antilles.

Like Comala in its bitter fertility and living death, Macondo is the site of the ruin of nature and the destruction of humanity. Together, they provide the novelistic transformations of narrative literary monuments (*Naufragios*, *La Florida*) that presided over the predawn of Latin American literature, telling stories of the New World's natural and human bounty and of the Old World's conquistadores, entrepreneurs, and institutions that transformed them. Twentieth-century Latin American fictional narrative takes stock of that transformation-as-destruction, but it was anticipated by the likes of Garcilaso's Guancane, holding in check, but hovering on the cusp of, events that at any time could erupt into deadly violence.

La Florida and *Naufragios* may surprise the reader with their pertinence to today's Latin American literary tradition. But it is this element of surprise that makes them worthy predecessors—that is, worthwhile pre-readings—of the Latin American novels so beloved and so enduring today. The expression *New World*, like *Guancane*, finds its full value in the literary system in which it resides. In their creation of Comala and Macondo, Rulfo and García Márquez have modified our conception of Guancane, of ancient La Florida, and of the New World itself. At the same time, Cabeza de Vaca and Garcilaso, who bequeathed to posterity the vast domains of La Florida and the province of Guancane, give depth to the human geographies of Comala and Macondo.

A recommended reading for students on all these principles is Borges's "Kafka y sus precursores."

NOTES

[1] For a fuller account of these arguments, see Adorno, *Polemics* 279–307.

[2] In his *Apologética historia sumaria*, Bartolomé de Las Casas took Cabeza de Vaca's account as the most authoritative source on the native peoples of La Florida, in particular, Cabeza de Vaca's report of having found neither idolatry nor human sacrifice in the immense territories and sea-lanes the expedition traversed. Las Casas relied on Cabeza de Vaca's *Relación* of 1542 rather than its edition of 1555, known today as *Naufragios*; the relevant portion of *Naufragios* is chs. 32–36 (see Adorno and Pautz 3: 137–39).

[3] I cite our facing-page, Spanish-language English translation text as well as our English-language paperback translation. The original foliation is reproduced in both.

[4] "[O]ur story does not give the lie to the cavalier, Álvar Núñez" ("[Y] con esto no desdice nuestra historia a la de aquel caballero"; *The Florida* 186; *La Florida* 131).

[5] The title of the work we know as *Naufragios* was published in a 1555 edition, which is the one Garcilaso cites, as *Relación y comentarios*, referring, respectively, to Cabeza de Vaca's participation in the North American Narváez expedition and his later governorship of the province of Río de la Plata in South America.

[6] Varner and Varner identify the eyewitness reporters (xxii). Garcilaso does not cite Guancane from the firsthand accounts of Alonso de Carmona and Juan Coles, from which he drew heavily, and Guancane does not appear in the firsthand accounts of the de Soto expedition that he evidently did not know: the account, published in 1557, of the Portuguese "Gentleman of Elvas" and those of the expedition's *factor*, Luis Hernández de Biedma, and de Soto's official secretary, Rodrigo Ranjel. There is no mention of a province Guancane by any of the firsthand de Soto chroniclers (Clayton et al. 2: 43n).

[7] The prefix *gua-*, common in the Taíno language, has been identified with the pronominal prefix *wa-*, which is equivalent to *our* in English (Arrom, "Notas" 77n122; see also Arrom, "Registro" 119–20).

[8] For these readings as well as an overview of Cabeza de Vaca's North American sojourn, see Adorno, *Colonial Latin American Literature* 56–62.

[9] For my classes, I tend to choose segments 1–3 and 24 of *Pedro Páramo* and the second (unnumbered) chapter of *Cien años*, electing the former for the eerie sense of silence of the no-longer-living Comala and the latter for the founding of Macondo.

WORKS CITED

Adorno, Rolena. *Colonial Latin American Literature: A Very Short Introduction.* Oxford UP, 2011.

———. *The Polemics of Possession in Spanish American Narrative.* Yale UP, 2007.

Adorno, Rolena, and Patrick Charles Pautz. *Álvar Núñez Cabeza de Vaca: His Account, His Life, and the Expedition of Pánfilo de Narváez.* U of Nebraska P, 1999. 3 vols.

Arrom, José Juan. "Notas al texto." Pané, pp. 57–82.

———. "Registro de voces taínas." Pané, pp. 118–21.

Borges, Jorge Luis. "El etnógrafo." *Obras completas,* pp. 367–68.

———. "Kafka y sus precursores." *Obras completas,* pp. 88–90.

———. *Obras completas.* Edited by Carlos V. Frías, vol. 2, Emecé, 1996.

Cabeza de Vaca, Álvar Núñez. *The Narrative of Cabeza de Vaca.* Edited and translated by Rolena Adorno and Patrick Charles Pautz, U of Nebraska P, 2003.

Clayton, Lawrence A., et al., editors. *The De Soto Chronicles: The Expedition of Hernando de Soto to North America in 1539–1543.* U of Alabama P, 1993. 2 vols.

Espinosa Galarza, Max. *Toponimia quechua del Perú.* COSESA, 1973.

García Márquez, Gabriel. *Cien años de soledad.* 1967. Edited by Jacques Joset, Cátedra, 2004.

———. *One Hundred Years of Solitude.* 1967. Translated by Gregory Rabassa, Harper and Row, 1970.

Garcilaso de la Vega. *Comentarios reales de los Incas.* 1609, 1617. *Obras completas del Inca Garcilaso de la Vega,* edited by P. Carmelo Sáenz de Santa María, Atlas, 1960–65. 3 vols.

———. *La Florida del Inca: Historia del adelantado Hernando de Soto, gobernador y capitán general del reino de la Florida, y de otros heroicos caballeros españoles e indios.* 1605. Edited by Emma Susana Speratti Piñero, Fondo de Cultura Económica, 1956.

———. *The Florida of the Inca: A History of the Adelantado, Hernando de Soto, Governor and Captain General of the Kingdom of Florida, and of Other Heroic Spanish and Indian Cavaliers.* Translated by John Grier Varner and Jeanette Johnson Varner, U of Texas P, 1962.

———. *Royal Commentaries of the Incas and General History of Peru.* 1609, 1617. Translated by Harold V. Livermore, U of Texas P, 1966. 2 vols.

Las Casas, Bartolomé de. *Apologética historia sumaria.* 1527–60. Edited by Edmundo O'Gorman, Universidad Nacional Autónoma de México, 1967. 2 vols.

Pané, Fray Ramón. *Relación acerca de las antigüedades de los indios.* c. 1498. Edited by José Juan Arrom, 3rd ed., Siglo Veintiuno, 1978.

Posse, Abel. *El largo atardecer del caminante.* Emecé, 1992.

Rulfo, Juan. *Pedro Páramo.* 1955. Edited by José Carlos González Boixo, Cátedra, 2008.

———. *Pedro Páramo*. 1955. Translated by Margaret Sayers Peden, Serpent's Tail, 1994.

Swanton, John R. *Final Report of the United States De Soto Expedition Commission.* 1939. Smithsonian Institution Press, 1985.

Vaccarella, Eric. "Echoes of Resistance: Testimonial Narrative and Pro-Indian Discourse in El Inca Garcilaso de la Vega's *La Florida del Inca.*" *Latin American Literary Review*, vol. 32, no. 64, July-Dec. 2004, pp. 100–19.

Varner, John Grier, and Jeanette Johnson Varner. Introduction. Garcilaso, *The Florida of the Inca*, pp. xxi–xxxiv.

Teaching the Picaresque
with the *Historia general del Perú*

Sara L. Lehman

American students love the picaresque. They have read *Huckleberry Finn, La familia de Pascual Duarte,* and *Moll Flanders.* They have seen *Oliver!* and read *David Copperfield.* They think Bart Simpson is hilarious. When students of Spanish learn that all these show a marked influence of a Spanish subgenre, they relish the connections between popular culture and their studies. They admire Lazarillo's wit as he siphons wine from his cruel master's jug. They laugh at Pablos's Bugs Bunny–style trickery when he poses as a raisin vendor and watches his pursuers race by unawares. They speculate with Francisco de Quevedo and Mateo Alemán about whether life will be better for their picaros in the New World.

Although neither Pablos de Segovia nor Guzmán de Alfarache found a richer life in the colonies, the picaresque did. Inventive writers such as Alonso Carrió de la Vandera and Juan Rodríguez Freile developed new ways of concealing novelesque stories within nonfictional frameworks. The form thrived in Mexico with *Infortunios de Alonso Ramírez,* by Carlos de Sigüenza y Góngora, and *El Periquillo Sarniento* and *Don Catrín de la Fachenda,* by José Joaquín Fernández de Lizardi. To study the picaresque is to engage the questions of literature and sociopolitics together: How does a modern reader separate history from fiction? Must one? How and when does the Spanish American novel emerge? How does one define genre in colonial literature?

These questions can be framed within the study of the second part of El Inca Garcilaso de la Vega's *Comentarios reales,* or the *Historia general del Perú.* This work narrates the story of the Spanish conquest and struggle for the wealth of Peru, but it is fundamentally an appeal for the legitimacy of a marginalized Spaniard: Garcilaso's father, Capitán Garcilaso de la Vega y Vargas. Following the rhetoric of both colonial historiography (the *relación*) and the picaresque novel, the author directs his appeal to an external "Vuestra Merced" who represents legitimacy—the state. He utilizes the autobiographical mode, positioning himself as an eyewitness and manipulating legal discourse in his telling of the "whole story." He also includes overtly picaresque episodes of robbery, mercantilism, trickery, and revenge, which he narrates in documentary detail through the use of suspense, dialogue, and irony.

Such episodes and characteristics make the *Historia general* a useful text for studying the picaresque in the Americas, which, as Wilfrido H. Corral observes, "appears at intervals, . . . in fragmentary form" (131). The diversity and extent of its presence is observed in colonial texts as varied as *Infortunios de Alonso Ramírez, Don Catrín de la Fachenda,* and *El Lazarillo de ciegos caminantes,* by Alonso Carrió de la Vandera, but the fragmentary nature identified by Corral is perhaps best illustrated through the *Historia general*. Although this second part of *Comentarios reales* is almost never used in colonial literature or history courses because of its density and length, I propose that, given the fact that the considerable picaresque episodes contained in the *Historia general* are presented by Garcilaso as interpolations, it is valid to extract them and read them as picaresque texts per se. Enrique Pupo-Walker agrees: "Las inserciones imaginativas . . . aparecen—al verlas en conjunto—como un componente significativo e integral del discurso" ("Imaginative insertions . . . appear—when taken together—as a significant and integral component of discourse"; 154; my trans.). The study of this *conjunto* reveals some of the most fascinating and characteristically picaresque tales to be found within the historiographical texts of the colonial Americas.

The remainder of this essay outlines two versatile ways of incorporating certain picaresque excerpts of Garcilaso's text in the undergraduate literature classroom. The first presents four episodes as a stand-alone unit in a picaresque course, pairing each with the traits that it most readily displays. As a body of narrative, these four episodes reveal the "picaresque chemistry" that Joseph Ricapito signals as the key ingredient to critical analysis (78). The second model considers a single almost hyperbolically picaresque episode, the study of which could form a complete lesson on the subgenre in a survey course. Both models offer concrete textual examples and illustrate their application to teaching the picaresque in ways that foster students' innate enthusiasm while laying the groundwork for solid analysis, meaningful class discussion, and well-informed projects on Garcilaso's important text, thus engaging students in the conversations of colonial scholarship.

Preparation

Both models will require some amount of instruction and definition of the picaresque before considering the examples in the *Historia general*. Particularly in the case of the survey course, showing video clips of *Huckleberry Finn*, *Oliver!*, or others as well as reactivating student knowledge of English-language picaresque novels will both raise consciousness and build confidence as students approach the subgenre. Contextualizing readings such as Daniel Eisenberg's "Does the Picaresque Novel Exist?," Harry Sieber's "Literary Continuity, Social Order, and the Invention of the Picaresque," and José Antonio Maravall's *La literatura picaresca desde la historia social* can inform discussions and alert students to the characteristics they should expect to find. Reading (in the picaresque course) or introducing (in the survey course) the picaresque's early and full-blown iterations as they are exemplified through iconic novels such as *Lazarillo de Tormes* and *El Buscón*, by Quevedo, could also illustrate the irony, picaresque values, and episodic structure that will be transposed to the Americas. However professors choose to present it, the very least that students need to understand, as I and many others have written elsewhere, is the development of the picaresque and its socioeconomic context in seventeenth-century Spain and the overwhelming commonalities of the subgenre, including first-person narrator, constant geographical and professional movement of the protagonist, commercial ambiance, satirical rhetoric, episodic structure, questioning of societal values, and picaresque themes.

Model 1: *Four Picaresque Tales from the* Historia general

Let us move to the first model: incorporating the *Historia general* in a picaresque course. It is assumed that the curriculum would include readings from both sides of the Atlantic and that the course would trace new developments in the genre when the picaresque "goes global"—that is, when it is transported and translated to a colonial context. With that background in mind, students are prepared to consider its key features (signaled in the subheadings below) as they appear in the interpolations of the *Historia general*.

Episodic and Entertaining: The Cruelties of Francisco de Carvajal

One of the best ways to approach the structure of the subgenre and the nature of the picaro is through the ongoing story of Francisco de Carvajal, aide to Gonzalo Pizarro. Like authors of picaresque novels, Garcilaso chose an episodic structure so that each adventure or misadventure in his character's life could be considered alone as an entertaining story with a moralizing message. Thus the Carvajal episodes marry the picaresque's (and indeed many literary genres') desire to *enseñar y deleitar* (inform and amuse) that is also, I would argue, typical of the *Historia general*. To extract a meaningful and self-contained body of episodes on Carvajal, it is useful to consider those that focus on his role as commander, which occupy several chapters from books 4 and 5.

Beginning in book 4, chapter 29, Garcilaso structures the Carvajal tale in mini-episodes that illustrate certain aspects of his character. With himself as first-person narrator and eyewitness, he relates Carvajal's cruel torture and killing of an arquebusier, followed immediately by an episode of a soldier's deceit and the commander's resulting anger and threats. Garcilaso infuses his story with suspense, using phrases such as "[d]exaremos con su enojo a Carvajal, en la persecución y alcances que dava a Diego Centeno, por bolver a dezir los que Gonçalo Piçarro deva al Visorrey" ("[l]et us leave Carvajal in his rage, chasing Diego Centeno, and return to Gonzalo's pursuit of the viceroy"; *Historia* 2: 101; *Royal Commentaries* 1041), thus employing the picaresque technique of multiple narrative perspectives and signaling the episodic nature of the Carvajal story.

When Garcilaso returns to the thread in chapter 36, he reminds readers with a simple "[c]omo atrás diximos" ("[a]s we said earlier") and goes on to narrate the trickery and attack of Carvajal's troops from the rear by his enemy Centeno. Here the author further develops Carvajal's character through dialogue and the depiction of him as "muy alegre y contento, viendo que llevava a su contrario al matadero" ("delighted at the thought that he was chasing his rival to slaughter"; *Historia* 2: 120; *Royal Commentaries* 1059) by driving Centeno into a ravine. At the end of this episode again Garcilaso jumps to a different narrative perspective, thus sustaining the suspense.

The rest of the story occupies five contiguous chapters, relating the events after Carvajal's capture by his own men (a subtle commentary on his character) and his condemnation by Pedro de la Gasca. In this portion of the narrative, Garcilaso presents a series of episodes that characterize Carvajal as a rogue, much like a picaro. He reveals that Carvajal

> ni tuvo amigo, pariente ni patriota, que entonces sus más amigos huían dél. Mas no por esso dexaron de visitarle muchos cavalleros muy principales, particularmente algunos dellos que eran moços libres y traviessos, los cuales ivan más a burlar y a triunfar dél que no a consolarle. Mas como Francisco de Carvajal era tan discreto y malicioso, conociéndoles la intención, triunfó e hizo escarnio dellos.   (*Historia* 2: 260)

> had no friend, relative, or countryman: even his most intimate friends avoided him. Nevertheless many leading gentlemen went to see him, especially some of the younger and naughtier ones, who went to mock him and triumph over him rather than to console him. But as Francisco de Carvajal was wise and wily enough to realize their intention, he triumphed over them, and made fun of them.   (*Royal Commentaries* 1198)

This characterization of Carvajal as both shunned and wily links him with picaresque novels such as *El Buscón* and *Don Catrín de la Fachenda*, whose protagonists are equally marginalized. Similarly, the six episodes that Garcilaso chooses to present in chapter 38 and the beginning of chapter 39 exemplify the witty banter and vaguely disguised insults typical of picaresque discourse. They also echo the spirit of *cofradía* ("roguish brotherhood") present in both novels mentioned above; all who knew Carvajal or were in captivity with him were greatly amused and even astonished at his sharp tongue.

The remainder of the chapter recounts the writings of other historiographers about Carvajal's cruel wordplay, while chapter 40 takes a more somber tone and narrates his death by hanging for war crimes. But rather than end the Carvajal episodes on a serious note, Garcilaso dedicates two more chapters to underscoring his role as a picaro in the text. Chapter 41 describes his attention to dress and physical appearance, his ironic expressions, and his love of wine. Like book 2 of *El Buscón*, it introduces a series of picaresque prototypes, including soldiers, a merchant, a friar, and a surgeon. Chapter 42 continues with six more episodes offering overt picaresque tropes such as scatological humor, reference to prostitution, bribery, and murder. It ends with a tale about Carvajal's continued revenge after his death, an obviously fictionalized episode. In short, the key elements of structure and character development can be traced in the Carvajal episodes that, like Quevedo's and others' novels, augment in intensity as they progress. By the last two chapters, the Carvajal story reads almost as a parody of the picaresque in its extreme presentation of the commonalities of the subgenre.

Commercial, Clever, and Critical: The Voyage of Rodrigo Niño

The episode of Rodrigo Niño occupies two chapters of book 6, although the protagonist is mentioned in book 4. Garcilaso's introduction to the digression is notable for its echo of picaresque discourse: "Por cortar el hilo a un discurso tan melancólico como el de los capítulos referidos, será bien que digamos alguna cosa en particular que sea más alentada, para que passemos adelante no con tanta pesadumbre" ("To interrupt the thread of a tale so melancholy as that of the aforementioned chapters, it will be well that we should say something of a more stimulating nature so that we may continue with less melancholy"; *Historia* 3: 31; *Royal Commentaries* 1247). Beginning, then, what José Durand characterizes as an episode of "arte y encanto" (383), Garcilaso relates the 1548 transport from Lima to Seville of eighty-six prisoners condemned to the galleys. Along the way, the poorly guarded prisoners begin to flee, and Niño, who is in charge, has to use his wits to preserve the rest of the crew from an encounter with French pirates. By the time they reach Seville, all but one of the prisoners have escaped, and Niño dispatches him roughly, preferring to face alone his punishment for their loss. He is condemned to pay a fine and serve in the military and is forbidden to return to the Indies, but he appeals to Prince Maximilian of Austria (then governing Spain) and is pardoned on the basis of inadequate support from the colonial government.

The pirate portion of the episode, in which Niño defies the corsairs through a musical ruse, has received the most critical attention. Pupo-Walker points out the novelesque tone of the scene as descended from the Byzantine subgenre, a known influence of the picaresque in America (84). As a response, Durand dedicates considerable effort and pages to documenting the identity of Niño and thereby the veracity of the digression. In fact, they are both right and signal two of the key characteristics of the picaresque. First, the episode takes place within a distinctly commercial ambiance, in which Niño's overland and transatlantic route matches that of the treasure fleets transporting riches (or galley slaves, in this case) from Peru to Seville. Second, the picaro relies on his cleverness to survive, often employing disguises and trickery. Pedagogically, the pirate portion alone serves as a superb representation of the picaresque in the *Historia general*.

Yet, like Sigüenzay Góngora in *Infortunios de Alonso Ramírez*, Garcilaso goes one step further and interprets the episode for his reader, signaling its critical message regarding colonial practices. Three times the narrator reiterates that the eventual escape of all the galley slaves was due to Niño being improperly provisioned by the colonial officials of Peru who had charged Niño with their guard and transport. Thus, studying the episode of Niño elucidates three of the key commonalities of the picaresque in Spanish America, allowing students to explore not just its characteristics but its purpose. In a course on the subgenre, the *Historia general* thus enters into dialogue with essential texts such as *Infortunios*, *Don Catrín*, and *Lazarillo de ciegos caminantes*.

Thematic and Testimonial: The Revenge of "So-and-So" Aguirre

The interpolation of "So-and-So" Aguirre occupies parts of two chapters and displays the picaresque values of honor and revenge in an episode worthy of Miguel de Cervantes or Lope de Vega. In the story, Aguirre is singled out for excessive punishment for having used more than his allotted number of Indian porters. After his whipping, the aggrieved Aguirre seeks revenge on the licentiate who misused him, first pursuing him for three years and four months and then murdering him in his bed. The sympathetic residents of Cuzco hide Aguirre and spirit him to safety in disguise. Pupo-Walker notes the episode's gradual "intensificación del plano imaginativo" ("intensification of the imaginative plane"; 183), which moves from dry fact ("En este tiempo entró en el Perú por Visorrey, governador y capitán general de todo aquel Imperio Don Antonio de Mendoça, hijo segundo de la casa del Marqués de Mondéxar" ["At this time there arrived in Peru as viceroy, governor, and captain general of the empire Don Antonio de Mendoza, second son of the house of the marquis of Mondéjar"; Garcilaso, *Historia* 3: 54; *Royal Commentaries* 1272]) to literary creation ("En aquella plaçuela halló dos cavalleros moços . . . y llegándose a ellos les dixo '¡Escóndanme, escóndanme!' sin saber dezir otra palabra, que tan tonto y perdido iva como esto" ["In the little square there he found two young gentlemen . . . and went up to them saying 'Hide me, hide me!' He was so wild and stupefied that he could not utter any other word"; *Historia* 3: 58; *Royal Commentaries* 1276]). The inclusion of suspense and imagined dialogue links the text with novelesque genres.

Additionally, themes that pertain to the picaresque are revealed in the last line of the interpolated tale: "Los soldados bravos y facinerosos dezían que si huviera muchos Aguirres por el mundo, tan deseosos de vengar sus afrentas, que los pesquisidores no fueran tan libres e insolentes" ("The unruly and swaggering soldiers used to say that if there were more Aguirres in the world and they went to such pains to avenge their wrongs, the investigators would mind their own business better and not be so high handed"; *Historia* 3: 59; *Royal Commentaries* 1278). This shift of narrative perspective signals to the reader the picaresque themes of pride, honor, revenge, and authority present in the Aguirre episode. Additionally, the picaresque's characteristic geographical movement, trickery, and role of appearances are intrinsic to the plot of the interpolation.

Furthermore, the Aguirre episode also invites discussion of testimony and eyewitness, as Garcilaso inserts himself three times in the narrative. At the beginning, he presents the alcalde mayor, "que yo conocí" ("whom I knew"; *Historia* 3: 55; *Royal Commentaries* 1273), who seized Aguirre from the line of soldiers. At the turning point, Garcilaso again asserts himself, saying, "En aquel tiempo un

sobrino de mi padre, hijo de Gómez de Tordoya . . . habló al licenciado Esquivel" ("At that time a nephew of my father's, the son of Gómez de Tordoya . . .
spoke to Esquivel"; *Historia* 3: 57; *Royal Commentaries* 1275). Toward the end
of the interpolation, he writes, "Passados cuarenta días del hecho, les pareció a
aquellos cavalleros (que el uno dellos se dezía fulano Santillán y el otro fulano
Cataño, cavalleros muy nobles, que los conocí bien, y el uno dellos hallé en Sevilla cuando vine a España)" ("Forty days after the deed, the gentlemen who were
hiding Aguirre—one of whom was called something Santillán and the other
something Cataño, both noblemen whom I knew well [I met one of them in Seville when I came to Spain]"; *Historia* 3: 58; *Royal Commentaries* 1277). These
three interventions underscore Garcilaso's position as a first-person narrator
while revealing the "enorme tensión intelectual y emotiva" ("great intellectual
and emotional tension") that results from the author's closeness to the events
(Pupo-Walker 87). In fact, Garcilaso's use of first person and his semantic choices
of *testimonio* ("testimony"), *documentar* ("documenting"), *yo vi* ("I saw"), *yo conocí* ("I met"), and *yo recuerdo* ("I remember") throughout his text reveals "a
process of comprehension and interpretation" akin to that of the picaresque,
where the protagonist-narrator puts a particular slant on events to serve his purpose (Anadón 151). Similarly, Garcilaso's interpolation of autobiographical passages reflects the author's inner ambition to achieve recognition while adding
depth to the events he narrates. The Aguirre episode, then, shares themes and
narrator construction with *Lazarillo de Tormes* and *El Buscón*.

Exemplary: The Rogue Contreras Brothers

The episode of the Contreras brothers occupies two self-contained chapters of
book 6. Like the picaresque, it opens by relating the foundational moment that
set Hernando and Pedro de Contreras on the path to ruin: during a restructur-
ing of the colony of Nicaragua their father is stripped of his post as governor and
of the Indians who had been granted to his family. Thus the sons decide to seek
revenge by starting a rebellion. They arm a band of similarly disgruntled soldiers to slay the bishop, steal ships, and lie in wait in the harbor of Panama with
the intention of ambushing President La Gasca upon his arrival and stealing his
treasure to compensate themselves for their service and losses. The band of
rogues succeeds in stealing more than three million pesos' worth of gold and
silver, together with pearls, jewels, and merchandise that they looted from shops
in Panama. Yet because of "disparates y locuras" ("follies and stupidities"; Garcilaso, *Historia* 3: 40; *Royal Commentaries* 1256) that lead them to attack many
of the chief citizens of Panama, the brothers lose all the treasure and thus their
revenge. When the Contreras brothers forbid the killing of said dignitaries, they
make enemies of their own roguish companions. Here Garcilaso introduces foreshadowing to build suspense: "[S]e enojó mucho Juan Bermejo, y le dixo que
pues era en favor de sus enemigos y en disfavor de sí proprio y de sus amigos,
pues no consentía que matassen a sus contrarios, no se espantase que otro día

72 HISTORIA GENERAL DEL PERÚ

ellos lo ahorcassen a él y a todos los suyos. Esas palabras fueron un pronóstico que se cumplió en breve tiempo" ("Juan Bermejo was greatly annoyed, and declared that if [Hernando de Contreras] wanted to favor his enemies and displease his friends by not letting them kill their enemies, he had better not be surprised if one fine day they hanged him and all his followers. This foreboding was soon fulfilled"; *Historia* 3: 41; *Royal Commentaries* 1257). Continued division of the rebels leads to the eventual loss of not only the treasure but also their lives, as chapter 7 relates.

One of the purposes of the picaresque is to illustrate through examples what *not* to do or how *not* to be; in other words, it seeks to raise a moral consciousness among its readers. Just as *Infortunios* would later argue for the reform of certain systems of empire by showing their dysfunctionality and *Don Catrín* much later would signal the need for education and just society through the depiction of a disengaged and selfish protagonist, the Contreras episode offers "role anti-models" for citizens of the empire. Garcilaso employs a variety of means to ensure that this message is clear. First, he continually characterizes his picaresque protagonists as foolhardy, boastful youths who are guided by misjudgment and "imaginándose que, sin tener contraste alguno, eran ya señores de todo el Nuevo Mundo" ("their belief that they were already masters of all the New World without any opposition"; *Historia* 3: 42; *Royal Commentaries* 1258). Second, he moralistically interprets the deaths of the Contreras brothers for the reader, observing, "Este fin tan malo y desesperado tuvo aquel hecho, y no se podía esperar dél otro sucesso, porque su principio fué con muerte de un obispo, cosa tan horrenda y abominable . . . no basta disculpa ninguna para hazer un hecho tan malo. Y assí lo pagaron ellos como se ha visto" ("Such was the hopeless and fatal end of this incident: no other result could have been expected since it began with so dire and abominable a deed as the murder of a bishop . . . no excuse can possibly justify so wicked an act. Their retribution we have already seen"; *Historia* 3: 44; *Royal Commentaries* 1260). Finally, in the chapter immediately following the episode, he reflectively contrasts the Contrerases' behavior with that of the "buen Presidente" ("good president") and "insigne varón" ("worthy man") La Gasca (*Historia* 3: 46; *Royal Commentaries* 1262). Thus, in semantics, moralizing passages, and the use of antithesis in the Contreras episode, Garcilaso's writing creates space for comparative study with Fernández de Lizardi and other American picaresque novelists who offer their protagonists as negative examples.

Model 2: A Single Episode for a Survey Course

For the other course model, using a single picaresque episode from the *Historia general* for a lesson in a survey, the most exemplary episode might be the picaresque novelette of Melchor Verdugo. Occupying just chapter 32 of book 4, this mini-novel has it all: an antihero, the role of fortune, trickery, a mercantile ambiance, pride, a voyage, piracy, misadventure, revenge, legal rhetoric, multiple narrative perspectives, suspense, and the use of first person. It tells the tale of "una novedad que causó mucho escándalo" ("an event that caused much scandal") by a man who "pretendió mostrarse . . . y hazer alguna cosa señalada" ("wanted to perform some noble feat to distinguish himself") in the service of the viceroy of Peru (Garcilaso, *Historia* 2: 108; *Royal Commentaries* 1047). Already the enemy of the Pizarrists, Verdugo acts quickly to escape his foes. He secretly arms himself, then lures twenty of the leading citizens of Lima to captivity in his house. He then seizes more in the street and leaves all his prisoners tied up on the beach while he embarks for Nicaragua in a stolen ship laden with valuable merchandise. Once there, his ship is taken (as are several others) by Captain Juan Alonso Palomino, and Verdugo's plans are momentarily foiled. Shifting gears, he aims to distinguish himself instead in Nombre de Dios and sails there in four frigates, seizing a ship of free Black sailors to serve as guides along the way. He loots and sets fire to a house occupied by several important captains. While the governor of Nombre de Dios prepares charges and revenge against Verdugo, he arms his men and a number of local citizens, launches cannon fire on the town, and escapes to Cartagena. The episode concludes with suspense and the possibility of future misadventures.

In this episode, the mercantile ambience is essential, manifesting in the references to Verdugo's wealth and resources, the ships he seizes, looting, and profit. Such a commercial atmosphere also implicates the picaresque's key themes of greed and pride, as Verdugo is intent on distinguishing himself through his daring deeds. Additionally, the classically picaresque themes of vengeance, the whims of fortune, and continual voyage exert an essential role in this episode. The piracy elements and legal rhetoric of the text again indicate common ground with narratives such as *Infortunios*, making the Verdugo episode a perfect microcosm of the picaresque in America.

The suspense of the Verdugo story is resolved in the last two paragraphs of book 5, chapter 2, which could easily be excerpted for the purposes of the survey course. It relates Verdugo's attempt to return to Nombre de Dios, his banishment, and his flight to safety in Spain, thus inverting Pablos's attempt to find a new life in America at the end of *El Buscón*. Here Garcilaso introduces the first-person perspective typical of the picaresque, writing,

> Yo le vi en la antecámara del muy católico Rey Don Felipe Segundo el año de mil y quinientos y sesenta y tres, bien fatigado y lastimado de que émulos y enemigos suyos resucitaron los agravios que en el Perú y en Nicaragua y en el Nombre de Dios hizo, por los cuales, según los acriminavan, temió que le quitaran el hábito, y assí era lástima verle el rostro, según el sentimiento que mostrava. (*Historia* 2: 149)

> I saw him in the antechamber of Philip II in 1563, when he was vexed and distressed by the charges his rivals and enemies had made against his

misdeeds in Peru, Nicaragua, and Nombre de Dios. He feared that these accusations would lose him his habit, and he took this so to heart that his face was pitiful to see.   (*Royal Commentaries* 1088)

Surprisingly, Verdugo is awarded the host of Santiago and allowed to return to Peru, thus ending the episode on an upswing of fortune stemming from the intervention of an official, similar to the conclusion of *Infortunios*. In sum, for its picaresque themes, antihero, misadventure, geographical movement, and links with exemplary novels, the mini-novel of Melchor Verdugo provides a perfect vehicle for approaching the picaresque in the colonies.

Through study of a unit of picaresque selections from the *Historia general* or even just a single episode, the characteristics and purpose of the picaresque in the Americas become clear, allowing us to view Garcilaso's text as Giuseppe Bellini does: as a "gran novela . . . de aventuras" ("great adventure tale") that teaches lessons about empire through "la magia . . . la invención, el estudio psicológico [y] la capacidad de observación" ("magic . . . invention, psychological study [and] observational capacity"; 51; my trans.). When we approach the *Historia general* as an example of the picaresque, not only do we find a manageable focus for exposing our students to this impressive work, but we also engage larger conversations about ownership, identity, and truth. Ultimately, those are the questions of both colonial historiography and the picaresque in the Americas.

WORKS CITED

Anadón, José. "History as Autobiography in Garcilaso Inca." *Garcilaso Inca de la Vega: An American Humanist: A Tribute to José Durand*, edited by Anadón, U of Notre Dame P, 1998, pp. 149–63.

Bellini, Giuseppe. "Sugestión y tragedia del mundo americano en la *Historia general del Perú* del Inca Garcilaso." *De los Romances-villancico a la poesía de Claudio Rodríguez: 22 ensayos sobre las literaturas española e hispanoamericana en homenaje a Gustav Siebenmann*, edited by José Manuel López de Abiada and Augusta López Bernasocchi, Gráficas Sol, 1984, pp. 49–63.

Corral, Wilfrido H. "Some Avenues into the Anglo-American Picaresque." Cruz, pp. 135–42.

Cruz, Anne J., editor. *Approaches to Teaching* Lazarillo de Tormes *and the Picaresque Tradition*. Modern Language Association of America, 2008.

Durand, José. "Rodrigo Niño, el de los galeotes." *Nueva revista de filología hispánica*, vol. 37, no. 2, 1989, pp. 383–404.

Eisenberg, Daniel. "Does the Picaresque Novel Exist?" *Kentucky Romance Quarterly*, vol. 26, no. 2, 1979, pp. 203–19.

Garcilaso de la Vega. *Historia general del Perú (Segunda parte de los* Comentarios reales de los Incas*)*. Edited by Ángel Rosenblat, Emecé Editores, 1944. 3 vols.

———. *Royal Commentaries of the Incas and General History of Peru*. Translated by Harold V. Livermore, U of Texas P, 1966. 2 vols.

Maravall, José Antonio. *La literatura picaresca desde la historia social*. Taurus, 1986.

Pupo-Walker, Enrique. *Historia, creación y profecía en los textos del Inca Garcilaso de la Vega*. José Porrúa Turanzas, 1982.

Ricapito, Joseph. "Formalism and Stylistic Analysis as Applied to *Lazarillo de Tormes*." Cruz, pp. 74–78.

Sieber, Harry. "Literary Continuity, Social Order, and the Invention of the Picaresque." *Cultural Authority in Golden Age Spain*, edited by Marina S. Brownlee and Hans Ulrich Gumbrecht, Johns Hopkins UP, 1995, pp. 143–64.

Natural History and the *Comentarios reales*

Yarí Pérez Marín

Given that it has not been the customary point of entry to the study of the *Comentarios reales* (*Royal Commentaries*), a reader may ask what would be especially valuable about exploring this canonical text with students through the lens of natural history. To begin to answer that question, and as a point of departure, I would offer two preliminary observations: first, the act of framing a reading of the work through the set of questions that arise from a consideration of this context highlights an already intrinsic feature of the project itself. The *Comentarios reales* devotes a substantial number of its pages to the subject, one that was at the very forefront of lettered culture in the mid-sixteenth and early seventeenth centuries. To put it another way, this approach restores Inca Garcilaso de la Vega to a certain company he kept—that is to say, to the books he read, written by some of the most widely circulated authors of the era who dealt with science and the natural world, like José de Acosta, Nicolás Monardes, and Juan Huarte de San Juan. Second, and more to the purpose of the MLA Approaches to Teaching series, inviting students to study the *Comentarios reales* through this frame is arguably equally useful to undergraduates and postgraduates being trained in literature departments as it is to those in history, including the history of science; in interdisciplinary programs on Latin American studies or early modern studies; or even pursuing degrees in the humanities more broadly. While a fact known to Hispanists for some time, the centrality of science to the story of Iberian expansion is a notion that has only recently enjoyed general critical acceptance. As Jorge Cañizares-Esguerra remarked over a decade ago, natural history, along with cosmography, can be said to have been "the backbone upon which the Portuguese and Spanish crowns built their mighty Christian monarchies" (Introduction 1). Yet it is the compelling nature of how this process was captured and disseminated to a wider world—in images, through the availability of new products and changing consumer culture, but above all in textual and literary representations—that enables our students to connect so profoundly with ways of seeing and modes of thought far removed from their own present-day experiences and imagination. What follows is a set of concrete suggestions for how to bring the *Comentarios reales* to the literature and history classrooms by way of natural history, although the potential to make connections beyond the models I propose is far greater.[1]

While the *Comentarios reales* addresses concerns relevant to natural history in many of its sections, book 8, chapters 9–25 (discussing plants, animals, and minerals in the Americas prior to contact with Europe), and book 9, chapters 16–31 (dealing primarily with plants and animals brought over by European settlers), are good places on which to anchor a close reading. Arranged thematically, with headings such as "De las esmeraldas, turquesas y perlas" ("Of Emeralds, Turquoises,

and Pearls") and "De la vid, y del primero que metió uvas en el Cuzco" ("Of the
Vine, and of the First One to Bring Grapes to Cuzco"),[2] they can be read sequen-
tially but also lend themselves to a partial selection, chosen either because of how
the subject matter connects with other materials being taught or because of the literary value or historical interest of a given passage, depending on the needs of the
curriculum. In addition, chapters 24 and 25 of book 2 (on medicinal herbs), chapter 10 of book 5 (on cattle, birds, and smaller animals), and chapter 6 of book 6 (on
organized hunts, or *chacu*) are recommended, and they help to explain lines in books
8 and 9 where the author alludes to having already touched upon those topics.

Book 8 of the *Comentarios reales* describes numerous crops and animals, including different types of corn and potatoes, peppers, agave, bananas, pineap-
ples, coca,[3] llamas, pumas, monkeys, large and small birds, and fish, as well as
precious stones, gold, and silver. Book 9 remarks on horses, cattle, fowl, domestic animals, wheat, grapes, sugarcane, and pomegranates, to mention but a few.
At the undergraduate level, these sections offer natural points of contact with
texts already frequently included in survey courses on pre-independence Latin
America taught in Hispanic studies and Romance languages departments. For
example, a possible course of study suitable to either a history or a literary studies setting would be an introductory module on early modern Latin America that
centered on the idea of encounter narratives and the key role the representation
of so-called New World nature played in them. It could showcase the *Comentarios reales* in the context of Christopher Columbus's coding of nature as marvelous in his letter to Luis de Santángel or in sections of his diary of the first
voyage. It could also be considered alongside Pero Vaz de Caminha's letter of
discovery, another document that purported to capture Indigenous reactions,
positive and negative, to European fauna and foodstuffs.[4] Parts of Gonzalo
Fernández de Oviedo's *Historia general y natural de las Indias*, such as the
famed passage on the pineapple (bk. 7, ch. 14), memorably analyzed by José Rabasa, would also yield interesting comparisons. Sections of the Florentine Codex, a project undertaken by Nahua students at the Colegio de Santa Cruz de
Tlatelolco under the tutelage of the friar Bernardino de Sahagún, or the less-
studied Badianus Codex, would be a worthwhile addition (see Sahagún; Pardo-
Tomás; De Vos). The latter, composed by the physician Martín de la Cruz and
translated into Latin by Juan Badiano, both men Nahuas from Xochimilco, is a
multilingual manuscript in book form that catalogues local medicinal plants and
insects, setting down their local names and providing brief recipes organized by
specific ailment. The codex is written in Nahuatl and Latin, but because the
entries are short, the hand-colored images striking, and the presentation accessible, students are usually very keen to engage with it. Both codices are available in facsimile editions, and integrating them into the classroom brings the
added benefit of giving students a chance to work directly with early modern
manuscripts and learn about Indigenous writing and approaches to visual illustration, often for the first time.[5] Moreover, studying these texts alongside the
recommended sections of the *Comentarios reales* underscores for undergraduates

the active role Indigenous scholars played in the intellectual life of New Spain and Peru, encouraging them to think about how non-Europeans in early colonial settings often adapted their own long-standing practices of knowledge production by mastering and refashioning tenets of Renaissance humanism to create new ways of understanding nature.

Texts from the end of the sixteenth century and the first decades of the seventeenth century, which began to express a sense of local pride and did so in part by turning to American nature, can also enhance a reading of Garcilaso's work. Recommended here would be Juan de Cárdenas's *Problemas y secretos maravillosos de las Indias* or Bernardo de Balbuena's *La grandeza mexicana*, with the latter's contention that Mexican flora is "un real jardín, que sin engaño a los de Chipre vence en hermosura, y al mundo en temple ameno y sitio extraño" ("a royal garden, which truly surpasses those of Cyprus in its beauty, and those of the world in its pleasant disposition and unique setting"; 99). Cárdenas's approach, in turn, mirrors Garcilaso's editorial decision of keeping separate the flora and fauna native to Peru from that which did not have Andean origins, anticipating the at times adversarial juxtaposition a comparison of books 8 and 9 yields. Only a few years before Garcilaso's work appeared in print, Cárdenas wrote:

> [No] tendrá Asia, África y Europa que quexarse, pues tiene y ha tenido más escriptores que dellas escrivan, que cosas que poderse escrevir. ¿Qué pudo dezir ni encarescer Plinio del cocodrillo, que no escriva el philósopho indiano del caimán desta tierra? Pues cotejadas sus propiedades con las del cocodrillo, son las del caimán muy notables y excelentes. . . . ¿Qué dixo Avicena de las tortugas, que no aya mucho más en nuestras indianas icoteas, pues ay algunas en cuya concha suelen caber casi seis hombres? ¿Qué escriben los auctores del lagarto que no digamos en las Indias de las iguanas?
>
> ¿Qué escrevió Dioscórides del erizo, que no se escurezca con las propiedades del armadillo de la Nueva España? . . . Pues yerbas, frutas, pescados y animales ¿qué libros serían bastantes para poderlo todo poner en summa?   (32)[6]

Asia, Africa and Europe need not complain, for they have and have had more writers to write about them than things to be written about. What could Pliny say or convey of the crocodile that the local philosopher does not write of the caiman of this land? For if its properties are compared with those of the crocodile, those of the caiman are more notable and excellent. . . . What did Avicenna say of turtles that there is not much more to be said about our turtles for the shells of some are so large that they usually can hold six men? What do the authors write about the lizard that we are not able to say in the Indies about iguanas?

What did Dioscorides write about the sea urchin that does not pale in comparison with the properties of the armadillo of New Spain? . . . Thus, herbs, fruits, fish and animals, what books would suffice to describe them all?

Similarly, Garcilaso's exposition of Peruvian nature is positive, stressing how the agricultural skills of the Inca had harnessed it to meet the needs of the people before the coming of Europeans. The land is fertile and receptive, features that Luis Millones Figueroa sees as supporting the case for a *"praeparatio agricola,"* which would be analogous to other parts in the text where Garcilaso argues in favor of Peru's *"praeparatio evangelica"*—that is, its ideal disposition to convert to Christianity thanks to the Incas' civilizing impact, which had laid the ground-work. The author's approach in book 8 is detailed and displayed systemically, reminiscent of the structure and methods of European natural histories and me-dicinal herbals of the time, even if different from them in scope.[7] While native natural products are painted as bountiful, descriptions tend to show restraint in their praise and are not characterized by the use of superlatives or an imagery of excess, traits that conversely will be typical of book 9. In that next section, the fertility of the Americas acquires a darker undertone, with abundance be-coming *overabundance* in the case of most of the non-native flora and fauna listed, and the language turning increasingly ambivalent or openly unfavorable.[8] As José Antonio Mazzotti, Ronald E. Surtz, and Millones Figueroa have noted in their respective studies of the *Comentarios reales,* Garcilaso's "doubly-folded discourse" on exuberance, to borrow Mazzotti's term ("Inca Garcilaso" 174), at once boasts a certain superiority of American fertility and serves a negative cri-tique of how the Andean landscape has been transformed as a result of Euro-pean settlement.[9] While admiration is expressed for animals like horses,[10] it is tempered by remarks on their superfluous presence given that the inhabitants of Peru "vivían muy contentos sin ell[o]s" ("lived very well without them"; *Co-mentarios* 674). Mastiff dogs, for example, were imported "no por la necesidad, pues no la había" ("not because of need, as there was none [for them]"; 685), and in the case of other animals, the weariness of owners who end up regretting the trouble of having brought them over in the first place is stressed, particularly after excessive propagation results in a lowering of the value of their investment: "Estos trabajos y otros mayores costaron a los principios las cosas de España a los españoles, para aborrecerlas después, como han aborrecido muchas de el-las" ("These and even greater efforts were demanded of Spaniards at first bring-ing things from Spain, only to later abhor them, as has happened with many of them"; 685); and he adds, "[P]or la mucha fertilidad de la tierra, hay tanta abun-dancia de todas estas cosas que ya dan hastío" ("Because of the land's great fer-tility, there is so much abundance of all of these things that they become tire-some"; 700).

Beyond the introductory format previously outlined, and particularly in ad-vanced undergraduate courses that run over the course of an entire semester or even the full academic year, greater space could then be given to tracing shifts in perspective: from providential images of paradise, to apocalyptic views of destruction and violence incorporating texts like Bartolomé de Las Casas's *Brevísima relación de la destrucción de las Indias* and colonial-era Nahua poetry, to the pragmatic, synthesizing critical approaches of writers like Felipe Guaman Poma de Ayala, thus moving from natural history to an exploration of the limits of discourses on wonder in New World historiography. The *Comentarios reales*'s depiction of a natural landscape that is in danger of being transformed from marvelous into monstrous would be particularly apt. According to Garcilaso, the rate of reproduction of alien flora and fauna in the Andes and the size of some of the produce are described as "increíble" ("unbelievable"; *Comentarios* 679) but also as endowed with "extraña grandeza" ("a strange large size"; 699), being "despreciables" ("loathsome"; 699) and "espantable[s]" ("frightening"; 704), disparaging adjectives absent in the previous book when describing the pre-Hispanic era that will appear time and again in book 9. Complementing what Surtz has termed Garcilaso's chronicling of a "vegetable aggression" (255) of foreign species, especially evident in chapter 29 where plants like mint and mustard are bluntly labeled "dañosas" ("harmful") and thrive despite "las fuerzas y la diligencia humana toda cuanta se ha hecho para arrancarlas" ("every possible human effort to eradicate them"; Garcilaso, *Comentarios* 701), would be a close reading of chapter 22 on vermin and rats "tan grandes que no hay gato que ose mirarlas" ("so large that no cat dares to look at them"; 686), animals not customarily given much thought in period natural histories.

Significantly, a reading attentive to issues of language reveals that the idea of monstrosity used to refer to the size and abundance of imported plants and animals resurfaces in value judgments about European mores. Garcilaso shares a childhood memory of going to see the first three bulls brought to Cuzco along with "un ejército de indios" ("an army of Indians"; *Comentarios* 678) who were "atónitos y asombrados de una cosa tan monstruosa y nueva para ellos y para mí" ("stunned and astonished at the sight of such a monstrous and new thing for them and for me as well"). Yet it is unclear if the reaction is caused by the sight of the animals themselves, which are not described as being especially large or as having any distinguishing features, or rather by the way they are being put to use, as the next sentence clarifies: "Decían que los españoles, de haraganes, por no trabajar forzaban a aquellos animales a que hiciesen lo que ellos debían de hacer" ("They said that the Spaniards, being lazy, to avoid working would force those animals to do their work for them"; 678–79).[11] In fact, if both books 8 and 9 are considered in their entirety, the first part of book 8 narrates the histories of Tupac Yupanqui and Huayna Capac, leaders worthy of admiration in the author's eyes, whereas book 9 shifts from Huayna Capac's reign to that of Atahuallpa, a ruler portrayed as cruel and illegitimate by Garcilaso. Thus the overarching framework linking discussions about pre-Hispanic nature to good rulers and colonial nature to a bad one colors the material by association. In a literature context, and depending on the scope and length of the course, the topic could be traced all the way to the nineteenth century, for example, to Andrés Bello's juxtaposition of European and American agricultural products in the "Silva a la agricultura de la zona tórrida" ("Ode to Tropical Agriculture") where one finds a binary juxtaposition of American and European nature, the former emerging as superior. But in contrast to the *Comentarios reales*, in Bello's independence-era context, America has carried out its own aggressive retro-appropriation of once-foreign nature. Autochthonous cochineal triumphs over Roman royal purple in "Silva," but so does originally Southeast Asian sugarcane over European honey. Natural foodstuffs, like coffee, brought over from the Arab world, are touted as now representative of America instead to the point of dissolving their former ties.[12] Let "la manzana y la pera en la fresca montaña el cielo olviden de su madre España" ("pear trees and apples forget their mother, Spain"), suggests Bello (lines 219–21; "Ode" 33).[13]

Graduate-level versions of the courses just outlined could go further in exploring early modern historiography related to natural history so as to include a consideration of figures like Bernabé Cobo and especially José de Acosta, an author who will likely be relevant to students' training regardless of whether they are based in literature or history departments and useful also in identifying points of contact with religious studies and anthropology.[14] As one of the primary authors acknowledged by Garcilaso, and depending on the flexibility of the specific graduate program, a module built around a comparative reading of the sections of Acosta's *Historia natural y moral de las Indias* (*Natural and Moral History of the Indies*) glossed in the *Comentarios reales* could form the skeleton of a seminar that branched out to explore key questions of the era, including (though not limited to) issues relating to natural history. Such a seminar would also provide the proper forum for an in-depth critical evaluation of the ample emerging scholarship on the place of natural history in colonial and early modern studies as well as the history of European global expansion. Given the interdisciplinary nature of the field at present, and the professional demands students will likely encounter should they pursue academic careers, it is essential at this level to provide them with greater awareness of the different kinds of materials that shape our understanding of the period and the ways in which texts and critical approaches alike are connected to one another.

One novel thematic graduate seminar that could be adapted to suit the needs of several disciplinary contexts would be a course highlighting the relevance of the *Comentarios reales* to science, in particular to early modern medicine. Although Garcilaso states that his objective is to describe staples, "las cosas que había en aquella tierra para el sustento humano" ("the things found in that land for human consumption"; *Comentarios* 578–79), not only does he venture outside this narrow focus into descriptions of plants that were, by his own admission, luxuries rather than basic necessities, like the *cuchuchu*,[15] but it is also striking just how many of the natural products he mentions are said by him to have medicinal properties. According to the text, beverages and ointments made of *zara* (corn) have been found by "médicos experimentados" ("experienced physicians") to have "otros muchos . . . provechos" ("many other . . . benefits"; 581); the "indios herbolarios" ("Indigenous medicine men") used quinoa flour "para

algunas enfermedades" ("for some illnesses"; 583); *ínchic* (sacha peanut) is used
to make "muy lindo aceite para muchas enfermedades" ("a very nice oil good for
many ailments"; 583); *palta* (avocado) is "muy saludable para los enfermos" ("very
healthy for those who are sick"; 586); *mulli* (peppertree) resin is useful to treat
urinary ailments and to maintain good dental health, whereas boiled *mulli* leaves
specifically could cure scabies and old wounds (587); maguey is "provechosa para
diversas enfermedades" ("beneficial for various illnesses"), including headaches
and facial skin discolorations (589); llama meat is not only tender and tasty but
also "sana" ("healthy"), so much so that "cinco meses mandan los médicos dar a
los enfermos, antes que gallinas ni pollos" ("doctors prescribe it to sick patients
for five months, above chicken meat"; 598). Indeed, it is the exception rather than
the rule in book 8 that the potential health benefits of a given animal or plant
are not deemed relevant. From Durand's research, we know that medical books
were part of Garcilaso's library, but it is the writing itself that lays bare a deep
affinity.[16] Even though products like tobacco and sarsaparilla receive little more
than a cursory mention in the *Comentarios reales*, the author still makes clear
to his audience that he is aware of their status in the medical world. "La zarza-
parilla," writes Garcilaso, "no tiene necesidad de que nadie la loe, pues bastan
para su loor las hazañas que en el mundo nuevo y viejo ha hecho y hace contra
las bubas y otras graves enfermedades" ("Sarsaparilla needs no introduction, for
its fame is secure given its achievements treating *bubas* and other serious ailments in the New and Old Worlds"; 595).[17] Moreover, he displays his dexterity
in the use of medical language when telling his readers that Inca medicine did
not have knowledge of "medicinas compuestas" ("multi-ingredient medicines")
but only of "simples" ("single-ingredient remedies"), a standard pharmaceutical
distinction at the time (150).

Garcilaso shows his competence as a reader of medical texts in other ways, by
alluding to tropes that would have been associated with the lighter side of medical practice in the Americas at the same time that they mark him as an insider
on the topic. One such example is found in the section on *ussun*, a fruit that
caused urine to turn "tan colorada que parece que tiene mezcla de sangre" ("so
red that it seemed it had been mixed with blood"; *Comentarios* 586). In the sixteenth century it was used by seasoned settlers to play tricks on young, newly
arrived doctors from Spain. They would be called to treat a feigned renal illness
and, horrified at the sight of the bloodred urine, would pronounce their patients
to be on the brink of death, only to see them refuse treatment and be none the
worse for it. A reader aware of this phenomenon would have recognized the subtle reference. Likewise, in the section on *papagayos* (parrots) where the text
pokes fun at the pretensions of the "doctors of Seville," who were often the tar-
gets of criticism in New World medical texts for claiming to be experts on the
botany of places they had never visited, the text reads, "En Sevilla, en Caldefrancos, pocos años ha, había otro papagayo que, en viendo pasar un cierto
médico indigno del nombre, le decía tantas palabras afrentosas que le forzó a
dar queja de él. La justicia mandó a su dueño que no le tuviese en la calle, so

pena que se lo entregarían al ofendido" ("In Seville, on Francos Street, some years ago there was another parrot who upon seeing a certain doctor undeserving of the title, spoke such insults to him that the man was forced to make a complaint. The authorities then ordered its owner to keep it indoors or risk having to relinquish the animal to the offended party"; 613). Not only do we laugh along with the author at the bird's candor, but the author signals to fellow medical enthusiasts that he too is aware of where one would go to buy the most up-to-date medicinal remedies in all of Spain: Caldefrancos.[18]

Garcilaso is a reader of medical literature and at times a former patient bearing witness to the positive effects of some of the natural cures he writes about. But in addition, the text even captures a moment where he practices medicine himself. In chapter 25 of book 2 we are told of a young man whom Garcilaso successfully treated with the *matecllu* herb:

> Yo se la puse a un muchacho que tenía un ojo para saltarle del casco. Estaba inflamado como un pimiento, sin divisarse lo blanco ni prieto del ojo, sino hecho una carne, y lo tenía ya medio caído sobre el carrillo, y la primera noche que le puse la yerba se restituyó el ojo a su lugar y la segunda quedó del todo sano y bueno. Después acá he visto el mozo en España y me ha dicho que ve más de aquel ojo que tuvo enfermo que del otro.
>
> (*Comentarios* 150)

> I used it on a boy who looked as if his eye were about to jump out of its socket. It was swollen like a pepper, the white of the eye indistinguishable from the black, being all one flesh, and it was half fallen on his cheek and the first night that I applied the herb, the eye was restored to its proper place and the second, he was completely healed. I have since seen this young man here in Spain and he has told me that he sees better out of that eye that was afflicted than out of his other one.

From a structural standpoint, the passage is an exact match to how cases were typically described in period vernacular medical literature, particularly in "flores," or medical compendia, which we know Garcilaso possessed. These were aimed primarily at surgeon-barbers and lesser medical practitioners rather than trained physicians. There is the dramatic establishment of the seriousness of the emergency, justifying intervention despite grim expectations; suspenseful narration of the cure; a wholly positive outcome; and, lastly, anecdotal patient testimony of the lasting success of treatment, often phrased in a witty fashion. Garcilaso writes as someone comfortable navigating the familiar tropes and the high-interest subjects of vernacular medical print texts on both sides of the ocean.

Two important sources that could be read alongside the *Comentarios reales* in this type of seminar would be Nicolás Monardes's *Historia medicinal* (published in English as *Joyfull Newes out of the Newe Founde Worlde*) and Juan Huarte de San Juan's *Examen de ingenios* (*The Examination of Men's Wits*), highly influential texts of the time. *Historia medicinal* achieved wide dissemination not just in Spain and America but all over Europe, enjoying twenty-five printings in the sixteenth century alone and becoming a standard reference in natural histories and medical books well into the seventeenth century. *Examen de ingenios* for its part was also widely read, translated into English, Italian, Dutch, French, and German, and was cited by some of the major literary figures of the day, like Quevedo and Lope de Vega. Both would be a good fit in this context since they can be traced back to Garcilaso directly: Monardes is mentioned by name in the *Comentarios reales*, and Huarte's *Examen de ingenios* is one of the books listed in the inventory of the author's library. Garcilaso's mention of Monardes is brief, to say the least. It occurs in chapter 15 of book 8, which is mostly on coca but touches upon tobacco and sarsaparilla near the end. The section reads: "Del arbolillo que los españoles llaman *tabaco* y los indios *sairi*, dijimos en otra parte. El doctor Monardes escribe maravillas de él" ("We already discussed elsewhere the shrub that Spaniards call tobacco and Indians *sairi*. Doctor Monardes writes marvelous things about it"), moving on immediately to the passage on sarsaparilla already quoted (*Comentarios* 595). Unlike the treatment afforded to other authors he alludes to, where more context on their identity is given, for Garcilaso and his readers Monardes apparently needs no introduction. Properly unpacking this connection sheds light on how natural history informs other important and commonly cited passages in the *Comentarios reales*, such as the following section:

> Otras muchas yerbas hay en el Perú de tanta virtud para cosas medicinales, que, como dice el padre Blas Valera, si las conocieran todas no hubiese necesidad de llevarlas de España [to the New World] ni de otras partes; mas los médicos españoles se dan tan poco por ellas, que aun de las que antes conocían los indios se ha perdido la noticia de la mayor parte de ellas.   (596)

> There are many other herbs in Peru so useful to medicine that, as Father Blas Valera says, if we knew them all there would be no need to bring [medicines] there from Spain nor from other parts; but Spanish doctors are so uninterested in them that even the ones that were previously known by the Indians are for the most part forgotten.

In *Historia medicinal*, Monardes had written:

> Y cierto en esto somos dignos de muy grande reprehensión, que visto que hay en Nueva España tantas yerbas y plantas y otras cosas medicinales que son de tanta importancia que ni hay quien escriba de ellas ni se sepa qué virtudes y formas tengan, para cotejarlas con las nuestras, que si tuviesen ánimo para investigar y experimentar tanto género de medicinas como los indios venden en sus mercados o tiánguez, sería cosa de grande utilidad y

provecho ver y saber sus propiedades y experimentar sus varios y grandes efectos, los cuales los indios publican y manifiestan con grandes experiencias que entre sí de ellas tienen y los nuestros, sin más consideración, las desechan y de las que ya tienen sabidos sus efectos, no quieren darnos ni noticia que sean, ni escribir la efigie y manera que tienen.   (*Herbolaria* 101)

And surely in this we are woorthy of great reprehension, that seeyng that there are in the newe Spayne, so manie Hearbes, and Plantes, and other thinges Medicinable, of so much importaunce, there is not any that writeth of them, nor is it understood, what vertues and formes they haue, for to accord them with ours: so that if men had a desire to search out, and experiment so many kinde of medicines, as the Indians doe sell in their Marketplaces and Fayres, it would be a thing of great profite, and utilitie to see and to knowe their properties, and to experiment the variable and greate effectes, which the Indians doe publishe, and manifest with great proofe amongest themselues, which they haue of them: wee of our parte without any consideration doe refuse it, and such as doe knowe their effectes, will not give us relation, nor knowledge what they are, nor write the efficacie and manner of them.   (*Joyfull Newes* fol. 25v–26r)

Garcilaso, in a sense, is the Peruvian answer to Monardes's statement about Mexico. Like this passage, there are various other moments in the *Comentarios reales* that engage in an intertextual dialogue. What is more, the editions of *Historia medicinal* published toward the end of the sixteenth century highlighted Andean nature, featuring a supposed "Letter from a Gentleman of Peru" where the man thanked Monardes for his efforts in letting people know about the benefits of local medicinal products. Because of the dates of publication, in all likelihood it is one of these editions that was read by Garcilaso. Exploring this largely uncharted terrain with graduate students could result in valuable contributions to our field.

Similarly, studying *Examen de ingenios* alongside the *Comentarios reales* would potentially shed new light on emerging scholarship analyzing the link between the natural and the human in relation to mestizaje.[19] In Garcilaso's opinion, as expressed in the last of the natural history chapters in book 9, "lo mejor de lo que ha pasado a las Indias . . . son los españoles y los negros que después acá han llevado por esclavos para servirse de ellos, que tampoco los había antes en aquella mi tierra" ("the best that has been brought to the Indies . . . are the Spaniards and the Blacks that they later took there as slaves to serve them, since they were also newcomers to my homeland"; *Comentarios* 707). "De estas dos naciones," he continues, "se han hecho allá otras, mezcladas de todas maneras, y para las diferenciar les llaman por diversos nombres" ("From these two groups others have emerged over there, mixed in every which way, and to tell them apart they are given different names" 707). Using humoral theory and physiognomy, and again considering the penetration of Huarte's ideas in Iberian intellectual circles at the time, the Spanish doctor had argued that different ethnic groups (*naciones*) of men possessed equally different intrinsic qualities that in turn explained disparities in aptitudes and levels of intelligence, as, for example, in chapter 2 of *Examen de ingenios*:

> Y vese claramente por experiencia cuánto disten los griegos de los escitas, y los franceses de los españoles, y los indios[20] de los alemanes, y los de Etiopía de los ingleses. Y no solamente se echa de ver en regiones tan apartadas; pero si consideramos las provincias que rodean a toda España, podemos repartir las virtudes y vicios . . . consideremos el ingenio y costumbres de los catalanes, valencianos, murcianos, granadinos, andaluces, extremeños, portugueses . . . ¿Quién no ve y conoce lo que estos difieren entre sí, no sólo en la figura del rostro y la compostura del cuerpo, pero también en las virtudes y vicios del ánima?   (247)

> And experience self-evidently shows how different are the Greeks from the Scythians, and the French from the Spanish, and the Indians from the Germans, and those from Ethiopia from the English. And this may be seen not only in regions that are far from one another, but if we consider the provinces around all of Spain we can distribute virtues and vices . . . let us consider the wit and the mores of Catalans, Valencians, Mercians, Grenadines, Andalusians, Extremenians, Portuguese . . . Who is unable to see and know how they differ from one another, not only in their countenance and in the features of their bodies, but also in the virtues and vices of the soul?

Huarte maintained that these qualities, even though originally shaped by the environment, would be retained by members of a given group for long periods of time even if they were to change their location, citing "gitanos" as one example: "con haber más de doscientos [años] que vinieron de Egipto a España los primeros gitanos, no han podido perder sus descendientes la delicadeza de ingenio y solercia que sacaron sus padres de Egipto, ni el color tostado" ("for although over two hundred years have passed since the first Gypsies came from Egypt to Spain, their descendants have not lost their delicate wit and cunning brought by their parents from Egypt, nor their toasted color"; 523). Further, Huarte is one of the few scientific sources in late sixteenth-century Europe where one finds a consideration of offspring whose parents were racially mixed. Making a case for his view that both male and female parents contribute seed to the generation of a child, Huarte turns to the "mulata" as supporting evidence:[21] "si un negro empreña una mujer blanca, y un hombre blanco a una mujer negra, de ambas maneras sale la criatura mulata" ("If a Black man beget a white woman with child, and a white man a Black woman, either way the child will be mulatto"; 665). It is reasonable to think that Garcilaso would have read these sections with attention, given that there are several moments in the *Comentarios reales* where he gives credence to physiognomy and humoral theory; for example in chapter 1 of book 7, where he explains that during Inca Yupanqui's rule, if conquered regions lacked sufficient levels of population, the policy was to take "indios de otras [provinces] de la misma calidad y temple, fría o caliente, porque no se les hiciese de mal la diferencia del temperamento" ("Indigenous people from other provinces with the same quality and climate, cold or hot, so that they would not be subject to negative effects from a difference in temperament"; 468). However, Garcilaso's own discussion of racial mixing differs from Huarte's, as well as from most other known usage examples. For instance, in Covarrubias's *Tesoro, mulato* is defined as "el hijo de negra, y de hombre blanco, o al revés" ("The son of a Black woman, and a white man, or the opposite"; 819). In the *Comentarios reales,* the coordinates are different: "Al hijo de negro y de india, o de indio y de negra, dicen *mulato y mulata.* A los hijos de éstos llaman *cholo*; es vocablo de la isla de Barlovento; quiere decir perro, no de los castizos, sino de los muy bellacos gozcones; y los españoles usan de él por infamia y vituperio" ("The child of a Black man and an Indian woman, or of an Indian man and a Black woman, are called *mulato* and *mulata.* Their children are called *cholo,* a term from the Windward Islands; it means dog, but not a thoroughbred dog but rather of mixed breed; the Spaniards use the word to insult and slander"; 708). The phrasing is ambiguous given that, depending on how it is read, either the children of "mulatos" would not belong to the same category as their parents or, if "éstos" refers back to the original "negros" and "indios" in the statement, then *mulato* and *cholo* are used interchangeably by the said "castizos." In addition, the text explains that the term *criollo* alone does not suffice to establish an individual's ethnicity as both "al español y al guineo nacidos allá les llaman *criollos y criollas*" ("both Spaniards and Africans born there [in the Americas] are called *criollos* and *criollas*"; 708). Thus Garcilaso can be said to enlist the language of physiognomy to make a different statement about the importance of context and who gets to have a say in establishing identity that gestures toward emerging scientific understandings but ultimately challenges their stability and authority.

An added advantage of reading Garcilaso, Monardes, and Huarte together is that it opens a discussion on the circulation of Hispanic natural history beyond Iberia and America, as well as the role all three played as translators of knowledge from other parts of Europe and the ancient world.[22] Indeed, the import of the *Comentarios reales* in European scientific circles beyond the Iberian Peninsula, particularly in England, where the text was first translated, is a topic that has not yet received its due critical attention.[23] The *Comentarios reales* was published in English in 1625 in book 4 of Samuel Purchas's *Hakluytus Posthumus; or, Purchas His Pilgrimes,* under the title "Observations of things most remarkable, collected out of the first part of the *Commentaries Royall,* written by Inca G. de la Vega."[24] Purchas was one of the followers of the famed Richard Hakluyt, the Elizabethan colonialist largely responsible for the dissemination of natural history about the New World in that country, as well as friend to the most influential engraver of images about America in the early modern period, Theodor de Bry. Translation then becomes yet another element pointing to Garcilaso's writing being read in the context of natural history, not only now but in his own time as well.

As many scholars of early modern historiography have remarked at various moments, the story of a small cast of Iberian juggernauts whose successful deployment of military prowess managed not only to deliver but to effectively secure control of the so-called New World for centuries to come is a narrative that has proven remarkably resilient in the popular imagination on overseas European expansion, despite the far more nuanced picture that colonial studies has and continues to draw, which all but unravels such a tale. There is a tangible disconnect between the gains that have been made by scholarship and specialized academic research on the one hand and still dominant, widely disseminated understandings of Latin American history on the other. The reasons as to why this is so are complex and respond to many factors, often varying considerably from one place (or one time or one political context) to another. All the same, superseded historical views continue to find expression and acceptance, for example, in state-sanctioned materials that historicize present-day notions of race and identity or in epic stagings of foundational encounters as imagined in popular culture outlets like television and film, mediums driven by the forces of a market economy rather than education but whose relevance to the public at large, and especially to young people, cannot be ignored. Therefore, from a pedagogical standpoint, offering students alternative and exciting ways of connecting with the past—ways that highlight and restore a consideration of sustained Indigenous agency in knowledge production, not just in pre-Hispanic times but throughout the vice-regal period, or that place the itineraries of well-known historical figures (salient as some of them may be still) in the larger contexts of imperial policies of territorial and political expansion—becomes an especially pressing endeavor. Beyond revitalizing the literary canon and demonstrating the relevance of Garcilaso's work to complementary fields of study, approaching the *Comentarios reales* from the vantage point of natural history encourages hands-on critical thought and independent comparative analysis on the part of students while offering a lively, rewarding reading experience of passages that put on display the author's sharp wit, his at times scathing sense of humor, the mastery of his prose style, and ultimately his affecting nostalgia for a fast-receding homeland, made ever more distant by the passing of time than by geography.

NOTES

[1] Most of the contextual materials suggested are available in English translation, and Harold V. Livermore's translation of the *Royal Commentaries* is available in both complete and abridged editions. All the period sources mentioned are available either in

modern editions or as free facsimiles for download from Web sites such as the *Internet Archive* (archive.org), the *World Digital Library* (www.wdl.org/en), *Google Books* (books.google.com), and *Biblioteca Digital Hispánica* (bne.es/es/Inicio).

[2] All translations not otherwise attributed are my own.

[3] According to Garcilaso, the coca plant "ha sido y es la principal riqueza del Perú para los que la han manejado en tratos y contratos" ("has been and is the principal source of wealth of Peru for those who have dealt with it in deals and contracts"; *Comentarios* 592).

[4] Unlike Columbus's claim that the Indigenous people of the Caribbean were utterly fascinated with all things European, Caminha describes a more ambivalent response in the Brazilian case: "Mostraram-lhes um papagaio pardo que o Capitão traz consigo; tomaram-no logo na mão e acenaram para a terra, como quem diz que os havia ali. Mostraram-lhes um carneiro: não fizeram caso. Mostraram-lhes uma galinha, quase tiveram medo dela: não lhe queriam pôr a mão; e depois a tomaram como que espantados. Deram-lhes ali de comer: pão e peixe cozido, confeitos, fartéis, mel e figos passados. Não quiseram comer quase nada daquilo; e, se alguma coisa provaram, logo a lançaram fora. Trouxeram-lhes vinho numa taça; mal lhe puseram a boca; não gostaram nada, nem quiseram mais" ("They showed them a cockatoo that the captain had acquired; they immediately held it and made signs toward land, as if to say that more were there. They showed them a calf: they paid no attention. They showed them a hen, they were almost horrified: they did not want to touch it; and later they took it, but very reluctantly. They fed them: bread, and cooked fish, sweetmeats, pastries, honey and figs. They almost did not eat, and if they tried something, they would spit it out. They brought them wine in a cup; as soon as they tasted it, it was clear they did not fancy it at all, nor did they want any more").

[5] Note that the English translation cited, *An Aztec Herbal*, reproduces only the text and not the drawings. The Mexican edition, *Libellus de medicinalibus Indorum herbis*, has two volumes: one is the facsimile of the codex, and the other, the Spanish translation.

[6] Millones Figueroa suggests the possibility that Garcilaso may have known Cárdenas, given the presence of an unidentified book in the inventory done by José Durand of his library listed as "Secretos naturales," though he acknowledges it cannot be established conclusively. Durand believes this title is either Jerónimo Cortés's *Fisonomía natural y varios secretos de la naturaleza* or Raimundo Lulio's *De secretis naturae*. I am inclined to believe Cortés as the more likely source given the similarity between his text and Huarte's in terms of subject matter and Garcilaso's interest in physiognomy. Although period marginalia in the British Library's copy of Cárdenas's book suggests that it was read in Europe at the time, there is limited evidence to suggest that the work was well known. See Pérez Marín 140–41. Lecturers teaching in contexts where the linguistic competence of students in Spanish cannot be taken for granted should note that the *Problemas y secretos maravillosos de las Indias* has not been translated into English.

[7] There is evidence that botanical and medical texts were popular with many different types of readers. They are mentioned in literature by the likes of Lope de Vega and Miguel de Cervantes; the latter goes as far as to make the character of Don Quixote a reader of herbals, telling Sancho after an unfortunate encounter with ewes and sheep where they are left battered and hungry that he would gladly prefer "un cuartal de pan, o una hogaza y dos cabezas de sardinas arenques, que cuantas yerbas describe Dioscórides, aunque fuera el ilustrado por el doctor Laguna" ("a quarter of bread, or a loaf and two pilchards' heads than all the herbs described by Dioscorides, even if it were the

one illustrated by doctor Laguna"; 226). Laguna's translation from 1555 was one of many versions then circulating of Dioscorides's *De materia medica*, originally a Greek source from the first century; his was distinctive in its use of high-quality illustrations.

[8] One exception to this trend are camels, which, according to the text, multiplied "poco o nada" ("little to nothing") in their new setting (681).

[9] See Mazzotti, "Inca Garcilaso" 174 and *Coros* ch. 3 (175–224); Surtz 254–44; Millones Figueroa.

[10] Garcilaso's personal interest in raising horses is well documented. See Millones Figueroa as well as Durand's inventory of the author's library, which lists two titles on the subject.

[11] The issue of inappropriate labor demands also appears in the section on monkeys (bk. 7, ch. 18) where the author humorously remarks on the belief that they possess the capacity to speak: "dicen los indios que [las monas y micos] saben hablar y que encubren la habla a los españoles, porque no les hagan sacar oro y plata" ("the Indians say that the monkeys know how to speak, but that they hide this from Spaniards lest they force them to mine for gold and silver"; 606).

[12] "Tú das la caña hermosa de do la miel se acendra, por quien desdeña el mundo los panales" ("You give sweet sugarcane, whose pure sap makes the world disdain the honeycomb"), writes Bello, followed by, "[B]ulle carmín viviente en tus nopales, que afrenta fuera al múrice de Tiro" ("Living red teems on your cactus plants, outdoing the purple of Tyre"; "Silva" lines 20–22, 25–26; "Ode" 29).

[13] The phenomenon would also be observed in reverse with select American products naturalized in Europe and even becoming representative of some of its regional cuisines, such as the case of corn (and much later tomatoes) in parts of Italy or potatoes in Britain.

[14] For a discussion on Garcilaso's reading of Acosta, see Zamora 85–128; Gastañaga Ponce de León; Surtz; Millones Figueroa.

[15] "Esta fruta [el cuchuchu] y el ínchic más son regalos de la gente curiosa y regalada que no mantenimiento de la gente común y pobre" ("This fruit [the cuchuchu] and the inchic are more of a delicacy for inquisitive and affluent people than for the common and poor folk"; 584).

[16] According to Durand, the inventory of Garcilaso's library included several medical compendia and books on natural history, natural philosophy, and cosmology, as well as a title on physiognomy, another on physics, possibly one on agriculture (for Millones Figueroa, it is Gabriel Alonso de Herrera's *Obra de la agricultura*), and two books on the care of horses that would have touched upon medical care. Further readings can be gleaned from intertexual allusions in the *Comentarios reales* and elsewhere in Garcilaso's oeuvre. See also López Parada et al.

[17] Although the term *bubas* is often associated with syphilis, present-day historians of medicine believe it may have been used in the early modern era to describe more than one pathogen with similar symptoms.

[18] The pharmacy on Francos Street was famous for being the best-stocked medicine shop in Seville, a city that in turn had claims to be among the most commercially cosmopolitan. Memory of this establishment has been kept in popular Spanish lore because of its association with the tale of a certain doctor whose lethal medicinal syrup was dubbed the "botica de Caldefrancos," owing to its excessive number of ingredients. See Chinchilla 133.

[19] See in particular Mazzotti, *Coros*, where he argues that the text offers a "caracterización del mundo natural como un cuerpo humano" ("characterizes the natural world as if it were a human body"; 225); see also Surtz's essay on the link between "botanical and racial hybridity." For more on the humoral transformation of Spanish temperaments in the Americas more generally, see Cañizares-Esguerra, *Nature* 64–95.

[20] Given allusions elsewhere in the text to the New World, the word here likely follows period usage of applying it both to Asia and America.

[21] Huarte argues that although both the male and the female contribute seed (*simiente*), one guides the process while the other offers nourishment, and the child's intelligence suffers a negative impact should the seed steering development come from the mother.

[22] For more on Garcilaso and issues of translation, see López-Baralt.

[23] One notable exception is Garcés's "The Translator Translated."

[24] Another early translation into French of the first part of the *Comentarios reales* would appear in 1633, undertaken by Jean Baudoin, who would go on to publish a translation of the second part in 1650.

WORKS CITED

Acosta, José de. *Historia natural y moral de las Indias.* Edited by Edmundo O'Gorman, Fondo de Cultura Económica, 2012.

——. *Natural and Moral History of the Indies.* Edited by Jane E. Mangan, translated by Frances López-Morillas, Duke UP, 2002.

Balbuena, Bernardo de. *La grandeza mexicana y compendio apologético en alabanza de la poesía.* 1604. Editorial Porrúa, 1997.

Bello, Andrés. "Ode to Tropical Agriculture." *Selected Writings of Andrés Bello*, edited by Ivan Jaksic, translated by Frances M. López-Morillas, Oxford UP, 1997, pp. 29–37.

——. "Silva a la agricultura de la zona tórrida." *Poesías, Biblioteca Virtual Miguel de Cervantes*, Universidad de Alicante, cervantesvirtual.com/obra/poesias-28.

Caminha, Pero Vaz de. "A carta de Pero Vaz de Caminha." *Biblioteca Virtual Miguel de Cervantes*, Universidad de Alicante, cervantesvirtual.com/obra-visor/a-carta-de-pero-vaz-de-caminha--0/html/ffce9a90-82b1-11df-acc7-002185ce6064_1.html#I_1_.

Cañizares-Esguerra, Jorge. Introduction. *Science in the Spanish and Portuguese Empires, 1500–1800*, edited by Daniela Bleichmar et al., Stanford UP, 2009, pp. 1–5.

——. *Nature, Empire, and Nation: Explorations of the History of Science in the Iberian World.* Stanford UP, 2006.

Cárdenas, Juan de. *Problemas y secretos maravillosos de las Indias.* 1591. Edited by Ángeles Durán, Alianza, 1988.

Cervantes, Miguel de. *El ingenioso hidalgo don Quijote de la Mancha.* 1605. Edited by Luis Andrés Murillo, Castalia, 1978.

Chinchilla, Anastacio. *Anales históricos de la medicina en general, y biográfico-bibliográfico de la española en particular: Historia de la medicina española.* Vol. 3, Imprenta de D. José Mateu Cervera, 1848.

Covarrubias, Sebastián de. *Tesoro de la lengua castellana o española*. 1611. Edited by Martín de Riquer, Alta Fulla, 1998.

Cruz, Martín de la. *An Aztec Herbal: The Classic Codex of 1552*. Translated by William Gates, Dover, 2000.

———. *Libellus de medicinalibus Indorum herbis*. 1552. Translated by Juan Badiano, Fondo de Cultura Económica, 1996.

De Vos, Paula. "Methodological Challenges Involved in Compiling the Nahua Pharmacopeia." *History of Science*, vol. 22, no. 2, 2017, pp. 210–33.

Durand, José. "La biblioteca del Inca." *Nueva revista de filología hispánica*, vol. 2, no. 3, 1948, pp. 174–85.

Garcés, María Antonia. "The Translator Translated: Inca Garcilaso and English Imperial Expansion." *Travel and Translation in the Early Modern Period*, edited by Carmine G. Di Biase, Rodopi, 2006, pp. 203–25.

Garcilaso de la Vega. *Comentarios reales: La Florida del Inca*. Edited by Mercedes López-Baralt, Espasa Calpe, 2003.

———. *Royal Commentaries of the Incas and General History of Peru*. Translated by Harold V. Livermore, U of Texas P, 1966. 2 vols.

———. *Royal Commentaries of the Incas and General History of Peru*. Edited by Karen Spalding, translated by Harold V. Livermore, abridged ed., Hackett Publishing, 2006.

Gastañaga Ponce de León, José Luis. "El Inca Garcilaso, José de Acosta, la injuria y el sarcasmo." *Hispanic Journal*, vol. 31, no. 2, Fall 2010, pp. 53–66.

Huarte de San Juan, Juan. *Examen de ingenios*. 1575. Edited by Guillermo Serrés, Cátedra, 1989.

López-Baralt, Mercedes. *El Inca Garcilaso, traductor de culturas*. Iberoamericana/ Vervuert, 2011.

López Parada, Esperanza, et al. "Selección de piezas comentadas." *La biblioteca del Inca Garcilaso de la Vega, 1616–2016*, Biblioteca Nacional de España, 2016, pp. 93–179.

Mazzotti, José Antonio. *Coros mestizos del Inca Garcilaso: Resonancias andinas*. Fondo de Cultura Económica, 1996.

———. "Inca Garcilaso: Migrancy and Modernity." *Review: Literature and Arts of the Americas*, vol. 42, no. 2, 2009, pp. 167–77.

Millones Figueroa, Luis. "Filosofía e historia natural en el Inca Garcilaso." *Biblioteca Virtual Miguel de Cervantes*, Universidad de Alicante, www.cervantesvirtual .com/obra-visor/filosofa-e-historia-natural-en-el-inca-garcilaso-0/html/02426810 -82b2-11df-acc7-002185ce6064_2.html#I_0_.

Monardes, Nicolás. *Herbolaria de Indias*. 1574. Edited by Ernesto Denot and Nora Satanowsky, Turner, 1990.

———. *Joyfull Newes out of the Newe Founde Worlde*. Translated by John Frampton, William Norton, 1577.

Oviedo, Gonzalo Fernández de. *Historia general y natural de las Indias*. Edited by Juan Pérez de Tudela y Bueso, Atlas, 1959. Biblioteca de autores españoles 117.

Pardo-Tomás, José. "Tlatelolco, espacio de ciencia mestiza, 1521–1579." *Catharum: Revista de ciencias sociales y humanidades del Instituto de Estudios Hispánicos de Canarias*, no. 17, 2018, pp. 89–97.

Pérez Marín, Yarí. *Marvels of Medicine: Literature and Scientific Enquiry in Early Colonial Spanish America*. Liverpool UP, 2020.

Rabasa, José. *Inventing America: Spanish Historiography and the Formation of Eurocentrism*. U of Oklahoma P, 1993.

Sahagún, Bernardino de. *El México antiguo*. Edited by J. L. Martínez, Biblioteca Ayacucho, 1981.

Surtz, Ronald E. "Botanical and Racial Hybridity in the *Comentarios reales* of El Inca Garcilaso." *Mediterranean Identities in the Premodern Era: Entrepôts, Islands, Empires*, edited by John Watkins and Kathryn L. Reyerson, Ashgate, 2014, pp. 249–64.

Zamora, Margarita. *Language, Authority, and Indigenous History in the* Comentarios reales de los Incas. Cambridge UP, 1988.

IDENTITY AND GENDER
IN THE *ROYAL COMMENTARIES*

Inca Garcilaso and Transnational Identity in Colonial, Postcolonial, and Neocolonial Contexts

Michael J. Horswell

Inca Garcilaso de la Vega, as an early modern, transatlantic subject, wrote his works in a context that has great resonance with the experience of many of our contemporary students. His subjectivity, like many of theirs, is marked by the intersection of social discourses in conflict, questions of identity, and experiments with self-representation. Born in Cuzco, Peru, to an Incan mother and a Spanish father, he had to confront the evolving discursive practices of their two cultural traditions, one from the emerging hybrid space of the imposed military and religious codes of conquest and later those codes of the "lettered city" of his European heritage (see Rama), and the other from the subjugated space of Andean oral tradition and the visual, iconographic media of his indigenous legacy. This transcultural negotiation led Garcilaso to develop a profound consciousness of the role that different means of representation would play in his later life as he began to translate and write about himself, his people, and the history of the confrontation he and others lived. As he developed a literacy in the practices of Renaissance print culture, he also left a record of how an author of the times positioned himself so that his voice would be heard, even from a relatively subaltern position. In addition, he also recorded the representational practices of the Incas, and, as scholars have argued, his texts, particularly the *Comentarios reales*, are linguistically, culturally, and structurally heterogeneous and polyphonic products of the two traditions (see Cornejo Polar; Mazzotti, *Coros*). In this sense, they represent the same kind of challenges and negotiations that many migratory subjects face today and voice processes of subjectivization with which many of our students readily identify.

Garcilaso wrote several *proemios*, or prologues, to his various works in which he expresses his most intimate thoughts about his place in the world and in which he lays out the discursive strategies he needed to project the necessary authority in order to be published and heard. Among the relevant themes found in these prologues, Garcilaso commented on the use of languages, the translation of words and concepts, the manipulation of history, the use of reliable and unreliable sources, the employment of rhetorical figures, and engagement with visual culture, among others. In this sense, Garcilaso offers us many lessons about the construction of arguments and discourses; he is the perfect model for our students who are immersed in their own processes of subjectivization and self-representation on social media and other outlets. These parallels encourage students to read Garcilaso more deeply because they can identify with his struggle in a world stratified by power and evolving at a vertiginous pace, and one in which the media of representation is evolving at an equally rapid rate.

This essay describes a pedagogical project I designed for a master's-level transatlantic studies course that addresses the themes of transnational identity and that also takes advantage of tools from the digital humanities in order to establish connections between the reading and writing practices of the sixteenth and seventeenth centuries and the cybernetic tendencies of today. The course opens with several weeks of readings devoted to the writings of Christopher Columbus, Alonso de Ercilla, and Álvar Núñez Cabeza de Vaca, as well as peninsular romances and *El Abencerraje*, all framed by critical and theoretical texts that inform the transatlantic turn in colonial studies and focus on the liminal spaces of imperial frontiers from a postcolonial perspective. I introduce key concepts from Barbara Fuchs, Barbara Simerka, Homi K. Bhabha, and Walter Mignolo in traditional seminar fashion, through lecture, student presentations, and discussion of the primary and secondary texts. We define and discuss terms like *mimesis, empire, colonial mimicry, otherness, stereotyping, locus of enunciation,* and *colonial semiosis,* among others, in order to prepare students for the reading of Garcilaso's works in the next part of the course.

Then we turn to a selection of Garcilaso's writings over the subsequent five weeks using a project-based approach. My students engage with Garcilaso's works by reproducing some of his techniques employed as a Renaissance writer bridging two distinct worldviews and cultural heritages: strategic self-representation and self-fashioning; the critical interpretation of historical sources; the incorporation of oral testimonies by informants; the use of commentaries, glosses, and marginalia; and the participation in collaborative writing. The simulation of these discursive practices is developed in a collaborative online space, where my students work in groups cooperating with one another on a series of activities that culminates in a final product that is mimetic of how early modern manuscripts and books were often palimpsests of the successive interventions in the imaginary of their active readers. This method incentivizes students to perform closer readings of texts that reveal the forces of colonial transculturation as well as speak to their own reality of contemporary globalization. Students reflect on the relation between the present-day compulsion to comment on everything (using *Facebook*, *Twitter*, etc.) and the practices by which early modern chroniclers and commentators strove to make sense of their equally complex and changing world. Above all, Garcilaso's texts present a diversity of themes still relevant to students at my public university in South Florida, many of whom have recently emigrated from Latin America or are first-generation university students from a variety of ethnic, racial, gender, and class positions.

The emergence of the digital humanities has contributed new tools, infrastructure, and techniques to complement and enhance more traditional literary analysis, including the use of digital databases and archives, the macroanalysis of textual corpora, the digital editions of literary and historical texts, the use of digital tools to facilitate comprehension and interpretation, digital mapping, and the use of digital platforms to present scholarship, among other innovations. Above all, the digital humanities facilitates the same broad question that humanists have always asked—what does it mean to be human?—but with the new twist of engaging the digital media in which we are immersed (see Pressman and Swanstrom; Borgman). In order for our students to effectively engage new media, both as private citizens and as future professionals, it is important to provide them academic experience with contemporary tools to express themselves and to intervene in the discourses that shape their lives.

My two primary objectives are, on the one hand, to do what we always do in literature classes: read, appreciate, and interpret texts and contexts. On the other hand, I want my students to be conscious of the media that interpellate the authors under study as well as themselves and of the technologies that play a role in the production of culture, both in our time and in the times we study. This requires linguistic, literary, visual, and rhetorical studies to appreciate and understand the codes employed by contemporary digital media as well as early modern media. This second objective of my project is to prepare students to not just consume the media and messages that surround them but analyze, question, and create the digital products in order to participate as critical thinkers in the diverse sociocultural discourses of their time. Studying Garcilaso's engagement with the challenges of his day, with attention to the discursive practices he employed, provides a model for examining our human condition in the twenty-first century. Furthermore, many of my students become teachers or proceed to PhD programs; therefore, another objective of this course design is to model new pedagogical methods that my students can adapt for their classrooms, whether they be face-to-face or online modalities. Given the recent emphasis on online teaching, this unit of my class is also adaptable to be delivered fully online.

Given the commonalities between my students and Garcilaso in questions of transnational identity, I start the class project with an activity in which all students write individual *proemios* to the larger project and share them with one another through a class discussion board. They read selections from Mignolo's *The Darker Side of the Renaissance* that include an explanation of the concept "locus of enunciation" so that they begin thinking about the relation between their positions and experiences in the world, discursive formations of power, and the articulation of difference that Garcilaso expresses. Before the students' *proemios* are due, we have discussed in class these concepts in relation to Garcilaso's translation of León Hebreo's *Dialoghi d'amore* and the prologue he composed for it (*La traduzion*). A student presents Doris Sommer's "At Home Abroad: El Inca Shuttles with Hebreo," and we read passages from Hebreo to begin to understand Garcilaso's intellectual affinity and stylistic apprenticeship displayed in his choice of translation. The close reading of Garcilaso's self-positioning, his relationship with his ideal readers, and the transatlantic context from which he writes provides students with a model and helps them articulate their own expression of the place from which they will work the rest of the semester. Of all his prologues to his works, this first one is perhaps the most autobiographical, thus introducing Garcilaso to the students through his own words and providing a preview of many of the themes that we will discuss during the rest of the unit. This first contact with Garcilaso's rhetorical prowess whets the appetite of the students and piques their curiosity to continue reading selections from *La Florida del Inca*, the *Comentarios reales*, and the *Historia general del Perú*. From the false modesty of his initial address to Philip II to his subtle reminders to the king of his family's loyal service to the imperial project to his final offering of the translation as a loving gift from a vassal to his lord, Garcilaso carefully constructs his locus of enunciation: a bicultural man of arms and letters seemingly devoted to the imperial project and conscious of the power of language and the unique potential of his voice, as he announces in the prologue, to write histories of the conquest of Florida and Peru. With this short piece, students are able to uncover the complexities of this position as well as to detect the ironies and counterdiscourses that hover just beneath the surface of Garcilaso's "appreciation" of the colonization and evangelization of his homeland. My students readily identify with these complexities because many of them are children of migration, profess hybrid identities, and feel divided loyalties to an original homeland and their new homes in Florida.

The discussion board activity allows the students to work through their own self-understanding and express their own positions while responding to their peers' self-fashioning. This is something most of our students are doing every day in the myriad social media outlets of contemporary culture. As we discuss the prologues written by the class, a comparative lens emerges through which the students can begin to appreciate the similarities and differences of the representational technologies used by Garcilaso and their self-representations of today. Students think deeper about how they present their stories and how their subject positions relate to others and to the greater society in which they live. While a tweet or a *Facebook* post might have seemed somewhat trivial before this exercise, students report that afterward they are more conscious of how they present themselves both in those casual interventions as well as in more formal writing. The conversation inevitably turns to examples of public figures of power who might be analogous to Philip II, the ideologies one might have to express to gain favor in today's society, the kind of language use that is appropriate for different contexts and purposes, the discursive strategies one might employ to achieve a goal, and so forth. Above all, instead of just analyzing the writing of Garcilaso, the student must actually write a similar piece, putting into practice the lessons learned in the reading.

This forum also extends the conversation beyond the time and space of our seminar, providing students who may not have spoken up in class an opportunity to comment on their classmates' prologues and their relationships to both Garcilaso and their peers. Some students choose to try to imitate the seventeenth-century writing style adopted by Garcilaso, while others write in a decidedly contemporary style. This playful approach to language use opens the class to later critical readings we do on Garcilaso's literary style and use of language (see Mazzotti, *Coros*; Zamora, "Filología"; Vaccarella). In a recent class, a student from Peru wrote in her prologue how she and her family were exiled by Fujimori in 1992 and how she could identify with Garcilaso's sense of displacement, denunciation of abuses of power, and strong desire to harmonize clashing cultures. A student born in the United States, on the other hand, could identify with Garcilaso's evolving subject positions as expressed in his changing names, for he himself had adopted a Spanish name after living in South America, a name that signified for him his bicultural identity. An added benefit of this activity is that I get to know my students' stories, interests, and abilities, all of which helps me place them in their project groups for the rest of the unit on Garcilaso and guide them on topics for their final papers. For example, for the student interested in name-change effects, I could recommend Christian Fernández's *Inca Garcilaso: Imaginación, memoria e identidad* and Mazzotti's "Garcilaso en el Inca Garcilaso: Los alcances de un nombre." Students also get to know one another, which helps build commonality for the group work to follow and for their overall socialization as fellow graduate students.

The second part of the project engages the students in a close reading of a chapter from one of Garcilaso's works while employing a digital technology tool to simulate the early modern custom from print culture of writing marginalia and commentary directly on the manuscript. As in the first part, this activity takes place outside of the seminar and in an online environment, parallel to seminar sessions in which we read and discuss other selections from his works along with relevant critical articles (e.g., Mazzotti, "Inca Garcilaso"; Vaccarella; Rabasa; Voigt; Martínez-San Miguel 101–41; Cornejo Polar). For this activity students use a Web 2.0 tool that is available for free and that allows them to collaborate on a document in real time from any computer: *Padlet*. While there are other collaborative tools that one could use for this activity (such as *Google Docs*), I found *Padlet* to be user-friendly, accessible from any computer, and aesthetically pleasing, given its parchment-like "wall" that looks like an old manuscript page. *Padlet* allows you to create a wall for each group in the class. The wall is an interactive space in which the students can read the primary text that I place there and then write commentaries and marginalia on the sides of the text, as if they were writing in the margins of a book. In addition, they can add images, video, links, and other texts to the wall. Each student's addition to the wall is instantaneously saved, and more than one student can work on the wall at the same time. By the end of the activity, each group has a record of its work to share with me and the rest of the class.

Before they start their reading and analysis, I introduce students to examples of commentary and marginalia from the early modern period. They consult the facsimile edition of Francisco López de Gómara's manuscript *La historia general de las Indias y nuevo mundo* that Garcilaso annotated, seeing for themselves Garcilaso's handwriting and his comments on the text. Available online at the *Biblioteca Virtual Miguel de Cervantes* (cervantesvirtual.com), this text provides the class with an introduction to reading practices in the colonial period and illustrates what students also read in Margarita Zamora's "Filología humanista e historia indígena en los *Comentarios reales*," which acquaints them with the practice of humanist philology, one of Garcilaso's principal discursive strategies. As Zamora comments, the notes and commentaries Garcilaso made on López de Gómara's text amounted to his "aprendizaje metodológico" ("methodological apprenticeship"; 553; my trans.) on how he could subvert the Spaniards' "interpretaciones negativas de la cultura incaica" ("negative interpretations of the Inca culture") and replace them with an Erasmian "hermenéutica reformadora" ("hermeneutics of reform"; 554) that expressed Garcilaso's version of the history of his people and their language and traditions. Understanding Garcilaso's exegesis leaves students with a greater sense of how he searches for the "truth" from the myriad sources he studies, forming arguments based on the early modern practice of philological analysis of ancestral languages and texts. Another resource I share with the students is *Annotated Books Online* (annotatedbooksonline.com), which is a digital archive of early modern books. There students can see other examples of marginalia and explore more about reading practices that included margins full of drawings, translations, glosses of key words, and counterarguments to the text. All these annotative practices are ones I encourage my students to use as they read Garcilaso's assigned texts in this second part of the project.

As with the prologue activity, after students see the authentic model, they then apply a similar methodology to Garcilaso's text by explicating a chapter I have placed on the *Padlet* wall for each group. Seeing the creative ways early modern readers interacted with their manuscripts inspires students to pursue a similarly active engagement with the text while also imaginatively annotating it using more contemporary digital techniques such as the insertion of photos, illustrations, maps, links, and memes to the margins of the text on the *Padlet* wall. Just as Garcilaso or other colonial readers might have expanded the text through philological commentary or illustration, students explicate the themes that interest them most, often providing glosses and illustrations to clarify for today's reader obscure classical or pre-Hispanic Andean cultural references. They are instructed to make commentary in relation to the critical and theoretical articles they have read in class in addition to Garcilaso's texts. By having the students work in small groups, a dialogue emerges among the group members that is more enriching than if this commentary were done individually. Again, because the activity takes place outside of class time and in the virtual space, the discussion of the text is extended and students have more time to think about their "interventions" and can respond better to the contributions of their fellow group members. Because the wall allows for visual components in addition to textual annotations, the digital marginalia permits students to see examples of objects, concepts, and artifacts they have not encountered before. Examples from recent classes of visual annotations included photos of quipus, maps of the antipodes, Andean flora and fauna, Inca symbols, and colonial paintings depicting Inca dynasties, among others; all were mentioned in Garcilaso's texts but were not clear in the students' minds as they read (see, for example, padlet.com/wall/d5sj47j7jp). Instead of this being instructor-driven, the students themselves identify their own gaps in knowledge and then offer the answers based on their research, which benefits the whole class while also guiding me on where I need to put more emphasis in class.

Perhaps the most useful outcome from this activity is the dialogue among the groups' members that emerges on the wall, one with results much better than the typical discussion board exchange many of us are used to having in learning management systems. This dialogue can take many forms, such as a simple question posed by one student and answered by other group members. Instead of having threads to follow, the *Padlet* wall allows students to present the comments written in the margins near the relevant topic in the primary text; other group members can add their annotations, move them around, and edit them at will. While sometimes these are fact-oriented questions or comments, others raise interpretive and theoretical issues students need to wrestle with outside of class time. The exchanges often lead to the development of creative marginalia employing irony and humor, such as the insertion of Garcilaso's face, taken from one of his portraits, into a photo of a contemporary scene from an Occupy movement demonstration, with the new tagline "Occupy Cuzco." Inspired by their reading of the final book of the *Historia general* and his "A los indios, mestizos, y criollos de los reinos y provincias del grande y riquísimo imperio del Perú" ("Prologue to the Indians, Mestizos, and Creoles of Peru"), and informed by Zamora's "Images of Colonialism in Inca Garcilaso's *Historia general del Perú*," this meme expresses a contemporary parallel with what Zamora calls Garcilaso's "dissident ethics" (184). Another student altered an Internet meme of four well-known literary theorists sitting in a circle discussing their ideas by adding Garcilaso as the object of their inquiry, with each commenting on Garcilaso from his disciplinary perspective (see es.padlet.com/wall/4ofbw7n6py). In addition to being fun, these kinds of annotation open up our readings to additional theoretical perspectives and historical parallels we may not have considered in class up until that point.

The apparent messiness of the wall (some annotations run into others, sometimes images slide down from their original position as others write onto the wall, etc.) at first bothered me, but then I realized that the seeming disorder of this digital marginalia is mimetic of the often chaotic annotations and sketches left in early modern manuscripts. What is left on the wall is a kind of digital palimpsest that records the students' interpretations, questions, and even errors, all of which provide the instructor an opportunity to use the walls in class to expand and clarify ideas raised in the online group work. In addition, the author of each annotation is identified by the tag that goes with the comment added to the wall; therefore, the instructor can evaluate the participation of each student in the group. The walls produced in *Padlet* continue to exist until the creator deletes them; they are private to the group or class, unless the creator opens them to unlimited access. I make each group's wall available to the whole class by sharing the URL in a class blog on our *Blackboard* site. Using the blog as the access point to the *Padlet* walls allows for students from other groups to comment on their classmates' walls on the blog but not on the other groups' walls. I require each student to visit the walls of the other groups so that they benefit from all the digital palimpsests they create, resulting in more follow-up commentaries that reveal other questions and issues conceived of by groups who have been working on other primary texts by Garcilaso.

Once the walls are complete, we dedicate the last in-person seminar on Garcilaso to oral presentations in which the groups present their walls to the class. *Padlet* walls can be projected onto a screen or smart board, and touching each annotation with the cursor expands the annotation to a large enough size to be read by students in a classroom. This is a nice pedagogical feature of the digital tool, since it allows the presenter or the instructor to zoom in on the most compelling of the students' work. I found the student presentations of their walls to be much more dynamic than most *PowerPoint* or *Prezi* presentations I have observed over the years, perhaps because the digital palimpsest was collaboratively produced with multiple overlays of interpretation, visually interesting, and highly creative, yet anchored in specific primary texts that we had all read. Because the identity of each annotator was clearly visible, there was no way a member could hide behind the work of their peers; this greater accountability seemed to have motivated a fuller participation of each group member than in other group work I have assessed in the past. Class discussions of the presentations required few prompts, as students were eager to decipher the marginalia on the walls, following the threads, getting the jokes, and expanding their understanding of Garcilaso's writings. In addition, students reflected on the digital tool and its product, comparing it to early modern media but also thinking through how digital culture surrounds them in everything they do. In a small way, this activity encouraged them to be active producers and not merely consumers of that culture, much like Garcilaso dared to make print culture his own for his purposes.

The final phase of the Garcilaso project is a formal, collaborative essay that each group writes on a theme of its choice. Students are encouraged to continue working on a theme that emerged from their group's commentary activity, or they can choose a different or additional primary text to analyze. The commentary activity helps the groups zero in on a topic, and the short essay they write allows them to formalize the close readings they have done in the previous phase of the project. My objective with this activity is for the students to gain experience formulating a research question, choosing source material, selecting relevant critical articles and theoretical principles to frame their argument, and using MLA guidelines. Since for many this may be their first graduate-level essay, working collaboratively answers many questions they have about research paper writing before the stakes are raised with the seminar's final, individual research paper at the end of the course. This assignment provides me with a midterm assessment of the students' writing and research abilities and helps me guide them better on how to improve these skills for their final seminar paper. The students write their short essay (six to eight pages) in a wiki on *Blackboard*. This platform allows me to hold each member accountable for their participation in the writing, since the wiki tool allows the instructor to follow each contribution, edit, and deletion from the text. The tool also allows students to work on the essay at any time and from any location, facilitating the group work without the necessity of face-to-face meetings. The wiki also allows for multiple drafts and edits, which is a good skill for students to practice.

Here again, I point out that students are simulating the process by which Garcilaso wrote his texts: they draw from multiple sources, annotated texts (the walls from the previous part of the project), and the oral discourse of students' brainstorming as they plan their collaboration. Since each student has become an "expert" on some aspect of Garcilaso through the seminar readings and presentations, they become analogous to an informant for the group during the writing process, a source for development of the paper much like the informants Garcilaso consulted when writing his histories. Students in the group must negotiate issues such as ideology, memory, bias, incomplete understandings, and so forth as they select what to include and what to leave out of their essays. They also take advantage of contemporary technologies that replace or supplement the letter with email or the archive's manuscript with digital facsimile, and in so doing they think about the commonalities and differences between themselves and early modern researchers and writers. To complete the experience, students post their essays on the class blog for peer review and instructor evaluation, thus converting themselves into authors with a readership.

Making the sixteenth and seventeenth centuries relevant to our students' lives is one of the challenges that we face in teaching colonial Latin American literature and culture to undergraduate and graduate students in American universities. Over the years, I have found that my students are most engaged when discussing issues that are pertinent to their life experiences or when analyzing historical texts that help them understand how things evolved to be the way they are in the present. In addition, students increasingly respond positively when engaging in reading and writing techniques advanced in the emerging field of digital humanities, whose tools allow for ever more radical decentralization of the classroom. My Garcilaso project responds to these two pedagogical imperatives. By linking the author's writings to issues of transnational identity in the specific colonial and transatlantic context in which Garcilaso wrote his monumental works, and by expanding that discussion to engage my students on these issues in contexts from which they themselves come, namely the postcolonial and neocolonial, I have realized better learning outcomes. The author's writings resonate with readers today given Garcilaso's reflections on universal issues as diverse as personal identity, language, race, ethnicity, gender, sexuality, migration, class conflict, memory, resistance, and adaptation, among others. Along the way, students also learn much about the media with which they can engage these controversial themes, much as Garcilaso did in his time.

WORKS CITED

Bhabha, Homi K. "The Other Question: Stereotype, Discrimination and the Discourse of Colonialism." *The Location of Culture*, Routledge, 1994, pp. 66–84.

Borgman, Christine L. "The Digital Future Is Now: A Call to Action for the Humanities." *Digital Humanities Quarterly*, vol. 3, no. 4, 2009, digitalhumanities.org /dhq/vol/3/4/000077/000077.html.

Cornejo Polar, Antonio. "El discurso de la armonía imposible (El Inca Garcilaso de la Vega: discurso y recepción social)." *Revista de crítica literaria latinoamericana*, vol. 19, no. 38, 1993, pp. 73–80.

Fernández, Christian. *Inca Garcilaso: Imaginación, memoria e identidad*. Universidad Nacional Mayor de San Marcos, 2004.

Fuchs, Barbara. *Mimesis and Empire: The New World, Islam, and European Identities*. Cambridge UP, 2001.

Garcilaso de Vega. *La Florida del Ynca*. 1605. *Biblioteca Virtual Miguel de Cervantes*, Universidad de Alicante, cervantesvirtual.com/portales/inca_garcilaso_de_ la_vega/obra/la-florida-del-ynca-historia-del-adelantado-hernando-de-soto -gouernador-y-capitan-general-del-reyno-de-la-florida-y-de-otros-heroicos -caualleros-espanoles-e-indios/.

———. *Historia general del Perú*. 1617. *Biblioteca Virtual Miguel de Cervantes*, Universidad de Alicante, cervantesvirtual.com/portales/inca_garcilaso_de_la_ vega/obra/historia-general-del-peru-trata-el-descubrimiento-del-y-como-lo -ganaron-los-espanoles-las-guerras-ciuiles-que-huuo-entre-picarros-y-almagros -y-otros-sucessos-particulares/.

———. *Primera parte de los Comentarios reales*. 1609. *Biblioteca Virtual Miguel de Cervantes*, Universidad de Alicante, cervantesvirtual.com/portales/inca_ garcilaso_de_la_vega/obra/primera-parte-de-los-comentarios-reales-qve

-tratan-del-origen-de-los-yncas-reyes-qve-fveron-del-perv-de-sv-idolatria-leyes
-y-gouierno-en-paz-y-en-guerra-de-sus-vidas-y-conquistas-y-de-todo-lo-que-fue
-aquel-imperio-y-su-republica-antes-que-los-espanoles-p/.

———. *La traduzion del indio de los tres diálogos de amor de Leon Hebreo.* 1590.
Biblioteca Virtual Miguel de Cervantes, Universidad de Alicante,
cervantesvirtual.com/portales/inca_garcilaso_de_la_vega/obra/la-traduzion
-del-indio-de-los-tres-dialogos-de-amor--0/.

López de Gómara, Francisco. *La historia general de las Indias y nuevo mundo.*
1552. *Biblioteca Virtual Miguel de Cervantes,* Universidad de Alicante,
cervantesvirtual.com/obra/la-historia-general-de-las-indias-y-nuevo-mundo
-fragmentos--0/.

Martínez-San Miguel, Yolanda. *From Lack to Excess: "Minor" Readings of Latin
American Colonial Discourse.* Bucknell UP, 2008.

Mazzotti, José Antonio. *Coros mestizos del Inca Garcilaso.* Fondo de Cultura
Económica, 1996.

———. "Garcilaso en el Inca Garcilaso: Los alcances de un nombre." *Lexis: Revista de
lingüística y literatura,* vol. 29, no. 2, 2005, pp. 179–218.

———. "Inca Garcilaso: Migrancy and Modernity." *Review: Literature and Arts of the
Americas,* vol. 42, no. 2, 2009, pp. 167–77.

Mignolo, Walter D. *The Darker Side of the Renaissance: Literacy, Territoriality, and
Colonization.* U of Michigan P, 1995.

Pressman, Jessica, and Lisa Swanstrom, editors. *The Literary.* Special issue of *Digital
Humanities Quarterly,* vol. 7, no. 1, 2013.

Rabasa, José. "'Porque soy indio': Subjectivity in *La Florida del Inca.*" *Poetics Today,*
vol. 16, no. 1, Spring 1995, pp. 79–108.

Rama, Ángel. *La ciudad letrada.* Ediciones del Norte, 1984.

Simerka, Barbara. *Discourses of Empire: Counter-Epic Literature in Early Modern
Spain.* Pennsylvania State UP, 2003.

Sommer, Doris. "At Home Abroad: El Inca Shuttles with Hebreo." *Poetics Today,* vol.
17, no. 3, Autumn 1996, pp. 385–415.

Vaccarella, Eric. "Echoes of Resistance: Testimonial Narrative and Pro-Indian
Discourse in El Inca Garcilaso de la Vega's *La Florida del Inca.*" *Latin American Literary Review,* vol. 32, no. 64, July-Dec. 2004, pp. 100–19.

Voigt, Lisa. "Captivity, Exile, and Interpretation in *La Florida del Inca.*" *Colonial
Latin American Review,* vol. 11, no. 2, 2002, pp. 251–73.

Zamora, Margarita. "Filología humanista e historia indígena en los *Comentarios
reales.*" *Revista iberoamericana,* vol. 53, no. 140, July-Sept. 1987, pp. 547–58.

———. "Images of Colonialism in Inca Garcilaso's *Historia general del Perú.*" *Review:
Literature and Arts of the Americas,* vol. 42, no. 2, 2009, pp. 178–84.

Writing as an Indian: Teaching the Other Inca Garcilaso and His Native Sources

Rocío Quispe-Agnoli

Inca Garcilaso de la Vega's *Comentarios reales de los Incas* (*Royal Commentaries of the Incas*) occupies an indisputable position in the canon of Latin American letters. A quick review of textbooks often used to introduce undergraduate students to Latin American and Hispanic literature shows the inclusion of a chapter about this author and a selection of texts from this work (Chang-Rodríguez and Filer; Varona-Lacey; Garganigo et al.; Ortega et al.; Rodríguez). The selection of passages in these textbooks tends to include "Proemio al lector" ("Preface to the Reader"), "El origen de los Incas reyes del Perú" ("The Origin of the Inca Kings of Peru"; bk. 1, ch. 15), and "Protestación del autor sobre la historia" ("The Author's Declaration about His History"; bk. 1, ch. 19). In addition to the information that may be found in textbooks, students may be prompted by their instructors to research the author, his work, and his context. Students usually conduct an Internet search that brings them to popular Web-based encyclopedias in which entries one can read Garcilaso's original name as his first descriptor: Gómez Suárez de Figueroa. This finding (also listed in textbooks) provokes immediate questions among students about the author's real and literary names and offers a valuable opportunity to discuss in class his individual and social identity. It also opens the floor for a conversation on the author's reasons for changing his Spanish name into an Inca-Spanish one with literary connotations (for although "Garcilaso de la Vega" alluded to his father's name, it is also an unavoidable reference to the early modern Spanish poet).

Instructors usually explain the author's choice of names as a rhetorical strategy used to obtain approval for the publication of his book. In order to claim his authority in the story he was about to tell, the author stated that he knew the story of the Incas better than any Spanish writer because of his ethnic affiliation. Furthermore, his self-proclaimed identity as an "Indian" was supported by his knowledge of Quechua and his ability to earn the trust of Inca noblemen, their relatives, and Andean people in general, who provided him with sources and abundant information concerning Inca history: "los cuales [los parientes de mis compañeros], sabiendo que un indio, hijo de su tierra, quería escribir los sucesos de ella, sacaron de sus archivos las relaciones que tenían de sus historias y me las enviaron" ("and they [the relatives of my schoolfellows], on hearing that an Indian, a son of their own country, intended to write its history, brought from their archives the records they had of their histories and sent me them"). The acknowledgment of his Indian identity encompasses also his competence in Quechua and his understanding of quipus, colored knotted strings used as record-keeping systems that could collect, among other kinds of information, historical events: "cada provincia tiene sus cuentas y nudos con sus historias anales y la tradición de ellas, y por eso retiene mejor lo que en ella pasó que lo que pasó en la ajena" ("for each province has its accounts and knots to record its annals and traditions, and thus preserves its own history much better than that of its neighbors"; Garcilaso, *Primera parte* 55; *Royal Commentaries* 50). In these statements students can read one of Garcilaso's major authoritative arguments to support his writing of Inca history: he was writing as an Indian.

In this essay I comment on "writing as an Indian" as a platform to teach *Comentarios reales.* The overall goal is to prepare students to think about and discuss the writer's exposition and explanation of his Inca identity, Andean sources (Inca oral traditions and data recorded in quipus), and reflections on Spanish authors who wrote about the Incas in his time. I propose a pedagogical approach to this text through the examination of the author's opinion of his native sources. In this way students are asked to scrutinize Garcilaso's attention to the tension between Spanish and Andean sources about Inca history and his revisions of such sources.

For the past fourteen years I have taught Garcilaso's *Comentarios reales* to undergraduate students from a variety of majors who seek a degree in Spanish or to fulfill the general education requirement in arts and humanities at my institution. As a specialist in Indigenous writings of colonial Spanish America, my pedagogical approach addresses the historical and literary context in which the text was produced and the linguistic reflection that the bilingual and bicultural author offered in his work to correct Spanish histories of the Incas as well as incorrect translations of key Quechua concepts. For the purposes of this essay, I use examples from an undergraduate course taught in English as part of the university program Integrative Studies in the Arts and Humanities. Open to sophomores, juniors, and seniors of any major, Latin America and the World: Native Latin America examines major issues of Indigenous cultures through the development of their native societies before and after the Spanish conquest. In contrast to other courses about the Spanish conquest of America, this class focuses on Indigenous sources from Mexico and Peru that told the history of European colonization from a native perspective. In agreement with the goals of Integrative Studies in the Arts and Humanities, this course seeks to assist students in becoming more familiar with different ways of knowing, in engaging critically with and learning about other societies while finding connections with their own experiences. Garcilaso's reflection about Inca history and its native sources in a context dominated by European writers and their points of view offers an ideal arena for the pedagogical goals mentioned above. To do this, I utilize a cultural rhetorical framework to trace, along with students, Quechua semiotic practices that subtly take place in *Comentarios reales* and reveal the history of the Incas as it could have been told from its native point of view.

Indigenous sources of Garcilaso's work consisted of information recorded and transmitted by means of communal oral performances. Such performances included the telling of oral traditions by native people of the Andes and the recitation of information recorded in quipus. In this way, teaching Garcilaso as an

Indian writer who spoke enthusiastically about his native sources implies the observation of Indigenous oral memory that was brought to life by means of two kinds of Inca rhetorical practices: material and visual (quipus) and oral performance (for example, recitations of traditions and memories, among other speech acts). In order to achieve the recognition of a native point of view in Garcilaso's work—that is, his "writing as an Indian"—students are taught first to identify oral narratives and then to envision the oral performance of the *quipucamayu*'s recitation of the contents of a quipu.

The identification of oral narratives can be achieved by looking for textual clues where memory was shared by Andean informants of the author. Such informants included his own relatives, the relatives of his schoolfellows, and other native people whom the author had interviewed. Textual clues may be easily identified through the narration of events by means of indirect citation: "decíanme" ("they told me"); "me contaban sus historias" ("they told me their stories"); "tuve noticia" ("I had news"); "me dieron noticia" ("I was told [by them]"). The source of *decir* ("telling") and *dar noticia* ("giving information") can be identified in the text with "otros muchos Incas e indios naturales" ("many Incas and Indians") and "la gente común del Perú" ("the people of Peru"), as well as specific individuals ("aquel Inca" ["that Inca"]) like one of the old relatives with whom the author held a conversation at a young age.[1] Such conversation, quoted in direct style, provides a very good example of oral narrative as a native source and is included in the passage selection of the five textbooks cited before. When asked by a young Garcilaso about the origins of the Incas and the beginning of their history, the author's uncle spoke in the following terms: "Sobrino, yo te las diré de muy buena gana; a ti te conviene oírlas y guardarlas en el corazón" ("Nephew, I will tell you these things with pleasure: indeed it is right that you should hear them and keep them in your heart"; Garcilaso, *Primera parte* 48; *Royal Commentaries* 41). The recognition of oral accounts in direct or indirect style is a first approach to introduce oral ways of knowing to students. It also emphasizes the importance of the oral word as a trusted way to preserve and transmit information that students may not be fully aware of given the weight given to the written word in modern and contemporary Western societies. Many examples of native oral stories can be examined and discussed as one of Garcilaso's authoritative strategies in *Comentarios reales*. The oral word is not only evidence of an Indigenous way of transmitting information, but the author associated it to historical truth about the Incas, as Margarita Zamora demonstrated in her 1988 study of Garcilaso's work (*Language*). In Garcilaso's time, historical truth was accomplished through interpretation of events authorized by classic and Christian traditions (Zamora, "Historicity" 338). Oral narratives about the Incas were then subjected to a corrective interpretation of their language by Spanish officials. In Garcilaso's reasoning, Inca tradition, recorded in the oral memory of Andean people, constituted the primary authoritative source in that matter.

To reinforce the authority of the Andean oral word, Garcilaso added to its performance a method that was highly regarded in European historiography to confirm true events: the eyewitness testimony. The author stated his firsthand experience as a privileged performance that validated the true nature of the historic events he told:

> Después de habérmelo dicho los indios, alcancé y vi por mis ojos mucha parte de aquella idolatría. . . . Yo nací ocho años después de que los españoles ganaron mi tierra y, como lo he dicho, me crié en ella hasta los veinte años, y así vi muchas cosas de las que hacían los indios en aquella su gentilidad, las cuales contaré diciendo que las vi.   (*Primera parte* 55)

> Apart from what the Indians told me, I experienced and saw with my own eyes a great deal of their idolatry. . . . I was born eight years after the Spanish conquered my country, and as I have said, was brought up there till I was twenty: thus I saw many of the things the Indians did in the time of their paganism and shall relate them and say that I saw them.
> (*Royal Commentaries* 50)

As said before, students can easily identify Inca oral sources in *Comentarios reales* because the author announced them clearly in his text. They are also useful for the next step in class: bringing students' attention to other Indigenous sources that were actively involved in the construction of Garcilaso's authoritative word. Such sources may be identified at first by observing occurrences of Quechua terms related to the recording and transmission of information such as *quipu*, *quipucamayu* (a quipu keeper and reader), and *yupana* (an accounting artifact). By identifying these terms in a close-reading analysis, the instructor can help students to discover Indigenous sources of knowledge that preceded the arrival of Spaniards to Peru. Searching for these Quechua terms trains students to observe the textual context in which they were used and their potential meanings. To help students understand Garcilaso's use of these terms, the instructor may present the information provided by other chroniclers that the author cited in his work as well as the meanings of these words in colonial and contemporary Quechua-Spanish dictionaries such as Diego González Holguín's *Vocabulario de la lengua general de todo el Perú, llamada lengua qquichua o del Inca* (*Vocabulary of the General Language of Peru, called Quichua*). I now turn my attention to the examination of quipus and *quipucamayus* in *Comentarios reales*, since this native source was often cited by the author. The instructor will be able to show students that quipus not only constituted an unusual system of record keeping but also played a role in understanding Andean oral performances before and after the Spanish conquest.

Elsewhere I have examined Garcilaso's thoughts on quipu as a reliable source of information for Inca history (Quispe-Agnoli). To understand the author's comments on quipus, it is necessary to make students aware of his citations of works by two late-sixteenth-century Jesuit writers about the subject: José de Acosta and Blas Valera. All three authors—Acosta, Valera, and Garcilaso—described the

Andean record-keeping system in its materiality and reflected upon its role in the production of historical narratives and the support of Inca administrative affairs. Garcilaso attributed his explanation of how quipus were made and read to an original manuscript by Valera that he said he owned (*Primera parte* bk. 4, ch. 26). He cited Acosta's *Historia natural y moral de las Indias* (*Natural and Moral History of the Indies*) to support his reasoning about language, writing, and history. Acosta's and Garcilaso's discussion of quipus led to the reflection about correspondences between Andean and European intelligence. This correspondence was an important topic for Garcilaso's overall project, because quipus confirmed the advanced level of Inca civilization and their right to free will and Christian salvation. However, while Acosta concluded that quipus could not constitute official systems of communication, Garcilaso saw quipu performance as a way to bring together European and Andean sources of information (Quispe-Agnoli 156–57). To understand this bridge between quipus and European writing, students pay attention to citations of quipus throughout *Comentarios reales*. They will find that Garcilaso acknowledged quipu as a reliable native source for statistical and historical records. Books 2, 5, and 6 include the majority of references to quipu, and students are asked to find and record these occurrences, the context in which they appear, and patterns that can lead them to understand the features and functions of quipu and its reliability as a native source of Inca knowledge. In book 2, chapter 13, for example, the author described the material characteristics of quipu and its role for Inca administration:

> La manera de dar estos avisos [de los jueces] al Inca y a los de su Consejo Supremo era por nudos dados en cordoncillos de diversos colores, que por ellos se entendían como por cifras. Porque los nudos de tales y tales colores decían los delitos que se habían castigado, y ciertos hilillos de diferentes colores, que iban asidos a los cordones más gruesos decían la pena que se había dado y la ley que se había ejecutado. Y de esta manera se entendían, porque no tuvieron letras . . . y del contar que tuvieron por estos nudos, que, cierto muchas veces ha causado admiración a los españoles ver que los mayores contadores de ellos yerren en su aritmética y que los indios estén tan ciertos en las suyas de particiones y compañías, que, cuanto más dificultosas, tanto más fáciles se muestran porque los que la manejan no entienden en otra cosa de día y de noche y así están diestrísimos en ellas.
>
> (*Primera parte* 96)

> The manner of making such reports to the Inca and the members of his Supreme Council was by means of knots tied in strings of various colors which they read as figures. Knots of certain colors meant the crimes punished, and small threads of various colors attached to the thicker strings showed the penalty meted out and the law that had been applied. Thus they made themselves understood without the use of writing. Later we shall devote a separate chapter to a fuller account of the method of

counting by means of these knots. It certainly often amazed the Spaniards that their own best accountants went astray in their calculations while the Indians were perfectly accurate in dividing and reckoning, and the more difficult the operation the easier it seemed. Those who operated the system did nothing else day or night, and thus became perfect and highly skilled in it.   (*Royal Commentaries* 98)

In this quotation students can observe the material description of quipus, their social function as record system, their effectiveness, and the dedication of those in charge of making and keeping them. In addition, the material aspect of quipu can be related to Garcilaso's use of *entretejer* ("interweave") in his work, for the author used this verb when he inserted texts from different sources in his account to make its reading more amenable at the same time that he was commenting on them. For quipus to work, explained Garcilaso, they needed to be part of an oral performance. This is, for example, the case of statistical quipu that worked in conjunction with an abacus-like artifact called *yupana*. *Yupana* contained geometric boxes where seeds or pebbles were placed and used for accounting. González Holguín associated quipu and *yupana* in his entry "*yupana qquellca, o quippu*. Las quentas por ñudos, o por escrito" ("*yupana qqellca, or quippu*: the accounts by knots or by writing"; 371). Garcilaso made clear the performance of quipu reading and *yupana* in book 5, chapter 16, when he explained how members of Inca society paid their tributes and how taxes were collected accurately in Inca times. The *quipucamayu*'s oral performance of a quipu was also crucial to the transmission of historical records. In *Comentarios reales*, the author described quipu as an accurate source of information linked to Inca oral memory and recognized its privileged position as a native source of Andean knowledge. In spite of Garcilaso's apparent agreement with Acosta's reasoning about the lack of letters in the Andes (bk. 2, chs. 8, 21), this apparent disadvantage seems to be palliated by the author's celebration of *quipucamayu*, *amautas* (philosophers), and *haravicus* (poets), whose quipus accomplished the purpose of setting the Inca records straight (bk. 2, ch. 27). In this sense, Garcilaso explained that quipu was the receptacle and source of Andean knowledge and needed to be activated by the speech acts of *quipucamayu*, *amautas*, and *haravicus*:

> También usaban otro remedio para que sus hazañas y las embajadas que traían al Inca y las respuestas que el Inca daba se conservasen en la memoria de las gentes, y es que los amautas, que eran filósofos y sabios, tenían cuidado de ponerlas en prosa, en cuentos historiales, breves como fábulas, para que por sus edades los contasen a los niños y a los mozos y a la gente rústica del campo, para que pasando de mano en mano y de edad en edad, se conservase en la memoria de todos.   (*Primera parte* 281)

Another method too was used for keeping alive in the memory of people
their deeds and the embassies they sent to the Inca and the replies he gave
them. The *amautas* who were their philosophers and safes took the trouble to turn them into stories, no longer than fables, suitable for telling
children, young people, and the rustics of the countryside: they were thus
passed from hand to hand and age to age, and preserved in the memories
of all.   (*Royal Commentaries* 332)

Garcilaso's claim regarding the oral performance of quipu and the important
role of oral memory and tradition is not surprising. At this point students could
be briefly introduced to the contents of a Spanish text about *quipucamayu* performance that was produced more than fifty years prior to the publication of *Comentarios reales*. In 1542 the Spanish governor Cristóbal Vaca de Castro
started the task of collecting information about the history of Inca kings. Since
gathering information from old Indian informants proved difficult because
some stories contradicted one another, Vaca de Castro sought more trustworthy
sources and ordered the capture of Indian *quipucamayus* (Collapiña et al.
19–20). By means of their quipus these men were forced to recite events of Inca
history to the interpreters of the governor, and their performances informed
Relación de la descendencia, gobierno y conquista de los incas ("Account of the
Descent, Government, and Conquest of the Incas"). These *quipucamayus* began their account by stating the importance of their social role, which could
be considered equivalent to historians (Lienhard 154). They said that knowledge was transmitted from father to son and they had been trained in the art of
quipu design and the technique of memorization. They were also taught to keep
their quipus updated (with what we would understand as corrections and editions) and to be ready to recite them when requested by Inca officials. This was
a lifetime profession, learned from childhood and carried on until a very old age
if not death. Furthermore, the Inca government assigned them a regular salary
for their work (Lienhard 155). Garcilaso's work repeated these ideas about the
social role of *quipucamayus*: "Las cuales pláticas tomaban los indios *quipucamayus* de memoria, en suma, en breves palabras, y las encomendaban a la memoria, y por tradición las enseñaban a los sucesores, de padres a hijos" ("Such
speeches were preserved by the *quipucamayus* by memory in a summarized
form of few words: they were committed to memory and taught by tradition to
their successors and descendants from father to son"; *Primera parte* 281; *Royal
Commentaries* 332).

In addition, each *quipucamayu* served an Inca king whose history he recorded,
kept, and recited. While *quipucamayus* were keepers of the information stored
in the quipu, they could be eliminated, since each Inca king could "rewrite" history and command the creation of new quipus by his *quipucamayus*. The process by which *quipucamayus* created, read, and used quipus to record information about historic events reveals not only that these were material sources but

also their association with the oral word to bring them to action. This is an aspect that was not well understood by European officials, learned men, or priests, and Garcilaso noted it in his work. Or if they did observe the oral performance of a quipu reading, it was an undervalued action in a Western society that privileged alphabetic writing as the valid means to record memories of the past. This latter aspect, called "incomplete dubbing" by José Antonio Mazzotti in his study of Garcilaso's work (47–55), is perhaps one of the least studied subjects in the scholarship of quipus.

In book 6, chapter 9, Garcilaso discussed one of the most difficult arguments to grant authority to his native sources. In Inca times, quipus were used to write: "En suma, decimos que escribían en aquellos nudos y reencuentros que se daban, hasta decir cuántas embajadas habían traído al Inca y cuántas pláticas y razonamientos había hecho el Rey" ("In short, they may be said to have recorded on their knots everything that had come to visit the Inca, and all the speeches and arguments the king had uttered"; *Primera parte* 281; *Royal Commentaries* 331). But this act of writing was incomplete without the speech act of the *quipucamayu*, crucial for the transmission of information: "Pero lo que contenía la embajada, ni las palabras del razonamiento ni otro suceso historial, no podían decirlo los nudos, porque consiste en oración ordenada de viva voz, o por escrito, la cual no puede referir por nudos" ("But the purpose of the embassies or the contents of the speeches, or any other descriptive matter could not be recorded on the knots, consisting as it did of continuous spoken or written prose, which cannot be expressed by means of knots"; *Primera parte* 281–82; *Royal Commentaries* 331–32).

That said, while the oral performance of *quipucamayus* was clearly effective in Garcilaso's account of native sources, Acosta, as other Spanish authors, did not consider them as sufficient as alphabetic writing. The instructor should invite students to think about this difference of opinion, for Acosta's problem was not actually the effectiveness of quipu but his lack of knowledge of Quechua. Garcilaso, instead, was a native speaker of the Inca language, which allowed him to understand the ways in which the Inca people recorded history. Once again, the instructor can refer to Garcilaso's citations of Valera's writing of Andean traditions originally recorded in quipus and recited by *amautas* (bk. 2, ch. 26). In contrast to Garcilaso's and Valera's opinions, Acosta concluded at the end of book 1 of his *Historia* that it was not possible to know the origin of the Indians because they lacked letters and therefore they lacked history (117–18). Garcilaso had another opinion: Andean oral memory could be activated in the speech act of *quipucamayus*, *amautas*, and *haravicus* who were the actual historians of the Incas (bk. 6, ch. 9). In this way, the author of *Comentarios reales* recognized the effectiveness of quipus and the role of oral memory and speech acts in the making of Inca history. Furthermore, he placed himself as a colonial *quipucamayu* who constituted the ideal mediator between Andeans and Spaniards: "Yo traté los *quipus* y nudos con los indios de mi padre. . . . Los curacas ajenos rogaban a mi madre que me mandase les cotejase sus cuentas porque, como gente sospechosa, no se fiaban de los españoles que les tratasen verdad en aquel particular" ("I used the *quipus* and knots with my father's Indians. . . . The *curacas* under the charge of others would ask my mother to send me to check their accounts, for they were suspicious people and did not trust the Spaniards to deal honestly with them in these matters"; *Primera parte* 283; *Royal Commentaries* 333).

The overall learning goal of approaching Garcilaso's work through his reflection of Indigenous sources helps students understand *Comentarios reales* as a text of Inca history framed beyond European historical discourses. In this way, the instructor is able to offer another perspective from which students can look at this canonical text of Latin American letters whose author, in his role of "writing as an Indian," gave us hints to uncover Indigenous ways of knowing that were included in his text side by side with European historical and literary discourses.

NOTE

[1] All translations not otherwise attributed are mine.

WORKS CITED

Acosta, José de. *Historia natural y moral de las Indias.* 1590. Edited by José Alcina Franch, Historia 16, 1987.

Chang-Rodríguez, Raquel, and Malva E. Filer. *Voces de Hispanoamérica.* 3rd ed., Thomson Heinle, 2004.

Collapiña et al. *Relación de la descendencia, gobierno y conquista de los Incas.* 1542. Ediciones de la Biblioteca Universitaria, 1974.

Garcilaso de la Vega. *Primera parte de los* Commentarios reales. Pedro Crasbeeck, 1609.

———. *Royal Commentaries of the Incas and General History of Peru.* Translated by Harold V. Livermore, U of Texas P, 1989.

Garganigo, John, et al. *Huellas de las literaturas hispanoamericanas.* 2nd ed., Prentice Hall, 2002.

González Holguín, Diego. *Vocabulario de la lengua general de todo el Perú, llamada lengua qqichua o del Inca.* 1608. Universidad Nacional Mayor de San Marcos, 1989.

Lienhard, Martin. *Testimonios, cartas y manifiestos indígenas desde la conquista hasta comienzos del siglo XX.* Biblioteca Ayacucho, 1992.

Mazzotti, José Antonio. *Incan Insights: Inca Garcilaso's Hints to Andean Readers.* Iberoamericana/Vervuert, 2008.

Ortega, Julio, et al. *Letras de Hispanoamérica: Nueva antología de la literatura de las Américas.* Vista Higher Learning, 2014.

Quispe-Agnoli, Rocío. *"Quipus,* memoria andina y filosofía del lenguaje en los *Comentarios reales de los Incas* del Inca Garcilaso de la Vega." *400 años de* Comentarios reales: *Estudios sobre el Inca Garcilaso y su obra,* edited by Elena Romiti and Song No, Aitana, 2010, pp. 155–67.

Rodríguez, Rodney T. *Momentos cumbres de las literaturas hispánicas: Introducción al análisis literario.* Prentice Hall, 2004.

Varona-Lacey, Gladys, editor. *Introducción a la literatura hispanoamericana: De la conquista al siglo XX.* National Textbook Company, 1997.

Zamora, Margarita. "Historicity and Literariness: Problems in the Literary Criticism of Spanish American Colonial Texts." *MLN,* vol. 102, no. 2, Mar. 1987, pp. 334–46.

———. *Language, Authority, and Indigenous History in the* Comentarios reales de los Incas. Cambridge UP, 1988.

Teaching Inca Garcilaso in the Context of Indigenous Writing, Thought, and Culture

Isabel Dulfano

The "Indian problem," referred to overtly by the Peruvian essayist José Carlos Mariátegui as a constant in Latin America, has drawn considerable attention from a wide array of disciplines and political spectra. The debate, initiated during the conquest, on the one hand perpetuated a condemnation of the Spanish exploitation of the vanquished through the dissemination of the Black Legend.[1] On the other hand, the Indian was considered a fomenter of disturbances by various government sources and a threat to imperial political and territorial domain as manifest in Indigenous peoples' insistent claims to resources, land, and cultural sovereignty. The controversy continued to arise in intellectual, political, and socioeconomic history, and its respective manifestations can be traced in canonical literature from Latin America and Spain. The underlying premise began with a probe of the human aspects of Indigenous peoples. Do natural law and natural right apply to Indigenous peoples? If so, are they noble or ignoble savages, examples of humanity in its natural state, capable of change, civilization, and redemption? After the conquest, the colonial encomienda system institutionalized land tract ownership in exchange for service by Spanish soldiers with corresponding enslavement of the Indian as property. This incited the polemic regarding the need for, or viability of, civilizing and reforming the natives through ecclesiastical or educational means. Intellectuals appraised arguments for centuries that ran the gamut from postulating fundamental ethnic and racial difference between Indians and whites to recognizing Indigenous rights for self-governance and citizenship. Although five hundred years have passed, these arguments are hardly settled; Carlos Monsiváis hailed the 1990s as the decade with the greatest proliferation of publications during the twentieth century about the Indian question. The centrality and gravity of this problematic is evident today around the world.

In the nineteenth century, as Latin American republics gained independence, the argument turned to addressing how the nations and corresponding ruling classes would either maintain the status quo of exploitation, oppression, and political exclusion or acknowledge through legitimate channels the Indigenous peoples' constitutional rights as members of the polity. Politicians and intellectuals assessed the ramifications of the entrenched inequality of economic, social, and class structures. Myriad forms of administrative, legislative, and judicial institutions of subjugation or possible channels to liberation were appraised with an eye to ascertaining the risk to the national project of transforming the situation of the native population (see Otero). Future strategies for assimilation, acculturation, pluriculturalism, integration, or separation of the Indigenous remained indecisive yet consistently controversial.

Within the context of this long-standing debate about the Indian problem, students of El Inca Garcilaso de la Vega, and specifically of his *Royal Commentaries*, come face-to-face with one of the first oblique criticisms inscribed informally against the European colonization of originary people in the New World. As the centuries passed, the social imaginary about the native populations would vacillate between the dichotomous representations of the Indian that this extensive work eruditely crystallized. In the spirit of official royal chronicler intimated in the title of the work, Garcilaso offered one of the first representations, as a son of Indigenous nobility and Spanish subject, of the "Indian" as a sentient, thinking, civilized human being, counterpart to the established paragons of the normative colonial empire and its denizens. The key philosophical and political stances delineated in this lengthy tome serve as essential anchors for students seeking to understand the complex characterization of Indigenous peoples through the present day. Moreover, as an anthropological ethnography, the text unveils an in-depth literary tableau of the minutiae of the lifeways and cosmogony of Garcilaso's maternal culture. For students of humanities, social sciences, and natural science, Garcilaso's rich compendium is a wealth of material and intellectual knowledge to be gleaned per their specific areas of expertise.

The approach I describe considers Garcilaso's corpus in the context of the Indian question. This Renaissance man serves as one of the initial articulators, in both senses of the word, of the Indigenous cosmovision project—debunking the conviction many held that *Indian* is synonymous with purely pejorative signifiers. Eloquently bilingual, he builds a bridge (an articulation) to the Spanish royalty by which they can cross over to a better understanding of the vanquished. The master of reconciliation and hybrid mestizo tries to "integrar armónicamente sus dos raíces" ("integrate harmoniously his two roots"; González Martínez 19; my trans.). Yet his treatise contrasts with the discourse that Western hegemony uses to establish an order of social and economic hierarchy ultimately oppressive of the natives. With this background, teachers and students will employ analytical tools from literary theory, literary analysis, and postcolonial and decolonization theory in their reading of the *Royal Commentaries*. Moreover, the text allows the opportunity to critically interrogate relevant terms emanating from the cataclysmic consequences of conquest: *mestizaje, Indianismo, Indigenismo,* and the broader spectrum of Indigenous identities that have seen depiction in canonical sources. As a corollary, aspects of the Indigenous cosmovision seep irreverently into the dominant mindset, from linguistic to conceptual frames of reference, as the reader inevitably is infused by the magnitude of his magnum opus.

This pedagogical project could be undertaken in a Spanish cultural or ethnic studies upper-division undergraduate class on Indigenous writing or expression and culture. Additionally, this content could be useful for a graduate-level seminar in literature or cultural studies or in a language pedagogy or world languages master's program. To date, undergraduate and graduate students majoring in Spanish have taken one iteration or another of this class, most recently under the course titles Indigeneity, Feminism, Activism; Indigenous Feminism; and Literary Representations of the Indigenous in Latin America, a foundational class. Moreover, these classes have attracted anthropology, science, ethnobotany, sociology, Indigenous language, and history majors. The approach is first and foremost literary, demonstrating the versatility of the text as a means to clarify and exemplify literary analysis in relation to period, techniques, and rhetorical and figurative practice. We examine themes, motifs, genres, images, literary devices, figurative language, plot, point of view, setting, and symbolism. Equally compelling is the application of postcolonial and cultural studies theory to frame the readings as a part of a cultural compendium of social and political tensions marking Latin American intellectual thought and history and the associated ongoing struggles of the Indigenous.

This essay outlines some of the ways to think about and integrate Garcilaso's book into a semester-long class in Spanish or Latin American literary, cultural, or ethnic studies. The pedagogical concerns of this class are geared toward inculcating a literary appreciation of the broad subject matter of indigeneity in terms of form and content. The *Royal Commentaries* is one primary text we read; however, additional literary oeuvres compose a Latin American canonical list of major works that represent and depict the Indigenous in literature. The narratives provide a view of the "imagined Indian" seen through the lens of hegemonic culture as it evolves or remains static over time. They also afford a glimpse at the evolution from mediated subject of inquiry to self-asserted and self-affirmed agent driving change. These include, for instance, Miguel León Portilla's *El reverso de la conquista* and *Visión de los vencidos*; Ángel María Garibay's *La literatura de los Aztecas*; Leon Mera's *Cumandá*; Mariátegui's *Siete ensayos de interpretación de la realidad peruana*; Jorge Icaza's *Huasipungo*; Rigoberta Menchú's *I, Rigoberta Menchú*; and Rosa Isolde Reuque Paillalef's *When a Flower Is Reborn*. Furthermore, students might watch video segments that complement the thrust of this material, such as *El futuro Maya: Voces del presente* and *500 Years: Life in Resistance*.

The aforementioned texts are presented in chronological order, accompanied with critical theory. Each illustrates various movements, genres, or literary tendencies, such as the historical chronicle; the Renaissance, baroque, Romantic, or realist style; the testimonial; or the Marxist essay. Students gain an appreciation for how Indigenous identity has been constructed by Western hegemonic and Indigenous authors, who exercise the literary style, discourse, and rhetorical devices of their era.

Typically, assignments involve weekly short written responses to specific questions reflecting the theme of the week. Simultaneously, students undertake an analysis of form such as identification of genre, period, and specific literary techniques employed by authors. Longer essays tend to be comparative in nature. Students of Garcilaso's works broaden their insights into the main arguments regarding the following topics: the complexity of the Indigenous writer and protagonist's agency or lack thereof; the psychological and physical trauma of colonization, its subsequent internalization, and decolonization efforts; the promulgation, exploitation, or erasure of the Indigenous worldview and subjectivity; and the adoption of particular literary forms to respond to and enunciate these motifs.

Although the formal structural elements of these narrative renditions of the Indian problem transform depending on the literary period, the aforementioned thematic concerns seem to be immutable and unsettled from the sixteenth-century conquest forward. Many are told through a Western, doctrinaire, parochial, and imperious lens. Even so, a noteworthy caveat is that many postcolonial theorists disagree with the concept of an "Indian problem," inverting the question such that the "problem" resides in the governing elites who must decolonize their mindset as much as accept a solution in consultation with and for the native populations in their nations. We define and discuss the concept of an "Indian problem" by summarizing the varied approaches and attitudes prevalent in Latin American society.

Taking one further step, we think about how change takes place, what kinds of solutions exist or might be advanced, and the insights gleaned from contemporary Indigenous alternative-knowledge producers. The preconquest poetry and narratives on Indigenous cosmogony lay out the tenets guiding the native peoples' intellectual mindset and worldview, some of which will be refuted or embraced by contemporary thinkers. From the seminal corpus of artistic, philosophical, historical, and literary thought, we acquire a foundational blueprint of these precepts from which to delve into the other writings and issues. The *Royal Commentaries* includes chapters on many underlying precepts for understanding the Incan empire during the pre- to postconquest period. The books make visible a plethora of information about Garcilaso's world from his childhood in Peru to the more mature view from afar in Spain and in later life.

Within the context of postmodernism, a tension exists between the Western tradition's tendency toward knowledge concentration in a few hands and the evolving relation between critical theory and praxis. Alternative channels as well as counter-hegemonic agents of knowledge dissemination—public intellectuals—find a space to propagate ideas. Garcilaso is a unique combination of organic (see Gramsci) and traditional intellectual. The former speaks with authority on behalf of the subaltern or a specific social class, whereas the latter is an erudite intellectual, described as disinterested, tied to the institutions of the hegemonic order, and a proponent of the Enlightenment's legacy of reason and truth. Walking a fine line in his figurative entreaty to the crown in the volumes, Garcilaso challenges and seeks to win consent through a conventional and counter-hegemonic discourse that elevates his Inca heritage without casting aspersions on his audience.

His text is written using two contrasting registers, reflective of these aforementioned definitions of intellectuals. The bulk is a historical, sociological, or political rendering, a traditional intellectual study in the history of the Inca civilization. For instance, in book 2, chapter 17, he outlines a philology of form, content, and performance practice for some Incan plays, including manner and location of presentation. There is a literary guide to poetry (versification and thematics), with explanations, transcriptions from memory, or translations by Blas Valera of various poems. It is one of only a handful of catalogs on the Incan literary expression. Chapters on philology and literary history, though few, are part of the comprehensive mapping of Incan culture and intellectual thought later reclaimed in the twentieth century, only to be redacted anew.

As a traditional intellectual, Garcilaso crafts a conventional expository report of Incan history as well as the religious, political, social, and economic facets of Incan lives. The breadth of subjects elucidated appeals to students of many disciplines, who can select particular chapters that focus on their specializations. His thorough accounting is encyclopedic. To name a few, scholars of religious studies, deities, and cosmogony would find useful book 1, chapters 9–11; for anthropologists, book 1, chapters 13–14, offers descriptions of living quarters, typical dress, and foods, augmented in subsequent books.

Although Garcilaso drew upon his own knowledge of the places he had lived until his departure to Spain, he also drafted more than 525 pages crammed with reference material. As observer, participant, or researcher, he described the underpinnings of ideas or events seen through the native perspective or told to him in his childhood. For some of the information, he did rely on oral accounts presented in interviews or filtered through personal encounters, which he acknowledged.

A preliminary subject listing includes horticulture, zoology, and botany (bk. 8, chs. 11–21; bk. 9, chs. 26–30); natural resources of the kingdom (bk. 8, chs. 23–25); geography (bk. 8, ch. 22); imperial history of conquest and descriptions of the region and peoples (bk. 2, chs. 18–19; bk. 3, chs. 2–14; bk. 7, chs. 13–29; bk. 8, chs. 1–8); layout of city, engineering feats, architecture, and interiors of domestic living spaces of Cuzco or Peru (bk. 1, chs. 8, 12; bk. 3, ch. 15; bk. 7, chs. 8–12); linguistic compendium (Advertencias; bk. 1, ch. 14; bk. 7, chs. 1–4); idolatry (bk. 1, chs. 9–11; bk. 2, chs. 1, 8–10); dress (bk. 1, ch. 13); forced reductions or migration of conquered peoples (bk. 2, chs. 17–19; bk. 3, chs. 2–12); religious sanctuary and personnel (bk. 3, chs. 21–23); history of Huayna Capac (bk. 8, ch. 8); genealogies of leaders; literary history and forms (bk. 2, chs. 27–28); traditional knowledge of astronomy and medicine (bk. 2, chs. 20–26); nomenclature; and social hierarchy. In fact, these comprehensive tomes reveal the material culture and intellectual legacy of the Inca on a monumental scale.

In only a handful of chapters does the organic intellectual emerge to directly address the reader in classical prose style, alluding to his role as ethnographer, interviewer, and compiler of information. First, the *proemio* (preface) not only offers a justification for his role as authentic narrator of the books but also attempts to raise the stature of the Incan culture in the reader's mind: "As a native of the city of Cuzco, which was formerly the Rome of that Empire, I have fuller and more accurate information than that provided by previous writers" (Garcilaso 4). The vindication of the Indian-not-as-problem is most clearly felt in these segments where he insists on and underscores his authority as "natural" of Peru.

In book 1, chapter 19, "The Author's Declaration about His History," and book 2, chapter 10, "The Author Compares What He Has Said with the Statements of the Spanish Historians," Garcilaso again positions himself as an organic intellectual. These sections read like an anthropological treatise, written by an individual who takes pains to mention his legitimacy as a denizen of Peru for twenty years and acknowledges the importance of many of the interviews undertaken with local people, even family members, in order to provide a credible recounting and testimony.

The tensions between these two narrators (organic and traditional intellectual) are subtle yet tangible, vying for attention throughout the narrative. The reader discerns the complexity of inserting a new paradigm of the Indigenous subject into a historical theater fraught with violent exploitation, discrimination, internalized colonization, and repressive structural barriers to the codification of Indigenous rights of sovereignty.

Ambivalence shrouds the narrative persona with regard to his performance as part organic and part traditional intellectual. This equivocation is characterized by both a baroque and a Renaissance sensibility in his prose. It is also deftly navigated in the oscillating use of first- and third-person pronouns. Deciphering these two voices and their corresponding styles is a core exercise for students to understand the nuanced differences between Renaissance and baroque writing (form and content) in the play between books and within individual chapters. Imposing balance and harmony of perspectives and authorial voice, typical of Renaissance discourse, the narrative weighs each point of inquiry through a privileged third-person narration of experts' opinions and historical accounts. On occasion, Garcilaso skillfully interjects first-person pronouns to underscore his authority as organic intellectual as well.

We note this interplay on the topic of physical bridge building versus diplomatic bridge building in book 3, chapter 15. Garcilaso's detailed specificity concerning various bridge-engineering projects, highlighted in the construction of the immense public works over the Desaguadero and Apurimac rivers, is juxtaposed, in the same chapter, with the characterization of diplomatic bridge building, supposedly out of pure kindness of heart, as a strategy for conquest, war, and politics. Recounting how the crown prince, accompanied by his heir, successfully convinces the caciques of Chayanta province to join the empire through rhetorical persuasion rather than violence is an astute tactic for humanizing and civilizing the Indian leaders.

It is fascinating for students to follow Garcilaso's trail of logic, which begins by weighing the philosophical arguments regarding the possibility of the existence of two worlds—old and new—followed by the interrogation of the plausibility of antipodes on a spherical Earth (bk. 1, chs. 1–2). These allusions to the other underscore the author's need to create a theoretical space to validate his mother's cultural heritage and vindicate the concept of Incan Indians as civilized beings. The rhetorical style of logic offers students an opportunity to learn about how to present contending theories in persuasive expository writing. It also exemplifies strategies for drafting a controversial assertion—in Garcilaso's case, the notion of "Indians as civilized" in the framework of conservative colonial thought. His elaborate recompilation of controversy-riddled theories, sources, and information (for example, introducing the etymology of Piru, the linguistic elements of Quechua language, and other cultural dimensions of a sophisticated Inca culture) illustrates both Renaissance style and baroque conceits and wordplay that students can further explore. Additionally, it is important to point out the immediacy and implications of his work for his intended audience: Doña Catalina, monarchs, and landed nobility.

Likewise, the grandiose and labyrinthine thought process associated with the baroque stylistic is exquisitely displayed in the book. Students can identify myriad ways in which Garcilaso uses baroque rhetorical devices to his advantage in order to scaffold his rationalization of Indigenous cognition and, consequently, set the Inca on par with his father's heritage. We note his determination, as organic intellectual in this accounting, to advance the concept of native people's knowledge production and dissemination as sophisticated and highly developed.

At variance with the rhetorical discourse of Garcilaso as organic intellectual, the twentieth-century Quiché Rigoberta Menchú explicitly defines "intellectuals" and knowledge producers as "quicker and able to make finer syntheses" (222) than others. Consequently, she claims intellectuals are spawned from a decolonized structure that does not privilege erudite scholars or cosmopolitan or urban leaders but rather those who "make revolution through struggle . . . with practical experience" (223), combining praxis and theorization. Addressed to the global audience and seeking urgent attention to the plight of the Indigenous Guatemalan people during the civil war, her message on collective consciousness varies from Garcilaso's in tone, content, and intention, illustrating the transformation of "intellectual" endeavors toward explicitly activist ends.

Another concept we interrogate in this class is the subject of violence and the Indian problem. Given that colonization was a violent process on many levels, classification of the types of literal and figurative violence executed against the Indigenous for over five hundred years elucidates some of the potential ramifications on Indigenous identity then and now. In a special section entitled *Indigenous Peoples: Promoting Psychological Healing and Well-Being*, an American Psychological Association panel acknowledged the multitudinous "scars and wounds of oppression" on the conquered people and their progeny of multiracial, -ethnic, and -cultural origins. Those labeled by the panel as "victims" of miscegenation suffer "continuous enactments of micro and macro symbolic and psychological vignettes of the original conquest/resistance" (Holliday i). To deal with the cicatrix left by colonization, identification and definition of the forms of violence perpetrated during the conquest through present day is instrumental. The characterization of these modalities of violence and their respective impact on the Indigenous peoples of the New World offers students a chance to delve into the topic from a perspective of the seventeenth century to modern times.

This shifts our focus to epistemic violence, described in Silvia Rivera Cusicanqui's "Violence and Interculturality: Paradoxes of Ethnicity in Contemporary Bolivia." Cusicanqui identifies forms of violence and repercussions on the Indigenous: border violence, domestic violence, internal (intimate enemy) violence, interethnic violence, sexual violence, and physical and psychological violence manifested by acculturating institutions, such as the military forces, all of which objectifies the Indigenous through physical and emotional abuses and strips them of their rights. We consider how the dominant power cultivates the myth of the noble savage and "conceals the most serious problem of physical/material and symbolic violence that the Indigenous suffer in the diverse arenas of their lifeworlds, in the constant crossing of borders, and in their migratory projects and complex identities" (Cusicanqui 278).

Indeed, violence shapes identity in many ways. The composition and conceptualization of subaltern identity is extremely complicated. Not only is it difficult for the Indigenous to define and give shape to their sense of self beyond the manifestations of violent effacement, but it is further complicated by the "intellectual [being] complicit in the persistent constitution of Other as the Self's shadow" (Spivak 24). Using postcolonial theories to decipher the persistent mechanisms and fallout of colonialism on identity construction, the following questions guide our discussion: How and why does Garcilaso frame his life history as a mestizo as well as focus on his mother's heritage in the context of the violence of colonization? In what manner does he depict an internalized image of the Indian, tackling these scars head-on, or in what way does he rupture or dismantle the stereotypical derogatory depiction through the example of his mother's regal lineage? What literal and figurative structural barriers of violence can we identify in these books as perpetuated on the Indigenous as well as by the Indigenous, and as repeating or undergoing metamorphosis in later authors' works? Is the Indigenous person in Garcilaso's work similar to the colonizer's portrait, or in what ways does it eschew the identity expounded in the other renditions of Indigenous identity?

Garcilaso's text becomes a counterpoint to the mediated autoethnography, autobiography, excoriating political exposés, and unofficial historical recording that became the hallmark of Latin American testimonial literature from the 1970s to the 1990s. Likewise, we can draw parallels to the anonymous codices, testimonials from the conquered people regarding that trauma and history, which were compiled by the Spanish friars in the 1500s. Juxtaposing Garcilaso's formal and contextual elements with Menchú's or the earlier narratives allows students to trace aspects of continuity and evolution in distinct forms of rhetoric and discourse that characterize Indigenous thought and sense of identity. Furthermore, these comparisons provoke the examination of historicity and ethnography in relation to fiction (Zamora 5), issues that overshadowed the unprecedented denouncement of Menchú's Nobel Peace Prize–winning narrative.

Postcolonial theory also queries subaltern subjectivity, one that is particularly compromised in any form of testimonial, including Garcilaso's: either the "oppressed . . . can speak and know their condition" (Spivak 25) or only through the intervention of a literate elite mediator does their story become known. The question of subaltern subjectivity thus asks students to weigh determinations of who ultimately constitutes the Indigenous as subject, as well as who is allowed to narrate the process of making them visible and heard, or who continues to perpetuate racist constructs. Students gauge the degree of symmetry or asymmetry in the relationship between the narrator or scribe of the various texts and the enunciator as insider or as representative of hegemony. We keep in mind that some "prevailing discourses about and around . . . indigenous people . . . are common *among mestizo-criollos* and not *with* or *among* the indigenous . . . fostered primarily by foreign authors, . . . who believe the indigenous question is exclusively the domain of minority studies" (Cusicanqui 275). Parting from a literary analysis of form, students situate subaltern discourse by classifying point of view, narrator, setting, and rhetorical devices or figures of speech that support or contradict this contention. In the case of Garcilaso, is he subaltern, other, or agent of authority?

The identification of the enunciator as insider or hegemonic representative, as much as determination of the geographical location or source of the discourse, is a related task. "Who is writing about what where and why?" (Mignolo 122); in other words, students must determine the "locus of enunciation." Underscoring the significance of who articulates the problem, how they do so, from which position of power or weakness it is spoken and who controls the dissemination and production of knowledge, where they are situated in relation to the North/South or East/West, what they choose to include, and finally when they do so is crucial. These questions guide this line of thought: What are the structural or figurative barriers to enunciation and representation of Indigenous reality? Does this discourse emerge exclusively in cosmopolitan city settings that respond only to one segment of the population? What language (e.g., Spanish or Quechua) is utilized? If Spanish is the universal lingua franca, how can a non-Spanish speaker have a voice when native tongues of origin are banned? How does language become a tool to control the discourse and maintain power in the hands of the hegemonic leaders?

Garcilaso's text is ideal for broaching the controversy that arose over the objectivity and authenticity of Menchú's *testimonio*, narrated to the editor and anthropologist Elizabeth Burgos-Debray in the twentieth century. Although a Nobel Peace Prize winner, Menchú was accused of fabrication, of telling a distorted version heavily tainted by personal bias, political machination, and deception in her accounts of her language acquisition; title to lands; and Indian cultural, social, political, and spiritual life in Guatemala during the civil war. Taken as a testimonial of sorts already in the 1600s, the *Royal Commentaries* sets the stage for confronting the very real problems and limitations of enunciation, truth, and fiction, with which Indigenous peoples will contend whenever attempting to insert their own discourse and subjectivity.

As a starting point, the preface of the *Royal Commentaries* in a veiled manner sets the methodology to be followed throughout the book. The author's aim is to figuratively elevate the Inca empire to equivalent status with Rome and the Roman Empire, a European crown jewel of religious and political power. Analysis of this preface invites comparison of the Inca empire with other imperial projects and their corresponding dynastic monarchies in Western and Indigenous cultures. In this regard Michael Horswell postulates a revisionist view of Incan royalty and mestizaje (miscegenation). Horswell queries how Garcilaso validates both sides in an economic, political, and cultural society and history that traditionally has disdained the Indigenous legacy of large segments of the population in Latin America (1–28). Garcilaso's intricate and tactful autoethnography walks the tightrope between Spain (oppressor) and Latin America (subjugated), between Western hegemony and servile other, promulgating aspects of a mixed heritage and opening a space for subjectivity through the continual figurative parallelism underscored from this start.

Garcilaso is a prescient precursor for problematizing Indigenous subjectivity, followed some four hundred years later by politically committed ethnographers and unofficial historians in the twentieth century who gave a voice and agency to the invisible, silenced, and exploited Indigenous as subject. Both Garcilaso's preface and Menchú's chapter 1 in particular offer radical alternatives to the articulation of the historically pejorative Indian as projected by and about the Indigenous. Menchú approaches the problem on the first page of her text by stating, "My name is Rigoberta Menchú. I am twenty-three years old. This is my testimony. I didn't learn it from a book, and I didn't learn it alone. I'd like to stress that it's not only my life, it's also the testimony of my people." Her gaze is filtered through the collective, and her insistence on retelling official history is brought into focus from the beginning, whereas Garcilaso insists on providing an apologetic gloss of the previous erudite "learned" accounts. He says "they have not described these realms so fully," pinpointing the brevity of earlier accounts that do not allow for in-depth understanding (4). "My purpose is not to gainsay them, but to furnish a commentary and gloss, and to interpret many Indian expressions which they, as strangers to that tongue, have rendered inappropriately." Ultimately his ostensible goal is

> with no other interest than to be of service to Christendom and to inspire gratitude to Our Lord Jesus Christ and the Virgin Mary His mother, by whose merits and intercession the Eternal Majesty has deigned to draw so many great peoples out of the pit of idolatry and bring them into the bosom of His Roman Catholic Church, our mother and lady.

In book 1, generally the narrator adopts a distanced, benevolent Christian-izing voice in the historical ledger, with occasional comments like "history obliges one to set down the whole truth" (1: 37; bk. 1, ch. 13). However, in chapter 15, the reader is privy to overt attribution to conversations at home with his prin-cess mother's remaining family members, who often gathered there in Cuzco to recount triumphs of their civilization and its current defeat. In particular, Gar-cilaso quotes an uncle, described as senior of the surviving familial sages and witness to Atahuallpa's tyranny and Spanish conquest. Garcilaso abandons the register of third-person narrator to admonish in the first-person plural, "[F]or everything said about them from other sources comes down to the same story as we shall relate, and it will be better to have it as told in the very words of the Incas than in those of foreign authors" (41). The inclusion of his presumed ver-batim conversations with this uncle, who repeats the oft-told oral annals of Inca heritage to be "kept in your heart," devolves away from traditional intellectual to the role as implicated organic intellectual.

The quotidian aspects of life in his mother's home, or in Inca society at large, can be compared with the digest provided by Menchú's *testimonio* about grow-ing up as an Indigenous girl from the rural highlands, migrating to the city, and becoming a political activist. Students can compare and contrast Menchú's sense of urgency in telling her *testimonio* so as to incite action to stop the killing in Guatemala with Garcilaso's aforementioned ostensible intention to gloss or in-scribe Inca history.

One successful essay-length assignment calls for an examination of the simi-larities and differences between Garcilaso and Menchú. Students identify the shared rhetorical and discursive strategies employed with regard to the "Indian problem"; analyze each interlocutor's relation to the Greco-Roman Western tra-dition and to their respective Indian culture in political, socioeconomic, cultural, linguistic, and ideological terms; discuss Menchú's allusion to the concealment of secrets about her culture versus Garcilaso's ostensible open, legalistic revela-tion and desire for His Majesty ("omnipotence") to "discover" the secrets of Inca culture parallel to his discovery of the New World (Garcilaso 1: 9–11; bk. 1, ch. 1); justify the extent to which the works are "examples of epic (epopeya) historical telling" (Stoll 79) or a subordination or supplementation of one's narrative to the "official" story; situate and contextualize narrative voices and their position along the continuum of Indigenous discursive history; conduct an analysis of Spanish, Quechua or Quiché, and Latin or Greek in the texts; identify variance in tone, audience, use of metaphor, rhetoric, and setting as epitomized by the genre of *relación* (letter of relation) versus the anthropological testimonio; and compare the orality of the texts.

For a seminar on Indigenous feminism, the analysis of the depiction of female characters in Garcilaso's volumes is a brief but important aspect of the interro-gation of the triply marginalized figure of the Indigenous woman, even the royal Indigenous woman. Book 4 contains several chapters characterizing women, in particular those living monastic lives, because, as Garcilaso decried, "all the

Spanish historians who have approached this question [what these women were, what their vows consisted of, and how they observed the rules] have passed it over 'like a cat on hot bricks'" (1: 195; bk. 4, ch. 1). Chapters 2–6 outline the duties, occupations, and hierarchy of the five hundred or more women in service of, or designated the wives of, the Sun. Other chapters enumerate rituals for coming of age and for raising children that are identified as common custom among all Indians of Peru, whether rich or poor, nobles or commoners (1: 212–13; bk. 4, ch. 12). Later chapters offer the portrait of life as a married woman or prostitute. The portraiture does not allow for agency of the female characters yet provides a sketch of life in the regime.

Garcilaso describes in some detail his relationship with his mother, growing up in her household and listening to the origin stories told by his uncle to him directly for his edification. He also writes of the gender roles of nobility and especially the chosen virgins, called "las escogidas" in Inca society (1: 5–8; bk. 4, chs. 1–3). The scant references to women or girls (bk. 1, chs. 15–17, 19, 25–26; bk. 3, ch. 21; bk. 4, chs. 1–9, 12–14) indicate two points. First, some critics have proposed the examination of point of view, specifically the lack of objectivity of the text in conveying an accurate portrayal of royal Incan women or other members serving the court and their respective roles. Second, the contradictory, stereotypical characterization of a too narrowly circumscribed group of women from the upper echelon of Incan society skews the spectrum to an atypical sample. Garcilaso manipulates the meager exposition of females to bolster his personal agenda, hence the limited repertoire of women is framed by the values of a Christian, Europeanized lens (see Mayea Rodriguez; Horswell 1–28; Heid). José Antonio Mazzotti, in his colonial semiosis, argues that Garcilaso's familiarity not only with Incan history but also with European "readings" of the Incas, as well as his mastery of the "rhetorical devices wielded by the Spanish historians," permits the reinvention and legitimization of Incan history, specifically of his mother's noble lineage in Cuzco, yet only her household is vindicated in the first part of the *Royal Commentaries*.

In undertaking a feminist analysis, determination of the degree of agency, or lack thereof, of the female characters is imperative. Neither the royal Inca queen or princess nor the panoply of other subservient females catalogued in his account exercise real power. The view of woman depends on her social class and position in the social hierarchy. If on the one hand Garcilaso recognizes the role of man and woman as civilizing agents necessary for the proliferation of society, there is an overriding ambiguity pervading his text. The majority of the women appear as objects of veneration or exchange as exemplified by the depiction of the founding mythic mother Reina Mama Ocllo. She is placed on a pedestal, similar to the Virgin of Guadalupe or as an angel in the house, responsible for providing a model of domesticity in a matronly, motherly version of the sanitized Indigenous cosmogony.

Therefore, Garcilaso's treatment of women reflects prevarication, a moderated lack of synchronicity with the social dictates of his times and those of the Inquisition in supposedly revealing the portrayal of women in the Incan empire. Miscegenation governs his worldview and influences the elaboration of the presentation. Required to follow the formulaic standards to prove his erudition and loyalty to the monarchy in Spain in order to be published, albeit in Portugal, his work would have to strictly adhere to those rules and codes. The subject matter of foreign women, particularly in a period when chastity, honor, virtue, and submissiveness were the norm, would be measured at best. Thus the narrator maneuvers in interstitial spaces, where what is not said becomes as telling as that pronounced. He limits himself to speaking mostly about women of the noble class, either of regal lineage or foreign, and thus enumerates a lengthy index of names in his native Quechua, as well as their corresponding functions or occupations, without giving them flesh and bones.

Students are asked to catalog the principal roles of women described in the text and their characterization and how the latter relates to their figurative, contradictory charge of being the main transmitters of cultural traditions and norms. If they appear subjugated and passive in public settings, and further constrained within the domestic sphere to ensuring the well-being of men and the ruler, how are cultural values transferred through a matrilineage? How does the depiction of the narrator's mother as the consummate, loquacious hub of Incan oral history telling—a magnet for surviving nobles who assemble at their home to hear her recounting of events—tie into this? Where does her authority within Incan society as the custodian of oral history and lineage, life giver, and responsible party for maintaining and inculcating the legacy in the progeny lie?

One might interpret Garcilaso's manner of speaking about women as emblematic of a broader strategy for passing muster before the rigorous censors of the Inquisition, respecting the social order of the moment as loyal vassal to king and God as well as reinforcement and exaltation of the virtues of the era of women's chastity, subservience, and honor. Having abandoned the apocalyptic religious customs detailed in several parts, his goal is to legitimize the grandeur and civilized aspect of the preconquest Incan empire. Women and other topics addressed in his book hence are pawns in the crafting of this illusion. The students of Garcilaso's text must weigh his guardedly idealized inscription of the Andean utopia (Flores Galindo) and its inhabitants, male and female, in order to opine on its efficacy, veracity, and ability to contest or convey an alternative narrative on the Indian question.

NOTE

[1] The *Encyclopedia Britannica* defines the Black Legend as "a term indicating an unfavourable image of Spain and Spaniards, accusing them of cruelty and intolerance, formerly prevalent in the works of many non-Spanish, and especially Protestant, historians. Primarily associated with criticism of 16th-century Spain and the anti-Protestant policies of King Philip II (reigned 1556–98), the term was popularized by the Spanish

historian Julián Juderías in his book *La Leyenda Negra* (1914; 'The Black Legend')" ("Black Legend").

WORKS CITED

"Black Legend." *Encyclopedia Britannica*, 11 Feb. 2020, britannica.com/topic/Black -Legend.

Cusicanqui, Silvia Rivera. "Violence and Interculturality: Paradoxes of Ethnicity in Contemporary Bolivia." Translated by Isabel Dulfano and Josef Raab. *New World Colors: Ethnicity, Belonging, and Difference in the Americas*, edited by Raab, Wissenschaftlicher Verlag Trier / Bilingual Press, 2014, pp. 275–91. Inter-American Studies 9.

Flores Galindo, Alberto. *In Search of an Inca: Identity and Utopia in the Andes.* Edited and translated by Carlos Aguirre et al., Cambridge UP, 2010.

El futuro Maya: Voces del presente (1998). YouTube, uploaded by UW Milwaukee Classroom, 21 Nov. 2011, www.youtube.com/watch?v=MXQ_xORzDEo&list =PLA3F9778C2CEEDE54.

Garcilaso de la Vega. *Royal Commentaries of the Incas and General History of Peru.* Translated by Harold V. Livermore, U of Texas P, 1966. 2 vols.

Garibay K., Angel María. *La literatura de los Aztecas.* 2nd ed., Joaquín Mortiz, 1970.

González Martínez, José Luis. "Garcilaso Inca de la Vega: Un hombre entre dos razas." *Revista de historia de América*, no. 110, July-Dec. 1990, pp. 19–35.

Gramsci, Antonio. "The Intellectuals." *Selections from the Prison Notebooks*, translated and edited by Q. Hoare and G. N. Smith, International Publishers, 1971, pp. 3–23.

Heid, Patricia. "Constructing a Peaceful Imperialism: Manipulating Gender Identity in the *Comentarios reales de los Incas.*" *Sixteenth Century Journal*, vol. 33, no. 1, Spring 2002, pp. 93–108.

Holliday, Bertha G. "We Bear the Fruits of Our Histories." *Indigenous Peoples: Promoting Psychological Healing and Well-Being*, American Psychological Association, Aug. 2010, apa.org/pi/oema/resources/communique/2010/08/august -special.pdf, pp. i–ii.

Horswell, Michael J. *Decolonizing the Sodomite: Queer Tropes of Sexuality in Colonial Andean Culture.* U of Texas P, 2005.

Icaza, Jorge. *Huasipungo: Novela.* 10th ed., Editorial Losada, 1975.

León Portilla, Miguel. *El reverso de la conquista; relaciones aztecas, mayas e incas.* 2nd ed., Editorial J. Mortiz, 1970.

———. *Visión de los vencidos; relaciones indígenas de la conquista.* 2nd ed., Universidad Nacional Autónoma, 1961.

Mariátegui, José Carlos. *Siete ensayos de interpretación de la realidad peruana.* 19th ed., Biblioteca Amauta, 1971.

Mayea Rodríguez, Liesder. "Un análisis de la representación y falta de representación del sujeto subalterno femenino u 'otro' en los *Comentarios reales* del Inca

Garcilaso de la Vega." *Espéculo: Revista de estudios literarios*, no. 46, 2010, webs.ucm.es/info/especulo/numero46/comreales.html.

Mazzotti, José Antonio. "The Lightning Bolt Yields to the Rainbow: Indigenous History and Colonial Semiosis in the *Royal Commentaries* of El Inca Garcilaso de la Vega." *Biblioteca Virtual Miguel de Cervantes*, Universidad de Alicante, cervantesvirtual.com/obra-visor/the-lightning-bolt-yields-to-the-rainbow -indigenous-history-and-colonial-semiosis-in-the-royal-commentaries-of-el-inca -garcilaso-de-la-vega-0/html/02426fb8-82b2-11df-acc7-002185ce6064_5.html.

Menchú, Rigoberta. *I, Rigoberta Menchú: An Indian Woman in Guatemala*. Edited by Elizabeth Burgos-Debray, translated by Ann Wright, Verso, 1984.

Mera, Juan León. *Cumandá; ó, Un drama entre salvajes*. 3rd ed., Espasa-Calpe, 1967.

Mignolo, Walter D. "Colonial and Postcolonial Discourse: Cultural Critique or Academic Colonialism?" *Latin American Research Review*, vol. 28, no. 3, 1993, pp. 120–34.

Monsiváis, Carlos. "Mexico's Cultural Landscapes: A Conversation with Carlos Monsiváis." Interview by David Thelen. *Rethinking History and the Nation-State: Mexico and the United States as a Case Study*, special issue of *Journal of American History*, vol. 86, no. 2, Sept. 1999, pp. 613–22.

Otero, Gerardo. "The 'Indian Question' in Latin America: Class, State, and Ethnic Identity Construction." *Latin American Research Review*, vol. 38, no. 1, 2003, pp. 248–66.

Reuque Paillalef, Rosa Isolde. *When a Flower Is Reborn: The Life and Times of a Mapuche Feminist*. Edited and translated by Florencia E. Mallon, Duke UP, 2002.

Spivak, Gayatri Chakravorty. "Can the Subaltern Speak?" *Colonial Discourse and Post-colonial Theory: A Reader*, edited by Patrick Williams and Laura Chrisman, Harvester Wheatsheaf, 1993, pp. 66–111.

Stoll, David. "Rigoberta Menchú and the Last-Resort Paradigm." *Latin American Perspectives*, vol. 26, no. 6, 1999, pp. 70–80.

Yates, Pamela, director. *500 Years: Life in Resistance*. Skylight Pictures, 2017.

Zamora, Margarita. *Language, Authority, and Indigenous History in the* Comentarios reales de los Incas. Cambridge UP, 1988.

Weaving Gender into the *Royal Commentaries*

Raquel Chang-Rodríguez

The following essay came about in response to the interest in gender issues when analyzing *Comentarios reales de los Incas* by Inca Garcilaso de la Vega in my graduate seminar on the chronicles of the early contact period. For part of a two-hour class, I concentrated on the ethnographic chapters of Garcilaso's masterpiece in which he describes the role of women who lived secluded in the *acllahuasi*, or "House of the Chosen Women," during the Inca empire. I set the stage for this discussion with an introduction on how elite women played an important role in Tahuantinsuyu and on a historical event of the early colonial years in which their agency was paramount. The responses this introduction elicited enabled the class to contrast and discuss Andean, Iberian, and contemporary issues related to the role of women. I then went on to Garcilaso's characterization of the Virgins of the Sun, who wove garments for this deity and, in turn, for the Inca (the king). In the discussion I explained the importance of the art of weaving—initially taught by the first Inca queen, Mama Ocllo—in the expansion of the empire and the consolidation of its values, and how the weavers of the Sun contributed to both. In addition, I aimed to show how these chapters were not isolated. Through them Garcilaso artfully links women and weaving to the wider critique of colonialism as projected in his magnum opus. Viewed in this manner, the chapters devoted to the weavers of the Sun offer a sharper lens to better understand the complexities of Inca civilization and *Comentarios reales* as well as the rhetorical skills of its author.[1]

Women played an important role in Andean culture and history during the Inca period. In this regard it is worth recalling their participation in ceremonies honoring the Moon, a deity associated with females and their role in society, and how elite women through marriage and other unions contributed to consolidating the Inca empire. The anthropological record points to a unique version of the myth of the origin of the Incas gathered by the chronicler Pedro Sarmiento de Gamboa. In this version it is Mama Ocllo, not her brother Manco Capac, who with her right hand throws the rod that, upon penetrating the earth, will determine the place of settlement of the clan in the area of Cuzco, then known as Guanaypata (Sarmiento de Gamboa 217). From a historical perspective later in the colonial period, we learn about *cacicas*, or female rulers who exercised authority on their own or through their husbands. Among them the most famous is Contarhuacho, Inca Huayna Capac's favorite, whose daughter, Quispe Sisa, also known as Inés Huaylas Yupanqui, was given in marriage to Francisco Pizarro by Atahuallpa and brought into the world a daughter and a son.[2] When Manco Inca Yupanqui rebelled, Contarhuacho responded to the request of help from her daughter. During the siege of Lima she sent more than a thousand Indians to provide relief to Pizarro and Quispe Sisa. This assistance saved the family of the princess and the newly founded Spanish city (Rostworowski, "La mujer" 23–38).

Andean chronicles offer a variety of information about women and their role in Inca society. An analysis of this record allows us to glimpse mainly the role of elite females and, to a lesser extent, that of women from other segments of society. Regarding the first group, the two versions of the early illustrated chronicle by the Mercedarian friar Martín de Murúa immediately come to mind. There, whether in the early Galvin manuscript or in the later Wellington version, one can see watercolors of the *coyas*, or Inca queens, elegantly attired. As for the second group of nonelite females, it is worth remembering the women codified in the ink drawings of *Primer nueva corónica y buen gobierno* (*First New Chronicle and Good Government*) by the native author Felipe Guaman Poma de Ayala. However interesting these iconic and linguistic registers are, in this essay I will focus on the first part of *Comentarios reales*.[3] My analysis centers on a segment of this chronicle often overlooked by critics: the Virgins of the Sun who lived in the *acllahuasi* in Cuzco. I contend that the chapters in which their role is described, often dismissed as ethnographic and thus hardly studied, are central to the author's narrative strategy. When extolling these women and their labor, the chronicler praises Inca culture while criticizing Spanish colonial rule.[4] Focusing on the segment devoted to the Virgins of the Sun, I propose to show how Garcilaso "weaves" women and their work into his historical project by emphasizing their contribution to the ritual character of Inca rule and the grandeur of its imperial order. The section of *Comentarios reales*—concretely the first six chapters of its fourth book—in which the chronicler underscores the importance of the Virgins of the Sun explains the centrality of their work as weavers and highlights related aspects of Inca justice.[5] These chapters echo key messages of Garcilaso's masterpiece.

Women of the Acllahuasi

The first three chapters of the fourth book describe the origin, the rooms, and the role of the women chosen as wives of the Sun in Cuzco's *acllahuasi*. As is often the case when the narrator refers to other descriptions of Inca customs, he begins his deliberation by correcting Spanish historians who address complex issues such as this in a manner as light "como gato por brasas" ("as a cat running on burning coals"; Garcilaso 1: 184; bk. 4, ch. 1). He brings up the popular saying in order to emphasize the casual way in which Europeans have treated matters related to Inca culture. According to the narrator, an issue worthy of much consideration is the "perpetua virginidad que las mujeres guardavan en muchas casas de recogimiento" ("perpetual virginity women kept in many official houses"). Thus, in his view, the permanent virginity of the chosen women who lived in the *acllahuasi* is an admirable Inca custom. In order to support this assertion, he details the constraints of life in the *acllahuasi* and the rules that contributed to preserving chastity. For example, the sovereign forbade the entry of men into these houses.[6] Garcilaso also notes the beauty and high lineage of these women while reiterating that they lived their lives in confinement as virgins.

When the chronicler details the complexities of life in the *acllahuasi*—the role of guardians and of *mamaconas*, or keepers of the rules; the severity of punishment if one fails in a task; and the origin and function of the maidens or Virgins of the Sun—we enter a totally feminine space forbidden even to the Inca lord.[7] Here women are responsible for several tasks: preparing the *çancu*, or sacrificial bread, for the Sun, and the *aca*, or ritual drink, for the Inca and his relatives (Garcilaso 1: 188; bk. 4, ch. 3). However, their most notable task is spinning and weaving clothes for the Sun, the Inca, and the *coya*, as the narrator explains: "El principal exercicio que las mujeres del Sol hazían

Figure 1. Weavers in the *acllahuasi*. Felipe Guaman Poma de Ayala, *Primer nueva corónica y buen gobierno* (c. 1615). GkS. 2232 4to. Courtesy of Royal Library, Copenhagen, Denmark.

era hilar y texer y hazer todo lo que el Inca traía sobre su persona de vestido y tocado, y también para la Coya, su mujer ligítima. Labravan assimismo toda la ropa finíssima que ofrecían al Sol en sacrificio" ("The main job performed by the women of the Sun was spinning and weaving everything the Inca wore, particularly his dress and headdress, and also for the Coya, his official wife. They also wove all the fine apparel offered to the Sun in ritual sacrifice"; 1: 187; bk. 4, ch. 2) (fig. 1).

The Garments of the Inca

As we know, clothing had a central role in Tahuantinsuyu. Through attire it was possible to identify the rank and ethnicity of each person as well as political, religious, and familial bonds (Ramos 117). In the particular case of the Inca elite, their exclusive garments became known as *cumbi* and were made from the finest wool of vicuña, sometimes mixed with hairs of bats or multicolored feathers (Ramos 116–18). These garments had the important role of affirming the concept of power within this high-status group and making it known to the governed. Thus, they proclaimed the royal standing of the Inca, reiterated his authority, and sent a message of opulence for all to see. According to the narrator of *Comentarios reales*, the *llautu* (braided headdress) from which the *mascapaicha* (red tassel) hung, the *uncu* (long sleeveless shirt), the *yacolla* (rectangular blanket), and the *chuspa* (bag for ritual coca) were woven in the *acllahuasi* by the select group of virgins dedicated to this activity. Among all these garments, the most elaborate was the *uncu*. Its abstract designs presented complex messages about Andean and universal hierarchies while exalting the figure of the Inca; since the ruler changed outfits according to the occasion being celebrated, most likely *uncu* iconography also set a particular interpretation of Andean history while linking the sovereign to a given ancestor (Mills and Taylor 14).

Among the various types of *uncu*, the most studied was formed by squares or *tucapu*, with designs of different colors arranged one after the other. According to some scholars, these abstract designs form a type of writing yet to be deciphered and understood (Zuidema, "Guaman Poma between the Arts" 37–85). In one of the precontact *uncu*, currently at the Textile Museum in Washington, DC, the *tucapu* are arranged like a checkerboard motif called *collcapata* (fig. 2). It has been speculated that the arrangement suggests the *colca*, or storage houses, where taxes paid in agricultural produce were kept. Therefore, the design seems to evoke communal concepts that linked the different social sectors of Tahuantinsuyu and strengthened its foundations throughout Inca dominion (Mills and Taylor 15). While this is not the only *uncu* pattern, it is known that the sovereign wore the shirt with the *collcapata* checkerboard design to the Inca Raymi, a celebration honoring the Inca, which was attended by individuals from all groups of the empire. The Inca also wore it when he inspected the different provinces under his rule, accompanied by the noblemen (Mills and Taylor 16). Thus, there is agreement among specialists to associate the *uncu*

Figure 2. *Uncu* with *tucapu*, c. 1452–1532. George Washington University Museum and the Textile Museum, Washington, DC.

that had *tucapu* in the *collcapata* design with the authority and person of the Inca ruler (Zuidema, "Guaman Poma and the Art" 151–202).

While viewers were unaware of the physical features of the weavers, they could judge and admire the quality of their work in the notable dresses of the sovereign. This is extremely significant because the concept of beauty in the Andes incorporates perfection in all aspects of a garment, from weaving to color and design (Phipps, "Garments" 19). Thus, from their confined space in the *acllahuasi*, the Virgins of the Sun established communication with the subjects of the Inca. Through their perfectly woven garments adorned with complex designs, they set aesthetic standards, asserted social and political hierarchies, and reiterated the divine character of the monarch as well as his earthly authority. Even though the garments were made for the Sun, the narrator explains that, as the Sun could not use them, the virgin weavers sent them to the Inca, who

> como a hijo legítimo y natural y heredero [del Sol] . . . El cual [el Inca] los recebía como cosas sagradas y las tenía él y todo su Imperio en mayor veneración que las tuvieran los griegos y romanos si en su gentilidad las hizieran sus diosas Juno, Venus y Palas. . . . Y porque aquellas cosas eran hechas por las manos de las Coyas, mujeres del Sol, y hechas para el Sol, y las mujeres por su calidad eran de la misma sangre del Sol, por todos estos respectos las tenían en suma veneración.   (Garcilaso 1: 188; bk. 4, ch. 3)

> as a legitimate and natural son and heir [of the Sun] . . . [the Inca] received them as sacred vestments; he and all in his empire had the garments in greater veneration than if Greeks and Romans in their gentility had garments made by their goddesses Juno, Venus, and Pallas. . . . And because those things were done by the hands of *coyas*, wives of the Sun, and made for the Sun, and the women because of their lineage were of the same blood of the Sun, for all these reasons they were greatly revered.

Hence women weavers and their *cumbi* cloth played a paramount role in proclaiming the established order as well as highlighting the human and divine character of the Inca lord. Both the mundane and the spiritual were combined in his royal person and affirmed by the elaborate attire he wore.

Venerated Vestments

The reference to antiquity cited above is instructive: just as Greeks and Romans would have revered garments made by Juno, Venus, and Pallas, the Incas and their subjects extolled the royal garments even more because they were made for the Sun by the chosen women of the *acllahuasi*. It behooves us to explore this comparison further. In the Roman pantheon Juno was considered a protectress and counselor of the state. As patron goddess of the empire she was called Regina (queen) and with Jupiter and Minerva formed a triad worshipped in several temples. As we know, Venus (Aphrodite), another goddess mentioned, is associated with beauty, love, and fertility. Pallas (Minerva), the third deity, is linked to wisdom, textiles, and just wars; with regard to her power, suffice it to recall how in book 6 of Ovid's *Metamorphoses* Pallas punished and transformed her rival Arachne in a weaving contest. By referring to these major deities from the classical world, the narrator again highlights the admirable work of women, be they from the ancient world or living in Inca times. When mentioning these goddesses of antiquity, the narrator cleverly stresses common values and standards of conduct shared by the Roman and Inca empires. Through this analogy Garcilaso binds the two superpowers through the work of women, be they classical goddesses or virgin weavers in the *acllahuasi*. Such an approach reiterates the positive assessment of the work of the Virgins of the Sun and of women's contribution in a framework that appears to transcend geographical, historical, and cultural boundaries.

It should be noted that elsewhere in the chronicle the narrator associates weaving and garments with the civilizing influence of the Incas, who clothed a population that was covered only with animal skins and tree leaves. Mama Ocllo, the first Inca *coya*, is in the center of this enlightening process in which textiles separate the civilized from the barbarians. In Garcilaso's version of the myth of origin of the Incas, she is the founder of the dynasty together with Manco Capac. As the first queen she teaches women how to spin and weave in order to clothe themselves: "[El Inca] mandó recoger el ganado manso que andava por el campo sin dueño, de cuya lana los vistió a todos mediante la industria y enseñança que la Reina Mama Ocllo Huaco havía dado a las indias en hilar y texer" ("[the Inca lord] sent to collect from the field cattle that had no owner, and he clothed all from their wool through the industry and teachings that Queen Mama Ocllo Huaco had given to female Indians in spinning and weaving"; 1: 52; bk. 1, ch. 21). It is then possible to bridge the gap—to weave the thread—between these early origins linked to Mama Ocllo's teaching and the subsequent splendor of Tahuantinsuyu, evoked by the royal garments made by the Virgins of the Sun. Obviously, throughout the ages women, and particularly those living in the *acllahuasi*, learned the lessons and perfected the training offered by the first queen and weaver. In this manner the narrator underscores the continuous and central contribution of women—the master teacher and queen Mama Ocllo and her successful female followers—to the civilizing task of the Incas, who first clothed a naked population and later consolidated their dominion through sophisticated garments promoting the authority and power of the Inca lords.

Crime and Punishment

The apotheosis of the Incas in this segment devoted to the weavers of the Sun occurs when the narrative voice details the penalties meted out to the women of the *acllahuasi* who breached their vows of virginity. They are buried alive and the men are hanged. Since this was deemed a small punishment for such a serious crime, "mandava la ley matar con el delincuente su mujer y hijos y criados, y también sus parientes y todos los vezinos y moradores de su pueblo y todos sus ganados, sin quedar mamante ni piante" ("the law also prescribed killing the offender with his wife and children and servants, and also their relatives and all neighbors and inhabitants of their village and all animals, without a living soul remaining"; Garcilaso 1: 188–89; bk. 4, ch. 3). The lands of the community were flattened and paved over so that the area could never be cultivated or repopulated. However, an explanation quickly follows:

> Esta era la ley, mas nunca se vio executada, porque jamás se halló que huviessen delinquido contra ella, porque, como otras vezes hemos dicho, los indios del Perú fueron temerosíssimos de sus leyes y observantíssimos dellas, principalmente de las que tocavan en su religión o en su Rey. Mas si se hallara haver delinquido alguno contra ella, se executara al pie de la letra sin remissión alguna, como si no fuera más que matar un gozque [perro pequeño]. Porque los Incas nunca hizieron leyes para asombrar los vassallos ni para que burlassen dellas, sino para executarlas en los que se atreviessen a quebrantarlas.   (1: 189; bk. 4, ch. 3)

> This was the law, but it was never applied since there was no one who had broken it, because, as we have previously mentioned, the Indians of Peru were very fearful and observant of their laws, particularly those dealing with their religion or their King. But if there were any who had broken it, the law was fully applied without exception, as if it were nothing more than killing a mongrel [small dog]. Because the Incas never made laws just to impress their subjects nor to be evaded by them, but to apply the laws to those that dared to break them.

It is surprising that from the observations about the offense and offenders and their punishment the narrator moves to praising the Incas and to extolling their obedient subjects and the prevailing order in Tahuantinsuyu. Such comments could not but bring those who read *Comentarios reales* or listened to it read aloud, whether in Europe or America, to contrast the Inca past and the present Spanish rule, to wonder what had changed the law-abiding subjects of the Inca, and, if native or mestizo, to reflect on what Garcilaso often called "el bien perdido" ("the ideal world lost")—that is to say, the glorious and perfectly organized Inca empire. Through the narrator's conclusion, once more the exemplary government of the lords of Tahuantinsuyu is showcased. His assertions serve to reaffirm Inca interest in the common good and, more important, the shared origin of all human beings through their use of reason to govern the empire. However, the narrator gives the final blow to the viceregal administration by pointing out that under the impeccable Inca rule—in obvious contrast to the imperfect colonial rule—laws were promptly and fairly applied and offenders duly and swiftly punished.

The Attire and the Text

In this context, it should be noted that the remaining Inca nobility settled in colonial Cuzco continued to use garments made of *cumbi* cloth. Some were
passed from one generation to another; others were freshly woven in different
areas by artisans of various origins. These garments followed traditional patterns
but also showed new designs (Ramos 117–19). Surely their use by native nobility
served as a reminder of the ritual component of their production in Inca times
as well as of their traditional royal users. It also contributed to remembering,
from the colonial present, the aesthetic standards and affirming purposes of
these outfits in the not so distant Inca period (see Phipps, "Textiles"). All led to
the evocation of a time of glory and privilege among the surviving descendants
of Inca royalty. Thus, it might be appropriate to suggest that among the indigenous and mestizo readership of *Comentarios reales*, learning about who produced these garments and for whom would bring to mind the Inca golden age
that colonial administrators were attempting to discredit.

  Viceroy Francisco de Toledo was well aware of the power of these outfits and
thus banned the use of dress in "Inca style" in 1575, three years after the beheading of Tupac Amaru I in Cuzco square (Phipps, "Garments" 27). Two centuries later, in the context of the rebellion of Tupac Amaru II in the southern
highlands of the Viceroyalty of Peru, the inspector José Antonio de Areche recommended the prohibition of clothing and images that would evoke the past glories of Tahuantinsuyu. He also advised the Spanish king to ban the circulation
and reading of *Comentarios reales*. Carlos III turned this recommendation into
law in Aranjuez on 4 April 1782.

In *Comentarios reales* the work of women in their capacity as weavers dates back
to the origins of civilization and progress in the Andes. As for the weavers of the
Sun, the narrator lists both their perpetual virginity and the *cumbi* cloth they
produced among the wonders of Tahuantinsuyu. In the context of this section
of the chronicle, the respect for Inca law and its strict application to offenders
are equally admirable. While underscoring all of this, Garcilaso praises the virgin weavers and the centrality of their work. He goes on to establish parallels
between the women in the *acllahuasi* and three goddesses of antiquity, respectively related to governance, love, and weaving. Through this analogy the author links two empires: the Inca, destroyed before it was made known (1: 49;
bk. 1, ch. 19), and the Roman, amply described and universally acclaimed. The
implication of this juxtaposition is apparent: when the glories of Tahuantinsuyu
are told by a writer familiar with them such as Garcilaso, the ancient Inca empire could be as admired as was the Roman empire.

  When the narrator explains how such beautiful and ritualized garments are
made, he indirectly brings to the fore their imitation and use in the colonial era
by the descendants of Inca royalty. In this manner the text rearticulates the

political message sent by this fine attire during Tahuantinsuyu. Moreover, in an era of Spanish hegemony, *Comentarios reales* boldly evokes the past glories of the Inca empire. So conjoined, the garments made by the Virgins of the Sun and the text drafted by Garcilaso bring to the mind of the reader or listener (particularly if native or mestizo) a past whose currency and significance colonial administrators wished to cancel. Viewed in this manner, the segment of *Comentarios reales* dedicated to the Virgins of the Sun and weavers of his garments becomes a strategic section of the chronicle from which key ideas emanate. In these chapters, traditionally viewed as ethnographic, Garcilaso goes far beyond the description of customs and traditions. He relocates the art of weaving and the work of women in the *acllahuasi* and elsewhere—the worthy disciples of the queen Mama Ocllo—and places them at the heart of the civilizing efforts of the Incas as much as in the center of their empire and its splendor. When Garcilaso reflects on the life of women in the *acllahuasi* and on the enforcement of laws in Tahuantinsuyu, the reader or listener is able to recall an ideal Inca past and to establish a contrast with the chaotic colonial present. Through the description of a space exclusively devoted to females, the role played by the weavers of the Sun, the perfect fabrics spun by them, and the penalties imposed on those who transgressed the laws of *acllahuasi*, Garcilaso's *Comentarios reales* sends a double message: of admiration for the women weavers in Tahuantinsuyu and of censure of Spanish colonial rule.

NOTES

[1] A longer version of this essay appeared in Spanish in my *Cartografía garcilasista*.

[2] Francisca and Gonzalo Pizarro were born of this union.

[3] All translations are my own.

[4] For analyses of gender variables in Garcilaso's work, see Heid; Guardia.

[5] In *Primer nueva corónica*, Guaman Poma characterizes the *acllas* as "monjas" ("nuns") and devotes a chapter to commentary on their age, rank, and the role of each category (1: 250). Supported by the testimony of several chroniclers, Rostworowski points to five types of *acllas*, or cloistered women: *yurac aclla*, of royal Inca blood and consecrated to the Sun; *huayrur aclla*, the most beautiful, some of whom were selected by the Inca as secondary wives; *paco aclla*, destined to ethnic lords with whom the Inca wanted to establish alliances or solid links; *yana aclla*, devoted to serving; and *taqui aclla*, who sang or played musical instruments during ritual celebrations (*Historia* 227).

[6] Despite these regulations, there were transgressions. In his *Historia general del Perú*, Murúa details a mythical breach of the code between the princess Chuquillanto and the shepherd Acoitrapa and also notes how guards searched the women when entering the *acllahuasi* (1: 17–25; bk. 1, chs. 91–92). Also see the facsimile edition edited by Cummins and Ossio (Murúa, *Vida*).

[7] It is worth noting that outside of the *acllahuasi* there were noblewomen who lived as virgins who were not subject to confinement. They were awarded the honorific title of *Ocllo*. An aunt of Garcilaso's had such a title and was venerated because of her age and chastity (1: 193; bk. 4, ch. 7).

WORKS CITED

Chang-Rodríguez, Raquel. *Cartografía garcilasista*. Universidad de Alicante, 2013.

Garcilaso de la Vega. *Comentarios reales de los Incas*. 1609. Edited by Ángel Rosenblat, Emecé Editores, 1943. 2 vols.

Guaman Poma de Ayala, Felipe. *Primer nueva corónica y buen gobierno*. c. 1615. Edited by John V. Murra and Rolena Adorno, translated by Jorge L. Urioste, Siglo Veintiuno, 1980. 3 vols.

Guardia, Sara Beatriz. "Vírgenes, coyas, mujeres. Garcilaso: Una visión de género." *Actas del congreso internacional "Las palabras de Garcilaso,"* edited by Marco Martos Carrera et al., Academia Peruana de la Lengua / Universidad de San Martín de Porres / Organización de Estados Iberoamericanos, 2010, pp. 249–72.

Heid, Patricia. "Constructing a Peaceful Imperialism: Manipulating Gender Identity in the *Comentarios reales de los Incas*." *Sixteenth Century Journal*, vol. 33, no. 1, Spring 2002, pp. 93–108.

Mills, Kenneth, and William B. Taylor, editors. *Colonial Spanish America: A Documentary History*. Scholarly Resources, 2006.

Murúa, Martín de. *Historia general del Perú: Origen y descendencia de los Incas*. 1613. Edited by Manuel Ballesteros Gaibrois, Wellington ed., Instituto Gonzalo Fernández de Oviedo Galciciana, 1962–64. 2 vols.

———. *Vida y obra: Fray Martín de Murúa*. Edited by Thomas Cummins and Juan Ossio, EY Perú, 2019, www.ey.com/es_pe/growth/la-historia-en-ey.

Phipps, Elena J. "Garments and Identity in the Colonial Andes." *The Colonial Andes: Tapestries and Silverwork, 1530–1830*, edited by Phipps et al., Metropolitan Museum of Art / Yale UP, 2004, pp. 17–39.

———. "Textiles as Cultural Memory: Andean Garments in the Colonial Period." *Converging Cultures: Art and Identity in Spanish America*, edited by Diane Fane, Brooklyn Museum / Harry N. Abrams, 1996, pp. 144–56.

Ramos, Gabriela. "Los tejidos y la sociedad colonial andina." *The Power of Images: Visual Representation in New Spain and Peru*, special issue of *Colonial Latin American Review*, edited by Nancy Farriss, vol. 19, no. 1, 2010, pp. 115–49.

Rostworowski, María. *Historia del Tahuantinsuyu*. Instituto de Estudios Peruanos, 1988.

———. "La mujer antes de Pizarro." *La mujer en la historia del Perú (siglos XV al XX)*, edited by Carmen Meza and Teodoro Hampe, Fondo Editorial del Congreso del Perú, 2007, pp. 23–53.

Sarmiento de Gamboa, Pedro. *Historia índica*. c. 1572. Edited by P. Carmelo Sáenz de Santamaría, Atlas, 1965, pp. 189–279. Biblioteca de Autores Españoles 135.

Zuidema, R. Tom. "Guaman Poma and the Art of Empire: Toward an Iconography of Inca Royal Dress." *Transatlantic Encounters: Europeans and Andeans in the Sixteenth Century*, edited by Kenneth J. Andrien and Rolena Adorno, U of California P, 1991, pp. 151–202.

———. "Guaman Poma between the Arts of Europe and the Andes." *Colonial Latin American Review*, vol. 3, nos. 1–2, 1994, pp. 37–85.

Inca Garcilaso on Women

Sara V. Guengerich

A graduate seminar in colonial Spanish American literature framing the intersections of gender, power, and racial identities allows for an in-depth discussion of Inca Garcilaso de la Vega's textual treatment of women in *Comentarios reales de los Incas* (*Royal Commentaries of the Incas*) and *Historia general del Perú* (*General History of Peru*). An important goal of the course is to understand that in colonial society the contingency in relations of power produced a system where racial and gendered identities were fluid rather than fixed.

The analysis of Garcilaso's works requires at least two class periods during the term and involves the discussion of background theory as well as excerpts from other texts of the period. *Comentarios reales* and *Historia general* provide numerous examples of women as mothers, wives, and colonial subjects, which must be read with a critical eye. In a general discussion on gender organization, students come with the preconceived idea that women in colonial society—as women in other societies across time—were perpetual minors under the tutelage of fathers and then husbands with no significant agency in the public sphere. But as we examine the primary sources and later theoretical works, the students learn that this model simplifies the analysis of women in the textual sources of this period. It is essential to counterbalance this viewpoint by emphasizing that the roles of men and women are not cross-culturally interchangeable, and they must be interpreted through the specific cultural matrix in which they were produced.

To establish a theoretical framework from which to begin this analysis, I ask my students to read Michel Foucault's "The Subject of Power" and selected chapters of Joan Wallach Scott's *Gender and the Politics of History*, which generated debates and perspectives about gender as a category of historical analysis and women's history since the late 1980s. Foucault's essay theorizes that power is exercised rather than inherent. Thus, men and women can exercise and contest power through a set of discourses. Following Foucault, Scott proposes to broaden the notion of "politics" by considering all unequal relations as "political" (27). She calls readers to challenge and dismantle a set of fixed and permanent binary oppositions and argues for a deconstruction of traditional concepts of power—in particular, male power.

As students apply these theories they begin to deconstruct traditional representations of gender, power, and racial identities that emerge from Garcilaso's texts. There are several passages from *Comentarios reales* and *Historia general* that could be used to teach these themes, but for the sake of brevity, I will focus this essay on the female addressees of both works, the references to the author's feminine ancestors, and his perceptions of Spanish and Andean women in colonial society.

The Female Addressees

Students' first task is to identify the addressees of *Comentarios reales* and *Historia general* and thus to determine Garcilaso's goals. Because the titles, subtitles, and illustrations of these sections are part of those verbal and nonverbal productions, they reveal an authorial intention and provide clues to guide the interpretation of the whole text (Zanelli 69n3). *Comentarios reales* is dedicated "A la Sereníssima Princesa doña Catalina de Portugal, Duquesa de Barganza [sic]" ("To the Most Serene Princess, the Lady Catherine of Portugal, Duchess of Braganza"), whose patronage he aimed to achieve. Although there is no evidence that Garcilaso gained her favor, the fact that his entire history of the Inca past was directed to this noblewoman deserves attention.

Doña Catalina was the sister of the emperor Charles V. Her marriage to João III of Portugal was part of a complex dynastic politics aiming to unite the noble houses of Spain and Portugal. Faithful to the tradition of her family and dynasty, she spared no effort in keeping alive the alliance of Portuguese and Castilian elites. To this end, she influenced the organization and composition of the houses in both kingdoms that formed around the marriageable young princesses. Her ultimate goal was to create courtly factions in Castile and Portugal with a common sense of identity in order to produce natural successions without the need of wars. This political miscegenation contributed to the creation of common social, political, and religious characteristics during her reign (Labrador 209–10, 224).

The elite marriage politics endorsed by doña Catalina coincided with Garcilaso's underlying purpose of justifying the marriages of elite indigenous women to Spanish conquistadores, which I explore further down. Yet, in order to appeal to the reader's sense of justice in sanctioning marriages between Spanish and Andeans, he first needed to establish the nobility of his indigenous ancestry. To do that, he attempted to equate both nobility traditions according to the humanist concepts of this period.

The humanist jurists and philosophers Bartolus of Saxoferrato, Brunetto Latini, and Erasmus conceived nobility as having three aspects: theological (bestowed by God), natural (i.e., innate virtues), and civil (bestowed by the community). While Bartolus proposes a connection between these three aspects of nobility, he leaves aside a discussion of theological nobility in discerning a noble's character. In contrast, Garcilaso makes theological nobility a main element of his discourse (Campbell 178; Rodríguez 77). Let us go back to his portrayal of doña Catalina de Portugal, which serves him as an example to write about the nobility of his own mother, Chimpu Ocllo. His praises of doña Catalina affirm not only her natural nobility but also her theological being when he writes, "Pues ya si miramos el ser de la gracia con que Dios Nuestro Señor ha enriquecido el alma de Vuestra Alteza, hallaremos ser mejor que el de la naturaleza (aunque Vuestra Alteza más se encubra), de cuya santidad y virtud todo el mundo habla con admiración" ("For when we behold the great grace with which our Lord God has enriched Your Highness' soul, we find that it exceeds those natural qualities [although your Majesty may conceal herself] of piety and virtue of which the whole world speaks with admiration"; *Primera parte* 15; *Royal Commentaries* 1: 3).

If doña Catalina is an example of the union of the three aspects of nobility, Garcilaso's mother, the Inca princess Chimpu Ocllo, is another. Chimpu Ocllo was a descendant of the Inca Tupac Yupanqui who ruled in the late fifteenth century. According to Garcilaso, contrary to what most Spanish historians had related, his mother's people were essentially monotheistic and had arrived through the exercise of natural reason at knowledge of the true God. Once they converted to Catholicism through the miraculous appearance of the Virgin, they defeated the devil and accepted the true God, a new faith, and baptism. Garcilaso's mother became a devotee of the Virgin, and his father was proudly called the "comendador del Ave María" ("Knight commander of the Hail Mary"; *Historia* 20; my trans.). These were enough reasons to devote his *Historia general* to the "Reina del cielo y suelo" ("Queen of Heaven and earth"), the Virgin Mary.

The Virgin, according to Garcilaso, allowed Chimpu Ocllo to acquire a state of grace. As she converted to Catholicism her noble blood became "más ilustre y excelente por las aguas del Santo Bautismo, que por la sangre real de tantos Incas y Reyes peruanos" ("more illustrious and excellent by the waters of holy baptism than by the royal blood of so many Incas and Peruvian Kings"; *Historia* 20; my trans.). Through this statement, the representation of his mother moves from the material to the spiritual realm. Thus, she can be compared with doña Catalina, who also embodied the union of the three aspects of nobility: theological, natural, and civil.

The comparison of these women's nobility both by lineage and by the spirit is often overlooked, but it is an important reference on how Garcilaso establishes the noble lineage and worthiness of his maternal side in *Comentarios reales* as well as in *Historia general*. Moreover, it is a strategy that empowers his mother and her people to be agents of the expansion of the Christian empire in the Andes.

Lineage, Language, and Limpieza de Sangre

Garcilaso's aim to compare Andean nobles with European ones is evident in his portrayal of his feminine ancestors. But students also need to look for the disjunctions in his gendered representations. Given the fact that his father was a Spanish hidalgo with an indisputable family history, Garcilaso focuses his attention on proving his mother's pure ancestry throughout his works. In doing so, he constructs a narrative informed by discourses on blood and lineage.

My pedagogical strategy in this section hinges on a comparison between excerpts from *Comentarios reales* and *Historia general* and humanist and medical treatises of the period. In addition to Garcilaso's works, students read portions of other colonial chroniclers' accounts on similar topics. The intertextuality of these sources along with Scott's challenge of fixed binary oppositions (e.g., men/women, ruler/ruled, public/private gender spheres, etc.) help the students question the idea of traditional gender roles and read Garcilaso's works more as political discourses.

I begin this section with Garcilaso's myth of origin that narrates the arrival of Manco Capac and Mama Ocllo, the first royal Inca couple, in *Comentarios reales*. The students read it in tandem with excerpts from Spanish authors such as Juan Luis Vives, Fray Luis de León, Juan de Betanzos, and Pedro Sarmiento de Gamboa. According to Garcilaso, the arrival of the first royal Inca couple helped "civilize" the pre-Inca Andean peoples. While Manco Capac instructed all the men, Mama Ocllo educated all the female population, teaching them "a hilar y tejer y criar sus hijos y a servir sus maridos con amor y regalo y todo lo demás que una buena mujer debe hacer en su casa" ("to spin, weave, bring up their children, and serve their husbands with love and joy, and everything else that a good wife should do at home"; *Primera parte* 69; *Royal Commentaries* 1: 67).

Spinning and weaving were considered the first "civilized" occupation of women, followed by raising their children and serving their husbands. Garcilaso's ideas about young women's first exercises are consistent with what Vives proposed for women's education in his book *Instrucción de la mujer cristiana*, an influential conduct manual for women. Vives writes:

> En la edad en que la muchacha pareciera apta para las letras y el conocimiento de las cosas, comience por aprender aquellas que al cultivo del alma pertenecen y las que conciernen al régimen y gobierno de la casa. . . . Aprenderá pues la muchacha, al mismo tiempo que las letras, a traer en sus manos la lana y el lino, dos artes que aquella famosa edad dorada y aquel siglo inocuo enseñaron a la posteridad, convenientísimas a la economía doméstica, conservadoras de la frugalidad, de la cual conviene sobremanera que sean las mujeres curiosas guardadoras. . . .   (92)

> When the young woman is ready to learn about letters and many other things, she should start learning those activities concerning the good governance of the house. . . . The young woman will learn to carry wool and linen in her hands, two activities that that famous golden age and that innocent century taught for posterity, so opportune for the household economy and to maintain frugality, and over which women should be in charge. . . .   (my trans.)

While Vives's conduct manual emphasizes the importance of these activities to the increment of a woman's family's estate, León adds that for women, "[el] servir al marido, y el gobernar la familia, y la crianza de los hijos . . . se debe al temor de Dios . . . todo lo cual pertenece al estado y oficio de la mujer casada"

("serving one's husband and administering the family and the raising of children
are the actions of one who is God-fearing . . . all of which are the duties of a
married woman"; 207; my trans). In comparing Mama Ocllo with the Christian
ideal of womanhood, Garcilaso suggests that it was her example that made the
rest of Inca women live exemplary lives.

His portrayal of the proto-Christian Mama Ocllo, however, is a willful oblit-
eration of other Inca myths of origin that offer a clashing version of the female
founders of Cuzco. Part 1, chapter 6, from Betanzos's *Narrative of the Incas* and
chapter 11 of Sarmiento de Gamboa's *History of the Incas* narrate a different
version of the Incas' origin, the Ayar siblings myth. According to these chroniclers, the four Ayar brothers, together with their sister-wives, left their place of
birth in search of fertile lands to settle. The students focus their attention on
Mama Huaco, the more forceful and bellicose of the sisters, who not only be-
rated her husband but also struck a man from a town near Cuzco and killed him
with a stone flung from her sling. She then split open this man's chest, took out
his lungs and heart, blew into the lungs to make them swell up, and displayed
them to the inhabitants of the town. The people fled in horror and fear, and the
group proceeded on to Cuzco.

As we discuss Betanzos's and Sarmiento de Gamboa's agendas in the portrayal
of the Incas, we also acknowledge the resilience of the oral tradition manifested
through these Spanish chroniclers' native informants. For the Andean informants
who repeated their oral narratives to these chroniclers, Mama Huaco may have
been a symbol of military, religious, or political power rather than a submissive
figure. Garcilaso's dismissal of Mama Huaco in favor of Mama Ocllo fashions a
process of gender transculturation where the gender anxieties caused by the former are domesticated by the latter.

In his narrative, Mama Ocllo, a figure from "time immemorial," sets an example for all Inca women with an emphasis on virginity, chastity, and exemplary
motherhood. Following her example, some Andean women such as the *acllakuna*
(women devoted to the cult of the Sun) became perpetual virgins. Others, such
as the Ocllo women, preferred living a virtuous life in and outside their homes.
The Ocllo women, writes Garcilaso,

> eran tenidas en grandísima veneración por su castidad y *limpieza* y por su
> *excelencia y deidad* las llamaban *Ocllo*, que era como nombre consagrado
> en su idolatría. . . . Yo alcancé a conocer una de éstas . . . [que] algunas
> veces visitaba a mi madre y, según entendí, era su tía, hermana de sus
> abuelos. . . .   (*Primera parte* 182; my emphasis)

> were greatly respected for their chastity and *high-mindedness*, as a mark
> of their *excellence and divinity* they were called *Ocllo*, a name held sa-
> cred in their idolatry. . . . I myself knew one of these women . . . she some-
> times visited my mother, and I understood she was her great-aunt, a sister
> to her grandparents. . . .   (*Royal Commentaries* 1: 204; my emphasis)

Not surprisingly, some of these excellent and divine women were his mother's ancestors, which once again legitimizes the historical figure of Chimpu Ocllo as an Inca princess in a state of grace. The allusions to the *limpieza* of the Ocllo women, and thus of his mother, serves to direct the class discussion toward discourses on purity of lineage.

The concept of *limpieza*, which originated in late medieval Castile, refers to "purity of blood." By the mid-sixteenth century, the ideology of purity of blood had produced a Spanish society obsessed with genealogy, in particular with the idea that having only Christian ancestors was a critical sign of a person's loyalty to the faith (Martínez 1). In the religious and medical contexts of this period, blood and other bodily fluids were thought to contribute to a child's physiology as well as his or her moral and psychological traits.

Theories inspired by the Greek physician Galen held that maternal blood nourished the child both inside and outside the womb, because breast milk was transformed menstrual fluid, or "blood twice cooked" (Martínez 48). According to these theories, a child acquired his purity of blood from his mother's milk. Garcilaso adapts this idea in his text to refer to his mother's role in his early life. His repeated assertion "esta lengua que mamé en la leche" ("the language I imbibed in my mother's milk"), which refers to his competency in the Quechua language, plays an important semantic role not only for its linguistics value but also for its capacity to define lineage.

As far as its linguistics value, as Margarita Zamora has shown, Garcilaso builds his authority as a native Quechua speaker among the Spanish chroniclers who barely comprehended the rudiments of the language. His insistence on his identity as a native speaker of Quechua and on his faithfulness to the original language in the translation of Quechua terminology, as well as the presentation of his narrative, point to his affiliation with a philosophy of language that is clearly humanist.

His adherence to humanism is also visible in the importance he gives to maternal breastfeeding in forming the moral and social identity of children. Authors such as León, Vives, Antonio de Guevara, and Pedro de Luján had begun an intense campaign against wet nurses and mothers who avoided breastfeeding (Rivera 208). Like them, Garcilaso repeatedly returns to this theme. He praises Inca women, particularly the female nobility, for breastfeeding their children. His text reads, "La madre propia criaba su hijo; no se permitía darlo a criar, por gran señora que fuese, si no era por enfermedad" ("The mother reared the child herself, and never gave it out to nurse, even if she were a great lady, unless she were ill"; *Primera parte* 188; *Royal Commentaries* 1: 212). Here Garcilaso argues that Inca women had always breastfed their children because they were good mothers who already practiced what the European humanists wanted all women to do.

As good mothers they could also be good wives, and together with the noble Spaniards, they would expand the Christian empire in America. Nonetheless, because of the concern over the purity of bloodlines, Spanish men preferred to marry the few young Spanish women who arrived in the New World before the 1560s. An interesting episode in Garcilaso's *Historia general* serves to contrast the idealized image of Inca women from the *Comentarios reales* with the wickedness of some Spanish women. Julie Johnson examines the episode of the return of the Spanish conquistador Pedro de Alvarado and his new Spanish wife to Guatemala, bringing along several young women from the Iberian Peninsula to become Alvarado's comrades' wives. During the festivities for these unions, the young Spanish women gaze out across the hall at their future husbands and express their shock at the broken-down condition of the old soldiers. Speaking of these "brave men," the women converse with each other, saying:

> —Dicen que nos hemos de casar con estos conquistadores.
> Dijo otra:
> —¿Con estos viejos podridos nos habíamos de casar? cásese quien quisiere, que yo por cierto no pienso casar con ninguno de ellos. Dolos al Diablo; parece que escaparon del infierno. . . .   (*Historia* 118)

> —They say we have to marry those conquerors.
> Another answered:
> —Are we going to marry those broken down old creatures? You can marry who you like, but I certainly don't intend to marry any of them. They can go to the devil: they are in such a state that they look as if they had escaped from hell. . . .   (*Royal Commentaries* 2: 733)

The women proceed to enumerate the soldiers' deformities:

> —[E]stán estropeados: unos cojos y otros mancos, otros sin orejas, otros con un ojo, otros con media cara, y el mejor librado la tiene cruzada una y dos y más veces.
> Dijo la primera:
> —No hemos de casar con ellos por su gentileza, sino por heredar los indios que tienen, que, según están viejos y cansados se han de morir presto, y entonces podremos escoger el mozo que quisiéremos en lugar del viejo, como suelen trocar una caldera vieja y rota por otra sana y nueva.
>   (*Historia* 118)

> —Some are lame and have some arms missing, and some ears, and some an eye, and some half their faces, and the best-looking of them has got one or two scars across his face.
> The first said:
> —We're not going to marry them for their looks, but to inherit their Indians: they are so old and worn out, they are certain to die soon, and then we can choose whatever young men we please instead of these dotards, like changing an old broken pan for a new whole one.
>   (*Royal Commentaries* 2: 733–34)

As Johnson notes, these exchanges, particularly the conversations among the Spanish women, are invented by Garcilaso to portray the surreptitious meeting between these "great heroes" and their future wives, "demonstrat[ing] a surprising boldness, lust for life, and outright greed on the part of the women" (27).

In reading these fabricated oppositions of good (Andean) and evil (Spanish) women in Garcilaso's works, the students are able to identify his underlying purpose, which is to demonstrate that a stable colonial society could emerge only from a fusion of Andean and European cultures in which noble Andeans and their descendants played the prominent role of expanding the Christian Spanish empire in America.

Women in Colonial Society

Garcilaso's vision of a stable society necessarily accompanies his criticism of the colonial world. Both the *Comentarios reales* and the *Historia general* provide an overview of colonial society as a disorderly space. Garcilaso complains that in colonial society the patterns of social rank and stratification among the Indians had been extensively reshuffled. In the early years of the seventeenth century, he writes, the Inca insignia made of *corequenque* (mountain caracara) feathers was being donned by plebeians. He recounts the episode of a commoner woman trying to pass as a descendant of the royal Inca elite by dressing as an Inca princess (*palla*). This story, he says, happened in Potosí around 1554:

> [H]ubo un papagayo de los que llaman loro, tan hablador, que a los indios e indias que pasaban por la calle les llamaba por sus provincias, a cada uno de la nación que era, sin errar alguna, diciendo Colla, Yunca, Huayru, Quechua, etc., como que tuviera noticia de las diferencias de tocados que los indios, en tiempo de los Incas, traían en las cabezas para ser conocidos. Un día de aquéllos pasó una india hermosa por la calle donde el papagayo estaba; iba con tres o cuatro criadas, haciendo mucho de la señora Palla, que son las de la sangre real. En viéndola el papagayo, dio grandes gritos de risa, diciendo "¡Huayru, Huayru, Huayru!", que es una nación de gente más vil y tenida en menos que otras. La india pasó avergonzada por los que estaban delante, que siempre había una gran cuadrilla de indios escuchando el pájaro; y cuando llegó cerca, escupió hacia el papagayo y le llamó zúpay, que es diablo. Los indios dijeron lo mismo, porque conoció a la india, con ir disfrazada en hábito de Palla.   (*Primera parte* 439)

> There was a parrot that spoke so well that when the Indian men and women passed by in the street it would call them by their respective tribes, saying "Colla," "Yunca," "Huayru," "Quechua," and so on, without any mistakes, as if it realized the meaning of the different headgear they used to wear in Inca times to distinguish themselves. One day a beautiful Indian woman passed down the street where the parrot was: she was

> attended by three or four servants, who treated her as a lady *palla*, or
> member of the royal blood. When the parrot saw her, it shrieked and
> laughed: "Huayru, Huayru, Huayru!" the name of the tribe that is looked
> down on by all the rest. The woman was very much humbled in front of
> the bystanders, for there was always a crowd of Indians listening to the
> bird. When she was opposite it, she spat at the bird and called it *súpay*,
> "devil." The Indians said the same, for it recognized the woman though
> she was disguised as a *palla*.   (*Royal Commentaries* 1: 525–26)

As fictional as this episode might be, it reveals a very real social pattern in colonial society. Indians ranked at the bottom of the social hierarchy took advantage of the flexibility of colonial society to pass as nobles, and they did so with
ease. Although the author, through the use of poetic justice, tells the readers
that in this case the deceitful *palla* was denounced, the colonial reality was another story. As Karen Graubart states, wearing the visual symbols of the vanquished rulers had great power for indigenous men and women struggling to as-
sert their status in the colonial hierarchy, as Inca costumes were evidence of
noble status and exception from tribute (137).

In examining Garcilaso's complaints about the fluidity of colonial society, I
also direct students' attention to episodes featuring a Black woman wearing pearls
(*Primera parte* 443; *Royal Commentaries* 1: 531), Spanish women disavowing
their husbands who wanted them to come to Peru (*Historia* 699; *Royal Commentaries* 2: 1424), and an Inca woman rejecting an imposed marriage with a
Spaniard (*Historia* 544; *Royal Commentaries* 2: 1230), because these are good
examples of how colonial subjects, including women from different ethnicities,
exercised power in colonial society.

In analyzing the textual treatment of women in these works, students gain a better understanding of Garcilaso and his intellectual and cultural environment. They
also learn to deconstruct his traditional representations of gender by comparing or
contrasting them with other discourses of the period. Reading Garcilaso's works
along with the humanist medical and religious treatises of this era unveils the process of intertextuality that lies at the heart of his goal of "vindicating the conquered
in the aggressor's own terms" (Zamora 9). Contrasting his texts with those of Betanzos and Sarmiento de Gamboa, the students become aware that gender roles are
not cross-culturally interchangeable. Finally, reading the various examples of
women's agency in the colonial world allows for a discussion of power within a system where racial and gendered identities were fluid rather than fixed.

WORKS CITED

Anadón, José, editor. *Garcilaso Inca de la Vega: An American Humanist*. U of Notre
    Dame P, 1998.
Betanzos, Juan de. *Narrative of the Incas*. 1557. Translated and edited by Ronald
    Hamilton and Dana Buchanan, U of Texas P, 1996.

Campbell, Thomas P. *Tapestry in the Renaissance: Art and Magnificence.* Metropolitan Museum of Art / Yale UP, 2002.

Foucault, Michel. "The Subject and Power." *Critical Inquiry*, vol. 8, no. 4, Summer 1982, pp. 777–95.

Garcilaso de la Vega. *Historia general del Perú.* Viuda de Andrés Barrera, 1617.

———. *Primera parte de los* Comentarios reales. Pedro Crasbeeck, 1609.

———. *Royal Commentaries of the Incas and General History of Peru.* Translated by Harold V. Livermore, U of Texas P, 1966. 2 vols.

Graubart, Karen B. *With Our Labor and Sweat: Indigenous Women and the Formation of Colonial Society in Peru, 1550–1700.* Stanford UP, 2007.

Johnson, Julie Greer. *Women in Colonial Spanish American Literature: Literary Images.* Greenwood Press, 1983.

Labrador, Félix. "La casa de la reina Catalina de Portugal: Estructura y facciones políticas (1550–1560)." *Miscelánea Comillas*, vol. 61, no. 118, Spring 2003, pp. 203–52.

León, Luis de. *Obras completas castellanas de Fray Luis de León.* Edited by Félix García, Biblioteca de Autores Cristianos, 1944.

Martínez, María Elena. *Genealogical Fictions:* Limpieza de Sangre, *Religion, and Gender in Colonial Mexico.* Stanford UP, 2008.

Rivera, Olga. "La leche materna y el sujeto de los descendientes en *La perfecta casada.*" *Hispanic Review*, vol. 70, no. 2, Spring 2002, pp. 207–17.

Rodríguez Garrido, José A. "Garcilaso Inca and the Tradition of *Viri Illustres* (Dedication and Prologue of the *Royal Commentaries*, Part II)." Anadón, pp. 71–89.

Sarmiento de Gamboa, Pedro. *History of the Incas.* Translated by Clements Markham, Dover, 1999.

Scott, Joan Wallach. *Gender and the Politics of History.* Columbia UP, 1988.

Vives, Juan Luis. *Instrucción de la mujer cristiana.* c. 1500. Espasa Calpe, 1940.

Zamora, Margarita. *Language, Authority, and Indigenous History in the* Comentarios reales de los Incas. Cambridge UP, 1988.

Zanelli, Carmela. "The Virgin Mary and the Possibility of Conciliation of Distinctive Cultural Traditions in the *General History of Peru.*" Anadón, pp. 59–70.

THE *ROYAL COMMENTARIES*, LANGUAGE, AND VISUAL REPRESENTATION

Inca Garcilaso and the Power of Language

Margarita Zamora

Against the vast backdrop of historical writing on the Spanish empire, Inca Garcilaso's *Comentarios reales de los Incas* stands out for its focus on and sensitivity to the myriad ways in which language expresses and imposes relations of domination and subordination, asymmetrical access to authority and agency, and inequalities in the social fabric. Replete with examples of the many ways in which words can be used to compel and constrain, intimidate and abuse, deride and condescend, Garcilaso's history of Peru can be read as an indictment of Spanish colonial language practices and policies.

In the *Comentarios reales*, he grapples with the forces of language at work in the colonial exchange—at times explicitly, but also through vivid literary renderings. Among the most striking of these is the interpolated story of the shipwreck of Pedro Serrano in the early chapters of the history of pre-Hispanic Peru (Garcilaso bk. 1, ch. 8). A metaphor for the historic encounter of Europeans and Amerindians, the story highlights the spoken word as an essential tool for survival, facilitating recognition of a shared humanity and the creation of a community, in the absence of which fear and conflict reign. The permanence, and therefore superiority, of writing as a vehicle for historical memory, but also its limitations with respect to the Quechua oral narratives, is addressed in "Proemio al lector" ("Prologue to the Reader"), a reflection on the Incan and European genres of history. In the story of the Indian porters transporting melons for a Spaniard, the invoice they are also carrying, together with their ignorance of writing, gives away the Indians' illicit consumption of two of the tempting fruit, exposing the power of the written word as an instrument of surveillance and control (bk. 9, ch. 29).

Perhaps the most penetrating look at language's force appears in book 9, chapter 31, of the *Comentarios reales*, where Garcilaso discusses colonial racial slurs. He had addressed these terms years earlier in *La Florida del Inca*, where the definitions provided are remarkably value neutral, as if intentionally sanitized of their derogatory intent. The same terms are revisited in the context of Peruvian history. This time, however, the definitions and commentary are strikingly different in tone and tenor. Garcilaso's voice becomes sharply contentious, underlining the stigmatizing aspects of the racist terminology and, at the same time, deploying an array of rhetorical devices to counter them. From the chapter's ironic opening sentence pairing as "imports" of equal value Black African slaves and Spanish conquistadores, Garcilaso moves methodically from one racial category to the next, eschewing the neutrality of the definitions in *La Florida* in favor of a critical attitude that ranges from ironic to sarcastic to blatantly confrontational. At times he simply underscores the derogatory connotations of a particular term: "A los hijos de éstos [los mulatos] llaman cholo; es vocablo de la isla de Barlovento; quiere decir perro, no de los castizos, sino de los muy bellacos gozcones; y los españoles usan de él por infamia y vituperio" ("Their children [of mulattoes] are called *cholo*; it is a word from the Virgin Islands; it means dog, not the pure bred but the rogue mutt; and the Spanish use it to dishonor and insult"; 2: 279).[1] At other times he counters racist language with a passionate defense of racial diversity and human dignity, most notably in his commentary on the term *mestizo*: "me lo llamo yo a boca llena, y me honro con él. Aunque en Indias, si a uno de ellos le dicen 'sois un mestizo' o 'es un mestizo', lo toman por menosprecio." ("I call myself [mestizo] openly and honor myself with that term. Although in the Indies, if someone says 'you are a mestizo' or 'he is a mestizo,' it is taken as disparaging"; 2: 279).

Linguistic considerations are at the heart of Garcilaso's historiographical project. In his prologue, he proposes a reinterpretation of the Spanish version of the history of the Incas, explaining precisely how he intends to proceed in his corrective revision. Much of the confusion, errors of interpretation, and vagueness in the Spanish histories, he notes, were the result of linguistic incompetence. Therefore, he offers himself, a native speaker of Quechua, to accurately translate and reinterpret many Quechua terms that the Spanish had misunderstood.[2] In a second prefatory chapter, "Advertencias acerca de la lengua general de los indios" ("Caveats about the General Language of the Indians"), he explains many of the specific characteristics of the Quechua language that confounded the Spanish, resulting in gross errors of interpretation.

As one continues reading, however, it becomes evident that Garcilaso's historiographical project is not confined to glossing and correcting common linguistic errors made by the Spanish historians. Instead, having established his linguistic authority over them, citing them only when correcting them or to corroborate his own narration of events, he undertakes a comprehensive reinterpretation of Inca history. Relying on the Quechua oral narratives he heard from his Inca elders in his youth and the supplemental information he obtained from his former Peruvian schoolmates, like himself native speakers of Quechua, Garcilaso fashions an unprecedented argument for his privileged access to historical truth and the historiographical authority to undertake a reinterpretation of the place of the Inca empire in world history.

At first glance, the argument appears straightforward enough: being a native speaker of the Quechua language afforded him a better understanding of the traditional narratives in which the Incas preserved their past than the Spanish historians were capable of. Garcilaso was acutely aware, nevertheless, that in Spanish colonial culture for a mestizo or an Indian to speak of language, authority, history, and truth was fraught with risks. Each one of those concepts was bound up with the Hapsburg ideology of empire and the institutions of the colonial state and, therefore, freighted with a thorny ideological charge. Considering why Garcilaso chose to build his revisionist historiographical discourse on Peru around those concepts promises to shed light on the resulting text and the profound connection between language and power in the colonial Hispanic world during the sixteenth and early seventeenth centuries.

That Garcilaso wields language ideologically, to give value to his historical work, should be evident enough by this point. What remains to be considered are the ways in which he wields language to attain agency and authority sufficient to criticize the conquest and colonial practices all the while correcting the canonical Spanish historians. What remains to be seen, in other words, is how Garcilaso establishes his position in the colonial intellectual field to counter competing versions of Inca history and culture. The question is hardly academic. The real-world stakes for the mestizo pro-Inca writer were enormous. Among the most critical were the freedom of expression without censorship, censure, or punishment; the ability to publish the work; market success and recognition by peers; and the attainment of the less tangible cultural capital of fame so coveted in the Renaissance. Although more difficult to weigh, the personal stakes of Garcilaso's Andean affections, loyalties, and commitments are palpable throughout the *Comentarios reales* and cannot be disregarded.

Little is known about Garcilaso's formal education other than what can be gleaned from the occasional autobiographical comments on the subject in his published works and personal correspondence. In a letter dated 1592 addressed to the antiquarian Juan Fernández Franco, he alluded to sporadic study of Latin up to the age of fourteen, after which time the last of the Spanish tutors who instructed the young mestizos of Cuzco left Peru. In the face of the increasing violence of the Peruvian civil wars, the students were forced to abandon their studies and dedicate themselves to the exercise of arms and horses. At his father's death, Garcilaso inherited a modest sum to travel to Spain. There is no evidence that upon his arrival there he made any effort to pursue a formal education. We know that he settled in Andalusia in 1560, where he eventually endeavored to make a name for himself fighting in the Wars of the Alpujarras. He describes his acquisition of the knowledge necessary for his literary and historiographical endeavors with an exquisite sense of irony, explaining that the scant recognition he received from the king for his efforts against the rebellious Moriscos, compounded by the idleness of civilian life, impelled him to study and write in order employ his time honorably.

What we know of Garcilaso's life as a translator and author suggests that he was essentially an autodidact. The lack of a formal education notwithstanding, his personal library, his intellectual friendships, and his own works place him in the humanist intellectual elite of Andalusia. Among the notable humanist scholars in Garcilaso's circle of acquaintances, the names of Ambrosio de Morales and Bernardo de Aldrete stand out. The former was a renowned humanist and historian, an eminent scholar at the University of Alcalá, who was residing at Córdoba when he became acquainted with Garcilaso's translation into Spanish of León Hebreo's Neoplatonic masterpiece *Dialoghi d'amore.* According to Garcilaso, Morales "honored me to the extent of adopting me as his son and accepting my work as his own" (qtd. in Varner 303). Aldrete, a canon of the Cathedral of Córdoba and a renowned philologist, had read versions of *Comentarios reales* years before it was published and cites Garcilaso in his *Del origen y principio de la lengua castellana* on the origins of the word *Perú.*[3] The inventory of the books that were in Garcilaso's possession at the time of his death in 1616 confirms a predilection for authors of the Italian Renaissance and classical rhetoric, including the treatises of Aristotle and Cicero and *De arte rhetorica* of Francisco de Castro, tellingly dedicated to Garcilaso by the author. The inventory also records an abundant number of titles on European and New World historiography, as well as numerous religious works, as would be expected of an educated Christian of that time. The languages and works represented in his library suggest that Garcilaso was comfortable reading in Latin, Italian, and French, as well as Quechua.

Garcilaso's European, book-centered education was preceded by what he refers to as the "pláticas" of the Inca elders that routinely took place in his presence at his mother's house (bk. 1, ch. 15). In English translation the term can be rendered as conversation, talk, or lecture. In Garcilaso's use of the term, the didactic connotations prevail as he describes how his great-uncle instructed him on the history of the Inca empire and its traditions and advised him to commit this learning to memory. The extent to which the young mestizo assimilated these lessons in the Quechua traditions and the techniques of oral memory was profound, allowing him to incorporate his uncle's narratives on Inca history in the *Comentarios reales*, faithfully translating extensive portions:

> Esta larga relación del origen de sus Reyes me dio aquel Inca, tío de mi madre, a quien yo se la pedí, la cual he procurado traducir fielmente de mi lengua materna, que es la del Inca, en la ajena, que es la castellana,

aunque no la he escrito con la majestad de palabras que el Inca habló ni
con toda la significación de las de aquel lenguaje tienen, que, por ser tan
significativo, pudiera haberse extendido mucho más de lo que se ha hecho.
(1: 42; bk. 1, ch. 17)

This lengthy narrative about the origins of their Kings was given to me
by that Inca, my mother's uncle, from whom I requested it, which I have
tried to translate faithfully from my maternal tongue, which is that of
the Inca, to the foreign one, which is Castilian, although I have not written
it with the majesty of the words spoken by the Inca, or the full signification that the words have in that language, which is so rich in meaning that
this account could have been a lot longer than it is.

Equally important as his mastery of Incan knowledge and oral memorization
is the fact that he considered it essential to his later intellectual endeavors as
literate historian and interpreter in Spanish of the pre-Hispanic Incan world.

Considering Garcilaso's intellectual sphere of influences yields one of the keys
to understanding his works. It reveals that he was exercised by language writ
large, viewed through the dual lenses of Andean oral culture and Renaissance
humanism. The array of concerns he addressed—the rhetorical force of language
and its myriad cultural manifestations, the commensurability of languages, translation between diverse tongues, philology and hermeneutics, and the place of
language in historiographical analysis and interpretation—betrays the breadth
and diversity of his knowledge and intellectual sophistication. It also marks him
as a consummate humanist, albeit with a decisively novel twist. His early life in
Peru as a bilingual and bicultural native speaker of Quechua enhanced his understanding of the strengths of alphabetic language with a deep appreciation for
the majesty and density of signification in the Quechua oral tradition as he strove
to capture historical truths. His experiences serving as personal secretary to his
conquistador father and as interpreter in the language of the Spanish colonial
system for his maternal Incan relatives must have heightened Garcilaso's awareness of a fundamental linguistic paradox: the creative and destructive forces at
work in and through language as social and political instrument. This discussion on the question of language in Garcilaso's works, therefore, is focused on
how Garcilaso's commentaries on the oral and written word engage with the dynamics of power inherent to Spanish colonialism.

Once the military conquest was achieved, the destructive forces at work in
the colonial enterprise were aimed at Inca culture, working through the imposition of the Spanish language, evangelization, and alphabetic writing to disrupt
and suppress the transmission and preservation of indigenous traditions. Garcilaso was acutely aware that diglossia reigned in the colonial Andes. Two disparate worldviews and their respective linguistic systems, *castilla-simi* (the language of Castile) and *runa-simi* (the language of the Quechua people), coexisted,

but only in the vertical and asymmetrical relations imposed by colonialism. The general language of the Inca empire had become under colonialism disdained and disregarded in all but the most utilitarian situations and functions. Thus, while the colonial Church made Quechua the official vehicle of catechization, blending its various dialects, rendering it alphabetic, and requiring it of those seeking ordination, it subordinated it to Castilian and Latin. Quechua also had a role to play in the juridical system of the República de Indios, the separate administrative unit established for Indian governance. In both of these arenas, knowledge of colonial Quechua was necessary, rendering it a worthy object of formal study yet ancillary to Castilian and its accepted uses circumscribed.[4] Moreover, as Garcilaso argued in his "Advertencias," colonial Quechua was not the same as the language spoken in Incan times but a bastardized form, corrupted by the linguistic incompetence of the Spanish and prescriptively discouraged usage and standardized to suit the colonial exchange.[5]

Although Garcilaso does not mention it in the prefatory chapter on the Quechua language, elsewhere in the *Comentarios reales* he shows how the breakdown of Inca cultural hegemony under colonialism led to linguistic chaos in the multiethnic world of Peru. The devastating effects of conquest on language as a means of effective communication is nowhere more evident than in the emblematic case of the mistranslation performed by the Indian Felipillo, brought by the conquistadores to serve as interpreter in the encounter between Francisco Pizarro and Atahuallpa at Cajamarca. The incident is narrated in part 2, book 1, chapters 19–28, of Garcilaso's history of Peru, devoted to the conquest and colonization of Tahuantinsuyu. Felipillo was not an ethnic Inca or even a competent speaker of Quechua, but a Puná islander of Tumbez ethnicity, a people who had successfully resisted conquest by the Incas. Garcilaso's contempt for this incompetent translator, who knew as little Spanish as he did Quechua, is matched only by his scorn of the Spanish for bringing a person of such scant linguistic abilities to mediate the momentous first diplomatic exchange between Pizarro and the Inca emperor. The communicative debacle that ensued, Garcilaso lamented, had ended in the massacre of more than five thousand Indians, many of them mere bystanders, and the arrest of Atahuallpa.

Tellingly, Garcilaso acknowledges that his revision of the Spanish accounts of the disastrous encounter at Cajamarca was based on eyewitness information recorded by the mestizo priest and Quechua native speaker Blas Valera and the quipu of Cajamarca, the knotted and colored cords with which native Andeans recorded their history—that is to say, on the oral testimony of the witnesses and the Quechua narratives that interpreted the information contained in the quipu. This privileging of oral sources in Quechua to revise Spanish written versions of the historic encounter at Cajamarca is not an isolated case but the rule throughout the *Comentarios reales*, most consistently and systematically applied to the task of accessing the truth about the history of Tahuantinsuyu before the arrival of the Spanish. In fact, Garcilaso goes so far as to affirm the centrality of the

Quechua sources and to explain when and how he obtained them. Premier among them were the Inca oral narratives of Cuzco he heard from his revered great-uncle Cusi Huallpa, which according to Garcilaso served as the source text for his reinterpretation of Inca history and culture.[6] These were supplemented by the narratives of other provinces, obtained by the historian from former schoolmates whose Indian mothers were not natives of Cuzco.

Although the Quechua narratives identified in the text as the privileged sources of Inca history were undoubtedly grounded in the pre-Hispanic Andean oral tradition, the intellectual work performed by Garcilaso with those sources was informed by the Renaissance humanist understanding of language, history, and the historiographical concept of truth that linked them. His sense of how the word becomes a privileged vehicle for gaining access to a past reality, a tool for rendering it in an authentic form in the present, and a means for mediating its interpretation is informed by the Renaissance traditions of text restoration, translation, and exegesis most closely associated with the humanist disciplines of grammar (understood as the historical study of a language through its canonical texts), rhetoric, and philology. This was precisely the work that attracted and elicited the admiration of Andalusian humanists like Aldrete and Morales, establishing Garcilaso as an authoritative voice on Inca history in Spain, in the Indies, and throughout Europe.

The historiographical applications of humanist philology had important European precedents in the works of the Italian Lorenzo Valla and the Frenchman Jean Bodin.[7] Closer to home, Garcilaso's association with a group of Andalusian intellectuals that included the Jesuit philologists and biblical scholars Jerónimo de Prado, Juan Bautista Villalpando, Juan de Pineda, and Pedro Maldonado de Saaevedra played a key role in the development of his philological acumen. Garcilaso's work was unique, however, in approaching an indigenous language philologically to derive conclusions about historiographical truth supported strictly on oral linguistic evidence. Working with his recollection of the oral narratives of Cuzco and the written versions of the provincial histories of the empire he obtained from former Peruvian schoolmates, Garcilaso crafted a version of Inca history grounded in the authority of the original language sources. This allowed him to claim a distinct advantage over the Spanish historians, whose linguistic limitations allowed them only a partial and inevitably inaccurate access to the historical truth. As Garcilaso the humanist philologist understood it, the creative linguistic force was channeled through the original language of a given culture. The essential link between knowledge of reality and its expression in words resided in the native language in which it was first thought and articulated. From this perspective, Quechua (as spoken by the Inca elite) came into view as both the vehicle of Incan knowledge and the privileged medium to access truth about Tahuantinsuyu and its history. As such, it was indispensable for understanding the world the Spanish aimed to transform and incorporate into Christendom and their new transatlantic empire.

In his "Advertencias," Garcilaso shows how ignorance of Quechua phonetics could lead to linguistic corruptions and errors of translation and interpretation. Throughout *Comentarios reales* he gives numerous examples of specific words that were misunderstood and corrupted by the Spanish. But the key to his historiographical methodology lies in the application of humanist philology to the reinterpretation of Andean history. Through a narrative that often reads like a philological exegesis on the Quechua oral version of the history of the Inca empire, Garcilaso develops a nexus of commentaries supporting an increasingly formidable argument on the fundamental connection between the original language and historical truth. Some have argued that the term *commentaries* in the title signals Garcilaso's adherence to the historical genre famously cultivated by Julius Caesar in *Commentaries on the Gallic Wars*. Readers familiar with both texts, however, are likely to notice more differences than similarities between the "simple narrative of events in a taut, concise style similar to that of the Ionic scientific notes" (Struever 31) characterizing Caesar's historiographical commentary and the fullness, copiousness, and didacticism of the full-scale history (*magistra vitae*) modeled in *Comentarios reales*. Garcilaso's commentaries—philological in form and hermeneutical and didactic in intent—create a hybrid historiographical discourse with the aim of accessing a previously elusive historical truth.

One of the most daring and consequential reinterpretations of Inca history and culture addresses the thorny question of pre-Hispanic religious thought and Spanish justifications for its eradication. Speaking about the temple of Pachacamac in the valley of the same name, and referring to the misconceptions of the renowned historians Pedro de Cieza de León and Jerónimo Román, who had interpreted this deity as demonic, Garcilaso counters that Pachacamac was the expression of an incipient monotheism. The Incas, he argued, approaching the concept of the true (Christian) God through the exercise of natural reason alone, as this name demonstrates, paved the way for the Spanish evangelization. He initiates the argument with a grammatical and semantic analysis of the proper Quechua name:

> Pachacámac: es nombre compuesto de *Pacha*, que es mundo universo, y de *Cámac*, participio presente del verbo *cama*, que es animar, el cual verbo se deduze del nombre *cama*, que es ánima. Pachacámac quiere dezir el que da ánima al mundo universo, y en toda su propia significación quiere dezir el que haze con el universo lo que el ánima con el cuerpo.
>
> (1: 62; bk. 2, ch. 2)

> Pachacamac: it is a noun composed of *Pacha*, which means "world universe," and *Cámac*, present participle of the verb *cama*, meaning "soul." Pachacamac means "he who gives soul to the world universe," and in its complete and proper signification means "he who does for the universe what the soul does for the body."

By means of a comparative philological exegesis of the original term contrasted to the Spanish corruptions, he then reveals its full semantic range and true signification, concluding that

> Pero si a mí, que soy indio cristiano católico, por la infinita misericordia, me preguntasen ahora "¿cómo se llama Dios en tu lengua?", diría "Pachacámac", porque en aquel general lenguaje del Perú no hay otro nombre para nombrar a Dios sino éste, y todos los demás que los historiadores dicen son generalmente impropios, porque o no son del general lenguaje o son corruptos con el lenguaje de algunas provincias particulares o nuevamente compuestos por los españoles.   (1: 63; bk. 2, ch. 2)

> But if one were to now ask me, who am a Christian Catholic Indian, through infinite mercy, "What is God called in your language?" I would say "Pachacamac," because in that general language of Peru there is no other name for God but this one, and all the other ones that the Spanish historians use are either corrupted with the language of some other particular province or newly composed by the Spanish.

The key to the philological commentary on the term *Pachacamac* is Garcilaso's assertion that there is no other name for God in Quechua, contradicting Spanish accusations that the Incas had numerous deities unworthy of veneration. The exegesis is philologically sound, albeit culturally misleading given the pantheistic nature of Andean religion. Not surprisingly, the commentary on Pachacamac constitutes the core of the chapter entitled "Rastrearon los Incas al verdadero Dios Nuestro Señor" ("The Incas Were on the Trail of the True God Our Lord"), cornerstone of Garcilaso's larger historical argument that Inca civilization was tending toward monotheism and, as such, constituted an essential stage in the conversion to Christianity of the Indian peoples of Peru.[8]

Against the prevailing Spanish view of Tahuantinsuyu as marginal or contrary to Christianity, Garcilaso countered with a reinterpretation of Inca civilization as *praeparatio evangelica*, rendering it central to the process of evangelization. Language is both the authority on which this interpretation is founded and its source. Historical truth about Tahuantinsuyu unfolds for the reader as an emanation originating in the original word, the authenticity of which is guaranteed by the perfect complementarity that exists between the verbal sign and its referent. Inscribing the historical argument in the discourse of humanist philology allowed Garcilaso to recover and restore the Quechua version of Inca history as a privileged primary source for writing the history of the Incas. In this way, he also secured his own cultural legitimacy, intellectual agency, and historiographical authority necessary to undertake the rehabilitation of Tahuantinsuyu and the critique of Spanish colonialism in the pages of *Comentarios reales*.

NOTES

[1] All English translations are mine unless otherwise attributed.

[2] Inca Garcilaso stretches the Spanish colonial definition of *Indian* to include himself, racially a mestizo, on linguistic grounds. See Zamora, *Language* 48–57 and "Mestizo" 182.

[3] For a more complete analysis of Garcilaso's intellectual influences and circle of acquaintances, see Zamora, *Language* 62–63.

[4] The first chair of Quechua was created at the Universidad Real y Pontificia in Lima in 1579.

[5] For a critique of Garcilaso's "Advertencias," see Cerrón-Palomino 36–69.

[6] This lengthy explanation of his Quechua sources can be found in bk. 1, ch. 19.

[7] Bodin devoted a chapter in his *Method for the Easy Comprehension of History* to the application of philology to historical inquiry.

[8] See also bk. 2, ch. 4, where the philological commentaries on *huaca* and *apachecta* complement this argument.

WORKS CITED

Cerrón-Palomino, Rodolfo. *Tras las huellas del Inca Garcilaso: El lenguaje como hermenéutica en la comprensión del pasado.* Latinoamericana Editores / CELACP / Revista de Crítica Literaria Latinoamericana, 2013.

Garcilaso de la Vega. *Comentarios reales de los Incas.* Edited by Aurelio Miró Quesada, Biblioteca Ayacucho, 1976. 2 vols.

Struever, Nancy S. *The Language of History in the Renaissance.* Princeton UP, 1970.

Varner, John Grier. *El Inca: The Life and Times of Garcilaso de la Vega.* U of Texas P, 1968.

Zamora, Margarita. *Language, Authority, and Indigenous History in the* Comentarios reales de los Incas. 1988. Cambridge UP, 2004.

———. "Mestizo . . . me lo llamo yo a boca llena y me honro con él": Race in Inca Garcilaso's *Royal Commentaries of the Incas* and *General History of Peru.*" *Inca Garcilaso and Contemporary World-Making,* edited by Sara Castro-Klarén and Christian Fernández, U of Pittsburgh P, 2016, pp. 174–94.

Incan Resonances in Inca Garcilaso's Prose

José Antonio Mazzotti

Inca Garcilaso was a master of Renaissance prose. The influence of León Hebreo, Baldassare Castiglione, Petrarch, and many other humanists is traceable in several passages of his works. However, as I have argued elsewhere (Mazzotti, *Coros* and *Incan Insights*), some of his selections of European topoi and images also remind us of similar elements within the Incan tradition. The goal of this essay is to offer a bicultural, transatlantic reading of the *Comentarios reales de los Incas* in order to appreciate the complexity of its prose.

The Importance of Formulas

A way to teach the *Comentarios reales* from a bicultural standpoint is to address the chapters that narrate the conquests of the Inca rulers. In the process of composing his work, Garcilaso seems to have started with the descriptive chapters—that is, those that give account of the institutions, administration, arts, religion, and political aspects of Incan society. He later added chapters that specifically narrate the expansion of Incan rule over new territories and peoples. This is the thesis that José Durand formulated based on different documents in which Garcilaso described the plan to write his masterpiece.

The work thus presents two different writing styles. The more ethnographic, descriptive one seems to be the style that Garcilaso first adopted to present his account of Inca society. However, soon in the text one finds the foundational tale of Manco Capac and Mama Ocllo, the two prince-siblings sent by their father, the Sun, to civilize the Indians. Their presence in the text is justified as coming from a genuine Incan source: the voice of Cusi Huallpa, Garcilaso's great-uncle. Cusi Huallpa's narration was "recitado" ("recited"; Garcilaso, *Primera parte* bk. 1, ch. 17, fol. 16v)[1] originally in Quechua, around 1554 or 1555 in Cuzco, according to Garcilaso, who at the time was still a teenager, eager to hear the stories of his maternal ancestors. Cusi Huallpa's tale of the foundation of Cuzco is translated, quoted, and paraphrased in chapters 15, 16, and 17 of book 1 of the first part of the *Comentarios reales* (fols. 13v–16v) in impeccable Spanish.

Whether real or fictitious, Cusi Huallpa's narrative and existence are pivotal to the entire text. His account establishes a sense of unity between the magnitude of the events being related and a particular narrative style that can be characterized as both formulaic and polyphonic. In my books *Coros mestizos del Inca Garcilaso* and *Incan Insights* I argue that Garcilaso later assumes this same narrative style when recounting other foundational acts and when signaling moments of special significance.[2] According to Garcilaso, the passage in question constitutes "la primera piedra de nuestro edificio" ("the cornerstone of our edifice"; *Primera parte* bk. 1, ch. 19, fol. 17v). It not only stresses the importance of

Cusi Huallpa's account of the mythical foundation of Cuzco but also establishes a "manera" ("manner"; see Garcilaso's prologue) of telling history in which Garcilaso's prose (with his plurality of voices) holds the discursive authority of an "Inca," or founding father.

The "manner" or style of this foundational event is shaped in the form of an epic narration, featuring several stylistic formulas or repetitive patterns that Garcilaso uses in other passages of the work when referring to other Inca rulers and their conquests. In my view, the internal composition of the text can be read as the presentation of successive foundational acts expressed through formulaic variations. (I will later explore the verbal resonance that some of the text's more paradigmatic passages could hold for a reader familiar with pre-Hispanic Quechua poetry.)

To begin with a basic analysis of the formulaic patterns, let us read a passage where certain verbal recurrences appear, announcing their presence throughout other passages of the *Comentarios reales*:

> Nuestro padre el Sol, víendo los hombres tales como te he dícho, se apíado y huuo lastima dellos, y embío del cielo a la tierra un hijo, y una hija de los suyos, paraque [sic] los doctrinassen en el conoscimiento de nuestro padre el Sol, paraque lo adorassen, y tuuiessen por su dios; y para que les diessen preceptos y leyes en que viuíessen como hombres en razon, y urbanidad, para que habitassen en casas, y pueblos poblados, supiessen labrar las tierras, cultiuar las plãtas y miesses, criar los ganados, y gozar dellos, y de los frutos de la tierra como hombres racionales, y no como bestias.
>
> (*Primera parte* bk. 1, ch. 15, fol. 14v)

> Our father the Sun, seeing humankind in the way that I have described, took pity upon them and felt sorry for them, and so he sent from the heavens to the earth a son, and a daughter of his own, so that they could teach [humans] the ways of our father the Sun, so that [those humans] would adore him and recognize him as their god; and so that [his son and daughter] could give [the humans] precepts and laws in which they would live in reason, and in urbanity, live in houses, and populated villages, knowing how to work the land, cultivate the plants and shrubbery, raise livestock, and benefit from them, and from all the fruits of the earth like rational beings, and not like beasts.

Cusi Huallpa presents the god Sun as a beneficial power to humanity, protecting and nurturing people and nature, teaching forms of civilization and how to live "like rational beings" ("capaces de razón"; fol. 13v). He asks in exchange only to be recognized as a true god and to be worshipped accordingly, for his ways are superior to those of other, false gods.

The mention of the Sun as a god, his infinite goodness and mercy, and the command to his children to convey his message and teach humans a superior way of life will be the same throughout the narration of those passages in which successive rulers expand the borders of the empire. The "warrior" chapters that present this concept of the Sun are as follows: Manco Capac (Garcilaso, *Primera parte* bk. 1, chs. 15–16), Sinchi Roca (bk. 2, ch. 16), Lloque Yupanqui (bk. 2, chs. 17–20), Mayta Capac (bk. 3, chs. 1–9), Capac Yupanqui (bk. 3, chs. 20–25), Inca Roca (bk. 4, chs. 15–19), Yahuar Huacac (bk. 4, chs. 20–24), Inca Viracocha (bk. 5, chs. 17–20, 25–29), Pachacutec (bk. 6, chs. 10–19, 29–36), Inca Yupanqui (bk. 7, chs. 13–20); Tupac Inca Yupanqui (bk. 8, chs. 2–8), and Huayna Capac (bk. 9, chs. 12–15). In all of them we also find consistent patterns of conduct and narrative formulas that repeat the original actions of Manco Capac and Mama Ocllo.

For example, one of the narrative elements of the *Comentarios reales* that could resonate with a previous Andean discourse is the formula that introduces the foundational act through the use of a specific syntactic structure. Garcilaso actually separates the subject of the sentence from its principal verb via the insertion of an adverbial phrase. In abbreviated form, the structure appears as subject + adverbial phrase + verb(s), with the adverbial phrase beginning with a gerund—often the verb *to see*. Recall, for example, Cusi Huallpa's statement crediting the Sun with the founding of Cuzco ("our father the Sun, seeing humankind in the way that I have described, took pity upon them and felt sorry for them"). Further on in the text, in the second paragraph of chapter 16, entitled "La fundación del Cozco, ciudad imperial" ("The Founding of the Imperial City of Cuzco"), another foundational moment occurs when Manco Capac and Mama Ocllo gather the inhabitants of the valley of Cuzco and begin to bring order to their new subjects. Importantly, this new act of foundation (effectively organizing Cuzco into two halves and establishing livelihoods for inhabitants based on masculinized and feminized activities) is expressed as follows: "Nuestros principes, viendo la mucha gente que se les allegaua, dieron orden que unos se ocupassen en prouuer de su comida campestre para todos . . ." ("Our princes, seeing the many people that came unto them, established an order so that some [people] should be occupied in providing food from the countryside for all . . ." (*Primera parte* fol. 15v). Here is the repetition of the same formula S+AP+ V(s) that characterized the Sun's initial act of sending his two children to earth.

In this way, the text not only infers that the children of the Sun should imitate the conduct of their father; it also performs an analogous imitation using these specific verbal signs. Therefore, as Cusi Huallpa's linear account continues, there appears, at the beginning of chapter 17, yet another foundational act using the same structure. And a similar one appears at the beginning of the foundational and expansion acts of the following rulers in the aforementioned warrior chapters. I call this recurrence a "formula of foundation."

A second type of formula, which I call "of requirement," also appears in the warrior chapters. Once the process of Cuzcan expansion begins, Garcilaso presents the actions of each Inca by way of imitation of the primordial acts of the Sun and the first Inca. In Cusi Huallpa's words, the Sun sent "un hijo, y una hija de los suyos, paraque [sic] los doctrinassen en el conoscimiento de nuestro padre el Sol, paraque lo adorassen, y tuuiessen por su dios; y para que les diessen preceptos y leyes en que viuíessen como hombres en razon, y urbanidad" ("a son, and a daughter of his own, so that they could teach [humans] the ways of our father the Sun, so that [those humans] would adore him and recognize him as their god; and so that [his son and daughter] could give [the humans] precepts and laws in which they would live in reason, and in society"; *Primera parte* fol. 14v). Clearly, the text presents the Incas as a civilizing force, and the portrayal is grounded in the Sun's two primordial directives: first, expand the cult of the Sun; and second, "humanize" people through laws of "reason" and "society." Each represents different aspects of a single pantheistic conception, a vision in which all elements of reality have a transcendent meaning as part of a transcendent order. The readiness to define what is human and what is not, implied in the passage above, fits an ethnocentric Cuzcan perspective, which both Cusi Huallpa and Garcilaso—as the central narrator—share. Interestingly enough, Garcilaso explicitly adopts the perspective only when he begins the direct narration of the foundational account, describing the expansion proposals developed by each Incan emperor.[3]

There are many examples of the narrator presenting Incan expansion in terms of the primordial directives. The Inca Yupanqui, for instance, "tenía este deseo [de llegar a Musu] por conquistar las naciones que huuiesse de aquella parte, para reducirlas a su imperio, y sacarlas de las bárbaras y inhumanas costumbres que tuuiessen y darles el conoscimiento de su padre el Sol, para que lo tuuiessen y adorassen por su dios" ("had the desire [to go forth to the Musu region] in order to conquer the nations that lived there, reduce them to his empire, rescue them from their barbaric and inhumane customs, and teach them of their father the Sun so that they would know him and adore him as their god"; Garcilaso, *Primera parte* bk. 7, ch. 13, fol. 179v). In another example, the Incan warriors "se atreuieron a persuadir a los Musus se redujessen al servicio de su Inca, que era hijo del Sol, al cual hauia enviado su padre dende el cielo para que enseñasse a los hombres a vivir como hombres y no como bestias; y que adorassen al Sol por dios" ("daringly persuaded the Musu peoples to submit to the service of their Inca, as he was the son of the Sun, sent from the heavens by his father to teach men to live as men and not as beasts, and to adore the Sun as their god"; bk. 7, ch. 14, fol. 180v).

Later in the text, the narrator claims that "el buen Inca Yupanqui . . . dixo. Ahora es mayor y más forzosa la obligación que tenemos de conquistar los Chiriguanas, para sacarlos de las torpezas y bestialidades en que viuen y reduzirlos a vida de hombres, pues para eso nos enuía nuestro padre el Sol" ("the good Inca Yupanqui . . . said: Our obligation to conquer the Chiriguana people is now greater and more pressing, because we must rid them of the blindness and bestiality in which they live and bring them into the life of men, since for just this purpose we were sent by our father the Sun"; Garcilaso, *Primera parte* bk. 7, ch. 17, fol. 183v). And during the subsequent conquest of "Chili" by the same Incan ruler, the narrator describes how the first Cuzcan warriors "enviaron mensajeros, según la antigua costumbre de los Incas, diziendo se rindiessen y sujetassen al hijo del Sol, que iua a darles nueua religión, nueuas leyes y costumbres en que viuiessen como hombres y no como brutos" ("following the ancient customs of the Incas, sent messengers ahead telling [the people of Copayapú] to surrender and give themselves over to the son of the Sun, that he would give them a new religion, and new laws and customs so they could live as men and not as brutes"; bk. 7, ch. 18, fol. 185r).

Likewise, following in the footsteps of his Inca predecessors, Huayna Capac

> mandó a los naturales della [la isla de Puna] y a sus comarcanos . . . , que dexassen sus dioses, no sacrificassen sangre ni carne humana ni la comiessen, no usassen el nefando, adorassen al Sol por universal dios, viviessen como hombres, en ley de razón, y justicia. Todo lo qual les mandaua como Inca, hijo del Sol, legislador de aquel Imperio . . .
>
> (bk. 9, ch. 4, fol. 229v–230r)

> ordered the inhabitants of [the island of Puna] and the surrounding areas . . . to give up their gods, to not sacrifice blood or human flesh, or eat that flesh, and to not practice sodomy, to adore the Sun as the universal god, and to live as men, ruled by reason and justice. All this he ordered as Inca, son of the Sun, legislator of that Empire . . .

The reader can follow with this analysis by looking at other warrior chapters.

A third type of formula is the "formula of validation." It consists of the frequent use that Garcilaso makes of phrases like "Hasta aquí Gómara" ("Up to here, Gómara") or "Esto dice Zárate" ("This is Zárate") when referring to previous passages from those Garcilaso is quoting. This usage is completely logical from a Spanish-speaking point of view, for there were no quotation marks in the seventeenth century to signal the beginning or the end of a quote from some other author. Nonetheless, the frequency in which Garcilaso uses this formula, compared with other chroniclers of the same period, indicates the resonance of a similar linguistic form that is mandatory in the Quechua language. In Quechua there is no indirect discourse; for example, one speaker cannot say literally, "John said that he would come early." The grammatical form in Quecha is "John said: I will come early, saying." This occurs because Quechua, like other Amerindian languages, stresses the veracity of an account based on the personal experience of the speaker. In other words, Quechua can render an account trustable only if the words of a third party are quoted literally. The recurrence of this formula is so high in Garcilaso's prose that it gives a "Quechua resonance" to it. In Quechua it is mandatory to close any quotation with words like *saying* or *said*. For this reason, the use of similar forms in Spanish may have sounded familiar to a Quechua-speaking reader in terms of the veracity of the quote or the account.

However, I want to stress again that this is not a backhanded argument about a Quechuanization of the Spanish of the *Comentarios reales*. On the contrary, my interest lies in locating moments of confluence between elements of the European and Andean narrative traditions and then suggesting to what extent this confluence and superimposition can enhance our understanding of this important work.

Syntactic-Semantic Couplets

Another important aspect of Incan resonance in Garcilaso's prose is the existence of the so-called syntactic-semantic couplets that are typical of Andean and Amerindian poetry in general. To identify their presence, we must remember the characteristics of the original 1609 and 1617 editions of the first and second parts of the *Comentarios reales.*

Interestingly, there is still no modern critical edition that respects every comma, capital letter, and period of the original or that addresses how modern textual modifications might affect the interpretation of the work. Because the punctuation of the original editions can often confuse modern readers, many scholars have been tempted to simply blame errors occurring during copying of the text and setting into type, especially when their readings concentrate solely on issues of content. However, even questions of content are affected by a close examination of the particular format in which this early-seventeenth-century text appeared, especially when one considers the dual diction that I have been attempting to recover in this analysis.

Let us go to an analysis of the prosody of the pivotal passage of the work that I have quoted before:

> Our father the Sun, seeing humankind in the way that I have described, took pity upon them and felt sorry for them, and so he sent from the heavens to the earth a son, and a daughter of his own, so that they could teach [humans] the ways of our father the Sun, so that [those humans] would adore him, and recognize him as their god; and so that [his son and daughter] could give [the humans] precepts and laws in which they would live in reason, and in urbanity, live in houses, and populated villages, knowing how to work the land, cultivate the plants and shrubbery, raise livestock, and benefit from them, and from all the fruits of the earth like rational beings, and not like beasts.

In the 1609 edition, there are eighteen demarcated syntactic fragments enclosed between commas and other punctuation marks. The original structure, then, requires a reading marked by numerous pauses. Closer study reveals that the fragments are grouped into parallel units, formed on the basis of both syntactic similarities and semantic compatibility (as I will discuss in detail below).

It is possible to group some of these eighteen fragments into pairs or triplets based on internal similarities. These parallel groupings may be referring to the "pairs or semantic-syntactic couplets" identified by Ángel María Garibay Kintana in his study of Nahua literature and elaborated in the much broader study by Dennis Tedlock on indigenous oral poetry of the Americas. Tedlock claims that "on the formal side of Mesoamerican and Andean poetics, there is a strong tendency toward quantified parallelism in the form of the semantic and/or syntactic couplet" (219). Now is not the time to discuss Tedlock's argument or a complementary one by Dell Hymes, which claims that semantic couplets are accompanied by formulaic openings and closings in oral poetic speeches (309–41). At this point, the focus must be on some of the groupings within the passage in question. In particular, it is important to ask why the demarcated pauses appear in places where there is no syntactic or grammatical need for them. Of course, one might argue that many texts from this period suffer from a similar abundance of commas and other punctuation marks. However, a rigorous philological analysis will demonstrate that parallel fragments appear more frequently in the foundational passages of the *Comentarios reales* than in analogous passages from the histories of Francisco López de Gómara, Jerónimo Román, or José de Acosta.

To begin with, given the tendency in the *Comentarios reales* to pause within a specific enumeration before almost every copulative conjunction (*y* [and]), it is possible to discern fragment pairs that become complementary through the use of a final punctuation mark. Such is the case with the fragment pairs: "and he sent from the heavens to the earth a son, / and a daughter of his own," "so that they would adore him, / and hold him as their god," and "so that they would live in houses, / and populated towns." One can also perceive groupings of up to four fragments (such as Tedlock has identified in Mayan verse [230]): "they would learn to work the fields, / cultivate the plants and shrubbery, / raise livestock, / and benefit from them." Read in this way, Cusi Huallpa's "recitation" begins to take on the appearance of verse. While this structure might have certainly been informed by European notions from the period, it could also represent a reworking of a sonorous-syntactic rhythm consistent with the meaning of the semantic couplet (or triplet or quadruplet) from the perspective of an Andean public.

Many passages from Cusi Huallpa's account can be subjected to this kind of analysis. Examples include the passage containing the Sun's speech to his children (bk. 1, ch. 15) and the passage describing what the "first savages" saw when Manco Capac and Mama Ocllo came to civilize them (Garcilaso, *Primera parte* bk. 1, ch. 16, fols. 15r–15v). As a way of illustration, it will be useful to spatially rearrange the latter passage into discernible fragments that have been clearly separated by punctuation marks. The result is as follows:

> Estas cosas y otras semejantes dixeron nuestros Reyes a los primeros
>   saluages,
> q̃ por estas sierras y montes hallaron,
> los quales viendo aquellas dos personas vestidas,
> y adornadas con los ornamentos que nuestro padre el Sol les hauia dado,
> (abito muy diferente del que ellos trayan)

y las orejas horadadas y tan abiertas,
como sus descendientes las traemos,
y que en sus palabras y rostro mostrauan ser hijos del Sol,
y que venían a los hombres para darles pueblos en que viuiessen,
y mantenimientos que comiessen,
maravillados por una parte de lo q̃ veyan,
y por otra maravillados de las promesas que les hazían,
les dieron entero credito,
a todo lo que les dixeron,
y los adoraron y reuerenciaron como a hijos del Sol,
y obedecieron como a Reyes:
y conuocandose los mismos saluages unos a otros,
y refiriendo las marauillas q̃ auían visto y oydo,
se juntaron en gran numero de hombres,
y mugeres[,]
y salieron con nuestros Reyes para los seguir donde ellos quisiessen
    lleuarlos.

Our Kings declared these and other similar things to the first savages,
who were found among these hills and forests,
and who upon seeing those two persons dressed,
and adorned with the ornaments given them by their father the Sun,
(very different from the dress [the savages] wore)
and with their ears pierced and wide open,
just as we their descendants now have,
and whose words and appearance showed them to be children
    of the Sun,
and who came to mankind to give him towns in which to dwell,
and stores of food to eat,
and being marveled on the one hand by what they were seeing,
and marveled also at the promises that [the Kings] made to them,
[the savages] gave total merit [to the two persons],
and adored and revered them as the children of the Sun,
and obeyed them as their Kings:
and these savages upon meeting one another,
and telling of the marvelous things they had seen and heard,
there came together a great number of men,
and women[,]
and they went out with our Kings to follow them wherever they
    would lead.

    I am not claiming that the Incan source had this particular structure, especially as it was uttered in Quechua. Obviously there is no way of knowing whether the Incan historical chants of the Cuzcan royal court were actually conformed in a similar way. The absence of pre-Hispanic Incan manuscripts makes any well-grounded philological comparison very difficult to perform. It does not, however, preclude one from discovering within the *Comentarios reales* a possible organization of syntactic fragments into groups of parallel or complementary meaning (examples include lines 9–10, 11–12, and 15–16) that coincide with the original pauses in the 1609 edition. An essential tool for this kind of analysis is Jean-Philippe Husson's research on the characteristics of the Quechua poetry quoted by Waman Puma (a.k.a. Felipe Guaman Poma de Ayala) in his *Nueva corónica*. Based on the many Quechua poems that Waman Puma included in his text, Husson was able to establish a series of characteristics proper to the verbal art of the pre-Hispanic Andes. The most striking feature of this poetry is that it is organized into pairs or "couplets" of complementary syntax and semantics.

Incan Symbols and Semantic Fields

The coincidence of European and Andean symbols and topics is also frequent in the chapters that speak of the foundation of Cuzco and some Inca monuments. For example, at the beginning of book 1, chapter 15, Garcilaso states:

> Viuiendo, o muriendo aquellas gentes de la manera que hemos visto, permitio Dios nuestro Señor, que dellos mismos saliesse un luzero del alua, que en aquellas escuríssimas tinieblas les diesse alguna notícia de la ley natural, y de la urbanidad y respetos, que los hombres deuian tenerse unos a otros, y que los descendientes de aquel, procediendo de bien en mejor, cultiuassen aquellas fieras, y las conuirtiessen en hombres, haziendoles capaces de razon, y de qualquiera buena dotrína: para q͞ quando esse mismo Dios, sol de justicia tuuiesse por bien de enuiar la luz de sus divinos rayos a aquellos idolatras, los hallasse no tan saluajes, sino mas dociles para recebir la fe Catholica, y la enseñança, y doctrina de nuestra sancta madre Yglesia Romana. . . .   (*Primera parte* fol. 13v)

> As these people were living, or dying in the way that we have seen, God our Lord permitted that from amongst them there should arise a morning star; someone who would illuminate that extreme darkness and offer people some notion of natural law, and of urbanity, and of the respect, that men should have one for one another; so that the descendants of that prophet, proceeding from good to better, would tame the savages and convert them into men, capable of reason, and of receiving any good doctrine: so that when this same God, the sun of justice finally decided it was the right time to send the light of his divine rays to those idolaters, he would find them no longer savage, but rather more docile and capable of accepting the Catholic faith, and the teaching, and doctrine of our holy mother Roman Church. . . .

The images of the darkest darkness, the morning star, and the sun of justice, which correspond to the three spiritual ages of the Andean world, are easy to identify within the European tradition. The sources are multiple (Mazzotti, *Incan Insights* 47–54). However, as it is said there, the three images also correspond to deities from the Inca pantheon, particularly the figure of the sun.

Given the dual characteristics of the Andean Sun god, I propose that the passage quoted can be read in two ways depending on whether one adopts an Andean perspective. In the Andean tradition, the Sun could have two completely different forms: that of the summer solstice sun (large, strong, luminous) and that of the winter solstice sun (small, weak, dull). The solstices of winter (June) and summer (December) in the Southern Hemisphere set the tone for different celebrations of the Sun god, which became two distinct entities throughout the year. For Garcilaso's text, the "sun of justice," identified in the Northern Hemisphere with the Leo constellation in the month of July, could be read as the weak winter sun in the Southern Hemisphere. The subtext would allow an interpretation of the temporal allegory of the Andean world as the opening toward a fourth period of spiritual and social flowering, with the primacy of the encomenderos and the Cuzco aristocracy at the peak of political power. This is, after all, the political agenda of the Garcilasian text.

Regarding the duality of the *Comentarios reales* with respect to Incan monuments and visual descriptions of the Andean realm, I will offer one representative example. Garcilaso states that the great northern fortress of Saqsawaman is located on a hill whose southern slope hangs perpendicularly over Cuzco. On that side the Incas built a single wall two hundred fathoms long; no greater protection was needed, given the chasm. On the other side, however, we find "tres muros, uno delante de otro, como va subiendo el cerro, tendrá cada muro mas de dozientas braças de largo. Van hechos en forma de media luna, porque van a cerrar y juntarse con el otro muro pulido, que està a la parte de la ciudad" ("three walls, one in front of the other, ascending the hill, each wall more than two hundred fathoms in length. They are made in the shape of a half-moon so as to enclose and join with the other burnished wall, which faces the city"; *Primera parte* bk. 7, ch. 28, fol. 193v), as seen in a graphic projection from my book *Incan Insights* (fig. 1).

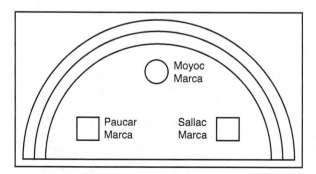

Figure 1. Saqsawaman, according to the *Comentarios reales*. From José Antonio Mazzotti, *Incan Insights: El Inca Garcilaso's Hints to Andean Readers*. Iberoamericana/Vervuert, 2008, p. 231.

The half-moon imagery used to describe the walls is striking, both because the symmetry of its three concentric semicircles provides an ideal spatial plane and because its relation to the actual architecture is debatable, as we shall see. Garcilaso's text, on the other hand, contains one of the only references we have to three interior towers, whose existence was in doubt until 1934, when the historian Luis E. Valcárcel found them buried in the earth. The Spanish had apparently begun to dismantle them shortly after the conquest, both to get stones for the rebuilding of Cuzco and to obliterate any religious power that native *cuzqueños* still vested in the towers. By the end of the sixteenth century, they had been destroyed. Garcilaso claims that the three towers formed "en triángulo prolongado, conforme al sitio" ("an extended triangle, conforming to the shape of the fortress"; bk. 7, ch. 29, fol. 195r)—that is, proportionally distant from the walls— and that he saw their ruins as a boy playing among the fortress walls and rooms with friends. The central, circular tower was called Moyoc Marca; the lateral, squarish ones were Paucar Marca and Sallac Marca. The similarity between Garcilaso's visualization of Saqsawaman and a stylized rainbow is clear.

We will examine the symbolic significance of the similarity later. For now it is important to note that the archaeological evidence partially contradicts the outlines we find in the *Comentarios reales*. The three front walls did run parallel to each other and were connected to the southern wall at both ends, but they were not curvilinear, as Garcilaso's half-moon suggests. Rather, they followed a zigzag pattern. Furthermore, the remains of the towers show that they were not positioned triangularly at all, so that the fortress in fact lacked an ideal symmetry (fig. 2).

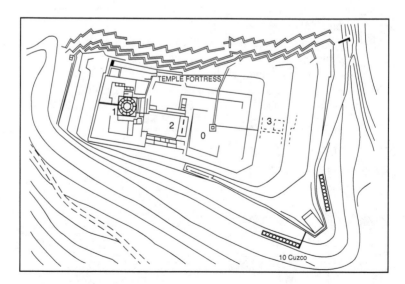

Figure 2. Aerial map of Saqsawaman. Note especially the location of the towers: (1) Moyoc Marca, (2) Sallac Marca, and (3) Paucar Marca. Reproduced with kind permission from Graziano Gasparini and Luise Margolies, *Inca Architecture*. Translated by Patricia J. Lyon, Indiana UP, 1980, p. 78.

It is unfortunate that most Spanish chroniclers emphasize Saqsawaman's military attributes only. Yet some, Pedro de Cieza de León in particular, noted early on that the indigenous people referred to it as Inti Wasi, "House of the Sun" (Hemming 65). Indeed Víctor Angles Vargas claims that its ritual function would have been the primary one, since it made little sense for an expanding empire to construct such a fortress at the city gates (43–48). R. Tom Zuidema suggests that Moyoc Marca represented the connecting point between the forces of the underworld and of this world. The very design of the tower, comprising underground levels analogous to its aboveground ones, made it possible to find "the squareness of the circle in Ancient Peru," since this vertical, cylindrical center had the power to rule the four quadrants of the Incan earthly universe (Zuidema 283–85). Some early chroniclers like Pedro Sancho even describe the towers as having five floors, and a passage from the *Comentarios reales* adds that "debaxo de los Torreones auia labrado debaxo de tierra otro tanto como en cima" ("beneath the towers, another had been wrought equal to the one above"; Garcilaso, *Primera parte* bk. 7, ch. 29, fol. 195r). Garcilaso bestows to the subsoil a labyrinthine character that the indigenous people themselves dared not penetrate unless, he insists, they were guided by "un ovillo de hilo" ("a ball of yarn"). (Here Garcilaso evokes the Greek myth of Ariadne and Theseus to reach a European public.)

The three zigzag walls on the northern side of Saqsawaman may have been built to represent three bolts of lightning extending from east to west, or vice versa. The Spanish chronicler Cristóbal de Molina points out that the cult of the god of thunder and lightning was inaugurated by the ninth Inca, Pachacutec, who ordered the construction of Saqsawaman and other temples dedicated to that deity. Pedro Sarmiento de Gamboa, a leading expert on the *wawqi*, or brother symbols of noble lineages, affirms that "Chuquiylla," or Chuki Illa, the lightning, was adopted by Pachacutec as his family totem, and the examinations of *panaka* (family clan) iconography undertaken by Horacio Urteaga (153), Arthur Demarest (35), and Zuidema (243) indicate the same. Chuki Illa was most likely a version of the pre-Incan deity Tunupa, also known in Quechua as Illapa, who lorded over all manifestations of the sky and was an important, though subsidiary, divinity (Demarest 35).

In the *Comentarios reales*, however, Garcilaso calls Illapa only an instrument of the Sun, not an independent deity. Given his importance to Pachacutec's *panaka*, one suspects that the selectivity so characteristic of historical tales from the Cuzco nobility explains Garcilaso's downgrading of him. We need to remember here that Pachacutec's family was a mortal enemy of Tupac Yupanqui's *panaka*, Garcilaso's family clan. Such an Andean reading does not preclude the more traditional approach of noting European classical and Renaissance tautologies at work in Garcilaso's text; rather, the transformation of the lightning bolt into an instrument of the Sun, the greatest visible Incan deity (*Primera parte* bk. 3, ch. 21), conjures up Jupiter and his lightning bolt. Garcilaso's "Romanization" of the Incas is quite explicit in part 1's "Proemio al lector," where Cuzco is compared with ancient Rome. Obviously Garcilaso is dialoguing with two very different publics simultaneously.

Garcilaso also speaks of Kuychi, the rainbow or *arco del cielo* ("sky arch"), as a minor figure in the Incan pantheon, yet its importance in the Andean universe is evident in many texts. In a myth frequently cited by Spanish historians, for example, the rainbow appears as a sign of a new era shortly before the founding of Cuzco, when the Ayar brothers arrive at the peak of the hill known as Huanacaure. Molina mentions the rainbow's importance, but critics have argued that his descriptions of the Andean world are permeated with European themes, in this case with the rainbow as the sequel to a flood. Molina and other Spanish chroniclers may indeed have interpreted evidence of a devastating flood in Incan history as proof of the Bible's universal truth; however, in pre-Columbian Andean mythology, destruction by water was a sign of cosmic renewal as well.[4] (The rainbow that follows is typically represented with three or four stripes rather than seven.) Other evidence of the Andean origins of the rainbow image can be found in ceramic and pictorial works.[5] In the Andean universe the rainbow represented a privileged natural element positioned on the axis of two worlds, imparting heavenly order to earthly chaos.

After the 1520s war of succession between Princes Waskhar and Ataw Wallpa, the rainbow was emblazoned on the coat of arms of the *panakas* that had survived Ataw Wallpa's massacres— that is, Garcilaso's mother's *panaka* and its allies. Later, because they had opposed Ataw Wallpa during the conquest and had submitted to Spanish rule, they were able to negotiate the privilege of blazonry and continued to bear their coat of arms. In part 1 of the *princeps* or first edition of the *Comentarios reales*, Garcilaso includes a personal coat of arms in which the left side is an Andean field. There, under a sun and a moon, a triple-banded rainbow emerges from the mouths of two sacred serpents (*amaru*), and a royal crêpe (*llawtu*) hangs between them (fig. 3).

Figure 3. Inca Garcilaso's coat of arms, with a half devoted exclusively to symbols of his royal Incan family, from the front matter of the first edition of the *Comentarios reales* (1609).

It is clear that a reading of the *Comentarios reales* from an Andean perspective yields more diverse and rich interpretations of the work than a strictly Europeanizing reading. For an advanced-level class on Garcilaso, the examples presented here can serve to develop topics such as miscegenation, hybridization, interculturality, colonialism, and the need to exercise decolonial readings of Garcilaso and other Andean authors.

NOTES

[1] Translations in this essay are my own.

[2] In fact, I will be quoting and summarizing some paragraphs from those books to explain my arguments.

[3] Curiously, it is worth noting that a similar presentation of a civilizing figure occurs in *Diálogos de amor*, León Hebreo's Neoplatonic work that Garcilaso translated from Italian into Spanish in 1590. Lisania de Arcadia (also called Demogorgon and Jupiter) is a mythical being and god. Hebreo writes, "Lisania de Arcadia, que yendo a Atenas, y hallando aquellos pueblos rusticos, y de costumbres bestiales, no solamente les dio la ley humana, pero tambien les mostro el culto diuino: por donde ellos le alçaron por Rey, y le adoraron por Dios, llamandole Iupiter por la participacion de sus virtudes" ("Lisania of Arcadia, who upon going to Athens, and finding those peoples to be primitive, and of beastly habits, not only gave them human laws, but also taught them divine worship: so that wherever they went they proclaimed him their King and adored him as their God, calling him Jupiter because of the sharing of his virtues"; Garcilaso, *Traduzion* fol. 79v). Garcilaso may have used these same features to introduce the Incas in the *Comentarios reales*. In any case, what interests me here is not whether the theme is of European or non-European origin but the particular way Garcilaso uses it to produce an effect of formulaic features.

[4] See Cieza de León, ch. 3, 8n; Molina, ch. 1; Acosta, bk. 6, ch. 19; Anello Oliva, bk. 1, ch. 2; Betanzos, ch. 1; López de Gómara, ch. 122; Sarmiento de Gamboa, ch. 6; Garcilaso, *Primera parte*, bk. 3, ch. 25.

[5] See Gisbert, figs. 121, 123, 125, 201, 203–05.

WORKS CITED

Acosta, José de. *Historia natural y moral de las Indias*. 1590. Edited by Bárbara G. Beddall, Valencia Cultural, 1977.

Anello Oliva, S. J. *Historia del reino y provincias del Perú*. Juan F. Pazos Varela and Luis Varela y Orbegoso, 1895.

Angles Vargas, Víctor. *Sacsayhuaman, portento arquitectónico*. Industrial Gráfica, 1990.

Betanzos, Juan de. *Suma y narración de los Incas*. Edited by María del Carmen Martín Rubio, Atlas, 1987.

Cieza de León, Pedro de. *Primera parte de la crónica del Perú*. Peisa, 1973.

Demarest, Arthur A. *Viracocha: The Nature and Antiquity of the Andean High God*. Harvard U Peabody Museum of Archaeology and Ethnology, 1981.

Durand, José. "Garcilaso y su formación literaria e histórica." *Nuevos estudios sobre el Inca Garcilaso de la Vega*, Centro de Estudios Histórico-Militares, 1955, pp. 63–85.

Garcilaso de la Vega. *Primera parte de los* Comentarios reales. Pedro Crasbeeck, 1609. Biblioteca Nacional del Perú, bdh-rd.bne.es/viewer.vm?id=0000009186&page=1.

———. *La traduzion del indio de los tres diálogos de amor*. Pedro Madrigal, 1590.

Gisbert, Teresa. *Iconografía y mitos indígenas en el arte*. Gisbert, 1980.

Hemming, John. *Monuments of the Incas*. Photographs by Edward Ranney, U of New Mexico P, 1990.

Husson, Jean-Philippe. "La poesía quechua prehispánica: Sus reglas, sus categorías, sus temas, a través de los poemas transcritos por Waman Puma de Ayala." *Revista de crítica literaria latinoamericana*, vol. 19, no. 37, 1993, pp. 63–86.

Hymes, Dell. *"In Vain I Tried to Tell You": Essays in Narrative American Ethnopoetics*. U of Pennsylvania P, 1981.

López de Gómara, Francisco. *Historia de las Indias y conquista de México*. 1552. Centro de Estudios de Historia de México, 1977.

Mazzotti, José Antonio. *Coros mestizos del Inca Garcilaso: Resonancias andinas*. Fondo de Cultura Económica, 1996.

———. *Incan Insights: El Inca Garcilaso's Hints to Andean Readers*. Iberoamericana/Vervuert, 2008.

Molina, Cristóbal de. *Relación de las fábulas y ritos de los incas*. Edited by Paloma Jiménez del Campo and Paloma Cuenca Muñoz, Iberoamericana/Vervuert, 2010.

Sancho, Pedro. *Relación de la conquista del Perú*. 1550. José Porrúa Turanzas, 1962.

Sarmiento de Gamboa, Pedro. *Historia índica*. 1570. *Obras completas del Inca Garcilaso de la Vega*, edited by P. Carmelo Sáenz de Santamaría, Atlas, 1965, pp. 189–279. Biblioteca de Autores Españoles 135.

Tedlock, Dennis. *The Spoken Word and the Work of Interpretation*. U of Pennsylvania P, 1983.

Urteaga, Horacio. *El imperio incaico en el que se incluye la historia del ayllo y familia de los Incas*. Gil, 1931.

Zuidema, R. Tom. "La cuadratura del círculo en el antiguo Perú." *Reyes y guerreros: Ensayos de cultura andina*, compiled by Manuel Burga, Fomciencias, 1989, pp. 280–305.

Incomparable Cosmologies:
Character and Motive in the March to Cajamarca

Sara Castro-Klarén

The *Historia general del Perú* was written and intended to be read as the second part of the *Comentarios reales de los Incas* by its author, Inca Garcilaso de la Vega. Although of immense importance for the discovery and understanding of the conquest of the Tahuantinsuyu by the small Spanish army led by Francisco Pizarro in 1532, the *Historia general* has not been nearly as widely read as the famed *Comentarios reales*. The encounter of the Inca Atahuallpa with the Spanish band of warriors, the subsequent capture of the unarmed Inca, and his execution after a long imprisonment, during which he paid an unimaginable ransom in gold and silver, are not only emblematic scenes of conquest but events with consequences that thunder down to our own times. That is why reading and understanding the narrative of this event in Garcilaso's hands calls for a double focus: one on the Spanish motives and actions and the other on Atahuallpa's actions and his mindset as he dealt with the appearance of strange bearded men on the coastal region of northern Tahuantinsuyu, the empire of the four cosmic quarters.

In class discussion students generally feel that they do not need to be aware of the temporal distance between "us" and the Spanish, but they quickly feel a distance from Atahuallpa. This sense of cultural and temporal distance starts with his name. That alone makes it harder for the students to consider Atahuallpa as not just the defeated leader who can be dismissed but rather the representative of a whole thriving culture that, despite a brutal conquest, survived and engaged the imposition of colonial rule that has resulted in contemporary Peru. One of the main objectives of this essay is to shorten that distance felt with respect to Andean culture and to place Atahuallpa's behavior, motivations, and mindset in a plane of intelligibility that students will be able to consider and appreciate as necessary to the serious understanding of the narrative of the conquest. The primary question is, What was Atahuallpa thinking?

The second question inquiring students bring up is the problem of sources. Prompted by Garcilaso's own discussion of his sources, students become skeptical about sources in this period of time when most Europeans were illiterate and especially with respect to the widely disseminated idea that since the Incas "did not have writing" they could not pass on any trustworthy memory of the past or the present. A discussion of the quipu system of recording information based on recent scholarly work is indispensable in the classroom dealing with any aspect of Andean culture. I will not present that discussion here. Scholars have clearly demonstrated that the quipu system of storing information was capacious and that the quipu also coded narrative memory (see Urton; Quilter and Urton). Garcilaso writes the story of the conquest of his mother's native land and civilization by cobbling together many contemporary eyewitness sources to which he had personal access while in Cuzco and the published chronicles of Spaniards. His Spanish sources were authored by participants in the conquest themselves. Garcilaso's Quechua-speaking sources included survivors of the fatal encounter between Pizarro and Atahuallpa in Cajamarca in 1532. "Lo oí a muchos indios, que visitando a mi madre, le contaban aquellos hechos . . . a estas relaciones se añade la que hallé en los papeles . . . del Padre Blas Valera, que fue hijo de uno de los que se hallaron en la prissión de Atahuallpa" ("I have also heard the version of many Indians who used to visit my mother and told her of these events. . . . To these is added the account I found in the papers of . . . Padre Blas Valera, who was the son of one of those present at the arrest of Atahualpa"; *Historia* 56; *Royal Commentaries* 671). In the *Comentarios reales* he identifies by name the Inca octogenarians who, with tears in their eyes, relate in his mother's house the events of first contact from the time of Huayna Capac's death to the execution of Atahuallpa (bk. 9, ch. 14). Garcilaso is extremely careful with the question of having and using responsibly the most trustworthy sources. He feels that the craft of the historian demands a critical awareness of all materials used in the composition of the story to be told, for his objective is the truth: "que la historia manda y obliga a escrevir verdad, so pena de ser burladores de todo el mundo y por ende infames" ("[that history] is bound and obliged to write the truth, under pain of becoming a deceiver of the world and so set down as a rogue"; *Historia* 56; *Royal Commentaries* 671).

The Quechua Dimension

Beyond the question of trustworthy sources, Garcilaso built an unassailable argument regarding the indispensable need to know Quechua in the *Comentarios reales*. Part of the inadequacy of Spanish historiography rests on the fact that without knowledge of Quechua, the Spanish really understood very little of Inca culture and cosmology. In the *Historia general* Garcilaso reiterates this point. Students exposed to other languages and cultures today generally appreciate this argument, and the introduction of Quechua terms and specially Andean cosmology is generally received with keen curiosity. In this segment of the class it is important to spend time discussing the scholarship available on Andean cosmology and the fact that our understanding has changed a great deal in the last fifty years. For the purposes of the classroom, *Filosofía andina: Estudio intercultural de la sabiduría autóctona andina*, by the ethno-philosopher Josef Estermann, is the most comprehensive and accessible text. It discusses in short but substantive entries key concepts and terms of Andean cosmology and social practices. Thus, neither the teacher nor the student can today deploy a reading strategy that is univocal, unilinear, or Spanish-centered. The doubly sided cultural and epistemological complexity of the events narrated call for a plurivalent orientation. Given the Andean or Quechua dimension, readers will need to pay attention to two radically different scenarios in action at the same time. This requirement produces a bifurcated point of view in the reading, for the scenarios do not belong to the same series but rather to incomparable cosmologies. The series of scenes are set parallel to each other as in a postmodern play or novel. Garcilaso does not submerge or subsume the line of the Inca sense of the event to what is going on from the Spanish point of view until they come to an explosive convergence in the scene of Cajamarca, when Atahuallpa is told by the priest Valverde to accept the word of God as contained in a small and strange object in order for him to be set free and avoid execution. Himself coming from both sides of the clashing civilizations, Garcilaso's point of view appears frequently tortured and twisted by the force of the impossibly bifurcated position he occupies in history: the illegitimate son of an Inca noblewoman and a Spanish conquistador.

Despite this impossibility or perhaps because of it, Garcilaso writes a history of the conquest that depicts the participants not as superheroes or base villains but rather as real men and women. His historical characters wrestle with dangerous and morally fraught choices. They are driven by passions. They make correct or misguided calculations while facing situations so new as to have no paragon in the annals of history. His emphasis on character and motive allows him to give the unbelievable events of the conquest a dimension of intelligibility that serves as a ground where it is possible to contest the charges of cowardliness that the Spanish leveled against Atahuallpa. That is one of the reasons a third focus in this essay will be a narrative that tells the story of greed and deception as the plane of intelligibility for the mind-boggling capture of Atahuallpa and the fall of the Tahuantinsuyu. Many other scenes and events in the *Historia general* can also be analyzed at the intersection of character and motive, itself a mainstay of all realistic narrative across cultures and epochs. But motive and character are bound and produced by specific cultures. That is why a fourth focus will be to culturally contextualize the story. I analyze the series of encounters between the Spanish and Andeans as a series of scenarios that, given the cultural determinants in play, adumbrate the final event in Cajamarca.

Cajamarca

Cajamarca is the city where Atahuallpa decided to take a long rest on his way back from Cuzco, where he had successfully waged war against and defeated his half brother Huascar. By virtue of his birth to an Inca *coya*, Huascar was the legitimate successor to the Inca Huayna Capac. But the old Inca, who loved his son with the Quito (non-Inca) princess exceedingly, decided to split the very large empire and name the two princes heirs upon his death. The Cuzco *panaka* (a term derived from the word *pana*, meaning "sister of a man" [Zuidema 54]), one of the nine royal *ayllus*, or ancestral lines, could not accept such a position, and civil war ensued. As he marched north toward Quito, Atahuallpa received many reports about strange-looking men marauding on the northern coast. It seems that Atahuallpa decided that it was time to meet the strangers. While the behavior of the Spanish is clearly motivated by greed and a ravenous appetite for power, the Inca's behavior remains a sort of mystery. There is a glaring asymmetry between the supreme power and resources of Atahuallpa and the small and common gold-hungry crew of Spaniards. The question for the class revolves around Atahuallpa's decision to welcome the Spanish with open arms and lavish gifts. Why was he not the first to strike? What kept him from seeing what we, in retrospect, clearly see: that the Spanish objective was to kill him and take over his realm? Students are intrigued, once they are aware of the profound cultural differences, by what may have been Atahuallpa's reasoning, his motives, and his character.

Honor and virtue were considered two powerful motivations in Renaissance historiography. The story of the Spanish invasion and conquest of Amerindian peoples and territories inverts that paradigm through the wanton destruction of the peoples and their civilizations in the Spaniards' unbridled search for gold. What prevails at the intersection of character and event is a paradigm of human action where greed and power trump all other motives and outcomes. Stimulated by unrestrained ambition, these men plot and murder under the shadow of hypocrisy and defended by the callousness of unfathomable cruelty gained over a lifelong familiarity with killing. However, Garcilaso himself had been a combatant in the king's war against the Moriscos in Spain. He knew valor firsthand. He also knew of the physical courage that war demands. Thus he applauds the Spanish warriors whose story is the mainstay of this book. His father was one of these men, and thus in the prologue he says that he writes this book, in part, to "celebrar . . . las grandezas de los heróicos españoles que con su valor y ciencia militar ganaron, para Dios, para su Rey y para sí, aquesse rico Imperio" ("celebrate the deeds of the heroic Spaniards that with their great valor and military science won for God, for the King, and for themselves that rich empire"; *Historia*; CF).[1] Notwithstanding this praise, by the time he wrote, the Spanish exploration of Amerindian lands and civilizations was known all over Europe to be simple pillage and massacres, as Bartolomé de Las Casas showed in his *Brevísima relación de la destrucción de las Indias.*

Garcilaso is unable, although he tries, to depict Pizarro or his men as "noble." Instead he must start with Pizarro's betrayal of his partner Diego de Almagro. When Pizarro returns from Spain with the necessary permit for further exploration and conquests to the south of Panama, he brings a title for himself and none for Almagro, although the old warrior had already put a considerable amount of money into funding the expedition. Pizarro was immediately accused by Almagro's associates of "malicia" ("malice"). They felt that Pizarro had cheated and deceived Almagro. For Garcilaso this deception lies at the root of Almagro's discontent and distrust of Pizarro, a mindset that "duró hasta que el uno mató al otro" ("which lasted till one killed the other"; *Historia* 46; *Royal Commentaries* 660). This deception, along with many others, drove the civil wars between the two men. Garcilaso's father got caught in them and was charged with switching alliances. His "nobility" had to endure questions and suspicion. Deception is thus established as the other great character mainstay and modus operandi among these warriors. Money, deception, malice, and greed play their fateful dynamic in this scene and in many more in this twisting story of conquest, of civil wars between Incas at first and Spaniards and their Indian allies later. Between 1532 and 1580 Peru knew nothing but war. Hundreds of thousands of men, women, and children died as victims of this war of conquest.

Action Gives Way to Speech

Garcilaso moves the Spanish ship quickly into the Inca geopolitical zone. Francisco Pizarro comes swiftly inland with his army, all the while making speeches to the effect that he comes not only in peace but as the pacifier of a land and peoples who are experiencing the tyranny of ignorant and unfit local rulers. Although Francisco Pizarro does not know any of the local languages, he proclaims his desire to bring justice to any who may have been the victim of Atahuallpa's rule. An attentive reader asks: Who does Pizarro think he is talking to? Why is Garcilaso reporting this speechmaking without questioning the impossibility of Pizarro communicating with his purported audience? The class discussion here should be prepared in the light of the doctrine of just war elaborated by the Spanish in the wake of the conquest of Amerindian peoples and civilizations. Pizarro is making speeches not for the Indians but for the historical and political record. He is covering his back and the king's rear guard in the European field of political warfare. Pizarro is seeding the path for the doctrine of just war and conquest to obtain when he kills Atahuallpa. The narrator, reporting on what the Spanish do, lets the Spaniards act out their farce with no comment. It is almost as if he wants to present the original invasion of Peru from the Spanish ideological point of view.

Having already learned in Tumbes about the march north from Cuzco by Atahuallpa and of the civil wars with his half brother Huascar by means of the interpreter Felipe, an adolescent Indian boy captured in the previous expedition, the Spanish see the opportunity to perpetrate the claim that either one of these heirs to the throne is the usurper of the rights of the other, and therefore it should be the Spaniards who should settle the matter by deposing them both. Garcilaso subtly intertwines Pizarro's political plans with the Spaniards' sighting of the beautiful cultivated fields, the large and well-fed populations, the ornaments of gold and silver common to all, and the general abundance of the land and the well-constructed towns and roads. Pizarro and his men seem absorbed in weighing the wealth of the Inca when they are surprised by an embassy from none other than Huascar, to whom Garcilaso refers as the "desdichado" Inca, now in prison in Cuzco. The narrative continues to adumbrate Atahuallpa's tragic end even when introducing Atahuallpa as "contento y ufano" ("full of satisfaction and pride"), savoring his defeat of Huascar and as yet unconcerned about the Spanish, the "gente extraña" ("unknown race of newcomers"; *Historia* 50; *Royal Commentaries* 665). Garcilaso here suggests that perhaps destiny rules over all vicissitudes (a Renaissance belief in *fortuna*) and it was Atahuallpa's destiny to be the last Inca.

Incomparable Cosmologies: The Puzzle

Atahuallpa's capture, deception, and execution is narrated in somber tones befitting the unwarranted death of a king, his empire, and a thriving civilization. These scenes are all told with the heavy rhythm of a funeral procession. Messages and embassies move slowly back and forth between Pizarro's men and the Inca king's courtiers. With each message that bears language and material offerings as means of communication, the tension grows. Garcilaso makes it clear that the parties are sinking even deeper into complete misunderstanding of the messages and their explicit and implicit meanings. Pizarro's intention to deceive Atahuallpa is always clear to the reader. Atahuallpa's intentions, with all the gifting and gallantry, remain a puzzle: Is he also deceiving? Is he overconfident? Or is he out of touch with what is going on as the Spaniards march deeper into his empire? Pizarro's simple principles of grab and kill are easy to fathom. The Inca's mind remains invisible. As with the capture of Montezuma in Mexico, the tension in these exchanges rises unbearably with each new report on the Inca's lavish gifts of gold, silver, precious jewels, and abundant food, for these only whet the Spaniards' appetite and determination to kill the Inca, the very act Atahuallpa is trying to avert. To the puzzle of Atahuallpa's blindness or highly flawed understanding of the menace he faced, Garcilaso offers the following explanation: Atahuallpa believed that the empire was doomed because his father, the Inca Huayna Capac, on his deathbed had prophesied that strange people would come and take the empire over. Given that Garcilaso spent years writing a book that proved the high intelligence and practical bent of the mind of the Incas, it stretches the imagination that a warrior like Atahuallpa would just collapse because of an improbable "prophecy." And yet the fact that Atahuallpa was puzzled by the nature of the Spaniards and did not react in time remains a brute historical reality. However, if we look carefully in Garcilaso's text, he offers other explanations of the event. But students will have to piece together this explanation by exercising a bit of textual detective work and analysis. The contextualization here calls for learning about Inca cosmology and social organization.

From the outset Garcilaso presents the mind of the Inca as suffused with the belief that the Spaniards were "hijos de su Dios Viracocha" ("sons of their God Viracocha") or "hijos del sol" ("sons of the Sun"; *Historia* 50; *Royal Commentaries* 665). However ambiguous these denominations as translated into Spanish may be, they represent a frame of mind that requires that the Spanish be treated not as enemies but certainly as equals. Nevertheless, the reader wants to know: Why did Andeans think so? What did they see in the Spaniards to think them *viracochas* or "sons of the Sun"? What did it mean to be "sons of the Sun"? Certainly Garcilaso himself reports that many in Atahuallpa's court did not think so and urged the Inca to attack and destroy the Spaniards right away. This discrepancy in the assessment of the Spaniards requires an explanation that Garcilaso does not offer. I venture here a hypothesis that can be further extended by reading into the appropriate scholarly literature.

First, all the evidence offered by Garcilaso seems to suggest that Atahuallpa, secure in his position as Inca, decided to wait till he himself met these strange men and made an assessment of their capabilities and intentions. After all, they were fewer than two hundred men and Atahuallpa had thousands of troops at the ready ("treinta mil hombres" ["thirty thousand men"; *Historia* 55; *Royal Commentaries* 670]). Second, in Inca cosmology, all humans are grouped into *ayllus*, or kinship of descent. *Ayllus* had their "origins" in material cosmic (sacred) features of the land, or *huacas*—lakes, caves, the ocean, rivers, water springs, mountains (Bauer 3–4).[2] The sun was worshipped as the sacred mythical ancestor (father) of the Inca *ayllu*. It is therefore not out of the question that these powerful and strange warriors would be thought to have the sun as their mythical ancestor as well. If the sun was their mythical ancestor, then they deserved respect. Third, when the Inca attacked other kingdoms such as the Wari or the Chimu, not only were the conquered allowed to continue to worship their *huacas* ("gods," as misunderstood by the Spanish), but their rulers were invited or coerced to join the Inca empire as Inca-by-privilege. The former rulers were not necessarily deposed, provided they became loyal subjects of the Inca. They were expected to come to Cuzco to pledge allegiance, bring tribute, and celebrate together the yearly festival of Sun worship. "Inca-by-privilege" were not "sons of the Sun," a denomination exclusively reserved for Inca kin, but they occupied an equivalent rank. In this respect R. Tom Zuidema writes that "Inca society . . . included various forms of hierarchical organization, that were, in part or in their totality, parallel to one another." Contextualized by Inca politico-cosmology, kinship rules, and war practices, Atahuallpa's language speaks of the "real" world and not of "gods." His messages do not indicate naïveté or ignorance. "Sons of the Sun," "brothers" (parallel relation), and even "sons of . . . Viracocha," the "creator God," entail more of a tentative but grounded approach before the unknown (54).

At this juncture, students begin to grasp the magnitude of the distance between Andean cosmology and our own. In play in the text and in our understanding of Atahuallpa's actions is the problematic rendition of terms deeply embedded in a language and culture without easy equivalents in another. Recent scholarship making use of a deep knowledge of Quechua, archaeology, and ethnographic studies has shown that the Incas' notion of the divine was completely different from the Western European notion of the divine. In fact the "divine" does not exist in Andean thought (Estermann, *Filosofía andina* 150–51). There is not such a thing as "God" in the Andes. This renders the notion of "su Dios Viracocha" an impossibility. The operative concept in the Andes is *pacha*—the invisible and visible set of relations that tie the cosmos together (144–45). In his *Filosofía andina* Estermann writes:

> Pacha significa el universo ordenado en categorías espacio-temporales, pero no simplemente como algo físico y astronómico . . . Es una expresión mas allá de la bifurcación entre lo visible y lo invisible, lo material e inmaterial, lo terrenal y lo celestial, lo profano y lo sagrado, lo exterior y lo interior . . . pacha es la base común de los distintos estratos de la realidad . . . pacha es la relacionalidad andina.   (144–45)

> *Pacha* means the universe ordered in space-temporal categories, but not simply as something physical and astronomic . . . [It] is an expression that goes beyond the bifurcation among the visible and the invisible, the material and the immaterial, the terrestrial and the celestial, the profane and the sacred, the exterior and the interior . . . *Pacha* is the common fundamentals of the different levels of reality. *Pacha* is the Andean relationality.   (CF)

Given Estermann's understanding, it is disconcerting to see that Garcilaso, who spends many pages explaining the notion of *huaca* in his *Comentarios reales* and tells of the Inca myth of origin in which the Inca kinship originates from four *pacarinas* (caves) in a mountain near Cuzco, does not take the opportunity to explain to his reader what was actually going on with the idea that the Spaniards were "sons of the Sun." However, if we look back in the *Comentarios reales*, Garcilaso himself is quite puzzled by the figure of Viracocha and Inca "religion" in general. As a Catholic, and one who claimed that the Incas were on their own way to monotheism, he wanted to make Sun worship among the Incas the prelude to their own discovery of the one true God, as he amply stated in the second chapter of the second book of the *Comentarios*, titled "Rastrearon los Incas al verdadero Dios Nuestro Señor" ("The Incas Glimpsed the True God, Our Lord"). In this sense the Incas were not behind or beneath the monotheism of Judaism or Christianity. They were not idol worshippers. On their way to monotheism, they could claim parity with Europe. In fact Garcilaso rejects categorically the idea that Viracocha was a god. Given Estermann's definition of *pacha* and the fact that there can be no transcendental plane of being compatible with the concept of *pacha*, it is clear that Atahuallpa is not confusing the Spanish with "gods." His intent may have been to make the Spaniards a sort of Inca-by-privilege, a sort of parallel *ayllu* of men not gods, as was the custom and practice in the Tahuantinsuyu. At a later point in the narrative, Garcilaso makes it clear that he would have preferred this outcome to the destruction of the Tahuantinsuyu.

Titu Atauchi's Double-Sided Speech

Atahuallpa's first embassy to Pizarro is carried out by none other than his brother Titu Atauchi. Titu Atauchi is to convey to the "sons of the Sun" that Atahuallpa wished to see them and serve them "[c]omo a hijos del Sol, su padre, y hermanos suyos, que assí lo creian él y todos sus vasallos" ("as children of his father the Sun and [as] his brothers, as he and all his vassals believed them to be"; Garcilaso, *Historia* 51; *Royal Commentaries* 665). Lest there be any doubt about the substance of these beliefs in Atahuallpa's mind, Garcilaso has Titu Atauchi deliver a speech that he says the ambassador was ordered to make. Breaking all the conventions of verisimilitude that he has imposed on his history, Garcilaso quotes it verbatim. In this text the Inca asks Pizarro for three things: that he consider Atahuallpa his friend, that he forgive any offenses that he might have received from ignorant vassals, and that he refrain from any more killings, "pues eres Inca, hijo del Sol" ("as you are an Inca and child of the Sun"; *Historia* 51; *Royal Commentaries* 666). Atahuallpa's rhetoric has long been mistaken for a sign of weakness and cowardliness. In fact, it should be taken for a greater deployment of Inca customary rhetoric in the face of enemies considered potential allies or Incas-by-privilege and what Estermann calls the ethical obligation of all *runas* (people on the *kay pacha*) to keep harmony undisrupted (*Filosofía andina* 168). Garcilaso shows and quotes from this rhetoric of harmony extensively in the *Comentarios reales*, when he narrates the many wars of conquest waged by the Incas on the polities that eventually formed the Tahuantinsuyu. Atahuallpa is asking the Spaniards to "honor" their new (parallel) status as "sons of the Sun." They should now be benevolent and forgiving, not cruel or deceiving. This is one side of the speech. But there is an underside to the speech also.

Titu Atauchi in the Grid of Colonialism

Titu Atauchi's speech does not only convey Atahuallpa's message. It is a double-sided and plurivalent text. It is a text produced by Garcilaso in the grid of Spanish discursive colonialism, and it needs to be contextualized as such, not just as a message originating purely from the precontact Andes. As such it occupies a crucial space in the Spanish rationale for conquest. This speech, as others that follow in these first scenes of contact, is more than a greeting. It is a legal and theological document. It is placed in the mouth of Titu Atauchi in order to factualize one of the myths (persuasive narrative) on which the "rightful" conquest of America was predicated. In this master text of colonization, the other submits of its own free will, thus liberating the conqueror from charges of usurpation and illegal conquest. The invention of this speech to be placed on the lips of the natives goes all the way back to Christopher Columbus. From his very first encounters with natives in the Caribbean, Columbus reports exchanging messages with them. The fact that none of the interpreters whom he carried on board knew any of the Caribbean languages did not matter. In the end he always got the message they gave to him correctly: the natives took the Spaniards to be gods and offered them their realm unconditionally. The speech made by Titu Atauchi is but one more reiteration of this master text elaborated in the forge of colonialism.

Even sophisticated rulers of empire such as Montezuma and Atahuallpa ceded their kingdoms to Spanish domain out of their own "free will." The underlining logic of the fallacious claim relates to the "fact" that Spain, and not France or England, had been providentially chosen by God to evangelize all non-Christian peoples. Although Hernando Cortés was not the first to play this hoax, his account of how Montezuma freely abdicated his throne in favor of the Spanish king constitutes the model for many of these speeches throughout the more than two hundred years of penetration and conquest of Amerindian civilizations. The pretended assumption here is that the Amerindian rulers lived with a sense of permanent guilt over the tyrannical way in which they ruled their people and that as soon as the Christians showed up on their shores, invested as they were with the pope's mandate to Christianize the world, they freely rendered their kingdoms unto the rightful rulers. The emphasis in this argument falls on the *free* abdication out of guilt, as well as on the identity of *rightful* rulers. Both terms are fundamental to Spain's providential reading of history. By putting this speech in the mouth of Titu Atauchi as mandated by Atahuallpa, Garcilaso is playing his full part in the maintenance of Spain's view of its providential place in the world's history. Students here will be interested in a lengthier explanation of the theory of providential history and its roots in the Bible.

The legal and cultural force of Titu Atauchi's double-sided speech is not confined to Spanish imperial historiography. It echoes right into the modern period, when scholars, still puzzled by these encounters, find, if not providential history as such, an undeniable cultural superiority as the explanation for these regicides. For example, Tzvetan Todorov argues in *The Conquest of America* that the explanation has to do with the difference between cultures that possess alphabetic writing and those that do not. It is a matter of cognitive superiority. Alphabetic writing gave Europeans a nimbler mind and culture. This was true even for those who, like Pizarro, could barely sign their names. Alphabetic writing allowed Europeans to have a more accurate view of the world and a better understanding of the reasons for human events. Despite the great libraries of Mexican semasiographic books and the Incas' extensive quipu records, Todorov claims that these forms of writing without words do not prepare the mind to deal with the unexpected, for they require extensive memorization, and such repetition of texts induces a lack of flexibility and diminished capacity to assess correctly the unexpected. The Inca rulers, being trapped in this oral culture, in a mythic frame of mind, believe that the Spaniards—the unknown—are godly manifestations sent to bring about the destruction of their realm. It is interesting to see that such modern explanations do not take into consideration the fact that Columbus himself followed a biblical geography that stood in his way of ever understanding where he was.

Why Viracochas?

But while Cortés and his hired biographer, Francisco López de Gómara—one of Garcilaso's many sources—may never have had any doubt as to the intellectual gifts given or denied to Montezuma, Garcilaso had just spent some thirty years collecting information and writing about the keen intelligence that animated the Tahuantinsuyu. Inca rulers deftly dealt with local rulers as well as Incas-by-privilege. The reader then must ask, How then could Atahuallpa be presented as such a mistaken and naive ruler as portrayed in this abject message to the invaders? Again, a careful reading of the speech shows that Atahuallpa is not making abject requests but rather using a rhetoric of guile to buy time, to keep the Spanish from attacking, as the Incas are accustomed to do even in the face of declared enemies, such as when the Chancas attacked Cuzco during the reign of Yahuar Huacac (Garcilaso, *Comentarios*, bk. 4, chs. 16–21). It is not that Atahuallpa believes that the Spaniards are the sons of the "god" Viracocha. In fact, Garcilaso appends to his narrative of the war with the Chancas a chapter where he explains why the Andeans in general called the Spaniards *viracochas* after the conquest (bk. 5, chs. 15–24).

This explanation goes back to the reign of Yahuar Huacac. This king had a son and heir who turned out to be extremely smart but not a good follower of orders and traditions. The father was worried about the kind of ruler that his questioning son might become, and he decided to exile him to teach him a lesson. While away from Cuzco and in exile, the adolescent prince had a dream in which a figure that identified himself as his uncle and brother of the founding couple Manco Capac and Mama Ocllo appeared to warn him of the Chancas' plans to attack Cuzco. This bearded man said that his name was Viracocha Inca: "vengo de parte del Sol, Nuestro Padre, a darte aviso para que se lo des al Inca" ("I come from the Sun, our father, to bid you warn the Inca") of the Chancas' rebellion. The figure then adds, "en todas ellas te socorreré como a mi carne y sangre" ("I will always succor you as my own flesh and blood"; Garcilaso, *Comentarios* 207; *Royal Commentaries* 231). The prince reported this dream to his father. Yahuar Huacac did not believe him. He took it to be an evil omen, although his diviners could not tell him why it had come in the form of a dream to this difficult son. The prince, who up until then had not been given a ranking name, took the name Viracocha for himself. He deposed his father and went on to fight the Chancas and win an impossible battle, probably with the assistance of the phantom of Viracocha. Chroniclers and historians agreed that this Inca who conquered the Chancas is in fact Inca Pachakutiq, the great reformer and founder of the "modern" Inca empire. The point here is that Viracocha identifies himself as kin of the Inca and not as a god. If anything, he is not a creator god, for such a concept would conflict with the overarching sense of *pacha*.

Zuidema, in *Inca Civilization in Cuzco*, has written incisively about Inca kinship rules, rules of descent, and most especially about the relationship between uncle and nephew in the political organization of Cuzco. A discussion of kinship rules is relevant here with respect to the term *brothers*, as translated into Spanish. Zuidema explains,

> These ten Inca lords were seconded by non-Inca lords and nobles who benefited from certain territorial rights in the valley [of Cuzco], which in turn guaranteed their representation at the Court. . . . The king formed with the non-Inca lords treaties that could lead to marriage alliances. . . . The rank order of these relatives was conditioned by that of the *chapas* that they governed, and *each rank was expressed by a kin term* that situated the individual in relation to the king.   (15; emphasis mine)

Clearly, what Atahuallpa had in mind by referring to the Spanish as "sons of the Sun" was simply "brothers," using a kinship term in order to indicate and accord the Spaniards' rank as non-Inca.

Further, in the text it is clear that it was not a flesh-and-blood Viracocha but a "phantom" that said in a dream that Viracocha was his name. There is no Viracocha other than the prince who took that name. Garcilaso explains why the name was applied to the Spaniards: "Porque el príncipe dijo que tenía barbas en la cara, a diferencia de los indios que generalmente son lampiños, y que traía el vestido hasta los pies, diferente hábito del que los indios traen, que no les llega más allá de la rodilla, de aquí nació que llamaron Viracocha a los primeros españoles que entraron en el Perú" ("As the prince said that it had a beard, unlike the Indians who are usually without hair on the face, and that it was dressed from head to foot while the Indians are clad differently and their dress does not go below the knees, the word Viracocha was duly applied to the first Spaniards who entered Peru"; *Comentarios* 258; *Royal Commentaries* 289). Therefore what is reported is the application of a word and not the deployment of a concept that contains a misunderstanding or insufficient act of cognition. The Inca did not think the Spanish were descendants of the "god" Viracocha, for, as Garcilaso states clearly again, the Inca had no other god than the sun and Pachacamac. But the Indians, after the conquest, invented Viracocha as a god to "adular a los españoles . . . A Viracocha y a los demás Incas tuvieron por hijos del sol" ("flatter the Spaniards . . . Viracocha and the other Incas were held to be children of the Sun"; *Comentarios* 251; *Royal Commentaries* 282). Thus, the key phrase "children of the Sun" refers to people now living on the visible and touchable plane of existence.

A Relational Cosmology Faces the Doctrine of Just War

Atahuallpa is not recognizing a great outsider "god" embodied in the presence or body of the Spaniards. The Inca Atahuallpa, whose cosmology is relational and not individual-centric, as is ours, is instead extending kinship status to the Spanish. Estermann explains that the principle of relationality along with the principle of reciprocation constitute two of the three fundaments for Andean thought:

> El rasgo más fundamental y determinante del pensamiento andino es la relacionalidad. La categoría básica no es el ente "en cuanto ente" de la metafísica occidental, sino la relación. La filosofía occidental tiene como fundamento ontológico la sustancialidad de todo lo que existe, sea en sentido realista como ser-en-si-mismo o sea en sentido transcendental como autonomía del sujeto. La existencia separada y nomadica es lo primero; la relación entre los entes particulares lo segundo. Para el *runa* quechua, la situación es la inversa: el universo es ante todo un sistema de entes interrelacionados, dependientes uno del otro, anárquicos, heterónomos, no sustanciales. ("La filosofía quechua" 38)

> The fundamental and determining characteristic of Andean thought is relationality. The basic category is not the being "as being" of Western metaphysics, but the relationship. Western philosophy has as ontological fundament the substantiality of all beings that exist, either in a realistic sense as being in itself, or in a transcendental sense as an autonomy of the subject. The separated and nomadic existence is first; the relationship among the particular beings is second. For Quechua *runa* [man], the situation is the inverse: the universe is first and foremost a system of interrelated beings, depending on one another, anarchic, heteronomous, not substantial. (CF)

In this system of relationality, correspondences and reciprocation encompass and predicate interactions in all three levels of existence: *hanan pacha*, or the space above; *kay pacha*, or the sphere of the here and now; and *uray/ukhu pacha*, or the world inside/within, the place of the dead and of the ancestors (Estermann, "La filosofía quechua" 38). The Spaniards are placed on the *kay pacha*. In that place they are comparable to the heads of Andean polities who by either conquest or negotiation entered the Tahuantinsuyu. Post-integration into the Inca realm, they are given the rank of Inca-by-privilege. It is in this sense that the Spaniards are accorded the title "sons of our father the Sun." Of course, the Spaniards heard not only what they wanted but also only what they could hear, given the precedent of Montezuma, their own sense of sovereignty ("I conquer, therefore I am"), and the lack of proper translation. Atahuallpa is not, as it has often been said, making offerings from a position of perceived weakness. To the contrary, he offers gifts, as is the custom in the Andes, from a position of unchallenged power, albeit, in the eyes of history, having mistaken the nature of the unknown.

Titu Atauchi underscores the invitation to join as "hermanos suyos" ("brothers"), as kin of the Inca (Garcilaso, *Historia* 51; *Royal Commentaries* 665). His humble request must be read as an entreaty to the Spaniards to behave as Incas, that is to say as protectors of the people. It is a call to stop the wanton killing. This speech is not a capitulation. Rather, it is a diplomatic interpellation to march on as possible allies and not as enemies ("pues eres Inca"; *Historia* 51; *Royal Commentaries* 666). Good, ethical behavior is expected from the "hijos del Sol." Atahuallpa's invitation is made within the Andean fundamental contract of correspondences and reciprocity, a contract that of course the Spaniards could not abide by, since it was beyond their imagination, their intentions, and their cosmology as a whole. In "La filosofía quechua," Estermann remarks on the impossibility of finding equivalents in Indo-European languages for Andean thought and practices (36–40). He coins the term *pachasofia* for this philosophy and *kosmologia* for this worldview because he thinks the Greek sense of the cosmos is the closest he can find for a possible comparison.

Requesting that the Spaniards behave as if they were Incas registers yet another meaning in this double-sided speech made by Titu Atauchi. Garcilaso here condemns the conquest for its wanton killing and relentless pillage. In doing so he disavows the doctrine of just war. Spain's claim to a right to intervene in the territories and business of other people by casting themselves as saviors is severely questioned in this request that the Spanish behave ethically as "sons of the Sun." Garcilaso counters the legal grounds for conquest that Pizarro had been trying to establish with his speeches addressed to nobody. Because Atahuallpa offers friendship rather than hostilities, the conquest is rendered illegal even under the cynical doctrine of just war.

Atahuallpa: Prophecies and a Bifurcated Portrait

Garcilaso's portrayal of Atahuallpa's motives and actions is elaborated by the dynamics of bifurcation. To the charges that Atahuallpa lacked courage, that like Montezuma he was a pusillanimous man afraid of his gods and of his courtiers, Garcilaso responds like the Aztec chroniclers did in Tenochtitlan: with the notion that Atahuallpa was disoriented by the prophecies his father and his oracles had made about an ominous catastrophe in store for the Tahuantinsuyu. In the *Comentarios reales* the author often deals with the importance of augury in the Inca court and the culture in general. The interpretations of dreams as well as signs written in the anatomy of animals' bodies are deciphering practices connected to daily life. Embalming practices gave Andeans unusual familiarity with the human body in health and in sickness. The attention to and study of nature and its health are attentively chronicled by Garcilaso so that the portrait of the culture is one of intense knowledge and curiosity about biological and climatological events. At the end of the *Comentarios reales* Garcilaso had drawn a picture of Atahuallpa that gathered all the attributes of the exemplary warrior and prince. Atahuallpa was indeed beloved by his father, for the prince was "de buen entendimiento y de agudo ingenio, astuto, sagaz, mañoso y cauteloso, y para la guerra belicoso y animoso, gentilhombre de cuerpo y hermoso rostro, como lo eran comúnmente todos los Incas y Pallas; por estos dotes del cuerpo y del ánimo lo amó su padre tiernamente" ("displayed a ready intelligence and understanding, and was astute, sagacious, and prudent: his mettle was brave and warlike, his bearing noble and his features handsome, as those of all the Incas and Pallas usually were. Because of these gifts of body and mind his father loved him tenderly"; *Comentarios* 230; *Royal Commentaries* 567). Such a splendid man could not act out of cowardice but was instead affected emotionally and intellectually by the strangeness of his father's illness—an illness that seemed to be spreading in the realm and that was as unknown to Andean medicine as the men who marauded on the coast.

It was reported that just before he died of a mysterious and terrible illness that ravaged his whole body with purulent sores (which turned out to be smallpox, to which Andeans had no resistance), the Inca Huayna Capac had predicted the end of the empire at the hands of unknown foreigners. In the *Comentarios reales* Garcilaso dwells on the origin and nature of this prophecy (bk. 9, chs. 12–15). It was not privately held by Huayna Capac and his court but was rather widespread in the realm. All Andeans knew about this prophecy because, according to Garcilaso, there had been a portent in Cuzco some three years earlier, in 1512 before the first ship was sighted on the coast in 1515. The oracles interpreted it to mean that pestilence and destruction were to visit the empire (bk. 9, ch. 14). On the day of the feast of the Sun, a huge eagle pursued by four falcons fell from the sky onto the central plaza of Cuzco. Upon inspection it was found that the eagle was sick with a plague of its skin that weakened its plumage and thus its ability to fly. The diviners interpreted that a great plague was to follow and that the empire was facing mortal peril. People also began dying of mysterious illnesses. By 1515 Huayna Capac had received news about some strange ships and strange people navigating on the coast of what is today Ecuador. Since then the Inca had paid close attention to news about the strange people on the coast, in part because this news seemed to dovetail with the Cuzco augury.

With this news and expectation in mind, it is not surprising to see that Atahuallpa felt somewhat discomfited when he learned that the strange people had actually disembarked and were on their way to see him. In this frame of reference, an extremely anxious and disoriented Atahuallpa makes sense. Atahuallpa, now in Cajamarca, is confronted with the arrival of these mysterious bearded men. He begins to suffer from a sort of cognitive dissonance. Thus he decides to placate the bad omens and contain the invaders, momentarily, with gifts. Atahuallpa is thus besieged by two forces, both equally hard to fathom and manage:

the prophecy wrapped up in the guilt of civil war and the unknown as embodied in the Spaniards. For Garcilaso, Atahuallpa's embassies to the Spanish are nothing more than gestures designed to cover up his fear: "Por no mostrar tan al descubierto la flaqueza de su ánimo cobarde" ("As not to display openly the weakness of his cowardly spirit"; *Historia* 53; *Royal Commentaries* 667–68). A combination of reasonable fears together with the occurrence of an extrarational portend turned Atahuallpa's bravery and war expertise into a cowardice and insecurity: "ni resistió ni usó del poder que tenía contra los españoles" ("he neither resisted, nor used his powers against the Spaniards"). And the matter should rest here, but Garcilaso flips again and precedes to offer now a further explanation for Atahuallpa's failure to destroy the Spanish and save his empire. This explanation lies beyond motive and action. It refers to Garcilaso's view of the conquest as part of God's plan for human history. Like most Spanish intellectuals of the time, Garcilaso believed in the thesis of providential history, and the conquest of the Tahuantinsuyu occurred, despite the incredible destruction of the people and the civilization, as a divine instrument to bring the Amerindian peoples to salvation under the aegis of the Catholic Church.

Speaking as if Stuttering

Despite his adherence to the providential explanation to make sense of the incredible events of Cajamarca, Garcilaso returns to his history with a full focus on providing a narrative and understanding of human deeds without the intervention of the divine. Garcilaso's wish is that a proper negotiation between Atahuallpa and the Spaniards had taken place for an agreement on joint (parallel) rule. Andeans and their civilization would have been spared the holocaust that was the conquest, and Spain would have gotten its flood of gold and silver. But this negotiation did not happen, not only because of providence but also because of the absence of intelligible translation. The debacle ensued because of the "torpeza de su interprete" ("clumsiness of his interpreter"; *Historia* 55; *Royal Commentaries* 669–70). Felipe, "el indio interprete" ("the Indian interpreter"), not only did not know enough Spanish to understand what he was being told by Hernando de Soto to say to Atahuallpa, but he did not know enough Quechua either, for he was from a small village on the northern coast and was a stranger to the elegant and elaborate ways of Cuzco courtly Quechua to which Atahuallpa and his military and political retinue were accustomed.

The scenes of Cajamarca are emblematic of the problem of translation, or rather mistranslation, that underscores life in postconquest Andes to this day and also colonial rule and domination in the world at large. When Pizarro decides to send his embassy to Atahuallpa, the young Indian Felipe takes on a central and indispensable role. In no way does his language skill compare with that of La Malinche, Cortés's translator, companion, and war strategist. Felipe is "torpe en ambas lenguas" ("he was . . . little versed in the general language of the Incas as in Spanish"; Garcilaso, *Historia* 55; *Royal Commentaries* 681). All the encounters that figure as preambles to the execution of Atahuallpa are predicated by and fraught with the problem of completely inadequate translation at the cultural and linguistic level. Garcilaso dwelled on the problem of translation at length in order to dis-authorize almost all Spanish chroniclers who wrote about Inca civilization. They misunderstood not only words, key concepts, and full sentences but the culture as a whole. Not surprisingly, Atahuallpa is disappointed and angered by the impossibility of communication and negotiation. Used to elegant, polished Quechua and elaborately respectful forms of address, he rejects the entire speech made by de Soto and "translated" by Felipe for its stuttering quality, improper Quechua, and general unintelligibility. Atahuallpa thunders, "¿Qué anda éste tartamudeando de una palabra en otra y de un yerro en otro, hablando como mudo?" ("What does this fellow mean, stammering from one word to another and from one mistake to the next like a dumb man?"; *Historia* 59; *Royal Commentaries* 674). Yet despite the general unintelligibility, Atahuallpa turns to his court and tells it that these men *resemble* the vision of Viracocha that the young Inca had and that he thinks these are "varones divinos" ("divine men"), or whatever phrase he may have used in Quechua, a phrase that remains unreported to our day.

Besides Atahuallpa's rejection of the message because of its unintelligibility, the exchange of speeches is underscored by its other side, for this moment also double-sided. The second or principal fundamental matter here is that de Soto's salutation is none other than a version of the *requerimiento* (Garcilaso, *Historia* 58–59; *Royal Commentaries* 673–74). The *requerimiento*—"a cynical piece of legal gibberish," as David Brading has called it (81)—is the companion text to the doctrine of just war. It requires that non-European polities submit instantly to the authority of the pope and to the king of Spain. To refuse to do so is to invite war and destruction. Garcilaso is intent on showing that, despite such insolence and offenses, Atahuallpa continued to receive the Spaniards in peace and without hostilities, for Garcilaso's objective is to underscore the peaceful reception given to the Spanish. From this scene to the capture and execution of Atahuallpa is but a few steps. It is all a foregone conclusion based on the mistake Atahuallpa made (prompted by Providence?) in thinking that the Spanish were "sons of the Sun," possible kin in a life of mutuality in the here and now, or the *kay pacha*, and the Spaniards' relentless pursuit of enrichment by conquest.

In this essay I have contextualized action by way of motive in the story of the march of both Atahuallpa and the Spanish to Cajamarca. The objective has been to offer the means by which the readers can gain a sense of the complexity of the narrative and the import of the speeches made in this theater of conquest. Understanding the conquest of the Tahuantinsuyu calls for full reference to the available scholarship of Andean civilization that avoids presenting a monologist Spanish point of view on the history of what would become Latin America. A second objective has been to dwell on the ambivalent position of Garcilaso as historian and narrator whose own personal and professional allegiances were not as much divided as plurivalent and the effect those switching positions has on our efforts to piece the story together at a high but critical level of intelligibility.

NOTES

[1] Christian Fernández has provided translations, marked by his initials, CF, of parts of the works of Garcilaso, such as the paratexts of both works, that are absent from Livermore's translation, and of quotations from the Estermann works.

[2] Michael J. Sallnow wrote, "The Andean landscape is imbued with sacredness. Human destinies are in part determined by chthonian powers, in the spirits of mountains, rocks, springs, rivers, and other topographic features, and generalized in the earth matrix, Pachamama" (qtd. in Bauer 4). Cosmological powers were worshipped in the landscape of their known world. The Spanish confused the *huacas* with gods from the earliest moments of contact. Even as late as the 1570s, when Juan Polo de Ondegardo wrote his *Informe* and his *Relación*, he insisted on calling the *huacas* "dioses" (Bauer 3).

WORKS CITED

Bauer, Brian S. *The Sacred Landscape of the Inca: The Cusco Ceque System.* U of Texas P, 1998.

Brading, David A. *The First America: The Spanish Monarchy, Creole Patriots, and the Liberal State, 1492–1867.* Cambridge UP, 1991.

Estermann, Josef. *Filosofía andina: Estudio intercultural de la sabiduría autóctona andina.* Abya-Yala, 1998.

———. "La filosofía quechua." *El pensamiento filosófico latinoamericano, del Caribe y "latino" (1300–2000): Historia, corrientes, temas y filósofos,* edited by Enrique Dussel et al., Siglo Veintiuno, 2009, pp. 36–40.

Garcilaso de la Vega. *Comentarios reales de los Incas.* Edited by Aurelio Miró Quesada, Biblioteca Ayacucho, 1985.

———. *Historia general del Perú (Segunda parte de los* Comentarios reales de los Incas*).* Edited by Ángel Rosenblat, Emecé Editores, 1944. 3 vols.

———. *Royal Commentaries of the Incas and General History of Peru.* Translated by Harold V. Livermore, U of Texas P, 1966. 2 vols.

Quilter, Jeffrey, and Gary Urton, editors. *Narrative Threads: Accounting and Recounting in Andean Khipu.* U of Texas P, 2002.

Todorov, Tzvetan. *The Conquest of America: The Question of the Other.* Harper and Row, 1982.

Urton, Gary. "From Knots to Narratives: Reconstructing the Art of Historical Record Keeping in the Andes from Spanish Transcriptions of Inka Khipus." *Ethnohistory,* vol. 45, no. 3, Summer 1998, pp. 409–38.

Zuidema, R. Tom. *Inca Civilization in Cuzco.* U of Texas P, 1990.

Teaching the *Royal Commentaries* with Visual Representations of the Exploration, Conquest, and Colonization of Peru

Giovanna Montenegro

"I myself was born in the torrid zone, in Cuzco, and was brought up there until I was twenty" (Garcilaso 1: 10). So says Inca Garcilaso de la Vega in his *Royal Commentaries*, thereby dispelling the notion that the torrid zone was uninhabitable. The author then decides to treat Incan history in the rest of his work through the lens of accepted geographical and cartographic conventions. Garcilaso asserts his mestizo identity through his rebuttal of ancient geography. This essay addresses instructors of courses in world literatures or great books of the Western canon of the modern era, but it can be also used in any other course related to colonial texts of the Americas, either in Spanish or in English, as it combines a reading of the *Royal Commentaries* with visual representations of the exploration, conquest, and colonization of Peru. The aim is to introduce students to the history, literature, and images of the colonization of the Americas. These modules will present students with the visual culture surrounding New World peoples and New World objects produced by Europeans, mestizos, and indigenous subjects.

Since the quincentennial of first contact between Europeans and the native Taínos of the Caribbean, or the "discovery" of America, there has been plenty of attention paid to the visual images that tell the story of the conquest, exploration, and colonization of the American continent. What exactly can undergraduates learn from exploring the visual culture of conquest while reading Garcilaso's *Royal Commentaries*? First, students can learn about the way in which the reproduction of maps and images detailing the conquest of the Americas was part of a print culture that sought to publish sensationalist accounts about the Amerindian "pagans" of the American continent. Second, students may also learn about genre in travel literature (the *crónica*, the travel narrative, the letter) and better understand that the history of cartography is inherently tied to a culture that privileged the "eyewitness" account.

The course in which I have taught the *Royal Commentaries* is a ten-week comparative and world literature undergraduate class titled Great Books of Western Culture: From the Middle Ages to the Enlightenment, which satisfies the university's general education and writing requirement. The course reading begins with Provençal love poetry and Andreas Capellanus's *The Art of Courtly Love* before moving on to Dante's *Inferno*, Shakespeare's *The Tempest*, and Cervantes's *Don Quixote* and ending with excerpts from Garcilaso's *Royal Commentaries* and Swift's *Gulliver's Travels*. As such, while the course includes many different works from the age of the troubadours until the eighteenth century, the latter part of the course focuses on travel and exploration. The grading requirements include four essays. The fourth essay prompt asks students to write a comparative study of the *Royal Commentaries* and *Gulliver's Travels* of about 1,500 to 1,750 words. In addition, students are assigned a group presentation. For example, during the course of ten weeks we had fifteen-minute group presentations on thirteenth- and fourteenth-century Florence, life in sixteenth- and seventeenth-century Spain, the Inca empire and the Spanish conquest, and philosophy and science in the Enlightenment. I devoted a week and a half (two to three course periods) to excerpts from part 1 of the *Royal Commentaries* in English translation (chs. 1–16).

Why Cartography and Geography?

Part 1 of the *Royal Commentaries* begins with chapters that seek to explain theories popular in Renaissance geography. I find that teaching this work allows students to further explore and think about the impact of geographic exploration and colonization after the "discovery" of the New World. After ample discussions in which students have grappled with the Caliban/cannibal dichotomy in Shakespeare's *The Tempest*, students may find Garcilaso's *Royal Commentaries* at first "too official" and "dry." However, teaching such a work encourages a creative pedagogical approach, especially as part 1 of the *Royal Commentaries* requires contextualization concerning the history of geography and cartography. Sections in part 1 include "Whether There Are Many Worlds; It Also Treats of the Five Zones," "Whether There Are Antipodes," "How the New World Was Discovered," "The Derivation of the Name *Peru*," and "The Foundation of Cuzco, the Imperial City." It also addresses such subjects as the religious customs, dressing habits, and political institutions of the Incas. Garcilaso's ethnographic descriptions of the Incas, his role as a historical *crónica* author, and the positioning of his work amid Renaissance geographical and cosmographical knowledge point to the necessity of introducing his work in a geographical context. Moreover, the material allows students to ponder the colonization of the Americas as well as the mestizaje implied in El Inca Garcilaso's authorship and his project. Below, I will describe a few visual materials that are easily available on the Internet and in libraries' and museums' map and image catalogs. Often these sites have images available for downloading that would be easy to integrate within any type of presentation software, such as *PowerPoint, Keynote,* or *Prezi.* Finally, I will give examples from a comparative student writing assignment on colonization and mestizaje in *Gulliver's Travels* and the *Royal Commentaries.*

Useful Objects: Portolan Charts and World Maps

The *Royal Commentaries* cannot be taught effectively without references to the contemporary geographical knowledge that Garcilaso had in mind in composing this work. You do not need to be an expert in the history of cartography to help students think critically about the purposes for which maps were made in the early modern period. It might be useful, for example, to pull up a few examples from the Middle Ages. A show-and-tell could consist of a tripartite (T-O) map, a mappamonde, and a zonal map.[1] The zonal map is the most interesting for students reading the *Royal Commentaries*. A Macrobius-style zonal map divides Earth into zones by temperature. There are northern and southern frigid zones as well as northern temperate, equatorial, and southern temperate zones. Many of these early modern maps also include information on the antipodes.

Garcilaso thought that geographical debate was relevant and decided to introduce his work with his opinions on sixteenth-century geographical conventions. This is particularly of use when students read chapter 1 of the *Royal Commentaries*. The author writes,

> [I]t seems proper to follow the usual custom of writers and discuss here at the beginning whether there is only one world or many, whether it is round or flat, whether it is all habitable or only the temperate zones, whether there is a way from one temperate zone to the other, whether there are antipodes and what they correspond to, and similar matters which the old philosophers treated very fully and curiously and the moderns do not fail to debate and describe. . . .   (1: 10)

Students can read this chapter and see how Garcilaso accepts and refutes contemporary geographical knowledge. In asking students why Garcilaso begins his *Royal Commentaries* by attempting to cover geography, we can discuss questions of genre. For example, the author doesn't engage in the flat-or-round-Earth debate but states merely that doubters "may be satisfied by the testimony of those who have gone round it, or the most part of it" (1: 10). He takes a similar approach to the questions of the "zones": those who still believed that the torrid zones were uninhabitable "may be assured that I myself was born in the torrid zone." Regarding the cold zone, he says, "I wish I could speak as an eyewitness of the cold zones" yet dares "declare to those who say that they are too cold to be habitable that I hold the contrary view, that they are as habitable as the rest, for it cannot reasonably be imagined, much less believed, that God should have made so much of the world useless, when He created the whole to be inhabited by man." Even in unpacking those passages students can begin to analyze questions of genre: for example, the importance of the eyewitness account, Christian rhetoric, and Garcilaso's defiance of ancient Western European geographical knowledge. He claims himself a child of the "torrid zone"; he rails against the ancients for thinking there was no snow under the equator—he refutes geographical knowledge that pairs colder climates with the northern frigid zone and instead points to altitude as a marker of temperature in Peru. Yet in the next shorter section he discusses the antipodes and the question of how New World peoples got to the American continent. There, he resolves that geographical conventions deal with "questions so obscure, I shall leave them, especially because I am less competent than others to enquire into them" (1: 12). Instead, he writes, "I shall deal only with the origin of the Inca kings and their succession, their conquests, laws, and government in peace and war. But before dealing with them it will be as well to say how the New World was discovered, and to treat of Peru in particular." Geography is a base from which to discuss the history of the Incas as Garcilaso sees it.

So what maps and images are useful for discussing navigation, exploration, colonization, and racial identity in the early modern period when reading the *Royal Commentaries* in a great books course? We can, for example, discuss the "practical" portolan charts that were faithfully redrawn by Genoan, Catalonian, Portuguese, and Mallorcan navigators and that depicted the known coastlines surrounding the Mediterranean. Within these, the land itself was usually left empty. Beyond the Mediterranean, these maps were also used to describe the American continent. One example that would be of interest to students deciphering the *Royal Commentaries* would be the anonymous sixteenth-century portolan chart of the Pacific coast of South America. The "Portolan Chart of the Pacific Coast from Guatemala to Northern Peru with the Galapagos Islands" is Spanish-made and includes two hands in the use of the toponyms.[2] It is one of the first maps that includes the Galapagos Islands. It also includes the Río Grande de la Madelena (Magdalena River) and Quito, signaled by a white church. It shows Granada and León in the upper part of northwestern South America. As a portolan chart, it includes wind roses, highly colorful birds, and the expected coastline, but it also goes beyond the requirement in the use of stylized and ornamented place markers. For example, Quito, León, and Granada are shown as places where there are *asientos*, or Spanish settlements—hence Quito's being symbolized by a church with many flags. Upon presenting students with this image, there are various questions that can be posed for discussion, including:

> Who was the author?
> Who was the intended audience?
> Were navigators actually using this map?
> What does the absence of native and indigenous places show?
> What does the mapmaker's preference for depicting towns in the Spanish
>   style show?
> How are nature and the environment depicted (for example, in the map-
>   maker's inclusion of birds)?

A simple exercise in looking at this map and asking such questions will lead students to realize that asking the same questions of images as we do of texts allows us to be better equipped to tackle both visual and textual literacy. A map, as any text that presumes it is factual or a key eyewitness account, is always made with intentions in mind. As soon as students grapple with the question of genre and authorship in mapmaking, they can apply those same principles to uncover some of Garcilaso's own problems with authorship.

Multiracial Identities in the Spanish Colonies

Another image emphasizes the multiracial colonial Spanish American society to which Garcilaso belonged. The painting in mind is the indigenous painter Andrés Sanchez Gallque's *Los mulatos de Esmeraldas* (1599), which is in the Museo de América's collection in Madrid, Spain. A digital file (watermarked) is easily found and downloaded from the museum's online catalog. Gallque, like Garcilaso, used a European language (pictorial in Gallque's case) to illustrate the submission of a multiracial population to the Spanish crown. The image, commissioned by Juan del Barrio de Sepúlveda for Felipe III, depicts three men described as mulattoes (as people of mixed African and indigenous descent were sometimes called during the sixteenth century): Francisco de la Arobe stands at the center of the frame accompanied by his two sons. The three men are adorned with jewels and wearing Spanish clothes, including ruff collars and silk robes, as well as indigenous nose rings crafted in gold. Francisco was the son of an escaped enslaved African man and an indigenous Nicaraguan woman who became the political leader of the Esmeraldas coast and the Arobe Maroon group. The "mulattoes" were descendants of those who had escaped slavery after Spanish boats capsized off the Pacific coast. They belonged to a community of Maroons, or *cimarrones*, and had become leaders (caciques) of a region populated by both Maroons and indigenous peoples. In exchange for the governorship of the region inhabited by descendants of enslaved Africans and their indigenous allies, Francisco swore allegiance to the Spanish crown. The painting shows how individuals negotiated their African, indigenous, and Spanish identities in a colonial context. By studying this painting and pairing it with the *Royal Commentaries*, students can ponder the hierarchy of Spanish colonial society in the larger colonial Peru and Garcilaso's struggle with the indigenous part of his mestizo identity. Art historians, for example, have focused on this painting as an exceptional example: "Finalmente, en relación con su autor, se trata de uno de los escasos ejemplos tempranos de una pintura firmada y fechada, elaborada además por un artista de origen indígena, aunque siguiendo el estilo y estética europeos" ("Finally, in regard to its author, it's a rare and early example of a signed and dated work, created by an indigenous artist, although following European styles"; Gutiérrez Usillos 8; my trans.).

This can be an opportunity to show students Miguel Cabrera's later eighteenth-century *casta* paintings from New Spain that detail how racial miscegenation in the Spanish colonies became codified further. It can lead to a discussion of racial identity and racial categories applied in a different Spanish colony to Amerindian and mixed-raced descendants, such as mestizo (descendants of an Indian and a Spaniard), mulatto (which became used mostly to describe descendants of a Black person and a Spaniard), and *lobos* (as mixed-race people from indigenous and African backgrounds began to be called in New Spain).

We discuss Gallque's painting before an online assignment on the *Royal Commentaries* that asks students to discover various themes and write a post on them on a class forum. For example, one student focused on Garcilaso's mestizo identity as a marker of his writing style. In a final review post, this student incorporated ideas such as nationalism, truth in history, and power, stating that

> Vega is, as mentioned, a mix of the two worlds, but gives his allegiance thoroughly to the Spanish side of things in this matter. He shows this in many ways, the first of which being the ratification of his Incan historical tales by Spanish historians. For every tale or story of Incan culture Vega writes, he sees fit to give it proof through documenting a trusted European historian's recounting of the same thing.

Students can ponder what it meant to "submit" to Spanish rule as the mulattoes of Esmeraldas appeared to have done. Likewise, as this student has done above, it forces us to explore the effects of mestizo identity upon the shaping of the historical genre as applied to the *crónica*.

Finally, the *Royal Commentaries* makes an excellent companion to the anglophone canonical world of Shakespeare's *The Tempest* and Swift's *Gulliver's Travels*. Reading the text and showing students maps and images begs students to reconsider the narrative of colonial history as Garcilaso struggles to define his stance as an author. For example, in a comparative essay on *Gulliver's Travels* and the *Royal Commentaries*, one student cited these texts as "two prime examples of texts that utilize the ridicule of the author's own nation in order to support or oppose colonialism. Swift's ridicule of his country comes in the form of criticizing its government, religion, and customs whereas Garcilaso de la Vega critiques Incan religion and history to show his support of European (Spanish) power." While we can argue against this particular viewpoint, it is helpful to see how students engage in a more nuanced analysis of the writing of history and the *crónica* genre, as in the case of this student's final paper:

> Next, we can see that Garcilaso de la Vega belittles his native Incan culture by using European historians to confirm relation of Incan history and religion, as well as by placing Christian themes onto his native tales. He first uses other historians to prove the truth of his tales in his recounting of how the name Peru came to represent the Incan country. He uses the writings of Pedro Cieza de Leon, stating that the man only used the term Peru when referring to a Spaniard who is speaking of the land (Vega 17). He goes on to explain that Incans never needed a term for their collection of lands, and that since his story matched Leon's it was proved true. Vega shows that the truth can only be brought forth by European writers here, which in turn belittles the history told by an Incan. Later on, Vega utilizes the same practice of ratifying his own writing with that of a European author multiple times, including the tellings before the Incas (Vega 33). Both of these, along with other pieces of his writing[,] reflect the idea that

Inca history cannot be true unless it is proved so by a European writer as well. Vega himself is part Incan, which is why he himself must use these methods in his writing. By doing this, Vega shows that the Incan culture is subservient to European or Spanish culture. Without Spanish ratification, the histories of the native people would be seen as meaningless ramblings; only with the help of European [confirmation] can the stories be shown to be true. . . .

I like to think of this student's last sentence alongside the painting of *Los mulatos de las Esmeraldas.* In a geographical area that effectively functioned as a lawless borderland, the mulattoes defended their territories against other Maroon groups such as the Ilescas (Gutiérrez Usillo 12). Juan del Barrio Sepúlveda was the *oidor* (official) who achieved the pact with the mulattoes and who later commissioned the work to mark this achievement for the king. Francisco de la Arobe (and his absent indigenous wife) would submit to the Catholic faith and become baptized in 1578. The European-style painting confirms the mixed-race mulatto as a European subject and as a symbol of submission. In Gallque's painting, Francisco's rich dress and jewelry exemplified to the other rebellious mulattoes of the regions that it paid to submit to Spanish will (Gutiérrez Usillo 18). Students can use Gallque's painting and Garcilaso's text to discuss to what extent the performance of a Spanish identity benefited (and restricted) the authors of both works.

NOTES

[1] Harley and Woodward's *History of Cartography* is key for deciphering some basic geographical and cartographic history and vocabulary. Also see this essay's appendix of works on cartography, geography, and race.

[2] Available from the Library of Congress Geography and Map Division Web site (hdl .loc.gov/loc.gmd/g4802c.ct001180).

WORKS CITED

Garcilaso de la Vega. *Royal Commentaries of the Incas and General History of Peru.* Translated by Harold V. Livermore, U of Texas P, 1966. 2 vols.

Gutiérrez Usillos, Andrés. "Nuevas aportaciones en torno al lienzo titulado *Los mulatos de Esmeraldas:* Estudio técnico, radiográfico e histórico." *Anales del Museo de América,* vol. 20, 2012, pp. 7–64.

Harley, J. B., and David Woodward, editors. *History of Cartography: Cartography in Prehistoric, Ancient, and Medieval Europe and the Mediterranean.* Vol. 1, U of Chicago P, 1987.

APPENDIX: Supplemental Bibliography
on Cartography, Geography, and Race

Arias, Santa, and Mariselle Meléndez, editors. *Mapping Colonial Spanish America: Places and Commonplaces of Identity, Culture, and Experience.* Bucknell UP, 2002.

Crone, G. R. *Maps and Their Makers: An Introduction to the History of Cartography.* Hutchinson U Library, 1966.

Gruzinski, Serge. *The Mestizo Mind: The Intellectual Dynamics of Colonization and Globalization.* Translated by Deke Dusinberre, Routledge, 2002.

Mignolo, Walter. "Cartas, crónicas y relaciones del descubrimiento y la conquista." *Historia de la literatura hispanoamericana: Época colonial*, edited by Luis Iñigo Madrigal, Cátedra, 1982, pp. 57–116.

Miller, Marilyn Grace. *Rise and Fall of the Cosmic Race: The Cult of Mestizaje in Latin America.* U of Texas P, 2004.

Penrose, Boies. *Travel and Discovery in the Renaissance, 1420–1620.* Atheneum, 1962.

Robinson, Arthur H., and Barbara Bartz Petchenik. *The Nature of Maps: Essays toward Understanding Maps and Mapping.* U of Chicago P, 1976.

Learning from Mistakes:
Interpretation in the *Comentarios reales*

Sarah H. Beckjord

When teaching part 1 of the *Comentarios reales de los Incas*, I encourage students to think about the prominent role that Inca Garcilaso de la Vega assigns to the imagination in his effort to re-create a "república antes destruída que conoscida" ("republic destroyed before it was known"; *Comentarios* 1: 49; *Royal Commentaries* 1: 51). Within the often ambiguous vision of the Inca past and emerging colonial society in the *Comentarios reales*, Garcilaso rehearses and reinvents a variety of philosophical, humanist, and Andean traditions.[1] He also explores the necessity, perils, and possibilities of the imagination: the term *imaginación* and its derivatives appear frequently in this work, and in a number of anecdotes the author stages spectacles or scenes in which characters or agents are represented in the act of imagining. Frequently, the coupling of desire and imagination in these scenes is portrayed as fostering misunderstandings and errors. By representing both invented and historical figures in the act of conjecturing and making mistakes, Garcilaso invites readers to reenact paradigmatic moments of the conquest in the theater of their own minds. By mimicking the act of interpretation in history, Garcilaso's performative scenes signal one way in which the text asks its readers not just to "see" but also to correct and transform the record of past. These exemplary scenes provide an accessible way for students to approach the text in a classroom setting as they make visible some of Garcilaso's rhetorical and pedagogical strategies.

I use this approach as a first step in undergraduate survey and advanced courses as well as in graduate seminars. To introduce the first part of the *Comentarios reales* to students, I review the author's biography and the genre of the commentary, which in the sixteenth century was considered a more flexible and personal form than a work of general or natural history, and provide background materials according to the students' level. For undergraduate survey courses, I recommend Rolena Adorno's *Colonial Latin American Literature: A Very Short Introduction* (63–76) as supplementary reading. For advanced undergraduate courses and graduate seminars, I contextualize Garcilaso's quarrels with the historians of Peru who preceded him during the term of Viceroy Francisco de Toledo and provide a bibliography of critical works, including those cited in this essay. A particularly useful introduction at this level is "Language and History in the *Comentarios reales*" (Zamora 39–61). I also make reference to Gonzalo Fernández de Oviedo's *Historia general y natural de las Indias* to contextualize Garcilaso's dialogue with the earlier *cronistas de Indias* ("chroniclers of the Indies"), to works by Juan Luis Vives on the writing of history, and to Garcilaso's Spanish translation of León Hebreo's *Dialoghi d'amore*. Depending on the number of classes devoted to Garcilaso's work, this approach can productively be combined with an examination of other topics of interest in the *Comentarios reales.*

Garcilaso's exploration of the value of the imagination looks back toward the classical tradition as it had been redefined in the early modern period.[2] In the writings of Vives, one finds an explanation of the view, common to many humanist thinkers and rhetoricians, that historical writings should contain vivid scenes that enable the reader to experience the past as present.[3] Vives conceives of the historian as a *sabio*, or wise man, in tune with the divine will and able to teach the truth about what lies beyond one's experience: "historia . . . efficit, ut praeteritis non minus videamos interfuisse, quam praesentibus, illisque perinde uti posse ac nostris" ("history makes it possible for us to see past events as if they were no less present to us than those occurring right now, so that we can exploit them as if they were our own"; 388).[4] Of particular relevance to the *Comentarios reales* is Vives's suggestion that the historian narrate events so that the reader can visualize them as if "present" before his or her eyes. Although in general Vives argues that chronology and accuracy should be respected in historical narrative, he allows that the historian may use agreeable digressions to foster exemplarity and to reach the widest possible audience (Beckjord, *Territories* 15–41). In the *Comentarios reales*, Garcilaso creates anecdotal scenes typical of humanist historiography that are performative in nature. By performative "scenes," I am referring to the work of Richard Schechner, who discusses "restored behaviors" or "twice-behaved" behaviors (22). In Garcilaso's anecdotes, we find scenes in which the faulty communication of past colonial encounters is repeated, rehearsed, and re-created.

Garcilaso's focus on error evokes not just the humanist techniques for capturing the interest of the reader but more broadly the *crónicas de Indias* tradition (the tradition of colonial Spanish historical accounts). As Victor Frankl notes, the colonial enterprise in the New World ushered in a historiography of "refutation" and "opposition," intended to affirm one version of events while simultaneously refuting competing accounts (96). Oviedo, in his *Historia general*, first published in 1535, attacked the notion of the ideal chronicler as envisioned by Vives. Like many of the New World chroniclers, he claimed his own authority—based not on formal academic credentials but on his own eyewitness experience in the Indies—as uniquely legitimate. Oviedo maintained that his direct experience and access to eyewitnesses gave him greater credibility than writers who, though erudite and rhetorically sophisticated, had never left Europe:

> Pero será a lo menos lo que yo escribiere, historia verdadera e desviada de todas las fábulas que en este caso otros escritores, sin verlo, desde España a pie enjuto, han presumido escribir con elegantes e no comunes letras latinas e vulgares, por informaciones de muchos de diferentes juicios, formando historias más allegadas a buen estilo que a la verdad de la cosa que cuentan; porque ni el ciego sabe determinar colores, ni el ausente así testificar estas materias, como quien las mira.   (9)

But what I write will be at least true history that eschews all the fables that in this case other writers, without getting their feet wet, have presumed to write from Spain in elegant Latin and Romance languages. They have used information from many sources, molding histories that are closer to good style than to the truth of what they tell: Just as a blind man cannot see colors, one who has not witnessed cannot testify in these matters as well as someone who has seen them.

The elegant style recommended by humanists like Vives, coupled with the dependence on the accounts of others, condemns the authors who write about the West Indies from Europe, in Oviedo's view. Oviedo's rival, Bartolomé de Las Casas, in his *Historia de las Indias*, would later engage in a systematic refutation of Oviedo by accusing the latter of false testimony that had twisted the truth and done grave damage to the native peoples of the Americas (Beckjord, *Territories* 92–111).

In adopting the form of the commentary, Garcilaso nods to these various themes in humanist and New World historiography yet takes a less confrontational approach than had the earlier *cronistas de Indias*.[5] In focusing on correcting the mistakes of those who lacked sufficient knowledge of Quechua language and culture to chronicle the Inca empire, he engages in a "vast enterprise of exegesis and interpretation" that challenges the authority of previous writers on Peru and on New World history on several fronts (Zamora 44). In asserting his mestizo identity as an erudite linguistic and cultural interpreter, Garcilaso debunks the idea that only wise male Europeans could be credible historians (Mazzotti, "Lightning" 210) as well as the notion that uninformed and linguistically incompetent witnesses could testify about a culture radically different from their own.

Indeed, the connection between experience and imagination in the making of knowledge becomes a frequent site of reflection in this work. In book 1, chapter 3, the author speculates that Columbus never could have imagined the westward route had he not benefitted from the experience of an earlier pilot (Garcilaso, *Comentarios* 1: 17). Frequently, the imagination has negative connotations: in book 1, chapter 1, Garcilaso imitates the custom common to many New World chronicles of addressing weighty philosophical issues, some of which were no longer in dispute: "Y a los que todavía imaginaren que hay muchos mundos, no hay para qué responderles, sino que se estén en sus heréticas imaginaciones hasta que en el infierno se desengañen de ellas" ("And to those who still imagine there are many [worlds], there is no answer except that they may remain in their heretical imaginings till they are undeceived in hell"; *Comentarios* 1: 9; *Royal Commentaries* 1: 9). In this same chapter, we find the word *imaginación* and its derivatives four other times to refute other authorities on a variety of points, such as the notion that the torrid zone of the earth was uninhabitable, and as a warning against those who with their limited human intelligence attempt to "tasar la potencia y la sabiduría de Dios, que no pueda hacer

sus obras más de como ellos las imaginan, habiendo tanta disparidad de un saber al otro cuanto hay de lo finito a lo infinito" ("confine the power and wisdom
of God to doing His works only as they imagine them, when there is as much
difference between their knowledge and His as between the finite and the infinite"; *Comentarios* 1: 13; *Royal Commentaries* 1: 11). Elsewhere in the text, desire and imagination are linked directly to *engaño*, or deception, and Garcilaso
frequently represents eyewitnesses who make mistakes because of their lack of
understanding. Often the reader has more information than the historical ac-
tors or characters represented in these scenes and thus can "witness" misunderstandings in action. By inserting performative scenes that, on the one hand,
recall the topoi of accounts by early European travelers and historians in the
Indies and, on the other, undermine assumptions concerning the primacy of
European eyewitness testimony and "natural" perspective in the face of cultural difference, Garcilaso invites the reader to revise the historical record
while exploring the necessity, perils, and promise of speculation for historical
understanding.

Garcilaso's imaginative anecdotes are often cautionary tales in which private
acts of the imagination have public or historical ramifications. A prominent example is the well-known story of the "deduction" of the name *Perú*. Garcilaso
attributes the territorial misnomer to an awkward meeting between unnamed
men accompanying Vasco Núñez de Balboa's early expeditions of the Pacific in
1513–15 and a native called "Berú." Caught unaware by the sight of the strange
Castilian ship, Berú, who was fishing in a river (*pelú*), "se admiró grandemente
y quedó pasmado y abobado, imaginando qué pudiesse ser aquello que en la mar
veía delante de sí. Y tanto se embeveció y enajenó en este pensamiento, que primero lo tuvieron abraçado los que le ivan a prender que él los sintiesse llegar"
("was lost in amazement and stood astonished and bewildered, imagining what
the thing he held on the sea before him could be. He was so distracted and absorbed in this thought that those who were to capture him had seized him before he perceived their approach"; *Comentarios* 1: 18; *Royal Commentaries* 1:
15). In the series of misunderstandings that follows, the Castilian explorers likewise carelessly give in to desire and imagination to impose a comically inappropriate, but enduring, name on the vast Tahuantinsuyu:

> Los cristianos entendieron conforme a su desseo, imaginando que el in-
> dio les había entendido y respondido a propósito, como si él y ellos huvi-
> eran hablado en castellano, y desde aquel tiempo . . . llamaron Perú aquel
> riquíssimo y grande Imperio, corrompiendo ambos nombres, como cor-
> rompen los españoles casi todos los vocablos que toman del lenguaje de
> los indios de aquella tierra.   (*Comentarios* 1: 18)

> The Christians understood what they wanted to understand, supposing the
> Indian had understood them and had replied as pat as if they had been
> conversing in Spanish; and from that time . . . they called that rich and

great empire Peru, corrupting both words, as the Spanish corrupt almost
all the words they take from the Indian language of that land.

(Royal Commentaries 1: 16)

Garcilaso's emphasis in this scene on the linguistic difficulties and undisciplined
imaginations of the explorers, who are unequipped and disinclined to communicate in any real sense, undermines the topical claims of *cronistas* such as
Oviedo and others concerning the value of direct experience.

The anecdotal digressions in the *Comentarios reales* model acts of interpretation in the work, thus appealing to the reader's imagination. Students readily
understand the literal level of these inventive episodes, which evoke and ironize
some of the commonplaces of the early literature of the conquest and colonization (such as the experience of shipwreck, the early encounters with the other,
and assumptions about the superiority of European over indigenous cultures).
The exempla are intimately connected to the larger philosophical and philological debates elaborated in part 1 of the *Comentarios reales*, as critics have noted.
The inventive interpolations, such as that of Pedro Serrano in book 1 or the story
of the melons in book 9, are often marked in the text through the use of hyper-
bole and create memorable patterns of scenes and images that echo and amplify
one another throughout the text, inviting the reader to puzzle over the connections between them and to consider the role of his or her own imagination as
mediating between perception and judgment.

The anecdote of Pedro Serrano (Garcilaso, *Comentarios* bk. 1, chs. 7–8) presents a variety of imaginative spectacles.[6] Serrano, a Castilian, is shipwrecked
on a deserted island: its vague cartographic coordinates and incongruent habi-
tat (barren and parched, but also humid from constant rainfall) become a stage
for encounters with a variety of others. When a desperate and hungry Serrano
chases turtles, their shells appear to him as shields of medieval weaponry (*adar-
gas, rodelas, broqueles* [shields and targes]), and he attacks them with knightly
fervor: "Con las muy grandes no se podía valer para volverlas de espaldas, porque
le vencían de fuerças, y aunque subía sobre ellas para cansarlas y sujetarlas, no
le aprovechava nada, porque con él a cuestas se ivan a la mar, de manera que la
esperiencia le dezía a cuáles tortugas havía de acometer y a cuáles se havía de
render" ("The largest [of the turtles] he could not contrive to turn over on their
backs, because they were stronger than he, and though he climbed on them to
subdue them by tiring them, it was no use because they could make their way to
the sea with him astraddle. So experience taught him which turtles he could attack, and which to abandon"; *Comentarios* 1: 27; *Royal Commentaries* 1: 28).
The verbs—*vencer, rendir*—conjure up the chivalric genre, yet the context of
battling turtles creates a scene more evocative of quixotic delusions of grandeur.
The jousting with reptiles moves toward ever more comic levels of animal hy-
perbole as the castaway, after years of exposure to the elements, grows a beard
so prolific that he starts to resemble a *jabalí* (wild boar). Later, when another
shipwrecked sailor washes up on the beach, Garcilaso depicts each castaway as

believing the other to be a demon. Only by invoking the Almighty out loud as they flee do they realize they are compatriots. As Margarita Zamora notes, this episode "functions rhetorically to entice the European reader to sympathize and identify with the unlucky Serrano, only to find that Pedro becomes the embodiment of the very image that Europe had shunned" (165). Once rescued, Serrano returns to "civilized" Europe as a traveling showman who exhibits his prodigious whiskers—now both proof of his hardships and his last, best hope for a royal recompense.

The Serrano episode picks up on earlier references (to newly named territories, to the importance of shared language and cultural traditions in overcoming conflicts, to the power of the imagination both to envision survival strategies and to misinterpret what is before one's eyes) and foreshadows later ones; it also encapsulates many of the author's overarching philosophical and philological perspectives in the book. While Serrano's feats with turtles ironize the image of the heroic explorer, elsewhere in the *Comentarios reales* the notion of chivalric honor appears to be taken seriously. In book 1, chapter 4, Garcilaso briefly registers the brutal beheading of Balboa, the first discoverer and adelantado of the South Sea (Pacific), by his rival (and father-in-law) Pedro Arias Dávila. In a work where, as José Durand has shown (88–137), historical questions of honor are paramount, this brief and blunt evocation of the violence that preceded Francisco Pizarro's conquest of the Tahuantinsuyu reveals a gaping chasm between conventional notions and discourses of honor and historical practice.

Another clue for understanding the role of the performative scenes in the *Comentarios reales* can be found in Garcilaso's Spanish translation of Hebreo's *Dialoghi d'amore*. Hebreo's work on love, written in Italian but soon translated into Spanish, Hebrew, Latin, and French, was an important Neoplatonic philosophical treatise of the day. In graduate classes, I provide students with a short selection from this text on the use of imaginative fables in historical narratives that explicitly links them to interpretation and memory. In Garcilaso's Spanish rendition of the second dialogue, Philo and Sophia converse on the value of poetic fictions, and Philo expounds on the justifications for including such fables in works of history or philosophy. The ancients, he explains, mixed literal, moral, and allegorical meanings in their works so as to preserve "secrets" of knowledge for readers who would be able to understand their profound or true meanings. When Sophia presses her interlocutor on this point, he notes that the brevity of poetic expression enables the author to intertwine efficiently many *sentencias*, or ideas, in an episode. Further, by mixing enjoyable fables with allegorical meanings, the author facilitates the comprehension of difficult points. Philo suggests that the use of fables may conserve complex ideas by appealing to a wide range of intellects over time: while simple minds will grasp the story alone, more sophisticated ones will be able to comprehend the moral meaning of a work, and superior ones will have the ability to see the allegorical meaning. With one single fable, then, the author can create a *manjar* (delicacy) for all kinds of readers, thus increasing the chance that important but difficult to understand knowledge will be remembered over time than if it were entrusted to a very few sophisticated readers (*La traduzion* 75–77).

Hebreo's principles of mixing styles and meanings and of appealing to a broad range of intellects recall medieval techniques for training the imagination that relied on creating rare and striking images. Mary Carruthers traces this technique in the readings of the ancient treatise *Rhetorica ad Herennium* by medieval authors such as Albertus Magnus: "What is unusual and marvelous strikes us and is retained in the memory more than what is ordinary . . . ; moreover, what is marvelous by its forceful impression on us causes us to remark it, and that engenders both inquiry and reminiscence" (141). Garcilaso frequently adapts vivid images from oral and written traditions on the conquest and molds them into telling performative scenes. In this way, Garcilaso's anecdotes, which often mix registers from different regions of the imagination (Martínez-Bonati 41–68), recall not just medieval mnemonic techniques but the author's own definition of *huacas*, not in the sense of a sacred object or divinity, but in that of an object that is extraordinary, marvelous, or monstrous and distinguished from others in a similar class (Garcilaso, *Comentarios* 1: 79–81; bk. 2, ch. 5). In this regard, Roland Greene has referred to Garcilaso's anecdotal interludes as "narrative *huacas*," noting that these stories "inflect and undermine commonplace notions and draw on humanist antecedents for their power to startle" while at the same time forcing the European reader to contemplate an Andean worldview (220, 228).

Garcilaso's short, imaginative interpolations function as exempla that model strategies of interpretation and echo scenes in the properly historical account, which, as is well known, was conceived in part to counteract the historiography produced as a part of the Viceroy Toledo's efforts to discredit the Inca dynasty and justify Spanish rule. I will just look briefly at two examples.

In book 7, chapter 27, Garcilaso describes the Inca fortress of Sacsahuamán, noting that many observers had postulated that the stonework was so astonishing as to seem to have been achieved not by humans but by demonic intervention (*Comentarios* 2: 146). Although Garcilaso refutes this hypothesis as erroneous with an extensive quotation from the Jesuit historian José de Acosta, who had described the stone constructions as produced by the skilled labor of a massive workforce, he soon returns to the supernatural hypothesis, this time by revealing the process of interpretation behind such a mistaken conclusion. He recalls a conversation with a priest from Montilla, who had visited Cuzco and witnessed the Sacsahuamán ruins: "Me dixo que antes de verlas nunca jamás imaginó creer que fuessen tan grandes como le havían dicho, y que después que las vió le parescieron mayores que la fama; y que entonces le nasció otra duda más dificultosa, que fué imaginar que no pudieron assentarlas en la obra sino por arte del demonio" ("Before seeing [the ruins] he would never have believed that they could have been so large as he had been told, and that when he saw them they seemed even bigger. Then there occurred to him an even more difficult problem—he could not believe they could have been set up unless by diabolic art"; *Comentarios* 2: 150; *Royal Commentaries* 2: 467). Here too Garcilaso presents a mistaken eyewitness in the act of thinking and imagining. His careful display of a mental process that moves from perception to image, and from imagination to considered thought, reproduces a scene in which the priest unsuccessfully negotiates his doubts and prejudices. Rather than solve the enigma before his eyes, the priest falls back on his initial misperceptions.

Garcilaso's treatment of pre-Incan cultures provides another interesting case in point. In the *proemio* to part 1 of the *Comentarios reales*, the author states that he lacks sufficient information to account for the history and culture of pre- and non-Inca groups in the Andes: "Escrivimos solamente del Imperio de los Incas, sin entrar en otras monarquías, porque no tengo la noticia dellas que désta" ("I write only of the empire of the Incas, and do not deal with other monarchies, about which I can claim no similar knowledge"; *Comentarios* 1: 8; *Royal Commentaries* 1: 4). However, in chapter 14 of book 1, he enumerates the "barbarian" qualities of these earlier cultures in extraordinary detail (Zamora 72–74). Yet Garcilaso interrupts this list, ostensibly for reasons of decorum, suggesting that his readers fill in the gaps: "A lo que cada uno quisiere imaginar y añadir a las cosas dichas, que, por mucho que alargue la imaginación, no llegará a imaginar cuán grande fueron las torpezas de aquella gentilidad" ("What I have not described as fully as necessary I leave each one to imagine and supply details: however he stretches his imagination, he will not realize how great was the savagery of these gentiles"; *Comentarios* 1: 38; *Royal Commentaries* 1: 39–40). Given the other instances of the coupling of desire and imagination ("A lo que cada uno quisiere imaginar") as a recipe for deception in the *Comentarios reales*, the invitation to imagine unspeakable *torpezas* would seem to indicate an authorial warning to the careful reader. Garcilaso seems to test the audience's memory here, offering the option to either imitate in the theater of the mind a scene that replicates the imaginative mistakes of careless interpreters or, perhaps, refrain from taking part in such a scene.

Like the narrative anecdotes, the imaginative scenes in Garcilaso's properly historical narrative are geared toward training the careful reader to see the mistakes of the past and also to visualize the complexities and contradictions of colonial experience. Although Garcilaso represents the imagination and its discontinuities in multiple ways in his *Comentarios reales*, it would be a mistake to conclude that this facet of his work confers a fictive quality on his history, as some critics have suggested (Pupo-Walker 85–105; Arrom 27–35). Rather, I would suggest the diverse spectacles of the imagination represented here function rhetorically to educate, inspire, and transform the possibility of historical understanding. In the space of his text, Garcilaso also draws on discordant regions of the imagination to represent disturbing realities that coexist with and sometimes shatter ideal ones. The possibility of an enlightened imagination in the *Comentarios reales* thus appears as a force capable of revealing essential similarities among strangers, of fostering the recognition and mending of past mistakes, and of facilitating at least the conception of a more harmonious future.

NOTES

An earlier version of this essay appeared in the collection *400 años de* Comentarios reales (see Beckjord, "Espectáculos").

[1] Among others, on humanist sources, see Durand; Pupo-Walker; Zamora; Mazzotti, "El Inca." On Andean traditions, see Mazzotti, "Lightning." On the diverse roles of the imagination in the *Comentarios reales,* see Arrom; Pupo-Walker; MacCormack.

[2] On the role of the imagination in Garcilaso's intercalated anecdotes, see, among others, Pupo-Walker 107–93; on the imagination in the portrayal of Andean religion, see MacCormack.

[3] For an overview of the broader humanist and philological currents in which Garcilaso participates, see Zamora 39–61.

[4] Unless otherwise attributed, translations are my own.

[5] On Garcilaso's use and modification of the genre of the commentary, see Zamora 52–61; Fernández 26–55.

[6] This episode has been much studied in, among others, Fernández Sosa; Pupo-Walker 58; Zamora 164–65. On the likely historical source for this narrative, see Ledezma.

WORKS CITED

Adorno, Rolena. *Colonial Latin America: A Very Short Introduction.* Oxford UP, 2011.

Arrom, José Juan. "Hombre y mundo en dos cuentos del Inca Garcilaso." *Certidumbre de América: Estudios de letras, folklore y cultura.* 2nd ed., Gredos, 1971, pp. 27–35.

Beckjord, Sarah. "Espectáculos de la imaginación: La interpretación histórica en los *Comentarios reales.*" *400 años de* Comentarios reales: *Estudios sobre el Inca Garcilaso y su obra,* edited by Elena Romiti and Song No, Aitana, 2010, pp. 15–33.

———. *Territories of History: Humanism, Rhetoric, and the Historical Imagination in the Early Chronicles of Spanish America.* Pennsylvania State UP, 2007.

Carruthers, Mary. *The Book of Memory: A Study of Memory in Medieval Culture.* Cambridge UP, 1990.

Durand, José. *El Inca Garcilaso: Clásico de América.* SepSetentas, 1976.

Fernández, Christian. *Inca Garcilaso: Imaginación, memoria e identidad.* Universidad Nacional Mayor de San Marcos, 2004.

Fernandez Sosa, Luis F. "Relectura de los *Comentarios reales*: Relato de Pedro Serrano." *Hispania,* vol. 62, no. 4, Dec. 1979, pp. 635–46.

Frankl, Victor. *El antijovio de Gonzalo Jiménez de Quesada y las concepciones de realidad y verdad en la época de la Contrarreforma y del manierismo.* Cultura Hispánica, 1963.

Garcilaso de la Vega. *Comentarios reales de los Incas.* Edited by Ángel Rosenblat, Emecé Editores, 1943. 2 vols.

———. *Royal Commentaries of the Incas and General History of Peru.* Translated by Harold V. Livermore, U Texas P, 1966. 2 vols.

———. *La traduzion del Indio de los tres diálogos de amor de Leon Hebreo, hecha del italiano en español por Garcilasso Inga de la Vega, natural de la gran ciudad del Cusco.* Pedro Madrigal, 1590.

Greene, Roland. *Unrequited Conquests: Love and Empire in the Colonial Americas.* U Chicago P, 1999.

Ledezma, Domingo. "Los infortunios de Pedro Serrano: Huellas historiográficas de un relato de naufragio." *Renacimiento mestizo: Los 400 años de los* Comentarios reales, edited by José Antonio Mazzotti, Iberoamericana/Vervuert, 2010, pp. 31–50.

MacCormack, Sabine. *Religion in the Andes: Vision and Imagination in Early Colonial Peru.* Princeton UP, 1991.

Martínez Bonati, Félix. *El Quijote y la poética de la novela.* Centro de Estudios Cervantinos, 1995.

Mazzotti, José Antonio. "El Inca Garcilaso Translates León Hebreo: *The Dialogues of Love,* the Cabala, and Andean Mythology." *Beyond Books and Borders: Garcilaso de la Vega and* La Florida del Inca, edited by Raquel Chang-Rodríguez, Bucknell UP, 2006, pp. 99–118.

———. "The Lightning Bolt Yields to the Rainbow: Indigenous History and Colonial Semiosis in the *Royal Commentaries* of El Inca Garcilaso de la Vega." *Modern Language Quarterly,* vol. 57, no. 2, June 1996, pp. 197–211.

Oviedo, Gonzalo Fernández de. *Historia general y natural de las Indias.* 1959. Edited by Juan Pérez Tudela Bueso, 2nd ed., Atlas, 1992. Biblioteca de Autores Españoles, 117–21.

Pupo-Walker, Enrique. *Historia, creación y profecía en los textos del Inca Garcilaso de la Vega.* José Porrúa Turanzas, 1982.

Schechner, Richard. *Performance Studies: An Introduction.* Routledge, 2002.

Vives, Juan Luis. *De tradendis disciplinis. Opera omnia,* edited by Gregorio Mayans y Siscar, vol. 6, Gregg, 1964, pp. 5–437.

Zamora, Margarita. *Language, Authority, and Indigenous History in the* Comentarios reales de los Incas. Cambridge UP, 1988.

The Andes in Appalachia:
Inca Garcilaso in a Hemispheric Curriculum

Kimberly Borchard

[A]unque las regiones y tierras estén tan distantes, parece
que todas son Indias.

[A]ll of these lands and regions, though far apart, are
regarded as the Indies.
    —Inca Garcilaso de la Vega, *La Florida del Ynca*
            (The Florida of the Inca)

Inca Garcilaso de la Vega is often touted as a cultural and linguistic intermediary
between the Spanish invaders and the surviving population of the Inca empire, as well as the voice for what he hoped would be an empowered mestizo
ruling class (Voigt 99–153; Zamora; Brading 1–23). For my students, Garcilaso
also serves as a geographic intermediary between early modern Peru and the
(North) American southeast or, more broadly, between colonial Latin America
and the contemporary United States. In the pages that follow, I outline how I use
Garcilaso to demonstrate the political and cultural continuity of the Americas
in the early modern Atlantic world. When viewed within a broad panorama of
authors engaged in a transnational polemic regarding the colonization of
today's southeastern United States, Garcilaso ceases to appear exclusively as
the voice of a distant, educated Andean elite and becomes one of many players
in the international dialogue that simultaneously described and shaped North
American colonization.

In the sample curriculum below, I offer students selections from a variety of authors concerned with the vaguely defined region first named in print as "Apalache" by Álvar Núñez Cabeza de Vaca in 1542. To begin, we compare selections from Garcilaso's *La Florida del Ynca* (*The Florida of the Inca*) and Cabeza de Vaca's *Naufragios*; next, we consider brief selections from René de Laudonnière's and Jacques Le Moyne de Morgues's accounts bearing witness to the disastrous French attempt to wrest control of Florida from the Spanish beginning in 1562, and the letters of the Spanish admiral Pedro Menéndez de Avilés documenting the massacre with which he put an end to those ambitions at the French settlement of Fort Caroline in 1565. We then return to the last pages of *La Florida* for what might be interpreted as Garcilaso's ultimate assessment of European endeavors in Florida following his cursory treatment of the French-Menéndez episode, as expressed by Florida natives. Finally, presaging England's eventual takeover of the region, we conclude the unit with a letter from Diego de Molina, a Spanish spy taken prisoner by the English on the Virginia coast in 1611, and excerpts from the account of John Lederer, a German who attempted the first westward crossing of the Appalachian Mountains from the Virginia colony in 1669.

Garcilaso and Cabeza de Vaca: Bounty and Poverty in Apalache

Whereas I habitually point out inconsistencies within and between colonial texts, I find that students usually engage the most with authors who point out such discrepancies themselves: intertextual commentaries and critiques both reveal authorial priorities and make the distant world of *indios* (Indians) and conquistadores more immediate for undergraduates struggling with the complexity of early *relaciones* (accounts) and *historias* (histories). Garcilaso's treatment of Apalache allows students to grasp the unsuspected proximity, in the early modern imaginary, of the familiar region of Florida to the distant one of colonial Peru. A close reading of select chapters of *La Florida* also encourages them to turn a critical eye toward Garcilaso's subsequent profession, in the *Comentarios reales*, that his work is not intended to "contradezirles [a los historiadores españoles], sino seruirles de comento y glosa" ("gainsay [the Spanish historians], but to furnish a commentary and gloss"; *Primera parte* xviii; *Royal Commentaries* 1: 4). Though I teach a broader selection from Garcilaso than that detailed here, of special import for the approach outlined in this essay are Garcilaso's efforts to explain the supposed inconsistencies between accounts of Apalache offered by Cabeza de Vaca and various participants in the Hernando de Soto expedition, as well as the final judgment of that expedition expressed at the end of *La Florida*. Both these selections cast the conquest in a critical light, complicating at least half of Garcilaso's assertion that he wrote his history with the dual intent of praising the heroism of natives and Spaniards alike (*Primera parte* xxxvii–xxxviii). The subsequent comparison of Garcilaso's final critique of the de Soto mission to Apalache with accounts of later explorers highlights the region's importance in the international competition to gain control over North America.

According to Garcilaso, the Florida natives encountered by de Soto on his northward treasure hunt warned him that the cacique of Apalache was awaiting his arrival, so that he and his warriors might "los matar y desquartizar a todos [los Castellanos]" ("kill and quarter the Spaniards"; *La Florida* 2: 95; bk. 2, ch. 3; *The Florida* 183).[1] Indeed, the expedition found itself persistently beleaguered by native attacks. When de Soto sent out three small reconnaissance parties, the two scouting out land to the north under the command of Arias Tinoco and Andrés de Vasconcelos returned to describe "muchos pueblos con mucha gente y . . . tierra . . . fértil de comida, y limpia de çiénagas y montes brauos" ("many populous villages as well as land . . . abundant in food and clear of swamps and extensive forests"). In contrast, the party that headed southward under the command of Juan de Añasco encountered "tierra asperísima y muy dificultosa, y casi imposible de andar por las malezas de montes, y çienagas" ("very rough and difficult terrain, almost impossible to traverse because of its woody undergrowth and swamps"; *La Florida* 2: 96v; bk. 2, ch. 4; *The Florida* 185).

Most striking in Garcilaso's commentary upon this testimony is his comparison of it with Cabeza de Vaca's account, in which he makes a decidedly incomplete reading of the latter text:

> De ver esta diferencia de tierras muy buenas y muy malas me parecio no passar adelante sin tocar lo que Aluar Nuñez Cabeça de vaca . . . escriue desta Prouincia de Apalache: donde la pinta aspera y fragosa, ocupada de muchos montes y çienagas, con rios y malos passos, mal poblada, y esteril, todo en contra de lo que vamos escriuiendo.
>
> (*La Florida* 2: 96–97; bk. 2, ch. 4)

> Having called attention to the fact that some of this land was very good and some very bad, I feel it wise not to continue my story without pausing to touch upon what Alvar Núñez Cabeza de Vaca writes of the province of Apalache. . . . Here he describes the country as rough and craggy; covered with forests, swamps, rivers, and troublesome passages; and poorly populated as well as sterile. . . . [A]ll of these characteristics are contrary to what we are writing.
>
> (*The Florida* 185)

Here, I ask that students return to *Naufragios*, which we read earlier in the course, and compare the passages on Apalache with Garcilaso's analysis of them. Decades before Garcilaso composed his history of Florida, Cabeza de Vaca had reported native accounts of a faraway "provinzia que se dezía Apalachen, en la qual avía mucho oro y . . . muy gran cantidad de todo lo que nosotros estimamos en algo" ("province called Apalachen, in which there was much gold [and] very great quantities of everything we held in esteem"; 1: 38, 39). Upon arriving there some months later, though, he bemoaned the "pobreza de la tierra" ("poverty of the land"; 1: 60, 61). Nevertheless, he also directly contradicted this charge with his detailed description of the region's great abundance of maize and wild game, as well as its ideal suitability for domestic livestock (1: 56, 57).

Rolena Adorno has referred to this discrepancy between "the impoverishment of the land about which [Cabeza de Vaca] wrote and the visions of wealth that he conjured up" as an "interpretative gap" (163–64). The more cynical among us might be tempted to infer that this gap was little more than cognitive dissonance born of the author's disappointment upon discovering only agricultural bounty, where he had hoped for gold. Given his propensity to mock Spanish avarice, Garcilaso might have taken this glaring inconsistency as an opportunity to comment upon the capacity of greed to blind Spaniards to the natural abundance of the land, or to inquire into the contrast between the behavior of the natives who encouraged Pánfilo de Narváez to continue to Apalache and exploit its wealth and that of those who warned de Soto he would be murdered there. Instead, his assertion that Cabeza de Vaca's account contradicted the reports of the de Soto expedition is outright misleading. In fact, Juan de Añasco's report of swampy woodlands blocking his path mirrors Cabeza de Vaca's complaint that "Apalachen" was "muy mala de andar por los muy malos passos y montes y lagunas que tenía" ("very difficult to traverse because of the very difficult passes and woods and lagoons it contained"; 1: 58, 59). Similarly, Cabeza de Vaca's rationale for leaving the region because "los indios nos hazían continua guerra" ("the Indians made war on us continually"; 1: 60, 61) foreshadows the subsequent admonishment to de Soto that the people of Apalache intended to continually assault his company in order to preserve the "reputacion que . . . auian ganado de ser los mas valientes y guerreros" ("reputation they had gained . . . as the most valiant and warlike people"; *La Florida* 2: 96; bk. 2, ch. 3; *The Florida* 183).

As he attempts to reconcile these purportedly antithetical accounts of Apalache, Garcilaso first suggests that Cabeza de Vaca and de Soto may have arrived at different villages within the same province sharing a common name (*La Florida* 2: 97; bk. 2, ch. 4; *The Florida* 186). However, in a twist typical of the tongue-in-cheek commentaries known today as the hallmark of his authorial voice, Garcilaso concludes with an alternate, obliquely damning explanation of Cabeza de Vaca's report: "[M]ucha parte de la relación que Aluar Núñez escriue de aquella tierra, es la que los Indios le dieron. . . . Y en la relación que le dauan es de creer que los Indios dirían antes mal, que bien de su patria por desacreditarla, para que los Españoles perdieran el desseo de yr a ella" ("A great part of Alvar Núñez' description of that land is what the Indians themselves gave him, and . . . the Indians would have given the Spaniards an unfavorable rather than a favorable account of their land, so that in discrediting it they would discourage them from coming there"; *La Florida* 2: 97; bk. 2, ch. 4; *The Florida* 186). Of pedagogical interest here is Garcilaso's choice to focus exclusively on Cabeza de Vaca's negative portrayal of Apalache. The unfavorable description to which he refers is a very short passage toward the end of the Apalache episode in which the residents of the town of "Apalachen" allege not that the entire province is poor and unpopulated, but that the region between its largest village and the next wealthy one is (Cabeza de Vaca 1: 59–61). Given Garcilaso's penchant for critiquing European misinterpretation of native sources, this lapse in his own reading, which provides the sole foundation for his assumption that the natives' priority is to deter further Spanish exploration, gives pause. Though Margarita Zamora was referring to Garcilaso's use of José de Acosta in the *Comentarios reales* when she wrote that "the pattern of citations and references actually distorts [the] work almost to the point of unrecognizability" (107), the same could well be said of his selective reading of Cabeza de Vaca.

French Visions of Apalatcy and the Spanish Response

Before moving on to Garcilaso's final assessment of the de Soto expedition—and by extension Spanish activity in the New World—I pause to give students a brief overview of the failed French colony mentioned in the final chapter of *La Florida*, as described by both French and Spanish participants. Because of limited time and in order to take advantage of Jacques Le Moyne de Morgues's stunning illustrations of the French voyages, I introduce selections of the French material in translation in class. I first give a brief timeline of French activity in Florida between 1562 and 1565, highlighting the French threat to Spain's economic and military control of the region. To reinforce the vision of North America beyond New Spain as a territory still disputed by European powers in the late sixteenth century, I cite Richard Hakluyt's assurance to Sir Walter Raleigh, from the preface to his 1586 translation of René de Laudonnière's *A Notable Historie*, that the English conquest of North America should go more smoothly than did Iberian conquests to the south, for northern indigenous peoples "are of better wittes than those of Mexico and Peru" and—as a result of their ostensibly superior intellects—will readily submit to the English crown and embrace Christianity (441–43). Next, I share passages from Laudonnière and Le Moyne announcing further indigenous reports of precious metals in "Apalatcy" (Laudonnière, *Notable Historie* 452, 466–67, 482, and *Second Voyage* 21–22, 35; Le Moyne, *Narrative* 42, 48). Finally, I present Le Moyne's gorgeous (if highly inaccurate) map "Floridae Americae Provinciae," with English translations of the Latin legends noting gold and silver in the northern mountains of "Apalatci," and his illustration "How the Natives Collect Gold in the Streams," complementing the latter image with the historian David Quinn's observation that no native peoples "north of Mexico" collected gold with such a technique (qtd. in Hulton 1: 215).[2]

After this overview of French Florida, students read selections from the letters of Pedro Menéndez de Avilés, dispatched by Philip II in 1565 to "quemar y ahorcar a los franceses luteranos" ("burn and hang the French Lutherans"; 131)[3] who had encroached upon his territory. In a letter dated 11 September 1565, Menéndez details his strategy to win over the Timucua in an alliance against the

French, as well as his feigned disinterest in their gold (131–38). On 15 October, he recounts his merciless assault on Fort Caroline.[4] Of greater importance than the gruesome slaughter itself for students' understanding of Florida/Apalache as a geopolitical hotspot is Menéndez's rationale for that slaughter. He first explains that the French had not bothered building more fortifications following their arrival, occupied as they were in celebrating

> nuevas que al nornoroeste de Santa Elena cien leguas, tienen la serranía que viene de las Zacatecas y que es de mucha plata, y han venido indios a ellos con muchos pedazos, y hallóseles destos pedazos de plata, que los indios de aquellas partes les traían, cantidad de cinco o seis mil ducados.
> (145)

> news that a hundred leagues to the north-northwest of Santa Elena [Parris Island, South Carolina] lies the mountain range that comes from Zacatecas and that contains much silver; and Indians have come to them with many pieces [of this silver], and they were discovered to have possessed a quantity of five or six thousand ducats of these silver pieces, which the Indians of those lands brought to them.

The source of this silver remains mysterious. However, Menéndez's estimation that the Appalachian Mountains lay a hundred leagues (roughly three hundred miles) north-northwest of Santa Elena is astonishingly accurate. This report of precious metals in the mountains to the north also seems to corroborate the illustration on Le Moyne's map.

Of equal or greater importance than the promise of silver was the intelligence gathered from a French captive, according to whom the French and English were conspiring to build a fort in Key West and use it as an outpost to pick off Spanish treasure fleets in the Caribbean. Yet this continuation of the piracy that had plagued Spain for decades constituted the least troublesome aspect of the plan: from Key West, the Anglo-French alliance would invade Havana, then Hispaniola, Puerto Rico, and, finally, the mainland, freeing all the African slaves and sowing chaos throughout the length and breadth of Spain's possessions (Menéndez de Avilés 146–47).

These passages from Menéndez's correspondence with Philip II are crucial in cementing the myth of Apalache as a northern El Dorado and a linchpin of competing European ambitions in the western Atlantic during the latter half of the sixteenth century. Menéndez feared not only that the French would discover the coveted Appalachian mines before the Spanish but that they would establish a trans-Appalachian route to the Spanish-controlled silver mines in Zacatecas, slashing a bloody path across the economic heart of the colonies by liberating the growing population of African slaves upon which Spain's economic might depended. It is therefore difficult to overstate the importance of his report to Philip II's increasingly panicked efforts to fend off rivals' incursions into North America.

To contain this threat, Menéndez proposed that he construct a fort in the Florida Keys where the French and English had intended to do so, thus protecting Spanish treasure fleets traveling between the mainland and the Caribbean. From there he would move on to settle Santa Elena and the Chesapeake Bay ("la bahía de Santa María"; 148). He hypothesized that half a league west into the Chesapeake, another saltwater channel led directly to the South Sea (149). Because of this underestimation of the length and breadth of North America, Menéndez believed a Huguenot settlement in Florida brought the French just one step away from sauntering down the mountains and seizing the silver mines of New Spain. Thus it was in the strategic interest of Philip II to consolidate control over the entire Atlantic coast, from Florida to Newfoundland. Finally, having secured the Chesapeake and access to both the Canadian fishing waters and the Appalachian mines, the Spanish could make the short trip westward to China and the Spice Islands (149).

With this sweeping plan, Menéndez imagined the Appalachian Mountains as the backbone of the Spanish empire in North America, stretching from a maritime entrance to Canada in the north to the Zacatecas silver mines in the south. Despite the catastrophic experiences of compatriots who had attempted to overcome the natives of Apalache during previous decades, Menéndez expressed confidence that with a few hundred more men the province "[c]on facilidad se allanará hasta la Nueva Galicia, que podrá haber como trescientas leguas" ("will easily be crushed [from here] to New Galicia, which might lie some three hundred leagues away"; 151). Once again misjudging the vastness of the continent, Menéndez anticipated the rapid conquest of all North America, resulting in a time when

> no habrá más que poblar en la Florida y se . . . caminará el camino a la Nueva España con facilidad y beneficiarse han muchas minas que hay de plata en aquellas tierras . . . y aun dentro de pocos años la plata que se beneficiare en aquellas minas y sierras de San Martín, se vendrá a estos puertos y a Santa Elena y a la bahía de Santa María . . . y de aquí y de Santa Elena a la bahía se Santa María es fácil navegación a España y breve.
>
> (152)

> we shall only have to settle Florida, and . . . the route to New Spain will be traveled with ease, and the many silver mines in those lands . . . will be exploited; and within just a few years the silver extracted from those mines and the mountains of San Martín will come to these ports and to Santa Elena and the Chesapeake Bay . . . and from here and Santa Elena to Chesapeake Bay, it is a short and easy voyage to Spain.

While contemporary knowledge of North American geography makes the impossibility of this scheme obvious, I explain to my students that Menéndez's hopes were not as quixotic as they might seem. During the previous four decades Spain had conquered first the Nahua and then the Inca civilizations, plundering un-imaginable wealth from Mexico to Peru while extending its empire across a dis-tance greater than the width of the continental United States. Why not imagine that a similar feat would be possible to the north?

The Final Vision of Conquest in La Florida del Ynca

After this glimpse into the perceived centrality of Florida/Apalache in the con-solidation of Spanish power, we return to the end of *La Florida*. Lisa Voigt has noted that the volume's final chapter, which begins with a detailed catalog of the missionaries who perished in failed conquest and evangelization efforts prior to 1568, "is difficult to reconcile with its mestizo author's reputation for the rec-onciliation of contraries" (99). Without mentioning either the massacre at Fort Caroline or his perception of the region's strategic importance, Garcilaso notes merely that Menéndez traveled to Florida three times to rid it of French cor-sairs, then turns his attention to seven natives whom the admiral brought back to Spain after his second voyage. They were greeted by Gonzalo Silvestre, one of the participants in the de Soto expedition who served as Garcilaso's informant. When Silvestre flaunted his knowledge of their homeland by asking "if they were from Vitachuco, Apalache . . . or other places where the Spaniards had fought," they responded contemptuously: "Dexando vosotros essas prouincías tan mal paradas como las dexasteys, quereys que os demos nuevas dellas?" ("Having left those provinces as desolate as you did, do you want us to give you news of them?"; Garcilaso, *La Florida* 350; bk. 6, ch. 22; *The Florida* 641). They then declared that they would prefer to strike him with arrows than respond to his questions, shooting arrows into the air to drive home their animosity.

Six of these Floridian hostages died shortly after baptism.[5] The sole survivor, a native of the Virginia Tidewater taken by Spanish explorers in 1561 and bap-tized Don Luis de Velasco following an audience with Philip II, would travel to Mexico and spearhead the murder of eight Jesuits to whom he had promised aid in their proselytizing mission to his homeland when they declined to invite a mili-tary detail for their protection.[6] Yet, despite Don Luis's feigned conversion and ruthlessness toward the unarmed religious men to whom he had promised aid, Garcilaso condemns any thought of revenge against him or his people. Rather, just as he puts the harsh final judgment of Spanish colonization into the mouths of Native American hostages, he puts a call for clemency in the hearts—or blood—of the slaughtered clergymen: "cuya sangre espero en Dios que esta cla-mando y pídiendo no vengança como la de Abel, sino mísericordia como la de Christo nuestro Señor, para que aquellos Gentíles vengan en conoscímiento de su eterna Magestad" ("I do trust God that the blood of these men is not crying out . . . for vengeance like that of Abel, but for mercy like that of Christ Our Lord, so that these pagans may come into the knowledge of His Eternal Majesty"; *La Florida* 351; bk. 6, ch. 22; *The Florida* 643). This dramatic call for forgiveness ends the cycle of violence and revenge plotted not only throughout the pages of *La Florida* but throughout the narratives of Le Moyne, Laudonnière, and Menéndez as well. It also vividly illustrates the vast sweep of early modern geopolitics, as one of the heirs to the Inca empire appeals to a Spanish audience, in a text published in Portugal, for the peaceful—and forgiving—settlement of what would eventually become the southeastern United States.

Apalache in Virginia

I conclude this unit with two revelatory glimpses into the continuing centrality of Apalache, beyond *La Florida*, in the Spanish and English colonial imaginations. The first is a letter presumably destined for Don Alonso de Velasco, the Spanish ambassador in London, composed by Diego de Molina in Virginia and dated 28 May 1613. Molina was a Spanish spy captured during a reconnaissance mission on the James River in 1611 (Tyler 217). He characterizes the English settlement in Virginia as "una hidra en su niñez" ("a hydra in its infancy") and "[una] plaça . . . muy aproposito para recogerse en ella todos los piratas de Europa" ("[an ideal] gathering place for all the pirates of Europe"; Molina, "Carta"; "Letter" 218). He then affirms that the English have already discovered profitable gold and silver mines that they have not yet begun to exploit; but when commercial mining begins,

> ay grandes promesas de que hallaran en las sieras mucha cantidad asi lo afirman los yndios y ofrecen de enseñar los lugares que ellos conocen y dicen que en los principios de los rios despues que an abajado de la sierra ay grande cantidad de granos de plata y oro, pero como no hagan caudal del, sino de solo cobre . . . no los cojen.   ("Carta")

> there are many indications that they will find a large number [of mines] in the mountains. So the Indians say and they offer to show the locations that they know and they say that near the sources of the rivers, as they come down from the mountains, there is a great quantity of grains of silver and gold, but, as they do not set any value on these but only on copper . . . they do not gather them.   ("Letter" 219)

These statements, included in a letter sewn into the sole of a shoe to be smuggled out of Molina's confinement (Tyler 223), reiterate the French accounts of gold in Appalachian waters and the promise—as old as the conquest itself—that the natives assign no value to such wealth and will, therefore, readily hand it over to the Europeans. Molina then repeats Menéndez's warning, penned a half century earlier, that the English intend to proceed down the mountains to invade Spanish settlements in the southwest (in this case New Mexico, rather than New Spain) and take over all the Caribbean colonies ("Carta"; "Letter" 219).

From this reiteration of Menéndez's belief in England's imminent appropriation of Appalachian gold, we move on to John Lederer's account of the first
English-funded efforts to reach that gold from the Virginia colony. Lederer was
a German, according to some a physician (Carrier 436), who attempted (and
failed) an Appalachian crossing three times between March 1669 and September 1670. Originally composed in Latin, Lederer's original text (now lost) was
translated into English by Sir William Talbot, proprietary secretary of the province of Maryland, and printed in London in 1672 (Cunz 181). In my class, we
focus on the account of Lederer's second journey, from 20 May to 17 July 1670.
Here Lederer makes two claims astonishing to readers of the previous 130 years
of accounts of Apalache. First, he claims to have passed through a village on the
banks of a vast lake by the name of Ushery, encountering there a people who
exist "in continual fear of the *Oustack*-Indians" who live on the lake's other shore
and fight with silver hatchets (Lederer 17–18). Readers of the French accounts
easily recognize "Oustack" as a variant of Laudonnière's "Houstaqua"—the hostile
chieftain who must be "subdued" in order to secure a path to the gold and silver
in the mountains (*Second Voyage* 21). Returning to Le Moyne's map of Florida,
one recognizes "Oustaca" as a native village near the northern Appalachian lake
where natives gathered gold and silver ("Floridae").

Though on this second voyage Lederer makes the strongest claims of nearing
the source of Appalachian gold, he turns back. He does not, however, retreat
out of fear of the formidable natives guarding the mines. Rather, it is another
warlike people who keep him at bay, when the Usheries warn him

> that two-days journey and a half from hence to the Southwest, a powerful
> Nation of Bearded men were seated, which I suppose to be the Span-
> iards. . . . I thought it not safe to venture my self amongst the Spaniards,
> lest taking me for a Spy, they would either make me away, or condemn me
> to a perpetual Slavery in their Mines.   (Lederer 18–19)

Cabeza de Vaca's 1542 report of native gold in Apalache, later transformed
into Menéndez's fear that the French would be the first to reach that gold, thus
morphs into a German belief in the existence of Spanish mines by 1670. Already mired in controversy during his lifetime, Lederer's account has continued to inspire everything from cautious praise (Cunz 175–85; Carrier 435–45)
to blatant mockery (Alvord and Bidgood 68) for more than three centuries. Yet
of greater importance here than the historical veracity of Lederer's claims is
the way in which his story may be used to close the circle of colonial rivalry
over Apalache/Apalatcy/Appalachia traced throughout the authors discussed
above.

In this international, multilingual drama of the European race to access fa-
bled Appalachian gold and build an empire in the North American southeast,
La Florida provides a continual point of reference, looking back at the first half
century of failed attempts at colonization and foreshadowing Spain's eventual

loss of the territory. That one of the first serious studies of European explorations of the region that gradually came to be known as Appalachia—that most idiosyncratically, paradigmatically "(North) American" of realms—should have been penned by Garcilaso—that most idiosyncratic, paradigmatic *indio mestizo del Perú*—helped me realize, while still a student myself, the artificiality of attempts to separate historical narratives produced within disparate linguistic and national traditions. It is from this intersection of colonial histories of the Northern and Southern Hemispheres that I teach the works of Garcilaso. By exploring the insertion of Appalachian (and southeastern American) history into Andean history in *La Florida*, I work to bridge the gap between the languages, geographies, and cultures that are all too often taught as mutually exclusive entities in college classrooms. Though our languages and nationalities are many, our history—as Garcilaso teaches us—has always been one.

NOTES

Part of the research for this essay would not have been possible without the generous support of a Rashkind grant from Randolph-Macon College in spring 2014. Many thanks are also due to Juan Pablo Gil-Oslé for not only obtaining but completing the arduous transcription of Diego de Molina's original letter; Lisa Voigt for her feedback on the first draft of this piece; and Nadine Zimmerli for making available her expertise on the most up-to-date scholarship in early American studies.

[1] It should be noted that although these early mentions of Apalache referred to the indigenous group of northwest Florida, the term would be applied farther and farther north until it eventually came to be associated with the mountain region stretching from the northeastern extreme of the United States into Georgia.

[2] These images were painted by Le Moyne in 1564 and later engraved and published by Theodor de Bry in 1591.

[3] All English translations of Menéndez are mine.

[4] Long assumed to have been constructed near contemporary Jacksonville, Florida, new research suggests that Fort Caroline may actually have been near Darien, Georgia ("Researchers").

[5] Though Garcilaso states that these natives traveled to Spain "de buena amistad" ("in good friendship"), the official account makes clear "that the Floridians in Spain were in fact taken as hostages to ensure the safety of the Spaniards left in Florida" (Voigt 100n2).

[6] For bibliography on Don Luis, see Voigt (101–02n3); Brickhouse.

WORKS CITED

Adorno, Rolena. "The Negotiation of Fear in Cabeza de Vaca's *Naufragios*." *The New World*, special issue of *Representations*, no. 33, Winter 1991, pp. 163–99.

Alvord, Clarence Walworth, and Lee Bidgood, editors. *The First Explorations of the Trans-Allegheny Region by the Virginians, 1650–1674*. Arthur H. Clark, 1912.

Brading, David A. "The Incas and the Renaissance: The *Royal Commentaries* of Inca Garcilaso de la Vega." *Journal of Latin American Studies*, vol. 18, no. 1, May 1986, pp. 1–23.

Brickhouse, Anna. *The Unsettlement of America: Translation, Interpretation, and the Story of Don Luis de Velasco, 1560–1945.* Oxford UP, 2014.

Cabeza de Vaca, Álvar Núñez. *Álvar Núñez Cabeza de Vaca: His Account, His Life, and the Expedition of Pánfilo de Narváez.* Edited by Rolena Adorno and Patrick Charles Pautz, U of Nebraska P, 1999. 3 vols.

Carrier, Lyman. "The Veracity of John Lederer." *William and Mary Quarterly*, vol. 19, no. 4, Oct. 1939, pp. 435–45.

Cunz, Dieter. "John Lederer: Significance and Evaluation." *William and Mary Quarterly*, vol. 22, no. 2, Apr. 1942, pp. 175–85.

Garcilaso de la Vega. *La Florida del Ynca.* Pedro Crasbeeck, 1605.

———. *The Florida of the Inca: A History of the Adelantado, Hernando de Soto, Governor and Captain General of the Kingdom of Florida, and of Other Heroic Spanish and Indian Cavaliers.* Translated by John Grier Varner and Jeannette Johnson Varner, U of Texas P, 1962.

———. *Primera parte de los* Comentarios reales. Pedro Crasbeeck, 1609.

———. *Royal Commentaries of the Incas and General History of Peru.* Translated by Harold V. Livermore, U of Texas P, 1966. 2 vols.

Hakluyt, Richard. *The Principal Navigations, Voyages, Traffiques and Discoveries of the English Nation.* MacLehose, 1904. 11 vols.

Hulton, Paul, editor. *The Work of Jacques Le Moyne de Morgues: A Huguenot Artist in France, Florida and England.* British Museum Publications, 1977. 2 vols.

Laudonnière, René. *A Notable Historie Containing Foure Voyages Made by Certaine French Captaines into Florida: Wherein the Great Riches and Fruitefulnesse of the Countrey . . . Are Brought to Light. . . .* Translated by Richard Hakluyt, 1586. Hakluyt, *Principal Navigations*, vol. 8, pp. 446–86.

———. *The Second Voyage unto Florida, Made and Written by Captaine Laudon-niere, Which Fortified and Inhabited There Two Summers and One Whole Winter.* Translated by Richard Hakluyt, 1586. Hakluyt, *Principal Navigations*, vol. 9, pp. 1–82.

Lederer, John. *The Discoveries of John Lederer.* Translated by William Talbot, 1672. Michigan U Microfilms, 1966. March of America Facsimile Series 25.

Le Moyne de Morgues, Jacques. "Floridae Americae Provinciae." *Brevis narratio eorum quae in Florida, Americae provincia, Gallis acciderunt, secunda in illam navigatione, duce Renato de Laudonnière classis praefecto, anno 1564,* by Le Moyne de Morgues, Theodor de Bry, 1591. *Barry Lawrence Ruderman Antique Maps*, raremaps.com/gallery/enlarge/20305.

———. "How the Natives Collect Gold in the Streams." 1564. *Library of Congress*, lcweb2.loc.gov/service/pnp/cph/3a00000/3a04000/3a04300/3a04313r.jpg.

———. *Narrative of Le Moyne an Artist Who Accompanied the French Expedition to Florida under Laudonnière, 1564.* 1591. Translated by Theodor de Bry, James R. Osgood, 1875.

Menéndez de Avilés, Pedro. *Cartas sobre la Florida (1555–1574).* Edited by Juan Carlos Mercado, Iberoamericana/Vervuert, 2002.

Molina, Diego de. "Carta." 1613. Archivo General de Simancas, Secretaría de Estado, legajo 2590, n. 47, folios 1–4.

———. "Letter of Diego de Molina, 1613." Tyler, pp. 218–24.

"Researchers Claim Discovery of America's Oldest Fort." *Heritage Daily*, 21 Feb. 2014, heritagedaily.com/2014/02/researchers-claim-discovery-of-americas-oldest-fort/102215.

Tyler, Lyon Gardiner, editor. *Narratives of Early Virginia, 1606–1625.* Charles Scribner's Sons, 1907.

Voigt, Lisa. *Writing Captivity in the Early Modern Atlantic: Circulations of Knowledge and Authority in the Iberian and English Imperial Worlds.* U of North Carolina P, 2009.

Zamora, Margarita. *Language, Authority, and Indigenous History in the* Comentarios reales de los Incas. Cambridge UP, 1988.

Inca Mummies and Mountaintop Sacrifice: Ethnohistory and the *Comentarios reales*

George Antony Thomas

A recurring concern in scholarship on the *Comentarios reales de los Incas* (*Royal Commentaries of the Incas*) is the veracity of Inca Garcilaso de la Vega's descriptions of Inca civilization (Spalding xxv–xxvii; Zamora 4–10). Historians, anthropologists, and archaeologists have often struggled with the question of how to employ the *Comentarios reales* in ethnohistoric research on the Incas. An excellent case study in regards to this topic is the archaeologist Thomas Besom's book *Of Summits and Sacrifice: An Ethnohistoric Study of Inka Religious Practices*, which employs a variety of primary sources from the colonial period in order to explain the discoveries of mummified children found buried atop Andean mountains. In attempting to understand the journey of a *capacocha* (also *qapac hucha* or *capac hucha*), a venerated maiden or child whose ultimate destiny was to be sacrificed, Besom's study considers a large number of sometimes contradictory colonial texts that offer clues as to the nature of *capacocha* sacrifice. This scholarly work was the inspiration for a classroom lesson in which students read excerpts of Garcilaso's descriptions of Inca religious practices along with alternative colonial accounts of *capacocha*. This interdisciplinary approach to teaching the *Comentarios reales* engages with the fields of anthropology and archaeology. In the context of an undergraduate survey course on the early literature of Spanish America, this activity serves to foment close readings of primary sources and to contextualize the *Comentarios reales* within a larger body of historical texts.

Since most students in an introductory survey of colonial Latin American literature first read a variety of accounts of the conquest of Mexico before being introduced to the *Comentarios reales*, they already understand that the representation of history in colonial texts is often conditioned by competing authorial interests and frequently responds to alternative accounts of particular events. Many anthologies highlight this facet of colonial textual production explicitly by presenting a series of texts that deal with the encounter between the Aztecs and the forces led by Hernán Cortés. In the anthology *Huellas de las literaturas hispanoamericanas*, for example, students read competing accounts of the conquest of Mexico by one of Bernardino de Sahagún's indigenous informants, Cortés himself, Bernal Díaz del Castillo, and Bartolomé de Las Casas. A similar approach can be followed in relation to the *Comentarios reales* by comparing selections from Garcilaso's work with excerpts from other colonial texts that discuss the conquest of Peru and Inca culture. Sabine MacCormack, Patricia Seed, and Antonio Cornejo Polar (13–58) have employed this methodology in order to analyze a variety of representations of Atahuallpa's encounter with the Spaniards in Cajamarca. Their scholarly articles comparing competing versions of this pivotal episode in Peruvian history would also be excellent secondary readings for the lesson I am suggesting in this essay.

Instead of focusing on narratives of conquest, this classroom activity centers on the topic of *capacocha*. Students will productively engage with the disciplines of anthropology and archaeology by comparing a series of primary sources that discuss Inca religious practices. This comparative methodology primarily considers the relation between archaeological evidence and textual sources that describe cultural practices and material objects, both of which are important sources for the writing of ethnohistory. While *capacocha* has been chosen as the springboard for the proposed activity, there are a variety of other topics that could similarly be employed. Instructors should consider the broad range of scholarship in Andean studies that incorporates observations from Garcilaso's *Comentarios reales* and other chronicles in order to elucidate our understanding of a variety of forms of Inca material culture, such as architecture (Dean; Niles), quipus (Brokaw; Quilter and Urton; Urton), drinking vessels (Cummins; Flores Ochoa et al.), or textiles (Pillsbury, "Inca-Colonial Tunics"; A. Rowe). While print or digital images of Inca artifacts could serve as the basis for such a lesson, instructors should also consider the feasibility of having students engage with such items firsthand in university or museum collections. These topics could also be employed in a subsequent lesson that would effectively complement the analysis of Garcilaso's commentary on *capacocha*, since he is often characterized as an "unreliable" source in relation to the topic of religious practices but "reliable" in regards to other facets of Inca culture (J. Rowe 196).

In order to introduce students to the material evidence of *capacocha* sacrifice, one effective strategy is to begin by showing excerpts from a National Geographic program on the archaeologist Johan Reinhard's expedition to Mount Llullaillaco, a volcanic peak on the border between Argentina and Chile in the province of Salta, Argentina. This video, entitled *Child Mummy Sacrifice*, provides footage of archaeologists unearthing three Inca mummies and the subsequent analysis of both the preserved remains and the variety of artifacts found at the burial site. Alternatively, or in addition to this resource, Reinhard and María Constanza Ceruti's book *Inca Rituals and Sacred Mountains: A Study of the World's Highest Archaeological Sites* contains a wealth of photographs and diagrams from the expedition. The Museo de Arqueología de Alta Montaña de Salta, which houses many of the artifacts and the mummies that were discovered, also maintains an informative Web site. The lesson begins with students viewing the first ten minutes of the video, which allows them to see Reinhard and his crew unearthing the mummies and artifacts from the ceremonial site at Llullaillaco. Working in harsh conditions and in an incredible setting, atop the mountain at more than twenty-one thousand feet above sea level, the archaeologists excavate three burial sites. They find a bewildering array of artifacts—such as ceramics, figurines, and textiles—as well as three incredibly lifelike "mummified" children who had been preserved by the extremely cold and dry environment: a seven-year-old boy in a red tunic ("el niño"), a fifteen-year-old maiden with intricately braided hair ("la doncella"), and a six-year-old girl with a silver plaque on her head who was struck by lightning at some point after her burial ("la niña del rayo").

As the video progresses, it becomes clear that the archaeologists will largely employ two different methods to explain these discoveries. First, the child mummies and accompanying objects are subjected to a rigorous scientific analysis. A secondary avenue is also pursued: the narrator in the video vaguely refers to "Spanish chroniclers," and these unnamed textual sources are used to create staged reenactments of the events leading up to the mountaintop sacrifice. These dual methodologies, the analysis of documentary sources versus the study of material artifacts, are also apparent in Besom's two-part study of *capacocha*. While his first book, *Of Summits and Sacrifice*, largely incorporates the former approach, his second book, *Inka Human Sacrifice and Mountain Worship: Strategies for Empire Unification*, primarily employs the latter strategy in order to formulate a theory on the purpose of human sacrifice within the Inca empire. After students have viewed the opening scenes of the video, they can be prompted to consider some of the pitfalls of employing either approach in isolation as well as the benefits of a complementary approach. Before students view the conclusion of the program, they will gain firsthand experience in studying documentary sources by reading colonial accounts of *capacocha*.

The pictorial evidence provided by the video and the initial discussion of how archaeologists engage with textual and material evidence will frame the subsequent reading activity. In selecting the texts to study in conjunction with the *Comentarios reales*, the choice should ultimately be informed by the objectives of the instructor and the reading level of the students. There are a large number of colonial texts that discuss *capacocha* and a variety of related topics, such as the Inca census, religious rites, and sacrificial practices. Besom provides an extensive list of documentary sources that specifically discuss *capacocha* and mountain worship (*Of Summits* 26–27, 66–67). Before students begin reading, it is important to underline that the topic of human sacrifice is one of the most controversial topics in colonial literature, since it often served as a mode of condemning Amerindian religious practices and reinforcing stereotypical notions of irrationality, barbarity, and otherness (Díaz Balsera 159–61). Nevertheless, as Viviana Díaz Balsera examines in relation to Las Casas's rewriting of the missionary Motolinía's descriptions of Mesoamerican human sacrifice, some authors attempted to portray such practices in a more sympathetic light or to suppress these controversial representations altogether. In a similar vein, Garcilaso's suppression of the topic of *capacocha* sacrifice can be viewed in relation to Las Casas's discussion of the topic in *Apologética historia sumaria*. More specifically in relation to the authorial models that Garcilaso attempted to contest, Margarita Zamora views his treatment of sacrifice in the *Comentarios reales* as a negotiation between the more tolerant approach of Las Casas and José de Acosta's condemnation of such practices in *Historia natural y moral de las Indias* (104–07).

The perspective of Gonzalo Fernández de Oviedo, who is also frequently characterized as the "enemy of the Indians" in relation to Las Casas, could also be considered (Myers). In short, instructors could emphasize the intertextual nature of the *Comentarios reales* and frame class discussion of representations of *capacocha* within the context of a body of colonial texts that were sometimes the product of missionary campaigns to eliminate native religious practices or were engaged with broader debates on the nature of indigenous civilizations.

While excerpts from the works of Acosta, Las Casas, and Oviedo could certainly be used in this activity, another method of proceeding is to prioritize texts that include details pertaining to extratextual elements, namely the types of material evidence encountered by archaeologists. With this focus in mind, students will compare a selection from the *Comentarios reales* (bk. 2, ch. 8) with descriptions of *capacocha* from three texts that are generally deemed to be "more trustworthy" from the perspective of anthropologists and archaeologists: Pedro de Cieza de León's *El señorío de los Incas* (*The Incas of Pedro de Cieza de León*), Bernabé Cobo's *Historia del Nuevo Mundo* (*Inca Religion and Customs*), and Felipe Guaman Poma de Ayala's *Primer nueva corónica y buen gobierno* (*The First New Chronicle and Good Government*). Significantly, none of these texts was published during the colonial period. This fact seems to confirm the notion that the mode of representing indigenous culture as well as the types of practices documented were significant factors in determining whether a work would be published (Adorno, "Censorship and Approbation" and "Censorship and Its Evasion"). In contrast to some of his contemporaries, Garcilaso was able to successfully negotiate the publication of both parts of the *Comentarios reales*. For this reason, it is informative to compare Garcilaso's strategies for representing Inca religious practices with those employed by Cieza de León, Cobo, and Guaman Poma.

The class activity adopts a comparative approach to reading the *Comentarios reales*, one that highlights the varying modes in which the authors address the subject of human sacrifice. As in Seed's and MacCormack's articles focusing on the varying accounts of Atahuallpa's encounter with the Spaniards written by a diverse range of authors, the selections on *capacocha* will allow students to compare a variety of perspectives: indigenous (Guaman Poma), mestizo (Garcilaso), soldier-chronicler (Cieza de León), and Jesuit (Cobo). For this reason, instructors should consider preparing a general introduction to each of the authors and texts before reading. Alternatively, or in conjunction with this lecture, students could be introduced to Joanne Pillsbury's *Guide to Documentary Sources in Andean Studies*, which is a particularly useful resource if the class will be asked to follow up on this activity by completing a more extensive research paper. Students can read the entries in the book that specifically discuss the life and work of Cobo (Hamilton), Cieza de León (Pease), Garcilaso (Mazzotti), and Guaman Poma (Adorno, "Guaman"). As a pre-reading activity, it is also a good idea for instructors to present key terms in Andean studies that students will encounter in the readings, such as *huaca*, *Tahuantinsuyu*, and *Viracocha* (along with their orthographic variants). An ideal means of doing this is to present Garcilaso's definitions and explanations of such terms as applicable.

In relation to reading the texts themselves, there are a number of options. The *capacocha* activity could be presented at the conclusion of the class session devoted to Garcilaso. After the class views the archaeological site in the preliminary portion of the video *Child Mummy Sacrifice*, the instructor could explain the activity and provide appropriate readings. If time permits, students could read all the assigned texts outside of class and the following session could be devoted to a comparative discussion of the assigned authors and texts. Alternatively, a method that more efficiently highlights the multiplicity of perspectives presented is to divide the class into groups of four and to have each student read and present one of the authors or texts to their group during the subsequent class. A third option, which is viable only in a longer class period, is to complete the entire activity during one class. Each group of students can be provided with either digital or paper copies of the four texts. After students are given an appropriate amount of time for silent reading in class, each group can commence its discussion of the texts.

As students read the brief selections by and about Garcilaso and his contemporaries, they should be prompted to prepare a summary of some of the key details pertaining to the life and work of each author. Additionally, students should be asked to identify two types of quotes from the texts in question: concrete information about the practice of *capacocha* as well as authorial opinions and commentary that relate to the potential biases or reliability of the author. For example, the excerpt by Garcilaso (*Comentarios* 1: 82–83; *Royal Commentaries* 1: 86–88) proposes that human sacrifice was a pre-Inca rite practiced by other indigenous groups and corrects earlier (nameless) historians who had advanced the notion that the Incas sanctioned such practices. The selection from Cieza de León (*El señorío* 103–06; *Incas* 190–93) broadly defines *capacocha* as the gifts or offerings given to idols but never mentions human sacrifice. Notably, the author relates that he gained this information about Inca rites from indigenous informants. Cieza de León's explanation of the practice of *capacocha* does, however, contain a graphic description of the slaughtering of animals and includes his condemnation of the rite as the work of the devil. In contrast, Guaman Poma's description of religious practices in each of the four quarters of Tahuantinsuyu (*Primer nueva corónica* 268–75; *First New Chronicle* 204–11) includes both pictorial representations of and textual references to the sacrificial offering of children. Nevertheless, Guaman Poma's vague references to this practice seem to refer to a distant past, and he reserves his condemnation for other, contemporary religious rites. The selection pertaining to the subject of immolation written by Cobo (*Obras* 2: 200–02; *Inca* 111–13), which is characterized by Besom as one of the most useful (*Of Summits* 15–16), provides a wealth of details that can be corroborated by the archaeological evidence discussed in the video. While this text does not include extensive religious condemnation by the Jesuit, Cobo does characterize the practice as "cruel and inhuman" (*Inca* 112).

Furthermore, some of his statements—such as his description of beating human hearts being ripped from the bodies of sacrificial victims—do not appear to be supported by archaeological evidence from *capacocha* sites, although these allegations could possibly apply to other forms of Inca sacrifice (Besom, *Of Summits* 54–55).

After students have finished their group discussions of the four authors and the variations in their descriptions of the practice of *capacocha*, it is useful for the class to make some collective observations on the nature of colonial chronicles and the formulation of a methodology of how to employ ethnohistoric texts in order to interpret archaeological evidence. Such a discussion could be supplemented by Besom's own observations on the topic (*Of Summits* 18–23) or Catherine J. Julien's comments on how ethnohistorians have employed documentary sources (178–80). If time permits, the lesson could conclude by viewing the remainder of the video *Child Mummy Sacrifice* and asking students to identify which pieces of information gained through the scientific analysis of the mummies were also contained in the colonial primary sources. It is also particularly useful to highlight the ways in which some details from the selected readings were chosen by the creators of the video in order to film a narrative reconstruction of the *capacocha* ceremony, one that is a modern retelling of Inca history. Such a form of analysis engages with the primary means by which many students in the twenty-first century encounter references to colonial texts like the *Comentarios reales*: in the staged historical reenactments that are featured in television programs like Michael Wood's *Conquistadors* or Jared Diamond's *Guns, Germs, and Steel*. As in contemporary literary criticism of colonial chronicles, these visual narratives can also be deconstructed in order to expose underlying contradictions and the ideological biases that influence their structure. Interestingly, Besom himself attempts to construct an entirely objective textual narrative based on archaeological evidence. This spine-tingling description of the journey of a *capacocha*, which appears as the prologue and the epilogue of his first book (*Of Summits* 1–3, 164–66), is a modern chronicle that attempts to connect the pieces of archaeological evidence in order to form a coherent story.

Approaching the *Comentarios reales* from a comparative perspective will allow students to see how representations of history, as a type of narrative, are often formulated by omitting particular details or emphasizing others. Teaching Garcilaso's work through an anthropological lens, and by employing a modern television program on the Incas as a point of departure, also addresses how contemporary historical narratives and scholarship are produced. One danger of employing *capacocha* as the main focus of this lesson, however, is that students often mistakenly interpret Garcilaso's statement denying the practice of human sacrifice to be evidence of the unreliability of his entire work. Faced with the discrepancy between the material record and the mestizo writer's words, students might wrongly assume that his text should be completely disregarded in ethnohistoric studies. As Zamora cautions, the work must be read in relation to the historical context in which it was produced: "If we were to subject the

Comentarios reales to a modern anthropological critique we might be tempted to criticize Garcilaso for what seem to us to be distortions of Andean reality. But in doing so we would be obliged to recognize that we are imposing our own discursive prejudices on a Renaissance work" (9). For this reason, it is important to conclude by identifying what particular narrative choices reveal about the *Comentarios reales* and the author himself. It is clear that Garcilaso's selection of topics as well as the rhetorical strategies employed in the *Comentarios reales* were meant to convey to the European reader that the Incas had a distinguished history that could rival the civilizations of the Old World. His work would contest previous chronicles that had represented indigenous peoples as being barbarous, uncivilized, and without history. Just as the archaeologist's narrative gives primacy to material evidence and the historical reenactment made for television selectively incorporates dramatic visual elements, Garcilaso chose to represent for a Christian audience the grandeur and complexity of Inca civilization in the most positive light.

WORKS CITED

Adorno, Rolena. "Censorship and Approbation in Murúa's *Historia general del Piru*." *The Getty Murúa: Essays on the Making of Martín de Murúa's* Historia general del Piru, edited by Thomas B. F. Cummins and Barbara Anderson, Getty Research Institute, 2008, pp. 95–124.

———. "Censorship and Its Evasion: Jerónimo Román and Bartolomé de las Casas." *Hispania*, vol. 75, no. 4, Oct. 1992, pp. 812–27.

———. "Guaman Poma de Ayala, Felipe (ca. 1535/50–ca. 1616)." Pillsbury, *Guide*, vol. 2, pp. 255–68.

Arias, Santa, and Eyda M. Merediz, editors. *Approaches to Teaching the Writings of Bartolomé de Las Casas*. Modern Language Association of America, 2008.

Besom, Thomas. *Inka Human Sacrifice and Mountain Worship: Strategies for Empire Unification*. U of New Mexico P, 2013.

———. *Of Summits and Sacrifice: An Ethnohistoric Study of Inka Religious Practices*. U of Texas P, 2009.

Brokaw, Galen. *A History of the Khipu*. Cambridge UP, 2010.

Child Mummy Sacrifice. Directed by Pamela Caragol Wells, National Geographic, 2009.

Cieza de León, Pedro de. *The Incas of Pedro de Cieza de León*. Translated by Harriet de Onís, U of Oklahoma P, 1959.

———. *El señorío de los Incas*. Edited by Manuel Ballesteros, Historia 16, 1985.

Cobo, Bernabé. *Inca Religion and Customs*. Translated by Roland Hamilton, U of Texas P, 1990.

———. *Obras del P. Bernabé Cobo: Historia del Nuevo Mundo*. Edited by Francisco Mateos, Atlas, 1956. 2 vols.

Cornejo Polar, Antonio. *Writing in the Air: Heterogeneity and the Persistence of Oral Tradition in Andean Literatures*. Translated by Lynda J. Jentsch, Duke UP, 2013.

Cummins, Thomas B. F. *Toasts with the Incas: Andean Abstraction and Colonial Images on Quero Vessels.* U of Michigan P, 2002.

Dean, Carolyn. *A Culture of Stone: Inka Perspectives on Rock.* Duke UP, 2010.

Díaz Balsera, Viviana. "On Barbarism, Demons, and Natural Reason: Las Casas's Rhetoric of Human Sacrifices in Pre-Hispanic Mexico." Arias and Merediz, pp. 159–66.

Flores Ochoa, Jorge A., et al. *Qeros: Arte Inka en vasos ceremoniales.* Banco de Crédito del Perú, 1998.

Garcilaso de la Vega. *Comentarios reales de los Incas.* Edited by Ángel Rosenblat, Emecé Editores, 1945. 2 vols.

———. *Royal Commentaries of the Incas and General History of Peru.* Translated by Harold V. Livermore, U of Texas P, 1989. 2 vols.

Guaman Poma de Ayala, Felipe. *The First New Chronicle and Good Government.* Translated by Roland Hamilton, U of Texas P, 2010.

———. *Primer nueva corónica y buen gobierno.* 1615. *Det Kongelige Bibliotek,* kb.dk/permalink/2006/poma/info/en/frontpage.htm.

Hamilton, Roland. "Cobo, Bernabé (1580–1657)." Pillsbury, *Guide,* vol. 2, pp. 229–41.

Julien, Catherine J. "Finding a Fit: Archaeology and Ethnohistory of the Incas." *Provincial Inca: Archaeological and Ethnohistorical Assessment of the Impact of the Inca State,* edited by Michael A. Malpass, U of Iowa P, 1993, pp. 177–233.

MacCormack, Sabine. "Atahualpa and the Book." *Dispositio,* vol. 14, nos. 36/38, 1989, pp. 141–68.

Mazzotti, José Antonio. "Garcilaso de la Vega, El Inca (1539–1616)." Pillsbury, *Guide,* vol. 2, pp. 229–41.

Myers, Kathleen Ann. "Las Casas versus Oviedo: The Polemic between the 'Defender of the Indians' and the 'Enemy of the Indians.'" Arias and Merediz, pp. 147–58.

Niles, Susan A. *The Shape of Inca History: Narrative and Architecture in an Andean Empire.* U of Iowa P, 1999.

Pease, Franklin. "Cieza de León, Pedro de (ca. 1518–1554)." Pillsbury, *Guide,* vol. 2, pp. 143–51.

Pillsbury, Joanne, editor. *Guide to Documentary Sources in Andean Studies, 1530–1900.* U of Oklahoma P, 2008. 3 vols.

———. "Inca-Colonial Tunics: A Case Study of the Bandelier Set." *Andean Textile Traditions: Papers from the 2001 Mayer Center Symposium at the Denver Art Museum,* edited by Margaret Young-Sánchez and Fronia W. Simpson, Denver Art Museum, 2006, pp. 123–68.

Quilter, Jeffrey, and Gary Urton, editors. *Narrative Threads: Accounting and Recounting in Andean Khipu.* U of Texas P, 2002.

Reinhard, Johan, and María Constanza Ceruti. *Inca Rituals and Sacred Mountains: A Study of the World's Highest Archaeological Sites.* Cotsen Institute of Archaeology Press, 2010.

Rowe, Ann. "Inca Weaving and Costume." *Textile Museum Journal,* vols. 34–35, 1995–1996, pp. 5–53.

Rowe, John Howland. "Inca Culture at the Time of the Spanish Conquest." *Handbook of South American Indians: The Andean Civilizations*, edited by Julian H. Steward, vol. 2, Government Printing Office, 1946, pp. 183–330.

Seed, Patricia. "'Failing to Marvel': Atahualpa's Encounter with the Word." *Latin American Research Review*, vol. 26, no. 1, 1991, pp. 7–32.

Spalding, Karen. Introduction. *Royal Commentaries of the Incas and General History of Peru*, by Garcilaso de la Vega, edited by Spalding, translated by Harold V. Livermore, Hackett, 2006, pp. xi–xxix.

Urton, Gary. *Signs of the Inka Khipu: Binary Coding in the Andean Knotted-String Records*. U of Texas P, 2003.

Zamora, Margarita. *Language, Authority, and Indigenous History in the* Comentarios reales de los Incas. Cambridge UP, 1988.

Religion in the *Royal Commentaries*

James W. Fuerst

Inca Garcilaso's portrayal of indigenous religion in the *Royal Commentaries* lies at the very heart of his revisionist project. In sixteenth- and seventeenth-century Europe, religion was viewed as the summit of human cultural achievement; along with knowledge of writing, it was the benchmark against which Europeans judged other peoples and cultures (including Amerindians). In Spain and its overseas possessions, Catholic orthodoxy was no simple matter of individual conscience but rather the law of the land, from which any divergence could be met with the harshest of penalties. This was especially so among the indigenous peoples of the New World, whose traditional practices and beliefs were viewed as idolatrous impediments that had to be swept away in favor of Catholic doctrine and who, as recent converts, were seen as particularly prone to backsliding and regression.

As the mestizo son of a Spanish conquistador and an Inca princess who called himself a "Catholic Christian Indian," Garcilaso was acutely aware of the importance of religion in his life and work, and it correspondingly occupies a central place among his concerns. His historical masterpiece, the *Royal Commentaries*, however, is neither a partisan text written to serve the campaigns of the Peruvian religious orders to extirpate indigenous idolatry that were spreading across the colony at the turn of the seventeenth century when it was written nor a work of positivist historiography that simply sought to convey the "facts" of indigenous religion to European readers. Rather, the *Royal Commentaries* takes root in the tradition of rhetorical historiography of the European Renaissance and in Andean oral histories, and it therefore has both argumentative and didactic aims. Accordingly, some of the information Garcilaso provides about Andean religions and the Inca solar cult is highly accurate, while in other instances he conspicuously alters the historical record or manipulates indigenous concepts and symbols to achieve his own ends. As such, closely attending to the presentation of indigenous religion in the *Royal Commentaries* provides students with a wonderful opportunity to see Garcilaso's major concepts and distinctions, arguments, critiques, and authorial methods at work in his narrative reconstruction and explication of crucial historical and cultural subjects.

In my course Conquests and Inventions of the Early Americas, we turn to Garcilaso toward the end of the semester with the benefit of having read selections from the debate over the rational capacities of Amerindians by Juan Ginés de Sepúlveda (*Democrates segundo*) and Bartolomé de Las Casas (*In Defense of the Indians*), as well as the account of Inca and Andean religion in book 5 of José de Acosta's *Natural and Moral History of the Indies*. A number of major themes and concepts already in hand, I can then have students focus on a close reading of select chapters within the *Royal Commentaries*, which is a deceptively rich and subtle work. Consequently, in what follows I will try to provide something of a road map through the core moments and ideas in the two prefaces to the first part of the *Royal Commentaries* as well as the crucial chapters on indigenous religion in books 1 and 2. In so doing I will limit myself to highlighting Garcilaso's principal rhetorical strategies and discursive reimaginings, which include the critical, revisionist stance of the work; calling the linguistic incompetence of previous historians to account as causing their misrepresentations of indigenous culture; dividing Peruvian history into two distinct ages; interweaving Andean and European notions and concepts; the providential justification of Inca civilization as *praeparatio evangelica*; and the use of Neoplatonic concepts and symbols. A more comprehensive list of books and chapters in which indigenous and Inca religion and associated topics feature is presented below, but all of the above, as well as some of Garcilaso's most famous passages, can be found within the two prefaces and books 1 (chs. 1–15, 18–19) and 2 (chs. 1–10) of the first part of the *Royal Commentaries*, making them an excellent starting point for nonspecialists.

Key Chapters in the First Part of the Royal Commentaries

> "Preface to the Reader" and "Notes on the General Language of the Indians of Peru"
>
> Book 1, chapters 1–15, especially 8–15 (idolatry of the First Age, origin of Incas), and chapters 18–19 (other myths of Inca origins, author's declaration about his history)
>
> Book 2, chapters 1–10 (Inca pantheon, meanings of *huaca*, comparison with other historians) and chapters 21–27 (Inca sciences, astrology, and poetry)
>
> Book 3, chapters 20–25 (temple of the Sun, Lake Titicaca)
>
> Book 4, chapters 1–5 (House of the Virgins) and chapters 21–22 (phantasm Viracocha appears to the Inca who will take his name)
>
> Book 5, chapters 21–23 (name of Viracocha, applied to Spaniards, temple of, and painting) and chapters 28–29 (Viracocha's prophecy, Garcilaso views his embalmed corpse)
>
> Book 6, chapter 5 (obsequies for death of an Inca), chapters 20–22 (first and second festivals held in honor of the Sun), and chapter 30 (Pachacámac and Rimac valleys)
>
> Book 7, chapters 5–7 (third and fourth solemn festivals dedicated to the Sun, nocturnal rite for purging ills from Cuzco)
>
> Book 9, chapter 10 (Huayna Cápac intuits Sun is not the First Cause of the universe) and chapter 15 (Huayna Cápac repeats and publicizes the prophecy of Viracocha)

Textual Analysis and Interpretation

Beginning with "Preface to the Reader" and "Notes on the General Language of the Indians of Peru" helps to introduce students to Garcilaso's argumentative, revisionist stance and intentions in the *Royal Commentaries*. In the preface the author famously promises not to contradict earlier Spanish historians but "to furnish a commentary and gloss and to interpret many Indian expressions which they [Spanish historians], as strangers to that tongue, have rendered inappropriately" (1: 4). In his "Notes" he provides a condensed Quechua grammar lesson and states that, in order to avoid further corruption of the language and additional intercultural misunderstanding, "I may be permitted, since I am an Indian, to write like an Indian in this history, using the letters that should be used in these words" (1: 5). These brief passages establish Garcilaso's general tone of critique, commentary, and correction and plant the seedlings of arguments regarding the brevity, incompleteness, and linguistic (in)competence of the Spanish imperial record that he will return to and elaborate later on, especially in book 1, chapter 19, "The Author's Declaration about His History," and book 2, chapters 4–5, regarding the many meanings of the word *huaca*.

The opening of book 1 (chs. 1–7)—which affirms the existence of antipodes but not their location (ch. 2), posits Antonio Sánchez de Huelva as the discoverer of the New World rather than Christopher Columbus (ch. 3), and dwells on how and why Peru was misnamed for three chapters (chs. 4–6)—further underscores the status of the *Royal Commentaries* as an alternate history that offers not only different accounts from the existing historical record but also a different perspective, as signaled in the prefaces. The tale of Pedro Serrano in chapter 8 relativizes the notion of "barbarism"—one of the central concepts used by Europeans in the sixteenth century to characterize cultural difference (Pagden)— by showing how two Spaniards marooned on a desert island do not recognize each other as men but rather immediately fear each other as the devil, until their language and religion (both men shout the Apostles' Creed as they turn tail and flee) restore to each his humanity in the eyes of the other. Worth noting is the easily missed comparison Garcilaso sets up between the natives of the New World, who he states are "usually smooth-cheeked and beardless" seemingly in passing in chapter 2, and Spaniards stranded for years in the New World, whose hair and beard grow to below their waist and who "no longer looked like human beings" when rescued by a passing ship (1: 11, 29). The apparently casual and indirect juxtaposition is indicative of Garcilaso's method and a good early example as to why his work should be read closely and carefully.

The ethical import of the tale of Serrano functions as a segue into Garcilaso's account of the idolatry of the First Age of Andean history in chapters 9–14, which he introduces as such:

> For the better understanding of the idolatry, way of life, and customs of the Indians of Peru, it will be necessary for us to divide those times into

two periods. First we shall say how they lived before the Incas, and then how the Inca kings governed, so as not to confuse the one thing with the other, and so that the customs and gods of one period are not attributed to the other. It must therefore be realized that in the First Age of primitive heathendom [*gentilidad*] there were Indians who were little better than tame beasts and others much worse than wild beasts.

(1: 30; bk. 1, ch. 9)[1]

Garcilaso's separation of the First and Second Ages—before Inca rule and during Inca rule, respectively—is as much *cultural* as it is historical. For instance, after describing the variety of gods some tribes had, Garcilaso states at the end of chapter 10, "Other tribes, such as the Chirihuanas and the people of Cape Passau (that is, the southernmost and northernmost provinces of Peru) felt no inclination to worship anything, high or low, either from interest or fear, but lived and still live exactly like beasts, *because the doctrine and teaching of the Inca kings did not reach them*" (1: 33; bk. 1, ch. 10; my emphasis). The point is repeated in chapter 12, in a discussion of the ways of life and government of ancient tribes: "Some of them, like those of Cape Passau and the Chirihuanas, *and other tribes not conquered by the Inca kings*, remain in that state of primitive strategy" (1: 35; bk. 1, ch. 12; my emphasis). On the one hand, this distinction follows the requirement of Renaissance rhetorical historiography to maintain a proper order of events (following the Ciceronian tradition of writing from which the *Royal Commentaries* stems), and on the other, it allows Garcilaso to portray the Incas as divine, civilizing agents of Peru who prepare the way for the preaching of the Christian gospel (see bk. 1, ch. 15). In these ways the distinction pertains to concepts within European frames of reference. Nevertheless, dividing historical and civilizational periods into different ages and epochs is also found within Andean accounts of history and indigenous myths, such as in the information collected from interviews with native sources in Pedro Sarmiento de Gamboa's *History of the Incas* or in the accounts of Garcilaso's contemporary the indigenous writer and artist Felipe Guaman Poma de Ayala in his *First New Chronicle and Good Government*, suggesting the presence of an Andean subtext or frame of reference as well. As many commentators have observed, the intertwining or superposition of distinct European and Andean concepts with separate and irreducible meanings within the *Royal Commentaries* is no mere coincidence in Garcilaso's work but rather an essential aspect of his method and intent, of which the division of Andean ages is an early example worth highlighting for students.

Having established the fundamental distinction between the First Age and the Second Age in chapter 9 of book 1, Garcilaso then vividly describes the savagery, brutality, and perversity reported to characterize the practices of indigenous peoples before the Incas—practices such as sodomy, incest, and cannibalism—and cites Blas Valera, Pedro de Cieza de León, and Acosta, three of his most frequently invoked sources, for corroboration. The sensational details of these chapters—especially chapter 11, which describes human husbandry in the service of cannibalism as well as graphic scenes of anthropophagy—create a dark contrast and foil to the advent of the Inca dynasty in chapter 15, while raising interesting questions for students to discuss about the extent to which the "others" of Europeans might also have their own stigmatized and marginalized groups. These passages also tend to overshadow Garcilaso's more modest and somewhat normalizing summation of the idolatry of the First Age: "some were barbarous beyond exaggeration in their life, customs, gods, and sacrifices. Others were simple about everything, like tame animals, or even simpler. Others had something of the two extremes" (1: 40; bk. 1, ch. 14).

All the opening material—the prefaces, the digressions, the repeated illustrations of Spanish ineptitude with indigenous language, the appalling state of Andean culture prior to the Incas—gradually builds up to the crucial and climactic moment of chapter 15, "The Origin of the Inca Kings of Peru." It opens with the providential rationale behind Inca civilization and rule:

> While these people were living or dying in the manner we have seen, it pleased our Lord God that from their midst there should appear a morning star to give them in the dense darkness in which they dwelt some glimmerings of natural law, of civilization, and of the respect men owe to one another. The descendants of this leader should thus tame those savages and convert them into men, made capable of reason and of receiving good doctrine, so that when God, who is the sun of justice, saw fit to send forth the light of His divine rays upon those idolaters, it might no longer find them in their first savagery, but rendered more docile to receive the Catholic Faith and the teaching and doctrine of our Holy Mother the Roman Church, as indeed they have received it.   (1: 40; bk. 1, ch. 15)

The presentations of God as the "sun of justice" ("sol de justicia") and the first Incas Manco Cápac and Mama Ocllo Huaco as a "morning star" ("lucero del alba") are Neoplatonic symbolizations that provide a Christian backdrop to the account of Inca origins. Following authors such as Bartolomé de Las Casas and Jerónimo Román, Garcilaso portrays the origin and expansion of the Inca empire as a divinely ordained *praeparatio evangelica* whose ultimate aim was to prepare the indigenous peoples of the Andes to receive the Christian gospel (MacCormack 234). The notion of *praeparatio evangelica* was first expounded by Eusebius of Caesarea in an eponymous fourth-century work and later by St. Augustine in *City of God* to account for the power and prestige of pagan Rome and the advantages that Roman civilization afforded the early Catholic Church. Garcilaso's use of the trope places the Inca empire on par with the achievements of the Romans, solidifying Cuzco's position as "another Rome." This providential explanation, furthermore, not only legitimizes Inca dominance over other indigenous peoples of Tahuantinsuyu—Quechua for "the four corners of the world" (1: 17; bk. 1, ch. 5)—but it also places the Incas in a privileged position in the European conception of universal (which is to say Christian) history as the necessary precursor to the establishment of the Church in the New World.

As important, the account of Inca origins is presented as a conversation between Garcilaso as a boy (still called Gómez Suárez de Figueroa then) and his maternal uncle Cusi Huallpa, linking it to Inca oral traditions and situating it in the specific Andean context of extended kinship groups called *ayllus*, which were structured internally and externally through complex systems of reciprocity (*ayni*). Inca rulers and elites, such as Garcilaso's mother Ñusta Isabel Chimpu Ocllo and her uncles (who were the sources of his history), belonged to royal *ayllus* known as *panakas*—matrilineal kinship groups centered in Cuzco whose coalitions and conflicts were the very substance of Inca political life (Rostworowski 7, 15–19). More specifically, Garcilaso identifies his lineage as descending from Cápac Ayllu, the *panaka* of Túpac Yupanqui, the eleventh ruler of the dynasty (bk. 8, ch. 8, and bk. 9, ch. 14), located in Hanan Cuzco (Upper Cuzco; bk. 1, ch. 16). The relevance is that each *panaka* kept a selective and encomiastic history of the deeds of its Inca founder and notable members as a family history in poems, painted panels, and quipus, and it is this particular family narrative that Garcilaso puts forward and privileges in Cusi Huallpa's speech. In fact, the foregoing chapters on the savagery of the First Age and the notion of *praeparatio evangelica* itself are repeated in condensed form and presented as true because they form part of the Incas' own understanding of their past, as conveyed by Cusi Huallpa. Further, the Christian and Neoplatonic symbolism of God as the "sun of justice" undergoes an immediate revision to resemble the high deity of the Inca solar cult from whom the Incas claimed both descent and political authority. In Cusi Huallpa's words, "God the Father" becomes "our father the Sun" (1: 42) who takes pity on the savages and sends them his son and daughter to rescue them from barbarism. The European version of *praeparatio evangelica* presented by Garcilaso in his role as narrator and the Inca myth related to him by Cusi Huallpa are so transparently connected as to be effectively the same story. Nevertheless, they are presented as *different versions* that arrive at the same, deeper truth—the truth that the Incas operated under divine mandate and that they were the legitimate and necessary forerunners of Christianity in Peru—and this is another, more complicated example of the intertwining of European and Andean meanings that is worth pointing out and discussing with students.

Chapters 16–18 respectively describe the founding of Cuzco, the peoples subdued by the first Inca, and additional myths about the Incas' origins, the last of which contain mention of a flood that some observers of the time equated with that of Noah in the Bible (Genesis 5:32–10:1). Rather than engage in theological controversies directly, however, Garcilaso deploys his familiar tactic of raising an issue and then backing away from it without giving his own view, while nevertheless encouraging readers to decide for themselves: "I do not venture on such profound matters: I simply repeat the fabulous accounts I used to hear my family tell in my childhood; let each take them as he wishes and apply whatever allegory he thinks most appropriate" (1: 49; bk. 1, ch. 18).

Chapter 19 of book 1, "The Author's Declaration about His History," extends and elaborates much of the foregoing. Garcilaso gives greater detail about his indigenous sources (including the quipus from various regions sent to him by his former classmates and friends), restates the contents of the history, and highlights both his privileged position regarding Inca religion—"they [his Inca relatives] told me, as if I were their own son, all about their idolatry, their rites, ceremonies, and sacrifices, the greater and lesser festivals, and how they were celebrated"—as well his status as an eyewitness to much of what he relates:

> Apart from what the Indians told me, I experienced and saw with my own eyes a great deal of their idolatry, festivals, and superstitions, which had still not altogether disappeared in my own time, when I was twelve or thirteen . . . thus I saw many of the things the Indians did in the time of their paganism [*gentilidad*] and shall relate them and say that I saw them.
> (1: 50)

To close out the chapter, Garcilaso returns to and extends the arguments he initiated in "Preface to the Reader" and "Notes on the General Language." He reaffirms his promise to "recount the same things Spanish historians have written . . . bringing forward where necessary their very words, so as to prove that I have not invented fictitious circumstances to credit my relatives . . . I shall merely act as a commentator to reveal and amplify much of what they have begun to say, but have left unfinished for lack of a full account." He then draws the earlier strands of argument together and makes the thrust more explicit:

> Much will be added that is missing in their histories but really happened, and some things will be omitted as superfluous because the Spaniards were misinformed, either because they did not know how to ask for information with a clear idea of the different periods and ages and divisions of provinces and tribes, or because they misunderstood the Indians who gave them it, or because they misunderstood one another on account of the difficulty of the language. The Spaniard who thinks he knows the language best is ignorant of nine-tenths of it, because of the many meanings of each word and the different pronunciations that a word has for various meanings, as will be seen from some words that I shall have to refer to. (1: 51)

It now appears that the seemingly innocuous "comment and gloss" on previous Spanish histories of Inca and Andean civilization have a much broader critical agenda and intent.

Garcilaso's direct treatment of Inca religion begins in book 2, with essential chapters 1–10 describing and explaining the idolatry of what he calls the Second Age, which began with the Incas. "What we call the Second Age [Segunda

Edad] and the idolatry practiced during it began with the Inca Manco Cápac," who bade the Indians to "hold and worship the Sun as their chief deity, persuading them to do so on account of his beauty and brightness," for "the many benefits the Sun conferred on them and how finally he sent down his own children to change their state from that of brutes to that of men." The Neoplatonic convergence of the beautiful, beneficial, and good within the divine is apparent, as is the interpenetration of moral and political justifications in the foundation of the Inca cult. Pachacámac, moreover, "the sustainer of the earth," is introduced for the first time as the one who "placed the Sun above all the stars in heaven" and therefore as an implicitly higher power (1: 67; bk. 2, ch. 1). Along with the simple arguments used by Manco Cápac to persuade the Indians to give up their earlier idolatry in favor of the solar cult and the extent to which they "regarded their kings as children of the Sun" and "worshipped them as divine," this chapter provides an initial description of the Inca pantheon as follows:

> They had no other gods than the Sun, which they adored for his excellent qualities and natural benefits, as more rational and civilized people than their predecessors in that First Age. And they dedicated temples of incredible richness to the Sun and although they considered the Moon to be the sister and wife of the Sun and the mother of the Incas, they did not worship her as a goddess or offer her sacrifices or build temples to her. They held her in great veneration as the universal mother, but did not go beyond in their idolatry. Lightning, thunder, and thunderbolts they considered to be servants of the Sun, as we shall see.   (1: 68–69; bk. 2, ch. 1)

Garcilaso will extend the Inca pantheon in later chapters (see below), but in the first instance he claims the Inca cult called for worship of the Sun and the Incas as his children, along with veneration but not worship of the Moon (following the distinction between *dulia* and *latria*—worship of God and veneration for blessed or saintly persons, such as the Virgin Mary, respectively—in Catholic doctrine) and reverence for lightning, thunder, and thunderbolts—"the three phenomena together are called *illapa*" (1: 69; bk. 2, ch. 1)—as servants of the Sun. Garcilaso elaborates on the indigenous names for, partial significances of, and respective places within Coricancha, the house or temple of the Sun, for each of these in later chapters (esp. bk. 2, chs. 21–27, and bk. 3, chs. 20–25) and includes the Andean deity Viracocha as a "modern god" in the Inca pantheon in book 2, chapter 27. In light of European and Catholic conceptions of divinity at the time, however, Inca religion as presented in the *Royal Commentaries* had arrived at the highest point that a non-Christian people could attain. In this sense, Inca idolatry would have been not only the least objectionable for late-sixteenth- and early-seventeenth-century Europeans—because it was based on such an obvious and appropriate use of natural reason—but also the easiest to overcome in favor of Christianity.

With Pachacámac, however, Garcilaso goes further in the next chapter, entitled "The Incas Glimpsed the True God, Our Lord." As the chapter begins, the
Sun is immediately revised from being the "chief god" to "a visible god" for "the
Inca kings and their *amautas*, who were the philosophers, perceived by the light
of nature the true supreme God our Lord, the maker of heaven and earth . . .
whom they called Pachacámac." Garcilaso then defines the term and swiftly corrects the translation of an earlier writer:

> The word is composed of *pacha*, "the world, the universe," and *cámac*, pre-
> sent participle of the verb *cama*, "to animate," derived from the noun
> *cama*, "the soul." Pachacámac means "him who gives life to the universe,"
> and in its fullest sense means "him who does to the universe what the soul
> does to the body." Pedro de Cieza (Ch. 78) says: "The name of this demon
> is intended to mean creator of the world, since *cama* means 'maker' and
> *pacha* 'world'" etc. As a Spaniard, he did not know the language as well as
> I, who am an Indian and an Inca.   (1: 70; bk. 2, ch. 2)

In condensed form, the sharp edge of Garcilaso's argument against Spanish
historians, even ones he admired and referred to often such as Cieza de León,
is revealed: the linguistic incompetence of Spaniards and Europeans led to their
misunderstanding indigenous practices and beliefs, which in turn led to their
misrepresenting those practices and beliefs to the point of demonizing indigenous peoples, which was then how indigenous peoples were viewed and treated
by other Spaniards and Europeans. This point is captured explicitly later in the
chapter, when Garcilaso writes that Indians "dare not tell these things with the
true interpretation and meaning of the words. They see that the Christian Spaniards abominate them all as works of the Devil, and the Spaniards do not trouble to ask for clear information about them, but rather dismiss them as diaboli-
cal, as they imagine" (1: 71; bk. 2, ch. 2).

Garcilaso's main discursive strategy, therefore, is to Christianize Inca religion
generally and the Andean god Pachacámac specifically. For instance, we have
already learned that Pachacámac was the first cause or prime mover of the world
universe as well as the implicitly monotheistic inspiration behind Inca adoration
of the Sun. Garcilaso goes on to say that he was an invisible and "unknown god"
("dios no conocido")—an allusion to the "Unknown God" of the Athenians referred to in the Bible (Acts 17:22–33)—whose worship consisted solely of inward
genuflection, whose name Indians dared not utter unless they were forced to,
whom they did not know because they had not seen, and therefore to whom they
dedicated neither temples nor sacrifices. The name *Pachacámac*, Garcilaso insists, which "Spanish historians so abominate because they do not understand
it, is 'God.'" Or again:

> But if anyone should now ask me (who by God's infinite mercy am a Cath-
> olic Christian Indian), "What is the word for God in your language?" I

should answer *"Pachacámac,"* because in the general language of Peru there is no word but this for God. All the rest given by the historians are generally incorrect. They are either not from the general language [of the Incas], or are corrupted from the tongue of a special province, or are merely invented by the Spaniards.   (1: 72; bk. 2, ch. 2)

One of the invented terms, he continues, is "'Pachaya chácher,' which they pretend means 'creator of heaven,' though it means 'teacher of the world,'" and accordingly, as expressed a few lines earlier, "the Spaniards in their histories give another word for God, *Tici Viracocha*, whose meaning neither they nor I can give" (1: 72; bk. 2, ch. 2).

In point of fact, however, Garcilaso is the only commentator of the time to claim that Pachacámac was the supreme deity of the Inca pantheon; all others—including Las Casas, Román, Cieza de León, Acosta, and Agustín de Zárate—report that Viracocha was the principal Inca deity (with variant names Illa Tecce Viracocha, Con Ticci Viracocha, or Ticci Viracocha Pachayachachi), making Garcilaso's preference for Pachacámac over Viracocha one of his most conspicuous, and often baffling, revisions of Inca history. Although he realized that Viracocha and Pachacámac were in fact two names attributed to the same deity, and the two are explicitly linked in the *Royal Commentaries* in a Quechua poem that Garcilaso found in Blas Valera's manuscript, of which Quechua, Latin, and Spanish versions are included in book 2, chapter 27, the most he is willing to admit is that "Viracocha is the name of a modern god" worshipped by the Indians (1: 128; bk. 2, ch. 27).

There are many possible reasons to account for why Garcilaso chose to alter the historical record so blatantly in his elevation of Pachacámac over Viracocha, such as fulfilling the prerequisites of Neoplatonic philology and hermeneutics or Neoplatonic theology (Zamora 122–28; MacCormack 332–49); the partisan and selective influences of Túpac Yupanqui's *panaka*, Cápac Ayllu, on the oral traditions he received and reported (Mazzotti 169–82); or exploiting Pachacámac's characteristics in Andean frames of reference (Fuerst, "'El Dios'" and *New World* 81–117). However that stands, it may simply be the case that Pachacámac was easier for Garcilaso to Christianize than Viracocha, who was an incredibly complex figure—a single, multiple godhead that manifested and unfolded into various personalities in accordance with a penumbra of diverse aspects and functions. Viracocha's numerous seasonal and meteorological transformations were not readily reconcilable with Christian notions of God, so Garcilaso may have had to demote him on those grounds. Nevertheless, as he creates a resemblance between Pachacámac and the Christian god (and the Christian god and Pachacámac for his Andean readers), he also draws a resemblance between Inca beliefs and Christian beliefs, by noting that before the arrival of the Spaniards the Incas had a cross in a "sacred place," one of the definitions of the word *huaca* (1: 73; bk. 1, ch. 3); that they believed in the immortality of the soul and universal resurrection; and that they had their own notions of heaven and hell:

> They believed there was another life after this, with punishment for the wicked and rest for the good. They divided the universe into three worlds. Heaven they called *Hanan Pacha*, "the upper world," where they said the good went to be rewarded for their virtues. They called this world of generation and corruption *Hurin Pacha*, "the lower world," and they called the center of the earth *Ucu Pacha*, meaning "the world below this," where they said the wicked went, and more explicitly they called it by another name *Çúpaipa Huacin*, house of the Devil.   (1: 84; bk. 2, ch. 7)

With a relatively modest and rationally grounded pantheon of Pachacámac, the Sun, and the Incas, which included worship of the one true God, and so many points of convergence between Inca religion and Christianity as he presents it, Garcilaso had little choice but to confront directly the many gods wrongly attributed to the Indians by the Spanish historians (1: 75–78; bk. 2, ch. 4). Again he deploys arguments made earlier in the text:

> The Spaniards attribute many other gods to the Incas because they are unable to distinguish the times and idolatries of the First Age from those of the Second. Moreover they are not well enough acquainted with the language to be able to ask for and obtain information from the Indians, and their ignorance has led them to attribute to the Incas many or all of the gods the latter removed from the Indians they subjected to their empire, and these subject peoples had many strange gods, as we have said.
>   (1: 76; bk. 2, ch. 4)

A particularly troublesome source of this error, he continues, "was that the Spaniards did not know the many diverse meanings of the word *huaca*. This, when the last syllable is pronounced from the top of the palate, means 'an idol,' such as Jupiter, or Mars, or Venus, but it is a noun and does not admit the derivation of a verb meaning 'to idolatrize.'"

In addition to this "first and main" meaning, *huaca* had many others; for instance, it could refer to a sacred article, temple, sanctuary, offering, oracle, or anything that stood out from the ordinary by virtue of its novelty, beauty, or ugliness. If the last syllable was pronounced in the back of the throat, *huaca* could mean "to mourn" (Garcilaso 1: 76–77), and yet "[b]ecause of these very various meanings, the Spaniards, who only understood this first and main sense of 'idol,' think that the Indians regarded as gods everything they called *huaca* and that the Indians worshipped all these things just as the Indians of the First Age had done" (1: 77). Garcilaso's philological exegesis of *huaca* and other Quechua religious terms, such as *apachitas*, *pacha*, *Pachacámac*, *Viracocha*, and *Tangatanga*, corrects the linguistic errors made especially by Acosta in *Natural and Moral History of the Indies* (Zamora 117–20; Fuerst, *New World* 177–213). Of course, Acosta explains the meaning of those terms in order to demonstrate the depth and precise nature of Peruvian idolatry as well as the clear relation between Inca religious practices and the counterfeit Church of Satan, and Garcilaso corrects Acosta to prove that the Incas, as we have seen, were divinely rather than diabolically inspired. He then cites Valera in support of his view in book 2, chapter 6, and discusses what the Incas sacrificed to the Sun in chapter 8, asserting "the Incas neither practiced them [sacrifices] nor permitted them to be made with men or children, even when their kings were sick (as another historian asserts)" (1: 87; bk. 2, ch. 8), a point to which he returns in chapter 10, the last in this cluster, where he compares what he has said with other historians' accounts. The central point Garcilaso makes, once again in contradiction to writers who have preceded him, is that the Incas did not perform human sacrifices. "I have gone into all of this," he explains, "to rebut the opinions of those who say the Incas sacrificed men and children, which they certainly did not. Some may think it does not matter, for it was all idolatry, yet so inhuman an accusation should not be made unless it is known for a fact" (1: 92; bk. 2, ch. 10). This, however, is another conspicuous divergence from the historical record as well as the historical reality, for the Incas did in fact practice human sacrifice—it was called *cápacocha*, it occurred during the festival of Cápac Raymi, and it included the interment of sacrificial victims, who appear to have been children.

Garcilaso's alterations of Inca religious practices and beliefs and his denial of human sacrifice pose a number of complex questions for students to consider and discuss, including the possible constraints under which the *Royal Commentaries* was written, Garcilaso's agenda in the work, the value of fidelity to "truth" or "fact" in light of potentially more urgent social and political realities, and how Garcilaso authorized himself to rewrite the Inca past in the first place, among others. In different moments I have taken different tacks in exploring these ideas with students, and by way of concluding I will share three. The first, mentioned earlier, is to delve back into the historical record, as it were, by comparing and contrasting book 5 of Acosta's *Natural and Moral History* with the chapters from the *Royal Commentaries* examined above. The second is to give students the passages on the "noble lie" in Plato's *Republic*, in which the philosopher kings fabricate a tale to explain the origins of the different social classes in the ideal state (93–94; bk. 3, 414b–415c). Garcilaso specifically alludes to the noble lie when he calls the tale of Inca origins a "fable" invented by Manco Cápac to win the esteem and allegiance of other Andeans (1: 64; bk. 1, ch. 25), and once they have read it, I ask students to reconsider the sections on the origins of the Incas and Inca religion in the *Royal Commentaries* in this light. Third, I have assigned Jorge Luis Borges's short story "Tlön, Uqbar, Orbis Tertius" and asked students to reflect upon not only the *Royal Commentaries* but also the various discourses of the New World that we have studied over the course of the semester through the lens of the story. As divergent as they are, each approach refocuses our attention on the constructedness of historical discourse and the multitude of factors and interests that can shape historical representations and narratives. The ingeniously crafted and relentlessly critical account of indigenous religion in the *Royal Commentaries* is a sterling example of just that, while also offering a revealing glimpse into Garcilaso's overall project, methods, and aims.

NOTE

[1] Instructors must take special care when teaching Garcilaso's *Royal Commentaries* in Livermore's translation. Livermore's version—the only complete translation of the first and second parts in English—is sufficiently readable for general consumption and therefore still a valuable resource, but it is frequently too inaccurate for research and scholarship. Livermore's rendering of *gentilidad* as "heathendom" in the passage quoted here, which he also renders as "heathen," "heathenism," "pagan," and "paganism" elsewhere, is a case in point. Garcilaso opts for *gentilidad*, or gentilism, in order to underscore the extent to which indigenous peoples of the New World were ignorant of Christianity solely by virtue of not having had previous contact with Catholic doctrine before the arrival of Spaniards and were therefore outside of the Church in the same way that gentiles were outside of Christianity in the New Testament. Garcilaso studiously avoids words such as *heathen* or *heathenism, pagan* or *paganism* due to the stigma of idolatry, barbarism, and cultural inferiority that such words carried in his day. This is one of several important instances where Livermore's translation tends to obscure, undermine, or even erase Garcilaso's intention and point.

WORKS CITED

Acosta, José de. *The Natural and Moral History of the Indies*. Edited by Jane E. Mangan, translated by Frances López-Morillas, Duke UP, 2002.

Borges, Jorge Luis. "Tlön, Uqbar, Orbis Tertius." *Collected Fictions*, translated by Andrew Hurley, Penguin, 1998, pp. 68–81.

Fuerst, James W. "'El Dios no Conocido' y la vuelta del mundo en los *Comentarios reales*." *Renacimiento mestizo: Los 400 años de los* Comentarios reales, edited by José Antonio Mazzotti, Iberoamericana/Vervuert, 2010, pp. 181–93.

———. *New World Postcolonial: The Political Thought of Inca Garcilaso de la Vega*. U of Pittsburgh P, 2018.

Garcilaso de la Vega. *Royal Commentaries of the Incas and General History of Peru*. Translated by Harold V. Livermore, U of Texas P, 1966. 2 vols.

Guaman Poma de Ayala, Felipe. *The First New Chronicle and Good Government: On the History of the World and the Incas up to 1615*. Edited by Roland Hamilton, U of Texas P, 2009.

Las Casas, Bartolomé de. *In Defense of the Indians*. 1552. Translated by Stafford Poole, Northern Illinois UP, 1974.

MacCormack, Sabine. *Religion in the Andes: Vision and Imagination in Early Colonial Peru*. Princeton UP, 1991.

Mazzotti, José Antonio. *Incan Insights: El Inca Garcilaso's Hints to Andean Readers.* Iberoamericana/Vervuert, 2008.

Pagden, Anthony. *The Fall of Natural Man: The American Indian and the Origins of Comparative Ethnology.* Cambridge UP, 1982.

Plato. *The Republic of Plato.* Translated by Allan Bloom, 2nd ed., Basic Books, 1991.

Rostworowski, María. *History of the Inca Realm.* Translated by Harry B. Iceland, Cambridge UP, 1999.

Sarmiento de Gamboa, Pedro. *History of the Incas.* 1572. Edited by Clements R. Markham, Dover, 1999.

Sepúlveda, Juan Ginés de. *Demócrates segundo; o, De las justas causas de la guerra contra los indios.* 1547. Edited by Ángel Losada, Consejo Superior de Investigaciones Científicas, 1984.

Zamora, Margarita. *Language, Authority, and Indigenous History in the* Comentarios reales de los Incas. Cambridge UP, 1988.

"Between the Tree of Memory and the Bark of History": Revisiting Inca Garcilaso's Sites of Memory

Dinorah Cortés-Vélez

As a veritable Renaissance savant and mestizo intellectual, Inca Garcilaso de la Vega holds a unique place within Latin American colonial letters. Garcilaso was born Gómez Suárez de Figueroa to an Incan noblewoman and a Spanish captain about seven years after the Spanish conquest of his native Peru. Not only have critics extensively researched Garcilaso's conundrum as a mestizo trying to reconcile two cultural inheritances in conflict,[1] but this particular situation has also had a tremendous appeal among general readership of Garcilaso's *Comentarios reales* (*Royal Commentaries*). The intimate way in which the tragic circumstances of the conquest of the Incan empire intertwine with the author's life renders a hybrid text[2] that is at once an exercise in historiography, history, and remembrance and a verbal monument to grief. The Incan empire was under siege; therein the need to remember in order to battle against conquest by oblivion.

The main goal of my inquiry is to chart the potential for experiential learning about self, identity, and remembrance through application to the *Comentarios reales* of Pierre Nora's concept of "sites of memory," as developed in his multi-volume project *Les lieux de mémoire*.[3] This essay aims to prove the viability of Nora's concept of "sites of memory" as a successful hermeneutic tool when approaching *Comentarios reales* in the classroom that will prove useful to professors interested in implementing a pedagogy of memory, one that will allow students to relate more experientially to some of Garcilaso's central concerns. It will show that the critical can become a successful springboard to the pedagogical and the pedagogical to the personal. I will probe Nora's concept feasibility as catalytic agent of students' own processes of personal and collective remembrance of their family mythologies, their ancestors, and their personal and familial histories. Examination of Garcilaso's own work of memory in *Comentarios reales* will be the basis for exercises in the language classroom involving exploration of the notion of *lieux de mémoire* in Nora's "three senses of the word—material, symbolic, and functional" (18–19). I will conclude with some reflections on the relevance of Garcilaso's work as historiographer, one that places *Comentarios reales* in the context of colonial domination and cultural clash.

El Inca: Between Memory and History

Although Nora's monumental study of remembrance focuses on "modern memory" (13) and offers a "typology of the memory sites that map the vicissitudes of

French national identity, especially since the revolution" (Ho Tai 908), I argue that Nora's concept of remembrance offers a wide pedagogical viability for studying an early modern writer like Garcilaso. Nora's conceptualizations of history and memory apply to Garcilaso's understanding of the will to remember and the need for the preservation of a collective memory. When applying Nora's concept of "realms of remembrance" to the work of Garcilaso, it is, of course, necessary to distinguish key differences in their conceptions of history as well. Nora conceives of history in the positivistic, modern sense of progress, while, according to Margarita Zamora, Garcilaso conceives of it as "a return to a more authentic version of ancient texts" with a necessary "emphasis . . . on language usage," which ultimately amounts to a "rhetorical conception of history" (14–15). In *Comentarios reales*, Garcilaso undertakes the mission of chronicling the rise, peak, and decay of the Incan empire through a monumental work of revision:

> Aunque ha havido españoles curiosos que han escrito las repúblicas del Nuevo Mundo, como la de México y la de Perú y las de otros reinos de aquella gentilidad, no ha sido con la relación entera que dellos pudiera dar. . . . Verdad es que tocan muchas cosas de las muy grandes que aquella República tuvo, pero escrívenlas tan cortamente que aun las muy notorias para mí (de la manera que las dizen) las entiendo mal. Por lo cual, forçado del amor natural de la patria, me ofrescí al trabajo de escrevir estos *Comentarios*. . . .   (*Comentarios* 1: 8)

> Though there have been learned Spaniards who have written accounts of the States of the New World, such as those of Mexico and Peru and other kingdoms of the heathens, they have not described these realms so fully as they might have done. . . . It is true that these have dealt with many of the remarkable achievements of that empire, but they have set them down so briefly that, owing to the manner in which they are told, I am scarcely able to understand even such matters as are well known to me. For this reason, impelled by my natural love for my native country, I have undertaken the task of writing these *Commentaries*. . . .
> (*Royal Commentaries* "Preface to the Reader")

For Christian Fernández, however, it is an "impossible task" to try to find a category in which to classify Garcilaso's complex discourse (230). Still, in spite of long-standing debates about its genre (history, memory, fiction, chronicle, commentary), Fernández defends the notion that *Comentarios reales* can be regarded as a history book, even if not in a positivistic sense of being a "truthful" account of the Incas. Instead, Garcilaso renders a "memoria colectiva andina" ("Andean collective memory"; Fernández 230; my trans.) in a manner faithful to the original (Zamora 8)—that is, faithful to his personal experience and interpretation of the Incan empire.

On the other hand, Nora's inventory of French national identity is necessarily founded on the idea of history as progress that builds nation-states.[4] Nora's central argument about the relation between memory and history is that historiography is "a history of history," or a turning of history over to its own methodologies and discourse, thereby revealing the fracture between a "real memory—social and unviolated" and history as a discourse that attempts to recapture the loss of "real environments of memory" (9, 8, 7). Nora describes historiography as a discourse about a discourse that reveals its own crisis because "[i]t operates primarily by introducing doubt, by running a knife between the tree of memory and the bark of history" (10). This analogy smacks of the crisis of language posed by poststructuralists. We might regard memory as signified, history as signifier, and historiography as a Derridean "dangerous supplement" or the Saussurean bar interposed between the two. The illusion of perfect "correspondence" persists as long as there is no awareness of the dividing line. The line reveals, however, potential multiple mutations of the signifier. In the same way, historiography turns memory into "a possible object of history" (10) even as it reveals the fracture between the two.

Nora's approach has been subject to criticism. It has been stated, for example, that such a stark contrast between memory and history is too simplistic (Ho Tai 920; Rothberg 4) and that "such a distinction comes close to paralleling the distinction between orality and literacy" (Ho Tai 915). To this point can be added that Nora's notion of "real memory," defined as memory unadulterated by the need to remember, suggests an essentialist and possibly primitivistic view reminiscent of the binary nature versus culture. It has also been pointed out that Nora's perspective presents too narrow a representation of France, thus foreclosing itself to the polyphony and polysemy it seeks to embrace (Ho Tai 910–13).[5] Nora's theory has been also described as a "nostalgia-tinged tale of decline [of memory]" (Rothberg 4), one that "embodies a top-down approach to its subject" (Ho Tai 921) insofar as it is conceived from a logocentric, European center.

For all its potential flaws, Nora's conceptualization still offers a unique pedagogical tool for experiential learning of the concept of remembrance within a traumatic context. According to Francisco Ortega, "instead of considering Garcilaso's writing as a direct response to any particular experiences, we should understand it as a mediated and accumulative reflection of the experience of catastrophe" (397). According to Nora, *lieux de mémoire* are a product of the interplay between memory and history intertwined in a reciprocal relation of overdetermination. Sites of memory are thus hybrid and subject to processes of continual mutation in their effort to "capture a maximum meaning in the fewest of signs," "to stop time," or "to block the work of forgetting" (19). Garcilaso's main agenda is none other than to erect a site of memory in testament to an Incan world rapidly vanishing. Garcilaso's tragic effort puts him in a bind, or at the crossroads "between the tree of memory and the bark of history" (10). By remembering the Incan past, Garcilaso attempts to save its memory from oblivion, but encoded in that very effort to remember is "the demise of memory"

(Rothberg 4). As Nora says, if there are sites of remembrance, it is because of the very disappearance of the realms evoked by such sites (7). However, Garcilaso must remember even if that act signals a disappearance, because in the face of the Spanish conquest of Peru, the era of the Incan empire has effectively come to an end, and someone ought to document what is disappearing and make memory of it.

Grief, Mourning, and the Work of Memory

In an oft-cited moving passage from chapter 15 of book 1 of *Comentarios reales*, Garcilaso relates the visits his maternal Incan relatives paid to his mother in Cuzco after the Spanish conquest. These visits themselves become a site of remembrance as the relatives mourn the world gone and confer about their grief:

> De las grandezas y prosperidades pasadas venían a las cosas presentes, lloravan sus reyes muertos, enajenado su Imperio y acabada su república. Etc. Estas y otras semejantes pláticas tenían los Incas y Pallas en sus visitas, y con la memoria del bien perdido siempre acabavan su conversación en lágrimas y llanto, diziendo: "Trocósenos el reinar en vasallaje". Etc.
> (*Comentarios* 1: 40)

> From the greatness and prosperity of their past they turned to the present, mourning their dead kings, their lost empire, their fallen state, etc. These and similar topics were broached by the Incas and Pallas on their visits, and on recalling their departed happiness, they always ended these conversations with tears and mourning, saying: "Our rule is turned to bondage" etc.
> (*Royal Commentaries* 1: 41)

During these mournful conversations, Garcilaso's relatives attempt to keep the memory of "their departed happiness" alive. In the face of the destruction brought about by the conquest and the fact that theirs was a society without a written language, such efforts prove to be insufficient.

At this very juncture—the one between what Nora calls "real memory" (of the Incas) and "history" as the demise of the realms evoked by their remembrance—emerges the figure of Garcilaso as a mestizo, a product of clashing cultures and, as fate would have it, future translator of his Incan heritage for the Spanish culture:

> En estas pláticas yo, como muchacho, entrava y salía muchas vezes donde ellos estavan, y me holgava de las oír, como huelgan los tales de oír fábulas. Passando pues días, meses y años, siendo ya yo de diez y seis o diez y siete años, acaesció que, estando mis parientes un día en esta su conversación hablando de sus Reyes y antiguallas, al más anciano de ellos, que era el que dava cuenta dellas, le dixe:

—Inca tío, pues no hay escritura entre vosotros, que es la que guarda la memoria de las cosas passadas ¿qué noticia tenéis del origen y principio de nuestros Reyes?   (Garcilaso, *Comentarios* 1: 40)

During these talks, I, as a boy, often came in and went out of the place where they were, and I loved to hear them, as boys always do like to hear stories. Days, months, and years went by, until I was sixteen or seventeen. Then it happened that one day when my family was talking in this fashion about their kings and the olden times, I remarked to the senior of them, who usually related this things: "Inca, my uncle, though you have no writings to preserve the memory of past events, what information have you of the origins and beginnings of our kings?"   (*Royal Commentaries* 1: 41)

Garcilaso recognizes the dire situation in which the lack of writing puts the Incan culture. As a palliative, he resorts to the Incan uncle as repository of memory. The latter accepts this role happily, as he responds to his nephew's inquiry, "Sobrino, yo te las diré de muy buena gana; a ti te conviene oírlas y guardarlas en el corazón (es frasis dellos por dezir en la memoria)" ("Nephew, I will tell you these things with pleasure: indeed it is right that you should hear them and keep them in your heart [this is their phrase for 'in the memory']"; Garcilaso, *Comentarios* 1: 40; *Royal Commentaries* 1: 41). This famous passage can be interpreted as a rite of passage for the young man. He is invested by his uncle, himself a site of memory, with the power to continue the labor of keeping alive the memory of "their departed happiness," or "la memoria del bien perdido." The nephew has the advantage over his uncle of having mastered the writing system of the vanquishers from an insider's perspective. Young Gómez Suárez de Figueroa is turned into a repository of memory, a site of memory on behalf of his Incan relatives.

A Pedagogy of Memory

A pedagogical application of Nora's theory to Garcilaso's dilemma includes close reading of passages pertaining to the tension between memory and history such as the ones quoted above. I first have student volunteers read these passages out loud. Then the class can delve into their nuances and complexities. Students are asked to identify the Incan conception of memory as revealed by these excerpts. Key words from the passages are jotted down on the blackboard as part of a brainstorming activity. Finally, students are asked to think about the role of memory in their own family histories and to individually write down their thoughts. This activity is followed by a plenary discussion where students are given the opportunity to share their personal insights with the class. At all times, students are reminded of the importance of continuing to reflect on the appeal of Garcilaso and his dilemma between memory and history for a contemporary readership.

The class following these exercises is devoted to group work where students are furnished with Nora's paradigm of *lieux de mémoire* "in three senses of the word—material, symbolic, and functional." According to Nora, these "three aspects always coexist" (19).

Material sites entail examination of Garcilaso's relation to sites singled out in *Comentarios reales*, such as the city of Cuzco, as well as his own family dwelling replete with remembrances and recuperation of family practices of his Incan relatives. One learning objective of this exercise is to shed light on students' own relation to certain material sites and into their own "family archives," an understanding that in turn produces a closer familiarity with Garcilaso's text. There is also reflection on the palpable materiality of certain sites of remembrance such as monuments, museums, cemeteries, and libraries. Field trips as a class to such places can be scheduled in order to give students a better grasp on the relation between material objects and remembrance.

Functional sites are approached from the viewpoint of the role of ritual in family reunions in order to answer the following question: what function or purpose does family ritual serve in individual and collective memory? Students are asked to reflect on the passages from *Comentarios reales* where Garcilaso remembers his maternal family gatherings and the grief that was shared in those reunions. The discussion is then extended to analysis of the value of family rituals like weddings and funerals that are close to the students' experiences.

The analysis of symbolic sites includes discussion on the solemnity of observance entailed in symbolic action such as "a commemorative minute of silence [that] serves as a concentrated appeal to memory by literally breaking a temporal continuity" (Nora 19). Group discussion delves into the topics of grief and remembrance in Garcilaso and in the text itself of *Comentarios reales* as a symbolic site of memory that constitutes a verbal monument to grief.

By the end of each of these modules on the three senses delineated by Nora for the word *lieux*—material, functional, and symbolic—students are asked to write response papers in preparation for class colloquies. The colloquies benefit from the individual feedback given to students on their initial papers. During each colloquy, we reflect as a class on the importance of sites of remembrance for "the illumination of the past" (Nora 10). Additionally, students are asked to reflect on how each type of site becomes a *lieu de mémoire*. For Nora, this occurs for a material site only if "imagination invests it with a symbolic aura" (19). The city of Cuzco, for instance, becomes for Garcilaso a sad example of a legacy—the one of the Incan empire—that is destroyed even before its richness is known by those who destroyed it. In book 1, chapter 19, of *Comentarios reales*, Garcilaso refers to Cuzco as "república antes destruída que conoscida" ("a state that was destroyed before it had been known"; *Comentarios* 1: 49; *Royal Commentaries* 1: 51). It is precisely the destruction of the capital city and its rich legacy that in Garcilaso's eyes (and in the eyes of all the Incas who witnessed it, for that matter) confers to Cuzco the necessary aura for becoming a site of aggrieved imagination and a material site of remembrance.

Without the benefit of the wheel or of mortar, and exclusively relying on man-power, the Incas managed to transport enormous rocks that they stacked so ever tightly "que apenas pueden meter la punta de un cuchillo por ellas" ("so that the point of a knife could scarcely be inserted between them"; Garcilaso, *Comentarios* 1: 146–47; *Royal Commentaries* 1: 464), thus building the fortifi-cations among which the magnificent fortress of Cuzco stands out. According to Garcilaso, "lleváyanlas arrastrando a fuerça de braços con gruessas maromas; ni los caminos por do las llevavan eran llanos, sino sierras muy ásperas, con grandes cuestas, por do las subían y baxavan a pura fuerça de hombres" ("They were in fact heaved by main force with the aid of thick cables. The roads by which they were brought were not flat, but rough mountainsides with steep slopes, up and down which the rocks were dragged by human effort alone"; *Comentarios* 1: 146; *Royal Commentaries* 1: 464). These rocks came to be known among the Incas as "piedras cansadas" ("tired rocks") because "[d]ezían que se cansó y que no pudo llegar allá, porque ellos se cansaron de llevarla; de manera que lo que por ellos passó atribuyen a la peña" ("[a]s it was never placed in the building, they say that it grew weary and could not be got there, for they grew weary of moving it: so that their own failings passed as an attribute to the rock"; *Comentarios* 1: 153; *Royal Commentaries* 1: 471). As Nora states, "A purely functional site, like a class-room manual, a testament, or a veterans' reunion belongs to the category only inasmuch as it is also the object of a ritual" (19). These rocks initially fulfilled the functional goal of being used for building edifices and fortifications, but with the Incan legacy under siege, these rocks acquired new meaning, becoming a functional site of remembrance or objects of ritual of remembrance of a world forever gone.

Symbolic sites allow for exploration of the mnemonic appeal of certain com-memorative actions, as is the case in book 1, chapter 15. Here Garcilaso describes the tales of his Incan uncle and the idea of keeping such tales in one's heart or memory. For Ortega, "the one character in Garcilaso that most dramatically per-forms this crisis [of knowledge] is Garcilaso's uncle, Cusi Huallpa, a noble Inca who informed him about the history of the Incas" (402). In the face of his neph-ew's questions about the history of their Incan ancestors, the uncle is more than happy to share, because it is advisable for the nephew to listen to them and to keep them in his heart, which according to Garcilaso's parenthetical explana-tion is another way for the Incas to refer to memory: "a ti te conviene oírlas y guardarlas en el coraçón (es frasis dellos por dezir en la memoria)" ("indeed it is right that you should hear them and keep them in your heart [this is their phrase for 'in the memory']"; *Comentarios* 1: 40; *Royal Commentaries* 1: 41).

This moment entails the solemnity of established observance that is proper to symbolic sites. It also turns young Gómez Suárez de Figueroa into the subject/object of a ritual of remembrance, and it has a symbolic aura. The uncle is "anoint-ing" the nephew as guardian of the family archive partly because the former recognizes that he is uniquely positioned to accomplish that mission. As a mes-tizo individual, Garcilaso was endowed since his youth with the linguistic and cultural tools to mediate between the culture of the conquered and the one of the conquerors. In the exchange with the uncle, Garcilaso is turned into a *lieu de mémoire*. As such he is a subject *mise en abîme* because, as Nora says, all *lieux de mémoire* are objects *mises en abîme*. In other words, in becoming himself a realm of remembrance in his role as historiographer or historian of the history of the Incas, Garcilaso's persona attests to the disappearance of a "real environment or memory" (Nora 7) or Incan *milieu de mémoire*. In this context, historiography operates as a principle of doubt about Garcilaso's own identity, about where his loyalties should be, about the fate of his family and of a people, and, ultimately, about the Incan legacy as a whole. This principle of doubt is like "a knife between the tree of memory and the bark of history." Garcilaso is thus "placed into abyss"; much like what occurs with the Droste effect, he stands between mirrors that reflect a hybrid, fractured, and confusing multilayered identity.

Collective Memory and Historical Revision

Garcilaso interrogates tradition in order to find a place for the Incan empire within the Judeo-Christian history of salvation. He does so by referring, in book 1, chapter 9, to two ages in the development of the Incan dynasty, the pre-Incan one and the Incan one.[6] As is mentioned in book 1, chapter 11, if the indigenous peoples of Peru who came before the Incas were idolaters and practitioners of cannibalism, not so the Incas, who were monotheistic. Contrary to Spanish belief, the Incas adored only the Sun their father, who they say instructed them through their founding parents, Manco Capac and Mama Ocllo, to bring the light of natural reason to the "savages" from the pre-Incan era (as described in bk. 1, ch. 15). Garcilaso's underlying argument is that the Christians were able to evangelize Peru thanks to the Incas' groundwork. Therefore, the Incas had a very important task within the Judeo-Christian history of salvation. This providential framework for Incan history operates as a symbolic site of remembrance. In this symbolic work, Garcilaso poses himself as a historiographer who pens a history of the history of the Incas, one that is revelatory of its own crisis because "to interrogate a tradition, venerable though it may be, is no longer to pass it intact" (Nora 10).

In his role as mestizo historiographer of the vanquished culture of his ancestors, self-doubt is an inevitable part of the process for Garcilaso. How can he authorize himself in front of the Spanish public for whom he writes without calling attention to the "lesser" circumstances of his birth from an unmarried interracial couple? How can he legitimize the Incas without betraying his professed loyalty to Catholicism and to the Spanish crown? How can he claim his rightful place as Renaissance savant with a vast European education but also claim firsthand knowledge of his Incan ancestry? The *proemio* (preface) of *Comentarios reales* reveals some of these doubts and hesitations:

En el discurso de la historia protestamos la verdad della, y que no dire-
mos cosa que no sea autorizándola con los mismos historiadores españoles
que la tocaron en parte o en todo; que mi intención no es contradezirles,
sino servirles de comento y glosa y de intérprete en muchos vocablos indios, que, como estranjeros en aquella lengua, interpretaron fuera de la
propiedad della. . . .   (*Comentarios* 1: 8)

In the course of my history I shall affirm its truthfulness and shall set down
no important circumstances without quoting the authority of Spanish historians who may have touched upon it in part or as a whole. For my purpose is not to gainsay them, but to furnish with comment and gloss, and to
interpret many Indian expressions which they, as strangers to that tongue,
have rendered inappropriately.   (*Royal Commentaries*)

This famous passage from *Comentarios reales* has been traditionally read as an
example of false modesty on the part of Garcilaso. Without denying that reading,
I want to propose that it is also indicative of the entrapments of a historiographical endeavor that places Garcilaso right in "the split between history and memory" (Nora 9). In this regard, there is false modesty in his remark about being a
mere provider of "comment and gloss" for the Spanish historians, but there is also
sincere self-doubt born out of the unstable subject position that he must inhabit.

Torn between Incan memory and the history of the conquest, Garcilaso is
"ready to confess the intimate relation he maintains to his subject" (Nora 10) as
he endeavors to craft a history of the history of the Incan rulers. His historiographical project paradoxically reveals that he "no longer unquestioningly
identif[ies] with [his Incan] heritage" (10). Garcilaso wants to place Incan civilization under the sign of history, but that very effort of preservation turns the
material preserved into a locus of remembrance and unveils the precarious "em-
bodiments of a memorial consciousness that has barely survived in a historical
age that calls out for memory because it has abandoned it" (12).

By furnishing students with such key notions as "sites of remembrance," I intend to facilitate a reading experience of *Comentarios reales* ultimately to show
them how the personal story can tell history at the macro level. As students delve
into the textual negotiations undertaken by Garcilaso, it is my hope to make apparent the work of memory that unveils him as a "guardian of memory" paying
commemorative tribute, even if from afar, to a world besieged by the European
conquest and colonization; a mestizo figure tragically entwined between memory and history and between the Incan and the Spanish worlds; a historian turned
"site of memory" by virtue of his personal work of memory, thus becoming an
"archive" of a world in danger of disappearing; a historiographer writing a history that explains its own makings; and, finally, a writer erecting a verbal monument to grief, which ultimately is an exercise in identification with and validation of his mestizo identity.

NOTES

I want to thank Dr. Michael Roeschlein for his valuable comments and insights in the process of editing this essay.

[1] For instance, Ortega delves into the notion of trauma understood from "a non-psychological rationality" and more "in its cultural and historical specificity" (400) in order to explore *Comentarios reales* as an "obsessive meditation" (398) born out of the catastrophic events surrounding the conquest of Peru.

[2] Fernández refers to the "discursividad heterogénea e híbrida" ("heterogeneous and hybrid discourse") of *Comentarios reales* (230; my trans.).

[3] *Les lieux de mémoire* was originally published between 1984 and 1992. For the purposes of this essay, I will use Nora's article "Between Memory and History: *Les lieux de mémoire*," in which he exposes his theory in condensed form.

[4] Rothberg says that Nora's theory "remains indebted to a rather traditional teleological view of modernity" (4).

[5] Rothberg speaks of "its reduction of Frenchness to the Hexagon" and "its elision of France's long and complex colonial and postcolonial history" (6).

[6] The title of this section is inspired by the following quotation by Nora: "Every great historical revision has sought to enlarge the basis for collective memory" (9).

WORKS CITED

Fernández, Christian. "La textualización de la memoria andina en los *Comentarios reales*." *Revista de Crítica Literaria Latinoamericana*, vol. 24, no. 48, 1998, pp. 229–39.

Garcilaso de la Vega. *Comentarios reales de los Incas*. Edited by Ángel Rosenblat, Emecé Editores, 1943. 2 vols.

———. *Royal Commentaries of the Incas and General History of Peru*. Translated by Harold V. Livermore, U of Texas P, 1989.

Ho Tai, Hue-Tam. "Remembered Realms: Pierre Nora and French National Memory." *The American Historical Review*, vol. 106, no. 3, June 2001, pp. 906–22.

Nora, Pierre. "Between Memory and History: *Les lieux de mémoire*." *Memory and Counter-Memory*, special issue of *Representations*, no. 26, Spring 1989, pp. 7–24.

Ortega, Francisco. "Trauma and Narrative in Early Modernity: Garcilaso's *Comentarios reales*, 1609–1616." *MLN*, vol. 118, no. 2, Mar. 2003, pp. 393–426.

Rothberg, Michael. "Between Memory and Memory: From *Lieux de mémoire* to *Noeuds de mémoire*." *Noeuds de mémoire: Multidirectional Memory in Postwar French and Francophone Culture*, issue of *Yale French Studies*, no. 118/119, 2010, pp. 3–12.

Zamora, Margarita. *Language, Authority, and Indigenous History in the* Comentarios reales de los Incas. Cambridge UP, 1988.

Casting Inca Garcilaso,
Comparatively Speaking

Nhora Lucía Serrano

[V]oyagers . . . thought that they knew where they were
going and ended up in a place whose existence they had
never imagined[; thus] the discourse of travel in the late
Middle Ages and the Renaissance is rarely if ever
interesting at the level of sustained narrative and
theological design, but gripping at the level of
anecdote. . . . [because voyagers found themselves] in
the shock of the unfamiliar, the provocation of an
intense curiosity, the local excitement of discontinuous
wonders.

—Stephen Greenblatt, *Marvelous Possessions:*
The Wonder of the New World

In any comparative literature and world literature class, the first required reading of the semester is crucial because it not only introduces students to the
course's methodological approach, thematic parameters, and theoretical terms
but also encourages them to think critically and globally. Put simply, the first
reading is an indispensable anecdote that navigates the semester's intellectual
itinerary. In particular, in today's era of transnationalisms, cultural identity de/
re-formations, and digital spaces, I have found that the first required reading of
a course beginning with or dedicated wholly to the early modern period (i.e.,
the age of European exploration, conquest, and colonization) must lend itself
readily to a multicultural and interdisciplinary framework so that students can
immediately apply knowledge gleaned from the classroom to their own sociopolitical engagement with the world. For example, in a survey or a seminar course
centered on the postcolonial travel narrative genre, or a digital humanities course
engaged with maps and national identity (e.g., a course on New World encounters, cartography, and literature, or on the Americas as a space where indigenous
identity is subsumed and erased and European identity is refashioned linguistically alongside the formation of new multicultural ones), the first required reading needs to grab the students' attention and be challenging and accessible to
them. Is there such an exemplary literary work that effectively lays the course
groundwork right out of the gate and also guarantees a successful first day of
teaching? Moreover, can a noncanonical literary text serve as a pivotal, methodological anchor that permits the college instructor to teach the rich cultural literary history of pre- and post-Columbian civilizations alongside European literary works throughout the semester? And, equally, can it address the theoretical
implications of language acquisition, exchange, and imposition to Spanish majors

and non-foreign-language majors alike? I propose Inca Garcilaso de la Vega's "The Story of Pedro Serrano" from *Royal Commentaries of the Incas* because it is an extraordinary and multifaceted little-known maroon tale that naturally welcomes a comparative approach and immediately enthralls students. Furthermore, "The Story of Pedro Serrano" complicates and enriches students' understanding of other primary texts—such as Michel de Montaigne's "On Cannibals," William Shakespeare's *The Tempest*, Thomas More's *Utopia*, and Daniel Defoe's *Robinson Crusoe*—that are covered later in the semester in sessions dedicated to the travel narrative, cultural identity, and the castaway thematic. This pedagogical essay thus brings "The Story of Pedro Serrano" to the forefront of course design and prevents it from being an overlooked and forgotten narrative of a castaway. In sum, my essay reconceptualizes Inca Garcilaso's story as an integral one for comparative literature and world literature courses that employ visual studies, digital humanities, and cultural studies approaches.

Introducing "The Story of Pedro Serrano"

In preparation for the first class of the semester—whether in an undergraduate or graduate seminar or an introductory course—I upload on the university's *Blackboard* platform Harold V. Livermore's English translation of "The Story of Pedro Serrano" from *The Oxford Book of Latin American Stories* alongside the original Spanish excerpt from the *Comentarios reales* (bk. 1, chs. 7–8). A week prior to the first formal day of instruction, I ask students to read the Livermore translation in advance. Although new students will inevitably show up on the first day because they are still "shopping" for classes, the seeming ease and brevity of the tale will not pose a problem for these newcomers; they will be able to spend ten to fifteen minutes in class reading this fictional account. During this time, I ask all the students—especially those who read in advance—to draw quickly two portraits of Pedro side by side on a single piece of paper: the first should show how this castaway appeared when he was first marooned on the island, and the second should show how the second castaway perceived Pedro in their first encounter later in the story. In addition, I ask them to draw a quick map of the island solely based on their reading. In an introductory undergraduate course, where some students may be shy and hesitant to draw, I permit them to draw in pairs, which helps to break the ice on the first day of the semester. These initial visual exercises are equally instrumental to future class discussions on many levels; not only do they encourage student interaction but they also set an interdisciplinary and critical tone for the course. Once the portraits and maps are done and are taped up on the classroom walls, the class is primed for discussion.

It is important, in particular for introductory undergraduate courses, to begin discussion with a quick recap of the story, delivered by two volunteers. Once the students reach the early point in the story where a shipwrecked Pedro first arrives on the island, we turn to their first portraits. We compare the students' different renderings, analyze the choices made to include or exclude certain details, and discuss how a castaway is portrayed in both verbal and visual terms. From the collection of images, ranging from scantily clad stick figures swimming to the island to beautifully drawn portraits of a young man kissing the soil with the shipwrecked vessel in the distance, students begin to comprehend what it means to be marooned both in literal and symbolic terms. Put simply, students remark that in the course of his extended time on the island Pedro undergoes a drastic outward transformation from civilized European to colonized native of the island. To further illustrate the physical and emotional archetype of a castaway, I show two movie stills of the actor Tom Hanks as the character Chuck Noland from the 2000 Robert Zemeckis film *Cast Away*. With much glee, students quickly compare and contrast their portraits of Pedro Serrano with Hanks's character. They also relate their maps to the island in the film and begin to interrogate their concept of an island.

It is then important that students return to Garcilaso's story and examine what actually transpires on the island—that is, how the island affects Pedro as well as how Pedro modifies the island. In this second part of the discussion, which takes place on the second day for an introductory course, I briefly outline Ferdinand de Saussure's concept of the linguistic sign in order to facilitate the conversation and to lay the foundation for future classes. From Pedro's refurbishing of turtle shells as water basins to the collection of sea pods, fish bones, and shredded pieces of his shirt to create tinder for his fire, students also consider the intrinsic transformation and appropriation of nature that is inevitably necessary for Pedro's survival on the island. Once the second castaway—a different European—arrives on the island, students remark that there is a clear contrast between the two men, especially in how they use language and engage with the island. Yet students are also drawn to highlight the similarities between these two castaways. For example, Pedro's audible recitation of the Apostles' Creed discloses that he is harmless, is approachable, and has maintained his Christian beliefs; religious language is the mediation for both men's salvation. I encourage students to make a list of these differences and similarities in order to work on a possible comparative thesis for a response or final paper on a castaway's identity and plight. In fact, in comparing both castaways' clothing and outer appearances, the students immediately glean how the island alters Pedro and all European Christian castaways. In returning to their island drawings, students also perceive how Pedro and his companion reshaped nature not only for survival but to reconstruct European civilization. Moreover, it is at this point in the discussion—whether on the first seminar day or on the second class day of an introductory course—that students are introduced to such basic concepts as colonialism and postcolonialism and are encouraged to interrogate what the terms *nature* and *civilization* signify to Pedro as well as to them.

For this particular discussion in an upper-level undergraduate or graduate seminar course, students must read in advance an excerpt from Saussure's *Course in General Linguistics* (65–70), short excepts from Ptolemy's *Geography* and José

Saramago's *The Tale of the Unknown Island*, and another excerpt from Mary Louise Pratt's "Arts of the Contact Zone." Without much ado, these assigned readings enable students to readily interrogate their second portrait of Pedro (how he is seen by the second castaway) and the role of language in verbal portraiture. I also introduce students to the rhetorical device of ekphrasis, a descriptive process in which one medium of art (e.g., prose or art) tries to connect with another medium (e.g., art or prose), so they can discuss the process of drawing directly from the story and vice versa. These discussions of ekphrasis and semiology help students quickly grasp how European languages, much like nature and Pedro's island, play significant roles in reshaping the body, self-perception, and identity of a castaway. In particular, Pratt's idea of the "contact zone" lends itself to the next natural query for this discussion: What happens when two languages, cultures, or sign systems intersect, clash, and inform each other? As students embrace these approaches and the idea of transculturation, Pratt's contact zone permits a fruitful exchange about social spaces, which is coincidentally a wonderful launching pad for later seminar class discussions on Montaigne's essay "On Cannibals." Furthermore, Pratt's contact zone and "The Story of Pedro Serrano" are good introductory readings for later discussions of Homi Bhabha's notion of liminality of hybridity, as discussed in *The Location of Culture*, and how it relates to the castaway trope in the travel narrative genre.

In a digital humanities course, the short excerpts from Ptolemy's *Geography* permit initial discussions on the meaning of the term *digital humanities* and how digital tools and methods such as *ArcGIS*, 3D printing, and data visualization can enable a richer understanding of mapmaking and all that it entailed in the age of discovery and conquest as well as inspire archival research from day one in the course. Moreover, the second seminar day could be conducted in the university's special collections, where students could begin archival research on maps and other material artifacts and ephemera related to Ptolemy. In particular, *ArcGIS*, used in conjunction with a university's holdings and other online collections, helps students use old maps to compile geographic data, analyze mapped information, and discover new geographic information. In a digital humanities course especially, class discussion of "The Story of Pedro Serrano" is a wonderful introduction to the use of digital tools and how they can assist students in interrogating the intersections of race, gender, culture, and material culture. After the introduction of these digital tools and a class visit to the university's special collections, the early class sessions conclude with a discussion of Saramago's *The Tale of the Unknown Island* and of what it means to map the unknown.

Written Assignments

Given how quickly the class period goes by, there is always much left to discuss about this story: the role of religion, Pedro's rescue, the death of the second castaway, the lack of name for the second castaway, the exhibition of Pedro in Europe, and Garcilaso's complex hybrid identity as the writer of this story. Consequently, I give students the opportunity to finish their discussion in the course blog or in the first response paper of the semester. This assignment not only provides students the opportunity to reflect further on this maroon story but also aids them in developing further analytical skills and appreciation for "The Story of Pedro Serrano." In the course blog, I require that students respond to one another, so the discussion is extended beyond the classroom.

The Course Blog

For each of my comparative literature and world literature undergraduate courses, whether survey or intermediate major courses, I create a blog on *Word-Press* where students post reflections and responses to the assigned readings and supplementary materials. In a digital humanities course dedicated to the travel narrative genre, the blog is most useful because students can post maps, videos, and images to elucidate their points. To facilitate the first few blog posts, I share the writing prompts for response papers that I give my undergraduate and graduate seminar students; these prompts assist in setting the critical and interdisciplinary tone for the rest of the semester. These online discussions serve to amplify in-class discussions; therefore, students are required to post original contributions as well as read their classmates' contributions on a given text before coming to class. This reading and writing activity is part of the ongoing homework, just like reading the primary literary works that are part of the class's workload.

I also encourage students to consider this site as a space where they are welcome to share any and all thoughts on the course readings, on works the students wish the class could read and discuss, on multimedia representations of travel narrative or the subjects of class discussion, and so forth. I emphasize that this is a site on which the student voice creates original content.

Response Papers

Throughout the semester my undergraduate and graduate seminar students are required to write weekly responses of at least four hundred words to the assigned readings. The writing assignments often include prompts to inspire and guide students' analytical approach. For "The Story of Pedro Serrano" I hand out the first three prompts listed below, from which they can select one (the first is an option for those who are fluent in or possess a reading knowledge of Spanish). The last four prompts are ones I offer during the weeks we read Montaigne, Saramago, Shakespeare, Aimé Césaire, and Defoe.

> *Translation*: Compare the original Spanish version of "The Story of Pedro Serrano" with its English translation and consider the challenges of translating this particular castaway story. In what ways does Livermore

alter both Pedro Serrano and, indirectly, Inca Garcilaso in order to appeal to a different audience?

Letter in a Bottle: Considering Mary Louise Pratt's idea of a "contact zone," if the second castaway were to write a letter to the Spanish crown about his encounter with Pedro, what would that letter say? How would he describe Pedro? the island? And why?

Letter in a Bottle: Considering Mary Louise Pratt's idea of a "contact zone," if Pedro were to write a letter to the Spanish crown about being a castaway and his adventures, what would that letter say? How would he describe the island? himself? And why?

Comparative Cannibals: Considering "On Cannibals" alongside "The Story of Pedro Serrano," how is Pedro Serrano (or how is he *not*) the Inca version of Montaigne's cannibal?

Comparative Islands: Compare and contrast the role of the island in Shakespeare's *The Tempest* with that of the island in Inca Garcilaso's story. How do Prospero's and Pedro Serrano's islands (or how do they *not*) affect their identities and destinies as well as their physical bodies?

Comparative Castaways: How is Pedro Serrano's fellow companion on the island (or how is he *not*) more of a castaway than Defoe's Friday? What makes these two men castaways?

Comparative Travelers: What would Pedro Serrano tell Saramago's traveler (i.e., the man who seeks the boat from the king) about islands, maps, and traveling? What would be his advice or warning? Be cognizant of how Pedro uses language to describe and delineate his meaning.

Mapmaking Assignments

Group Cartography Project

In introductory undergraduate courses, especially those with many or all first-year students, I build upon the initial group work of drawing the portraits of Pedro Serrano and the map of his island by assigning a group cartography project in which students consider the tenets of cartography in the early modern period. In the second week of the semester, I ask the students to form groups of two or three. This collaborative mapmaking assignment requires them to create by hand a collage mapping the island from either "The Story of Pedro Serrano" or Saramago's *The Tale of the Unknown Island* (using, for example, other maps and images from newspapers, magazines, and images printed from the Internet). The assignment does not require special artistic ability but should reflect students' understanding of the intentions, understanding, implications, assumptions, ramifications, and effects of the voyage represented by the map. The assignment is meant to interrogate the genre of mapmaking as well as our readings in a hands-on manner. In addition, each student will turn in an individual two-page response that speaks to the collaborative process.

Virtual Literary Map Journal Project

In an upper-level undergraduate course, I build upon the initial group work by assigning an intermedia project that incorporates students' archival research in the university special collections. Each student will produce, in lieu of a research paper, a virtual "story map," or map journal, that will be housed on the course blog. The overall objective of this intermedia assignment is to demonstrate, by selecting and discussing maps and other images, how the selected text (i.e., the literary space) inscribes sociopolitical and geographical boundaries and forms or deforms cultural identity. During the semester, our educational technologist offers workshops that will teach students how to use *ArcGIS* to create the journal.

Both projects open class discussion of the literary space and its relation to cartography. The final products from both assignments are always awe-inspiring and truly demonstrate how students interpret the language in visual terms. If possible, I find the opportunity during the semester to showcase the projects in an exhibition space or in a campus presentation by the students.

Comparing Inca Garcilaso de la Vega

As a contemporary of Shakespeare and Montaigne, Garcilaso is an important writer to study comparatively and in (English) translation because his works offer what may be an unaccustomed picture of the New World and of the "native"— that is, a textual portrait of alterity. In particular for a seminar class, right after "The Story of Pedro Serrano," I assign Montaigne's "On Cannibals" because it argues wonderfully how language is used to distinguish difference and establish alienation. To further develop this argument, I break students into small groups and ask them to analyze the final clause of this renowned essay: "ils ne portent point de haut de chausses" ("they do not wear breeches"). I ask some groups to focus their conversation on the clothing, while others I ask to focus on who the "they" are. After ten to fifteen minutes, we compare the groups' findings. We discuss not only the role of clothing as a marker for gender, ethnicity, and social class identities but also how the addition or lack of certain clothing distinguishes one culture from another and how civilization has been defined.

At this point, I ask students to consider that Pedro is the man who Montaigne claims is wearing breeches; after all, in "The Story of Pedro Serrano" he travels throughout Europe after he is rescued. The ensuing comparative analysis produces new insight into the maroon tale. In essence, Montaigne's last sentence permits students to see how the end of Garcilaso's story reverses Montaigne's story and turns the gaze back onto the European. In other words, students begin to engage with comparative discourse by having two stories speak to each other. For example, Pedro literally takes off his clothes on this island and begins to live like Montaigne's cannibal—that is, without a European language. However, students are encouraged to consider his reversal as an ironic consumption of language itself, because Garcilaso needs the Spanish language to uncover its earlier histories and chronicles of the "discovery" of the Americas; he himself writes a new version of the history of Peru and the Incas. At this time, I also introduce selections from Felipe Guaman Poma de Ayala's *El primer nueva corónica y buen gobierno* to further enrich and complicate our discussion of cultural identity construction, language differences, and alterity and resistance in writing.

This line of inquiry sets up potential comparative research papers on the writing of history as well as a comparison between Shakespeare's Prospero and Caliban (the assigned reading for the next week) and Garcilaso's Pedro Serrano. It also sets the stage for later discussion of the Caribbean and identity if Césaire's *A Tempest* is an assigned reading. As a final thought, I propose that students consider writing a response paper on Pedro as the Inca version of Montaigne's cannibal. In these papers, students analyze how Pedro is in a dialogue with his European counterpart, the cannibal who doesn't wear breeches—a dialogue, I point out, that runs counterpoint to Montaigne being in discourse with Garcilaso. For those seminar students interested in pursuing this line of inquiry for a final research paper, I recommend that they read Margarita Zamora's *Language, Authority, and Indigenous History in the* Comentarios reales de los Incas, because in it she argues that "The Story of Pedro Serrano" is "[an] allegory of the encounter between the Old World and the New" (165).

In conclusion, as a charming, unexpected precursor to Defoe's *Robinson Crusoe* or Césaire's *A Tempest*, "The Story of Pedro Serrano" is indeed the perfect literary introduction to broaching these questions of colonial subjectivity, history, and identity within a postcolonial context because it proffers to the student a complex hybrid perspective. Instead of first reading about alterity through a fictional character such as Montaigne's cannibal, More's Utopian native, Shakespeare's Caliban, or Defoe's Friday, students truly engage with a firsthand account of hybrid subjectivity and alterity. "The Story of Pedro Serrano" is thus a foundational comparative text for courses that employ postcolonial theory as their overarching framework. It is clear that Garcilaso's story aptly inscribes the castaway's cultural and social disorientation as well as educating the modern college student about what it means to be cast away in a new setting and survive new experiences.

Sample Reading Schedule

Based on a fifteen-week semester, the following reading schedule is one I have used for a comparative literature course entitled Lost Civilizations, whose focus is on castaways, new worlds, and travel narrative, and where I have successfully taught "The Story of Pedro Serrano" as I discussed above. I also include alternative texts that could be assigned in another possible course on mapping in the global early modern era. In this schedule I have included two films from which I show select stills during class, and which I screen, when possible, in their entirety outside of class. While

Zemeckis's *Cast Away* fits quite naturally with the course readings and early discussions on "The Story of Pedro Serrano," Jerry Hopper's *Secret of the Incas* is a cinematic gem for a course dealing with contact zones. A precursor to the Indiana Jones movie franchise with Charlton Heston in the role of adventurer Harry Steele, *Secret of the Incas* presents an interesting interpretation of Pratt's idea of social spaces "where cultures meet, clash, and grapple with each other, often in contexts of highly asymmetrical relations of power, such as colonialism, [and] slavery" (*Imperial Eyes* 4). Equally curious and worthy of discussion is Ridley Scott's *The Martian*, which prompts viewers to think of space exploration in similar terms. All in all, I propose to students that they consider that in the modern era, Pedro Serrano has been possibly transformed into a complex and fraught adventurer, explorer, and colonialist.

Week	Reading
1	Inca Garcilaso de la Vega's "The Story of Pedro Serrano"
2	Michel de Montaigne's "On Cannibals," José Saramago's *The Tale of the Unknown Island*, and selections from Felipe Guaman Poma de Ayala's *El primer nueva corónica y buen gobierno*
3–4	William Shakespeare's *The Tempest*
5–6	Daniel Defoe's *Robinson Crusoe* or Aimé Césaire's *A Tempest*
7–8	J. M. Coetzee's *Foe* or Thomas More's *Utopia*
9–10	Juan José Saer's *The Witness*
11–12	Excerpts from Michael Crichton's *Jurassic Park* and Jules Verne's *Journey to the Center of the Earth* or Sir Arthur Conan Doyle's *The Lost World*
13	Selections from Jorge Luis Borges's *The Book of Imaginary Beings*
14–15	Selections from Paola Ramos's *Finding Latinx: In Search of the Voices Redefining Latino Identity* and Alejo Carpentier's *The Lost Steps* or Cataline de Erauso's *Lieutenant Nun*

Films Screened outside Class

Cast Away (2000)
Secret of the Incas (1954)
The Martian (2015)

WORKS CITED

Bhabha, Homi K. *The Location of Culture*. Routledge, 1994.

Cast Away. Directed by Robert Zemeckis, Twentieth Century Fox, 2000.

Césaire, Aimé. *A Tempest: Based on Shakespeare's* The Tempest: *Adaptation for a Black Theatre*. Translated by Richard Miller, Theatre Communications Group, 2002.

Defoe, Daniel. *Robinson Crusoe*. Edited by Kathleen Lines, Knopf, 1993.

Garcilaso de la Vega. *Comentarios reales de los Incas*. Edited by Aurelio Miró Quesada, Biblioteca Ayacucho, 1985. 2 vols.

———. "The Story of Pedro Serrano." Translated by Harold V. Livermore. *The Oxford Book of Latin American Short Stories*, edited by Roberto González Echevarría, Oxford UP, 1997, pp. 38–42.

Greenblatt, Stephen. *Marvelous Possessions: The Wonder of the New World*. U of Chicago P, 1991.

The Martian. Directed by Ridley Scott, Twentieth Century Fox, 2015.

Montaigne, Michel de. "On Cannibals." *The Essays of Montaigne*, translated by John Florio, AMS Press, 1967, pp. 100–07.

More, Thomas. *Utopia*. Open Road Media, 2020.

Pratt, Mary Louise. "Arts of the Contact Zone." *Profession*, 1991, pp. 33–40.

———. *Imperial Eyes: Travel Writing and Transculturation*. Routledge, 1992.

Ptolemy. *Ptolemy's* Geography: *An Annotated Translation of the Theoretical Chapters*. Edited and translated by J. Lennart Berggren and Alexander Jones, Princeton UP, 2002.

Saramago, José. *The Tale of the Unknown Island*. Vintage Digital, 2011.

Saussure, Ferdinand de. *Course in General Linguistics*. Philosophical Library, 1959.

Secret of the Incas. Directed by Jerry Hopper, Paramount Pictures, 1954.

Shakespeare, William. *The Tempest: With New and Updated Critical Essays and a Revised Bibliography*. Edited by Robert Langbaum, Signet Classic, 1998.

Zamora, Margarita. *Language, Authority, and Indigenous History in the* Comentarios reales de los Incas. Cambridge UP, 1988.

NOTES ON CONTRIBUTORS

Rolena Adorno is the Sterling Professor of Spanish emerita at Yale University. Her books include *Guaman Poma: Writing and Resistance in Colonial Peru* (1986, 2000), *The Polemics of Possession in Spanish American Narrative* (2007), *De Guancane a Macondo: Estudios de literatura latinoamericana* (2008), *Colonial Latin American Literature: A Very Short Introduction* (2011), and, with Roberto González Echevarría, *Breve historia de la literatura latinoamericana colonial y moderna* (2017). She is the coeditor of print and digital editions of Felipe Guaman Poma de Ayala's *Nueva corónica y buen gobierno* (1980, 1987, 2001, 2004). Her books have been awarded prizes by the MLA, the American Historical Association, the Western Historical Association, and the New England Council of Latin American Studies. Adorno is a fellow of the American Academy of Arts and Sciences, an honorary associate of the Hispanic Society of America, an honorary professor at the Pontificia Universidad Católica del Perú, and a recipient of the MLA's Award for Lifetime Scholarly Achievement. She has been honored with the Enrique Anderson Imbert Award of the North American Academy of the Spanish Language, and she has held the senior chair in Countries and Cultures of the South at the Library of Congress.

Damian Bacich is professor of Spanish and chair of the Department of World Languages and Literatures at San José State University, where he teaches courses on translation and literatures of early modern Spain and Spanish America (including the southwestern United States). His research focuses on issues of intercultural contact in the Ibero-American borderlands. He has published essays on Inca Garcilaso de la Vega, translation in the early modern Iberian world, and the Spanish colonial presence in California and the American Southwest. He is also a translator and published a new English translation of León Hebreo's *Dialogues of Love* together with Rossella Pescatori (2009) as well as *Documents Concerning the Revolt of the Indians of the Province of New Mexico in 1680* with Juan Antonio Sempere (2017).

Ralph Bauer is professor of English and comparative literature at the University of Maryland, College Park. His publications include *The Cultural Geography of Colonial American Literatures: Empire, Travel, Modernity* (2003), *The Alchemy of Conquest: Science, Religion, and the Secrets of the New World* (2019), and the coedited collections *Creole Subjects in the Colonial Americas: Empires, Texts, Identities*, with José Antonio Mazzotti (2009), and *Translating Nature: Cross-Cultural Histories of Early Modern Science*, with Jaime Marroquín Arredondo (2019).

Sarah H. Beckjord is associate professor of Hispanic studies at Boston College. Her research focuses on historical and literary representations of colonial Spanish America, and she has published articles and book chapters on Bernal Díaz del Castillo, Gonzalo Fernández de Oviedo, Inca Garcilaso de la Vega, and other subjects. Recent publications include "Nature as Book and Stage in Gonzalo Fernández de Oviedo's *Chronicle of Nicaragua*" in *Reading the Natural World: Perceptions of the Environment and Ecology in the Middle Ages and Renaissance* (2020), "La imaginación performativa: Figura e imagen de Ignacio de Loyola" in *Teología política e imagen* (2019), "'Deseo saber': Escenas neoplatónicas en la *Historia general del Perú*" in *Revista de crítica literaria* *latinoamericana* (2017), and "Love: Spanish America" in *Lexikon of the Hispanic Baroque* (2014). Her first book was *Territories of History: Humanism, Rhetoric, and the Historical Imagination in the Early Spanish Chronicles of the Indies* (2007), and she is currently working on a second book on the role of spectacle in the works of Garcilaso.

Kimberly Borchard is associate professor of Spanish at Randolph-Macon College, where she teaches courses in Spanish, Latin American colonial literature, and Spanish for social justice. Her book, *Appalachia as Contested Borderland of the Early Modern Atlantic, 1528–1715* (2021), highlights the European obsession with Appalachian mineral wealth during the sixteenth and seventeenth centuries. Reframing Appalachian history within the fields of Latin American, early American, and Atlantic history, Borchard's research provides a critical study of the enduring myth of Appalachian wealth and its dire human and environmental consequences. Drawing on sources in Spanish, Portuguese, French, Latin, and English, Borchard emphasizes the international, polyglot nature of colonial Appalachia, foregrounding the region as a locus of imperial rivalry in the early modern period.

Sara Castro-Klarén is emerita professor of Latin American culture and literature in the Department of Modern Languages and Literatures and founder of the Latin American Studies Program at Johns Hopkins University. She is also a member of the Academy at Johns Hopkins. Castro-Klarén has served on numerous boards, including the MLA and Fulbright boards of directors. She has also served on the editorial boards of many professional journals such as *Modern Language Notes, Latin American Literary Review,* and *Colonial Review.* With John Beverley she has been the editor of the influential series *Illuminations,* published by the University of Pittsburgh Press. She is the author of *The Narrow Pass of Our Nerves: Writing, Coloniality, and Postcolonial Theory* (2011) and coeditor of *Inca Garcilaso and Contemporary World-Making* (2016). Castro-Klarén has also written books on José María Arguedas and Mario Vargas Llosa. She is the editor of the Blackwell *Companion to Latin American Literature and Culture* and is currently preparing a second, revised edition of the *Companion,* which will appear at the end of 2021.

Raquel Chang-Rodríguez is distinguished professor of Hispanic literature and culture at City College and the Graduate Center, City University of New York. Her books and editions include *Talking Books with Mario Vargas Llosa* (2021), *Literatura y cultura en el Virreinato del Perú: Apropiación y diferencia* (2017), *Cartografía garcilasista* (2013), *Entre la espada y la pluma: El Inca Garcilaso de la Vega y sus* Comentarios reales (2010), and *Beyond Books and Borders: Garcilaso de la Vega and* La Florida del Inca (2006). The founding editor of *Colonial Latin American Review,* she is the recipient of fellowships and awards from, among other institutions, the NEH, the New York Council for the Humanities, the Council of Learned Societies, and the Inter-Americas Society of Arts and Letters, as well as an honorary associate of the Hispanic Society of America and corresponding member of the Peruvian and North American academies of the Spanish language. In 2016 Chang-Rodríguez received the Enrique Anderson Imbert Award of the North American Academy of the Spanish Language, an affiliate of the Royal Academy of the Language (Madrid). She is profesora honoraria of the Universidad Nacional Mayor de San Marcos and holds an honorary degree from the National University of Athens, Greece.

Dinorah Cortés-Vélez is associate professor of Spanish at Marquette University. She specializes in colonial Latin American literatures and cultures and is also interested in the literatures of the Hispanic Caribbean, especially Puerto Rican poetry. She has published several scholarly pieces on Sor Juana Inés de la Cruz, including a chapter in a forthcoming volume on the Mexican nun's critical reception during the twentieth century, to be published by the Instituto de Estudios Auriseculares. She has completed a scholarly book manuscript entitled "'Sin que a uno u otro se incline': La filosofía de género de Sor Juana Inés de la Cruz," currently under review, and has published three books of fiction and a chapbook of poetry.

Isabel Dulfano is a professor at the University of Utah. Her current research engages autoethnography by Indigenous women who reframe the narrative of their lives and the respective challenges of agency, activism, and unmediated subjectivity. Her recent manuscript, "Walking on (Y)our Sacred Path: Indigenous American Women Speak Out on Identity and Activism," transcribes interviews with native women from the Americas in 2016–18. The discussions focus on how Indigenous identity informs definitions of activism and social change work in many different professional fields. She has translated Silvia Rivera Cuscicanqui, Irma Velasquez Nimatuj, and Luz Maria de la Torre and has coedited, with Linda Maier, *Woman as Witness: Essays on Testimonial Literature by Latin American Women* (2004) and *Indigenous Feminist Narratives: I/We: Wo(men) of an(Other) Way* (2015).

Christian Fernández is the director of Hispanic studies in the Department of World Languages, Literatures, and Cultures at Louisiana State University. He is a specialist in Latin American studies. His teaching and research interests include literary theory, colonial and postcolonial studies, transcontinental studies, and Latin American narrative. Fernández is the author of *Inca Garcilaso: Imaginación, memoria e identidad* (2004) and coeditor, with Sara Castro-Klarén, of *Inca Garcilaso and Contemporary World-Making* (2016). His most recent book is *Imaginar la nación: Güiraldes, Gallegos, Lugones y Borges* (2020). He has lectured on these authors and many others in Europe, Asia, the United States, and Latin America.

James W. Fuerst is a Nuyorican author and assistant professor of writing at Eugene Lang College of Liberal Arts, where he teaches fiction and literature. He received his PhD from Harvard. His first novel, *Huge*, was published in 2009. His most recent academic work is *New World Postcolonial: The Political Thought of Inca Garcilaso de la Vega* (2018).

Sara V. Guengerich is associate professor of Spanish at Texas Tech University. She specializes in the literature and history of the colonial Andes. Her research and publications center on the analysis of the discursive production of colonial subaltern subjects in colonial manuscripts in the context of the Spanish conquest and colonization of Peru and its connections to the early modern Atlantic world. Her work has been supported by institutions that include the John Carter Brown Library and the Newberry Library and has appeared in various peer-reviewed journals. She is coeditor of the collection *Cacicas: The Indigenous Women Leaders of Spanish America, 1492–1825* (2021). Her current book project, "Daughters of the Inca Conquest: Inca Women under Spanish Rule," explores the role of indigenous noblewomen in the delineation of a neo-Inca identity that was key to preserving the cohesiveness of this group during the colonial period.

Michael J. Horswell is professor of Spanish and Latin American literature and dean of the Dorothy F. Schmidt College of Arts and Letters at Florida Atlantic University. He is the author of *Decolonizing the Sodomite: Queer Tropes of Sexuality in Colonial Andean Culture* (2005) and coeditor of *Submerged: Alternative Cuban Cinema*, with Luis Duno-Gottberg (2013); *Baroque Projections: Images and Texts in Dialogue with the Early Modern Hispanic World*, with Frédéric Conrod (2016); and *Sexualidades periféricas: Consolidaciones literarias y fílmicas en la España de fin de siglo XIX y fin de milenio*, with Nuria Godón (2016).

Sara L. Lehman is professor of Spanish in colonial literature and director of the Latin American and Latino Studies Institute at Fordham University. A specialist in transatlantic studies, she is the author of several books and articles on seventeenth-century discourse, including *Sinful Business: New World Commerce as Religious Transgression in Literature on and of the Spanish Colonial Period* (2010). Lehman has also published critical editions of Antonio Vázquez de Espinosa's *Tratado verdadero del viaje y navegación* (2008), José Joaquín Fernández de Lizardi's *Don Catrín de la Fachenda* (2015), and Carlos de Sigüenza y Góngora's *Infortunios de Alonso Ramírez* (2011) and *Don Catrín de la Fachenda* (2013). In her interdisciplinary and comparative approach to colonial studies, the notions of greed, commerce, and allegorical voyage that she explored in *Sinful Business* inform her exploration of genre and discourse in the sixteenth, seventeenth, and eighteenth centuries.

José Antonio Mazzotti is the King Felipe VI of Spain Professor of Spanish Culture and Civilization and professor of Latin American literature at Tufts University. He has taught at Harvard, MIT, Brown, and the University of Pavia (Italy) and given seminars in Madrid, in Seville, and at several universities in the United States and Peru. In 1996 he founded the nonprofit International Association of Peruvianists, and he is director of *Revista de crítica literaria latinoamericana*. Among his books are *Coros mestizos del Inca Garcilaso: Resonancias andinas* (1996), *Poéticas del flujo: Migración y violencia verbales en el Perú de los 80* (2002), *Incan Insights: El Inca Garcilaso's Hints to Andean Readers* (2008), *Encontrando un inca: Ensayos escogidos sobre el Inca Garcilaso de la Vega* (2016), *Lima fundida: Épica y nación criolla en el Perú* (2016), *The Creole Invention of Peru: Ethnic Nation and Epic Poetry in Colonial Lima* (2019), and twelve volumes of poetry. He received the 2018 José Lezama Lima International Poetry Award from Casa de las Américas, Cuba, for his book *El Zorro y la Luna*. He has also edited several volumes on Latinos in the United States, Latin American colonial literature, Peruvianist studies, José María Arguedas, Amazonian languages, and literary theory.

Giovanna Montenegro is assistant professor of comparative literature and Spanish at Binghamton University (SUNY). Her interests include colonial Latin America and the early modern Habsburg realms, especially colonial travel narratives and cartography. Her book, *German Merchant Capitalism: The Story of the Welsers' Venezuela Enterprise (1528–1556) and Its Cultural Memory*, is forthcoming in 2022. Her articles have appeared in *MLN*, *Transit*, *Trópico absoluto*, and the *International Yearbook of Futurism Studies*. She received the 2019 LASA-Venezuela section Best Article Humanities Award for "'The Welser Phantom': Apparitions of the Welser Venezuela Colony in Nineteenth- and Twentieth-Century German Cultural Memory," published in *Transit: A Journal of Travel, Migration, and Multiculturalism in the German-Speaking World*. Montenegro also works on the twentieth-century transatlantic avant garde and visual culture.

Yarí Pérez Marín is assistant professor in the Department of Hispanic Studies at Durham University, England. She has received awards from the Mellon Foundation, the Social Science Research Council, and the Woodrow Wilson Foundation and has been a fellow in residence at the John Carter Brown Library. In her book *Marvels of Medicine: Literature and Scientific Inquiry in Early Colonial Spanish America* (2020), she examines texts written in Spain and colonial Mexico in which American nature takes center stage in the ongoing feud between Renaissance humanism and experiential modes of knowledge production. Her analysis makes a case for the incorporation of scientific writing into current discussions on early modern historiography and literature.

Rocío Quispe-Agnoli is professor of colonial Latin American literature, American Indian and Indigenous studies, and women's and gender studies at Michigan State University. She is the author of *La fe andina en la escritura* (2006), *Durmiendo en el agua* (2008), and *Nobles de papel* (2016), for which she received the 2017 LASA-Peru Section Award, and coeditor of *Women's Voices and Textual Negotiations in Latin America, 1500–1799* (2017) and *Colonial Latin American Literatures in Transition* (forthcoming). She is the editor in chief of the *Journal of Gender and Sexuality Studies / Revista de estudios de género y sexualidades*.

Nhora Lucía Serrano is the associate director for digital learning and research at Hamilton College. She is a medieval and early modern scholar whose areas of focus include Latin America and transatlantic studies, editorial cartoons and graphic arts, book history and print culture, and technology-enhanced learning and educational innovation. Serrano was a recipient of an NEH Summer Institute grant and a Smithsonian National Postal Museum and World Philatelic Exhibition Scholarship. She was a visiting scholar of comparative literature at Harvard University, a Mellon University Press Diversity Fellow at MIT Press / MIT, and a 2018 Eisner Industry Awards judge. She has served on the MLA forum GS Comics and Graphic Narratives and presently serves on the MLA forum TM Book History, Print Cultures, Lexicography. Serrano is the editor of *Immigrants and Comics: Graphic Spaces of Remembrance, Transaction, and Mimesis* (2021) and coeditor of *Curious Collectors, Collected Curiosities: An Interdisciplinary Study* (2010), and her published essays have appeared in *The Oxford Handbook of Comic Studies*, *MLA Approaches to Teaching Orhan Pamuk*, *X-Tra Contemporary Art Quarterly*, *Museological Review*, and other venues.

George Antony Thomas is professor of Spanish and chair of the Department of World Languages and Literatures at California State University, San Bernardino. His scholarship focuses on colonial Latin American literature. His research interests include gender studies, indigenous studies, material and visual culture, and the history of the book. His most recent publications include chapters in *The Routledge Research Companion to the Works of Sor Juana Inés de la Cruz* (2017) and *Latin American Textualities* (2018).

Margarita Zamora is a literary critic and cultural studies scholar specializing in Spanish American literature and culture of the colonial period. She received her doctorate from Yale University and is professor emerita of the Department of Spanish and Portuguese and the Latin American, Caribbean, and Iberian Studies Program at the University of Wisconsin, Madison. Her publications include *Reading Columbus* (1993), winner of the MLA's Katherine Singer Kovacs Prize, and *Language, Authority, and Indigenous*

History in the Comentarios reales de los Incas (1988). She is coeditor of *Cuba: Contra- puntos de cultura, historia y sociedad* (2007) and *Narradores indígenas y mestizos de la época colonial (Siglos XVI–XVII): Zonas andina y mesoamericana* (2016). Zamora's articles have appeared in *Cultural Critique, Hispanic Review, Insula, MLN, Modern Language Quarterly, Revista iberoamericana, Revista de crítica literaria latinoameri- cana, Revista crítica de ciencias sociais,* and *The Americas,* among other journals on culture, history, linguistics, literary studies, and social sciences.

SURVEY RESPONDENTS

Ralph Bauer, *University of Maryland, College Park*
Sarah H. Beckjord, *Boston College*
Kimberly Borchard, *Randolph-Macon College*
Galen Brokaw, *State University of New York, Buffalo*
Raquel Chang-Rodríguez, *City University of New York, City College and the Graduate Center*
Dinorah Cortés-Vélez, *Marquette University*
Isabel Dulfano, *University of Utah*
Sara V. Guengerich, *Texas Tech University*
Michael J. Horswell, *Florida Atlantic University*
Anne Lambright, *Trinity College*
Sara L. Lehman, *Fordham University*
Mark J. Mascia, *Sacred Heart University*
Ana María Metcalfe, *Seminole State College*
Luis Millones, *Colby College*
Giovanna Montenegro, *State University of New York, Binghamton*
Yarí Pérez Marín, *Durham University, England*
Rocío Quispe-Agnoli, *Michigan State University*
William E. Schutmaat, *Corporación Universitaria Reformada, Colegio Americano*
Patricia Seed, *University of California, Irvine*
Nhora Lucía Serrano, *Hamilton College*
Robert Simon, *Kennesaw State University*
Sarah Smorol, *University of Hawai'i, Mānoa*
George Antony Thomas, *California State University, San Bernardino*
María Zalduondo, *Texas Christian University*